Embraced

Jordan Jantz

Receives Lifetime Achievement Award as a Beacon of Light unto the World with the Voice of Hope!

A book for the entire family, rated PG.

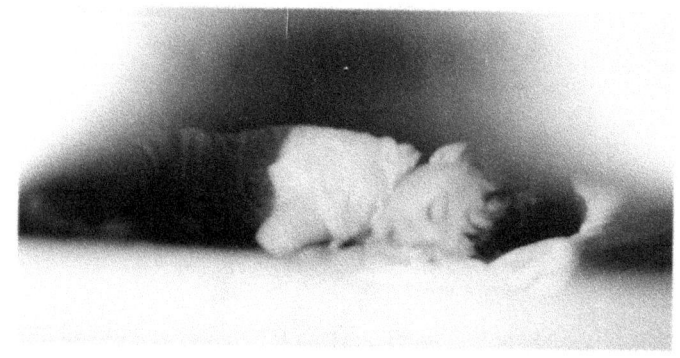

Hush little James, don't you cry.
There will be no little boy tears in heaven.

Copyright © 2016 Jordan Jantz
All rights reserved.
Revised Third Edition

Publisher:
Jordan Jantz Underground 4 Saving the Lives of Children

ISBN-13:
978-0692639979
ISBN-10:
0692639977

YOU KNOW, the smallest thing can change your life. In the blink of an eye, something happens by chance when you least expect it. It sets you on a course you never planned, to someplace you never imagined. Where will it take you? Sometimes, finding the light will take you through the deepest darkness. At least, that's how it was for me.

Everyone has their own destiny.

Not everyone makes the choice to follow it.

I'm lucky I did.

DEDICATED

By GRACIOUS PERMISSION To
HER MAJESTY
CHARITY,
SERVICE DOG
THAT WILL NEVER BE REPLACED.

Thank you for fourteen years of dedicated service to your
owner who lives with challenges that
you have been able to control.
You are my blessing from God.
There will be no other like you.
This book is dedicated to licensed service dogs everywhere.

The US Department of Justice defines
Service Animals as dogs that are individually trained to do
work or perform tasks for people with disabilities,
under Title II and Title III of the
2011 Americans with Disabilities Act.

For more information:
www.ADA.gov
ADA Information Line:
800-514-0301 (voice)
800-514-0383 (TTY)

EMBRACED

*My best friend turns 15 this year.
Isn't she beautiful, at her age?*

Charity was essential to every step of the production of this book. Her seamless cooperation and editorial skills are unmatched.

IN MEMORY OF:

ALL OF MY BROTHERS WHO HAVE MARCHED in the band and sung in the choir with me, throughout life.

My memory of all we have shared will be forever embedded in my heart. I keep the memories of our times growing up as adults to now middle aged men. It is sad to see so many of you who have left my life from this terrible disease called AIDS.

Silence equals Death, and I will never keep silent over the reality of the people I love who have touched my life. So many people have been stricken with AIDS:

The artists, the musicians, and the producers of many extraordinary artistic fashions and designs for clothing are no longer possible to be recreated since your lives have been removed from this earth.

Until we meet again, you will always be a blessing of gratitude for coming into my life. I understand there are no more tears in heaven.

I lived in my biological dad's car when he would go to the bar. I was told I was the best little boy in the world for being so quiet. Daddy would even sleep in the car with me until it was daylight. He was so good to me, getting me away from being in a small closet and to be in such a big car was so nice to play with toys in the backseat of the car, while daddy drank after work.

JORDAN JANTZ

VIEW FROM JORDAN'S BALCONY, PORTLAND

VIEW FROM RONNIE'S RANCH, MOWEAQUA

JAMES LEE BOND SITTING ON TOP OF WHERE HE AND HIS DAD SPENT MANY SOBERING NIGHTS TOGETHER

JORDAN JANTZ

TABLE OF CONTENTS

Acknowledgements	XVI
Benefit to the Christmas Box House	LXXN
Personal Invitation	LXXVI
Chronology	LXXIX
Bibliography	LXXX
Voices on Amazon	LXXXIII
Voice of Hope Information	CX
Permissions	CXIII
Interview	CXIII
Embraced Synopsis	CXLIX
Special Messages	CLII
Message from the Compilers	CLIV
Illustrations	CLVI
Introduction	CLVII
Prelude and Foreword	CLXIII

EMBRACED

CHAPTERS OF EMBRACED

Chapt.		Pg.
1	The Spirit of Valentine's Day	1
2	Far From Heaven	34
3	Who do I belong to?	47
4	You Can't Pray the Gay Away	53
5	Giant of a Man	71
6	Family Home Evening in Portland	85
7	Lifetime Achievement Award	97
8	Going the Extra Mile (Hello, are you there?)	123
9	Where is the Love and Where did it GO?	128
10	Aunt Marion's Boy Since Age Three	130

11	Brothers Forever with Embraced Love	135
12	Washing the Feet of Those you Love	142
13	Why was I the only one sold?	152
14	A Magical Memorial Day with a Gift of Love	160
15	I hear you are gay, and I was told you have AIDS	169
16	Lake Decatur	172
17	Cornfields and Soybeans Forever, Oh My	178
18	Family Home Evening in Decatur	181
19	Holy Ghost Revival Elevated to Heaven	188
20	Aunt Marion's Life-Long Protection of Me	196
21	Follow the Yellow Brick Road	216
22	Group Therapy	225
23	Mother's Bistro	230
24	My Father Who Paid the Price	253
25	Christmas Box House – Pay it Forward	277

EMBRACED

26	False Truths Cost a Fortune	290
27	Love Moved Mountains; A Mustard Seed of Faith	294
28	Be Where You are Celebrated Not Where You are Tolerated	299
29	Kitchen Table: The Night My World Changed	313
30	Phone Therapy: Are you There, Can you Hear Me?	325
31	Cracker Barrel and Shopping Therapy with Aunt Marion and Charity	331
32	Flashbacks with the Kidd Kaddilacs	350
33	Election Year: Decatur Country Club	363
34	Bishop's Blessing in Decatur	375
35	Hung Out to Dry	384
36	Aunt Marion Finds the Blind Side	386
37	Sabbath in Moweaqua	391
38	Mama's Mistake No Refunds and No Returns	395
39	Uncle Bill's First Time Out	402
40	Mama States: Why Don't You Stick It Up You're a**?! Sister States: I Disconnect From You. You are Unhealthy.	406

JORDAN JANTZ

41	Feeding the Homeless in Downtown Portland	419
42	I Have an Uncle and it is my Father's Brother! I LOVE Him!!!	428
43	Christmas In Utah with my Spiritual Family	438
44	New Year's Eve Some Like it Hot, Hot, Hot!!!	448
45	Holiday of Love, Sharing Faith, Hope and Charity	457

THE HEART OF THE SEA

46	Love can Touch your Life Once and Change your Destiny Forever	460
47	Cotton Candy, Sugar Daddies and Plastic Fantastic	467
48	Some Men Were Not Meant to be Fathers … and That's OK	474
49	Letting Go of Hollywood	478
50	Speedo Model	481
51	My Shame and Pain in Sharing the Truth of My Life. Will it ever Stop?	488
52	Doctor's Orders	490
53	Spencer, no Man has Given Me the Gift of Love and Family Until I Met You. I Will Never be the Same Again.	492
54	My Life Growing Up in Southern California	497
55	New Year's Eve in Time's Square	505

EMBRACED

Epilogue	509
My Favorite Dream	511
Final Thoughts on Reality	515
Montage of Embracements	519
About the Author	620
Biographical Facts	628
Appendix	637
Memories to Take With You	645
Final Curtain Call	648
Connect with Jordan	658

JORDAN JANTZ

ACKNOWLEDGMENTS

**To my medical team
for all the patience and time
given to embrace this moment in life:**
I thank you for the grace that you have
extended in my blessing from being my
Primary Health Care Team in Portland, Oregon.

What it takes is a certain kind of person to be special.
It takes someone who is really wonderful,
Someone who lights up this little corner of the world
With feelings of friendship of love and understanding
It takes a truly unique personality and a knack for making
Life happier and more rewarding.
It takes someone who's willing to make the time it takes
Individuals who are able to open up and share their
Innermost feelings with another.
It takes those who make the path of life
an easier and more beautiful journey
It takes a rare combination of many qualities.
It takes a certain kind to be special.
It takes special individuals exactly like you.

James Lee Bond

XVII

To my landlords
for all your encouragement.
Having been a tenant for several years, I want this place to be my home until I leave this planet, because of the truth and trust we have built through the decades.
Thank you, Jordan and Pam, for the life you opened up for me. I am <u>forever grateful</u>. I want to thank you both so much for taking the time to be there when I needed a home. Thanks for seeing me through so much. I love my home and I love and respect what you have done for me, all these years. Thank you for taking the hours out of your own precious days to make a little more sunlight shine in mine. Thank you for being a generous team with beautiful spirits in a world that could use a million more people just like you. Thanks so much for giving and continuing to give us this beautiful residence. We all are grateful for the life you have shared in giving us new light.

To the heads of the departments that coordinate all the services for my life at home and medically,
I express my gratitude. You all make my life abundant.
THANK YOU, for giving me a home that I will enjoy 'til I see my new life after this life is over. It is a blessing to call this my home and know I have the expert care of management and facilities that have so many amenities for someone such as myself. And thank you, for all you have done for helping me give the quality I can to others by sharing acts of kindness in our community where I live.

You are everything and more, all of you! You are very important to me. And I'll try to tell you why, in this little, short message that explains that you and I share so much of what is good about life. So many experiences that only you and I know, and so many personal feelings and emotions that we have shown only in

XIX

working and moving into the facility when we created it to be our home. With you, the ordinary times turn into great times, and all of you have given this to me. Simple conversations turn into honest, truthful talks. That's what I receive from the services in my apartment and in my home at Rose Schnitzer Tower. It is an honor to have Cedar Sinai and Harsch Investment Properties come together along with the Jewish Community to provide what God would want for *all* His children. What a blessing the Jewish Community is in my life, for I will always enjoy a Passover with my Jewish community of friendships, from past to present. All of you, here, have given me the best. Thank you for my home, and taking care of the things that I can't do on my own. I value the kindness I have received from all of you at Rose Schnitzer Tower.

To my photographer
who made me look 21 again, you worked miracles.

I have loved every day we have shared.
I have cherished every memory we've made.
I have appreciated the uniqueness and the sweetness and the wonder of you, more than my words can ever say. What a beautiful soul you have, and what a blessing you are, as my friend. I am so grateful to you for giving me such a wealth of things to treasure. You never stopped thinking of me. Thank you for the precious feelings and the priceless moments. Thank you for an amazing amount of encouragement and understanding. Thank you for the comfort of feeling so close and letting me know I can always count on you. Thank you for all the gifts you've given, all the smiles you've inspired, and all the things you've always done to make my life a Voice of Hope.

To Sam Adams,
My favorite mayor in Portland,

XX

EMBRACED

Thank you, for being such a great representative of honesty and truthfulness about one's own fallibility. Whether we are involved in politics or whatever, the circumstances at hand, nobody is beyond reproach. You have stood by me and I thank you for walking the miles that you have walked with me as a friend and as a politician. We have shared many wonderful opportunities to see life grow into wonderful blessings for both you and for me. Despite the gossip that we both endure in our life from being in the public eye, we are free from within from the judgment of others, because we have both put the truth of our life out on the table for everyone to see our faults and our failures. Jesus has drawn the line in the sand, Sam, for you and me, and he without sin can cast the first stone. Never let anything be an affirmation in your life because affirmations are things that do not last or stay around, they are only for the moment. Your friendship has taught me much about living in the public eye and it has been my dream for you to enjoy Washington DC and have the best life possible, after all the things people have to say about people who are going someplace. All we can do is let it go, let it go, let it go. And rise above.

To Nicki and Billy,

thank you for believing in me and being my cheerleaders. There are a few absolute gems in this world. They are the people who make a tremendous difference in other people's lives through the smiles they give, the blessings they share, and the way they warm the hearts of everyone around them. Those rare and remarkable people are so deserving of every hope and happiness. They are the people who are incredibly personal, enormously thanked, and endlessly appreciated for everything they do in my life. Two of those wonderful, rare individuals are most definitely YOU. Thank you for not walking out when others ran.

The day Gram and Aunt Helen sent me to California to live

XXII

To the Cascade AIDS Project

I've been blessed to serve you for the past thirty years. I've loved every moment of seeing our growth in Portland, Oregon. Downtown is a Mecca of liberation for all humanity that comes together and share the values of love and respect.

That's why I choose to always remember the kindness from Cascade AIDS Project, and the integrity and confidentiality it has for human beings who desire help and hope. Now, after receiving, I can give back what you have given to me. Only now, I choose to utilize my life to transform the lives of children. Thank you, for planting the seed of love from the community that has stood by me since I was a teenager and that's all of you, who are gay in the Pacific Northwest. Thank you for being my family when there was no family to be found.

To my pharmaceutical representatives,

you are the best. Without you, things just wouldn't work. I am grateful for western medicine and what it has had to offer me in my life-transformation. It is a blessing to have all of you remain in my life for the past seventeen years, along with all of my medical providers and professional medical representatives, stepping up to make sure my life is not left behind.

To the family who took me from the life I had for my first five years of life in Decatur, Illinois,

All of you have and are going to always have a special place in my life. I can only say, **thank you for saving me from life that would have soon ended up with death,** if I had continued to live with my biological mother in Decatur. God only knows whatever

XXIV

happened to Robyn, my biological half-sister. I know she had to have really had it impossible to survive. But you stepped outside of the box and got to know me and desired something that you saw special that nobody else saw. And I thank you for saving my life and I have no regrets because I know I would be dead if my biological dad would not have given the opportunity for me to have another home that he felt would be best, and I want my adopted father to always know it will never come any better than him. I pray he never reads this book or finds out about it, or any of my adoptive family, for I will always love them into eternity.

In remembrance of the Jantz Family

It has been an incredible spiritual awakening of who God really is. Never did I realize that God loved me as a gay man, even when I was told I am an abomination and that I am not a child of God, because a child of God has standards that I don't have. You've opened my eyes and I realize today that my standards rise above most religious organizations throughout the world and my spiritually devout faithfulness to the Savior, Jesus Christ, is one of monogamy. I am honored to say that *nobody* will ever talk me again into becoming a part of a family that says that they will be conditionally forever in my life or that we are forever family. How desperate and shaming it is for me today! I'm so thankful we all have moved away from the shame we have brought upon the name of Jesus Christ. I have feared for my life as all of my friends throughout the world know, to remember that many of you would love to see the end of the last call of my life come to pass. I'm grateful to be open about the hatred that I received, and the manipulation that has given me growth and maturity to never believe in *religion* again. I will never be a religious person, after my experience as Jordan Jantz, for I am Latter-day Saint Christian that happens to emotionally and mentally deal with the consequences of severe misfortune of living with the desire to

JORDAN JANTZ

belong intimately in a family. Much embarrassment surrounds my life as I must sign my name *Jantz* for believing a dream that has been a dream throughout my life. Thank you for the reality that it is time to wake up. I wish you all happiness but most of all, may you find contentment away from me, as I have found a new life with meaning and value in my life today, just as I am. Much regrets of taking the name, Jantz. No more plastic fantastic, for me. No more adoptions and no more marrying anybody again, just to belong to a family. The truth has set us all free.

To my Production Team,
you all are a blessing to the Christmas Box House and this book could not have been produced without you. You know who you are.

Has anyone ever told you what a wonderful group of people you are? I hope so. I hope you've all been told dozens of times, because you all are amazing. And just in case you haven't heard those words in a while, I want you to hear them now. This book, *Embraced,* could not be done without you. I owe you so much and I realize that my dog could not have gotten you to do anything without her love in her heart for all of you, who are writing your corrections and finding spelling errors, and all the normal mishaps of completing a true story. You deserve to know that I appreciate all of your labor. It takes special people to do what you all do for me. It takes people who are rare and remarkable to show me that I can become an author and to make the lives of everyone around me nicer and brighter with my story. It takes someone like me to be able to see the miracle in you and what you have given to me.

EMBRACED

To Ty Mansfield
President and Founder of North Star International and Founder of Voices of Hope International

I want to thank you for the most honorable time of my life, receiving the lifetime achievement award as a Beacon of Light touched me, transformed my heart to the reality that in the past I believed so many lies, so I am ready to say, "Enough is enough! God has done more for me through the Church of Jesus Christ of Latter-day Saints in letting me have the blessing of honesty and not persecution of the consequences of my same gender attraction and realizing it is a part of my identity of who I am today. God has created me to make a choice to have abundance of health and happiness as a man who desires Jesus Christ, dealing with same gender attraction, and it is not a sin to be living with same gender attraction and be gay!" FINALLY there is a ministry that can be real, that marriage is not the answer or the cure to dealing with same gender attraction, and *thank you, Ty,* for this blessed opportunity to be a Voice of Hope in a world with so many persecution of people like many of us who desire to follow Jesus Christ, but are mocked for the fact that we actually believe He loves us, just as we are. Thank God you came in to my life, and opened my eyes that God loves me and died for me and does not expect me to be walking around with a boastful false attitude that I am a "heterosexual man and have been set free from the spirit of homosexuality." Thank you, that those days are GONE. I am free to live and walk the light of the spirit of the Holy Ghost as my comforter and not man.

To Jewel Adams,
for always believing in me and going the extra mile, you are my Oprah Winfrey.

I adore you. You are a very special person. I want you to know

EMBRACED

how amazing you are. I want you to know how much you are treasured and celebrated and quietly thanked. I want you to feel really good about who you are, about all the great things you have done for me. I want you to appreciate your uniqueness, acknowledge your talents and abilities. *Realize what a beautiful soul you have.* You gave me so much sunshine in a time in my life that I needed to be inspired with much joy. I am very lucky to know you. You give me many reasons in my life to smile these days. You are a beautiful author and a beautiful sister in Christ and my friend.

To Jewell Burcham,
for the genealogy.

This book would never have been written, if you had not found out that I have biological family alive. I thank you for all your work and time. I hope nothing will come between the bond of friendship we've made, and that I will always be able to be there for you, as you have been there for me. will have shared truths and treasured memories. You have done my genealogy work for the entire biological family and worked very hard with Ancestry.com. I never dreamed that I would find out that I have family. Now, because of you, I have a brother, and a sister-in-law, and a niece and nephew and an uncle that I adore! Wherever you go, you will be in my heart, your hand will be in my hand, as friends forever.

To my brother, Ronnie Bond,
you have a special place in my heart that
I will take with me into the next life.

I see so much of myself in you.
Thank you for not running.
You are my angel and I will always love you.

XXX

When life isn't easy and you wonder if anyone understands what you are going through, I want you to reach out to me. Even though we find ourselves miles apart, don't ever forget that my heart is filled with so many hopes for your happiness. I want you to feel like you can tell me everything that is on your mind. I want to be able to help you find a lot more smiles and make your days more joyful and filled with all the serenity you so dearly deserve. You are my brother and I love you. I am older, and you will always be my *little brother*. I love you to pieces! I wish I would have always had you in my life, for I always dreamed of what it would be like to grow up with a brother.

To my sister-in-law, Lisa Bond,

1 thank you for the instant connection we have made. Thank you for bringing your love for me to the table.
You will never be replaced. I love you and
I thank you for sharing your family with me.
If I could have a wish come true, I would wish for nothing but wonderful things to come to you in your life, which is so precious to me. May troubles, worries, and problems never linger, may they only make you that much stronger and able and wise. And may you rise each day with sunlight in your heart, success in your path, answers to your prayers and that smile that I love so much. Remember that I will always love to see you and be able to spend time with you. Always there for you, your brother-in-law, Jimmy.

To Hannah and Zach,

I think the world of you.
Do you both know what you are to Uncle Jimmy? You are the most special two kids I will ever have the privilege of knowing or having in my life. I really mean that. The older I get the more I understand how rare it is to be blessed *with two wonderful kids* like

JORDAN JANTZ

you, a niece and a nephew. You deserve to receive the best in return. One of my heart's favorite hopes is that the happiness you give away will come back to warm both of you each and every day of your lives. I want you to both to appreciate your uniqueness and acknowledge your talents, strengths and abilities. Realize what a beautiful soul each of you has. You inspire so much joy in your Uncle Jimmy's life. You are very special in giving to so many people and giving them a reason to smile. There are so many moments when I am quietly in awe of the two of you, even from Portland Oregon, when I think of what I have missed not seeing the two of you growing up, if I had *only known* that I was an uncle, or had a brother, or a family that might honestly, truly walk hand in hand with me …would have been a life-changing moment for all of us. But God had things planned and your grandpa Bud did the best he could do. He sold me to a good family in California, and then fifty years later, WOW! I have a niece, nephew, a wonderful sister-in-law, and my brother, your father, *who I just adore*. When I see the two of you I realize that I have missed out on a portion of my brother's happiness, for the two of you have brought so much happiness into your mom and dad's life, which makes me very proud, as an uncle, to know the joy you inspire. You are both not plastic fantastic, just laid back and real. It opens my eyes to all the wonderful qualities about you both. I see goodness and kindness. I see compassion and understanding. And I have seen a twinkle in both of your eyes, a gentle reminder to me that I am in the company of two people who have big hearts, with beautiful ability to love their Uncle Jimmy, no matter what the circumstances are in life, I know you are not ever embarrassed of anything about the love I have for the two of you. I appreciate the closeness that I have for the two of you in my heart. I only wish I could have been with the two of you from the very start. I think you two are the most precious nephew and niece in this world and I will be blessed forever because I know what my biological brother and sister-in-law and niece and nephew are a part of me.

Long hours practicing performances for the next production

To North Star International
Thank you all for honoring me with
The Beacon of Light Award!!
It is a blessing to receive this life-time achievement award from all of you, to meet Oprah Winfrey and share the story of my life was amazing.
All of you made this possible and continue to reach out and lift up God's torch that all of us with same gender attraction can be honest, truthful, walk with integrity and hold our heads high as Latter-day Saint Christian men and women of God. You are a blessing, North Star, when other same gender ministries claim to walk in love and embrace the sheep of Jesus Christ and leave the 99 and go after the 1 who is without, that is what you *do* and *have done for me*. It is an honor to be a Beacon of Light within the Church of Jesus Christ of Latter-day Saints, in this ministry of North Star International and to be considered a Voice of Hope.

To Voices of Hope
All of you have opened the hearts of
people throughout the world with me.
What a blessing to be sharing this adventure with all of you who are working on Ty Mansfield's wonderful project, called the Voices of Hope project. What an international project this has become, and what an incredible opportunity it was for all of you to honor me with the Beacon of Light award as a Voice of Hope and a lifetime achievement of sharing the Gospel of Jesus Christ unto the nations. This is the most honorable award any man could ever be awarded as far as I am concerned. No money, no title, and no earthly pleasure could give me the happiness and peace of knowing that Jesus Christ is the reason for my voice being a voice

EMBRACED

of hope and my light being a Beacon of Light to the world. Only through Jesus Christ are all things possible for Jordan Jantz. Thank you for loving me as family and as your brother without shame.
— Jordan and Charity

Jordan in the middle, waiting to meet his new family

To Evergreen International

You have been the beginning of my introduction to living in peace with hope, not being ashamed of having same gender attraction. WOW, I could even open my eyes and go to church and not try to hide the fact that I am gay.
I can go to church and sing to Jesus Christ and *not lie* and say, "Oh, I just have same gender attraction but I'm not gay." No more excuses to people. No more reasonings to people. I'm done trying to take back ground that doesn't suit my life. I left that ground where it was at, and I don't want it back in my life, if it is not

JORDAN JANTZ

going to suit God's testimony for me to walk on. I need safe ground and safe people, like all of you, to make this life work for those who have been broken-hearted as children and as adults. We all have come together and merged as a hive of bees working for the purpose of God's glory for those like me, who are same gender attracted and love Jesus Christ, over all.

To Allen Oyler,

You are more important than words could express. I have grown into living a life that I never dreamed was possible because of men like you, and most do not hold true as you do. The friendship, incredible conversations and get-togethers with you and your family have meant more to me than going on some extravagant trip. For me, experiencing the basic American family life is like watching an I Love Lucy program; I can watch it and laugh but not ever embrace the moments of laughter within my own life. You have given me more than any other man in God's Kingdom and taken time to open your life and family up to me, when the majority only does this during home teaching or visiting the members in the church. You and I surpass everyone. And, you surpass my doubts for I know I never need to question anything that you would ever tell me. I would do anything for your family and you. We are eternal friends and I love you from my heart and soul, which I understand is so much of my character of who I am and why I am the way I am in my life.

To First Christian Church of Moweaqua, Illinois

I have heard and visited this beautiful church. My brother, Ronnie Bond, and my sister-in-law, Lisa Bond, and my niece and nephew, Hannah and Zach Bond, have taken me to church on Sunday. I enjoyed the teaching and the way you are reaching people through the life-changing message you shared with me of Jesus Christ. I

XXXVII

am very excited to hear about my niece and my sister-in-law who went on a team of twelve, leaving for Haiti last November. The group was working at a children's orphanage for a group called Children of Promise Orphanage to make walkers and wheelchairs for children with special needs. They also help with construction and projects and medical care. Pictures of the group along with a wheelchair and the walker they made were available on display, at the church. And, I'm very grateful to know that there is a well-established church that explores faith that finds answers, giving no room for doubt, causing all to **draw to near and go far**, as children of God. I love your vision statement that states *"reaching people through the life changing message of Jesus.'* Learning how to Moweaqua reaches people through the message of Jesus Christ in the village where my brother and his family live. There are so many people that have prayers that get whispered, and so many hopes that fill the heart. There are wishing stars that spend their entire evenings to all the things I have longed for throughout my life, as a little boy and as an adult. I have seen the most beautiful stars at night in the village of Moweaqua. Driving through the cornfields, what a lovely little village! I only wish there were apartments available, but then again, would it take away from the feeling of the village? It made me feel like I was in Mayberry in Andy Griffith Show. I never dreamed that if I asked and believed well enough, reality could provide things that turned out so right as really going to the First Christian Church on that beautiful Sunday morning, with my family. I couldn't have asked for a blessing more wonderful than meeting all of you at the First Christian Church in Moweaqua. It was a meaningful event that I long for again. Thank you for embracing Ronnie, Lisa, Hannah and Zach Bond. – Love, Ronnie's brother who was a first time visitor who embraced the time of worship with his family here on earth as I will also, in heaven. What a day of rejoicing that will be. *When we all see Jesus, we will sing and shout for victory! We win in the end.*

EMBRACED

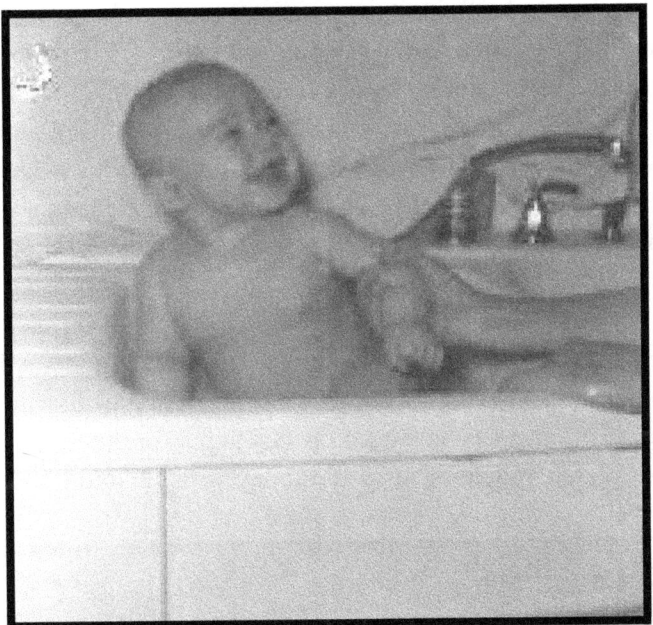

First real bath, a Polaroid moment

To LDS Family Services around the world,

ALL of you have given me the best of what I can offer to the world here in my life, with you, which is to share the purpose of the gospel and the love for other people, letting go of my own personal needs and desires and embracing children who are fatherless. All this makes me realize what God did for me. I know I will never be God himself, but I sure would like to have a heart after God's own life that He had for so many that He touched and healed. LDS Family Services has helped so many of my friends who have dealt with their families breaking up due to their same gender attraction. It is amazing that people can say, "If you will just get married, it will go away." I praise the Lord that you all are on board in teaching that you *cannot pray the gay away*. That is long-overdue and it is all because of you and

JORDAN JANTZ

God's plan for LDS family services to become a home-base for healing in the lives of Latter-day Saint Christians in our church, so that they can come out of the closet and walk into the LDS Family Services and be embraced with the love of Jesus Christ and the hope that they can have a transformed life and not be judged for putting the truth on the table. I pray we all can make the pact to not talk bad about the gay and lesbian people in church, for they are as close to the Savior as anybody else. In God's eyes, He has no room for being a respecter of persons. I'm on that page, also. Been there, done that, and I have worn out the t-shirt. And I am done with the "national coming out day" for me, it is time to claim the ultimate life that has now been opened to me for the first time in fifty years. Will you walk this journey with me into eternity?

Friends for 30+ years, Jordan and Billy at Mother's Bistro.

EMBRACED

To Affirmation LGBT Mormon Families & Friends,

CARE OF THE PRESIDENT of AFFIRMATION,
Mr. Randall Thacker,

It has been a great blessing to have been invited to many of the Affirmation events throughout the years. I'm a devoted gay Latter-day Saint Christian who is elated to see the Affirmation Community hold on to many values that are life-touching to us, that live with same gender attraction. My hat is off to all of you who have stood by me along with all the community of brothers and sisters who share my attraction from Seattle to Portland to Idaho, for the Pacific Northwest is my territory where ground has been broken for gay and lesbian people to stand and turn to the happiness that is naturally given to us out of love, for us all being children of God. Thank you for remembering me in your prayers and may the blessings of living a truthful life always be a light that lights the way for the truth to set us all free. Thank you for walking side-by-side when others turned and ran from me.

To The Well,

Eric and Annabelle Davis

The two of you have stood out as pillars, holding me on each side, throughout the past two decades that we have shared incredible moments of our lives. I'm so elated to have an honest minister as a friend. I love your non-judgmental attitude towards me and my Christianity as a Latter-day Saint, whereas many ministers have literally – to my face – said, "How can you be a part of this church or this ministry outreach when you are in a church that doesn't the Word of God and is not a Bible-based church!?" How sad it is to hear this when my honesty came from the ability to be honest in front of God that I am gay and that I do love Him. To see so many

A BENEFIT FOR OUTSIDE IN
and the HOMELESS YOUTH

Dear Randall Thacker and All Throughout the country who are affiliated with the Affirmation Community,

It was my grateful heart that was touched by all of the Affirmation Group in Portland, Oregon who had asked me to help deliver the incredible gifts and blessings that were put together by the Affirmation Community in Portland, Oregon. Thank you for extending your invitation to me to help, for I will do all I can to share the love I have for others, through the love that I have for Jesus.

XLII

Friends are friends forever if the Lord is the Lord in them.

XLIII

I've been told that when a friend dies, you then have an angel to call by name. I have been blessed to have many friends waiting for me on the other side.

XLIV

put their expectations and chains of public notoriety for them, to make it a sink or swim. I cannot be that way. I'm in a church-based Bible-teaching Gospel-filled Church of Jesus Christ of Latter-day Saints, and to judge puts horrendous bandages on people and creates wounds, spiritually, when love could repair the sores that life has made. I will no longer affiliate in any manner with ministries that are bullying their people that come in for help, not knowing what kind of help is needed and so they allow their hearts and lives to be all wrapped up in performance. My God and my blessings received from God are not received by works or actions. They are given because of Love. And that's the way that Eric and Annabelle Davis have groomed me to walk as a Latter-day Saint Christian, for they have both said several times, "There has never been any church that has reached out and walked the walk and not the talk as the Latter-day Saint Church people have with you." They have allowed the truth to be spoken, the truth that you can have same gender attraction and be gay and open about who you really are and tell the truth and honor your Heavenly Father with respect. That is what Eric and Annabelle Davis give to me and that is more than money could buy. I will hold on to this relationship until the day that I am transformed into my new life, because what we share is not plastic fantastic. It is not a friendship based on works. It is not a relationship based on getting my monthly home teaching done, or a Sunday relationship. I love you, Eric and Annabelle. Thank you for supporting me in my church and in turning my life toward leaving a legacy behind for the lives of children.

To Russell Ballard,

I'm so thankful to have had time with you in my stake conference in Beaverton. All of my friends came to meet you and were amazed to meet you and your loving spirit of kindness. I know that you have opened the hearts of many

JORDAN JANTZ

BE THE CHANGE YOU WISH TO SEE ON EARTH
AND MAY LIFE TREAT YOU WELL
LOTS OF LOVE FROM ME AND CHARITY

men like me who have same gender attraction and I am grateful that your son is on board with working with the missionaries here in Portland. I admire your son for he is doing is something that affects the world, in sending out the missionaries that teach the gospel. You and your son have both touched my life. I'm not the type to just say *thank you* but I will say, I am honored that you would embrace someone that is not plastic fantastic, like me, and support them with love and embrace in their hope and embrace the lives of God's children who are different but never give up, and choose the right. Thank you for your support is everything to me becoming embraced in my church.

To Pastor William T. Turner,
Trinity Full Gospel Pentecostal Church of Christ,

I SAY BLESSSINGS TO YOU, Pastor Turner and Sister Turner, for it is an honor to walk in the path of Christ's love throughout downtown Portland with you and the Full Gospel message that you are teaching! You have helped me to let go of the people that do not suit my future. And I want to say, thank you. You are a light in this life of mine. And, coming and visiting and bringing guests where I know they will be filled and touched by the spirit, more than any other church I know. I have never felt so many people in any church, ever, embrace their attendees like this incredible black gospel church, and that is the boat I'm on with my church, today.

I'm not in to a *Sunday relationship* with people. I am in a life-time commitment with brothers and sisters in Christ. No time for the plastic fantastic. Until we are glorified in heaven together as brothers I love you, _Jordan Jantz, your church is a breath of fresh air.

JORDAN JANTZ

To Fred and Marilyn Matis,
Words cannot express the impact of hope on a life! Still, these words are from a child of God who needed your light and loving encouragement through disabilities put upon me in my life. I thank you and <u>I love you!!!</u>

To the family, friends and professionals that handed out promises as life-long relationships,
I can only respond to the true reality of abandonment. But, you are all who you are and created to be the person you are, and to feel comfortable with the life-choices you all have made. Never did I expect to be fooled by so many that claim to be family and claimed to this day, to have had feelings in their life for me. Impossible! Pure, impossible, unreality and a total façade, making such blurred understanding of why we were ever even family or friends to begin with. For my realization is opening to me now, the surmountable emotional cruelty for not being who you wanted me to be, to a new life so that at last I understand why people like me hold on to people like you. Children that have been damaged never believe they can have anything of value. Reality - God restores all broken children and puts them up as His prize, as he did me. My life is so much better off without all of you in it. Thank you, for leaving so that I could be the man of God that is not *religious,* walking in a prideful spirit. That's not my group. And neither are any of you, so thank you for letting go and letting me be the man I am called to be.

Prominent political friends in government celebrating Oregon's new State Senate What a festive evening filled with love.

XLIX

JORDAN JANTZ

Political Election Celebration in Downtown Portland for the new US President

L

To Banfield Pet Hospitals,

I have the <u>best</u> veterinary for my dog, Charity, and I'm so grateful because women are so attentive to the emotions of being gentle to animals. I have so much integrity and respect for Banfield Veterinarians in Northwest Portland, for the care of my *healthy* almost-fifteen-year-old barkless Basenji from Egypt who is essential to my life. Basenjis are the dogs of the Pharaohs, of African descent, and my Aunt Frieda picked Charity out which is even more special, because any kind of love that has ever come into my life, I hold on to. That's how Charity came into my life with her loving heart opening my cold heart, protecting myself from others who knew the word and actions that would break the spirit and soul of a human being. I am grateful for what I have today. I can let go of yesterday as if it never happened, because of Charity, which name means the Pure Love of Christ.

To the Gay and Lesbian Community:

It has been since I was nineteen years old that I met many of you here in Portland, Oregon, who have embraced my life. Then, I never knew what to expect, but you can expect this from me. Today, as always, we have made a major life pact to one another, since family and friends and loved ones have died and deserted all of us. To most families, the individuals don't comprehend how close we are and the love and kindness and intimacy we have in holding up others to see the love that radiates from within the brokenness that has shredded our hearts. But with all of us being honest, I'm going to let you know, I will be here for you no matter what. When you need someone to turn to, I'll be here for you. ALL of you. I will do whatever it takes as a brother from the gay community and give as much as I can, as I have in the past. I will not desert any of you, for I am in no way better off

JORDAN JANTZ

without you. Today I am not without you, we are just closer in spirit and in truth. Many churches and religions will misrepresent you. I will not allow that to ever happen. To help you find your smile and to get you back on steady ground again after the world has ripped us apart, ever since Harvey Milk and his experience with me back in 1974 and 1975, I will forever remember the broken gay men and women on the streets of San Francisco who were beaten to a pulp for claiming to be gay or lesbian. And today we all still live with people wanting to put the identity of gay or lesbian on us so that they can push us away. They love the fact that some of us have attached ourselves to the main identity as a gay man or gay woman. Don't believe a word they say. That is not our identity. It is their manipulation. I will not tolerate anyone messing with the community that stood up when my families left me and walked away because I was not what they had hoped I would turn out to be. I will listen with my heart and I will do my best to hear the things and the dreams as I have in the past, with many of you, but I can't quite find the words that open the reality of what it is like for you and me who do believe in another life after this life. Please forgive them, for they do not know what they do, although they claim to run ministries for men and women who are 'broken' with same gender attraction. *They know not what they do.* And remember, <u>I will never betray the trust you have put in me</u>. I will do my best to see you all through. If there are decisions to be made, I may offer a direction for you to go in. If there are tears to be dried, I will tenderly dry them. I want you to feel completely at ease about reaching out to me for the rest of our lives and throughout our old age as men and women that have dealt with same gender attraction throughout life until the day God takes us home. I don't ever want to forget this life and what I've experienced. You couldn't impose on me if you tried, by asking me to help you, in any format. It is simply impossible. I am here for you, with happiness and peace of mind. We are so closely interwoven throughout our life that we are inseparable, as same gender attracted men and women who desire to live in truth and light. I will truly, deeply and completely care about you every day, you can count on that. I hope it will invite a little more serenity in your life to know you are not alone and I hope it will encourage a brighter day. I'm not going anywhere; I promise you that. There will not be a ministry that will be successful in this world if it doesn't open its heart to the reality that there is not one person that is infallible and has never made a mistake and the shame of the reality that that mistake even happened, unless it is to come to your side and to hold out a hand to you, be at peace, until we meet again. I will be by your side, through thick and thin. Let's all be set free, from other people's judgments and our own judgments.

TODAY ON MARCH 14, 2016, the very day that is the anniversary of Jordan's Baptism (that the entire gay community attended), Jordan's gay friends – musicians, artists, political officials - now celebrate with Jordan both his transformation anniversary <u>and</u> the submission of this Second Edition of *Embraced,* just this morning. A dinner event will be hosted by the Portland gay community at the Old Town Spaghetti Factory. **"Portland, I thank you so much for the wonderful gay friends that have walked with me for more than thirty years. I will never turn my back on you!!"** - Jordan

Also this same week, the North Star Convention returns and though Jordan is not able to attend this year, Jordan is overcome with joy that there will be a new Beacon of Light presentation and recipient who can encourage the whole world to do good and embrace truth with unconditional love.
"North Star, you are *all* in my heart!" - Jordan

JORDAN JANTZ

To Spencer Wallentine,

The goodness you give me is a goodness that came from your first knock on my door, inviting me to share a conversation. This little letter is for you, Spencer.
This is a thank you for having a heart that is so big and a mind that is so open. You never judged me; you never looked at me as though I was weird or different. You embraced me and with a spirit that had a lot of love, and I really felt God's spirit when I first met you, that you would be not-plastic-fantastic, but true-blue. Your message of gratitude for *me* is incredible. You inspire me with your wonderfulness. You are the first person I think of whenever I have something to share, and you are the last person in the universe I would hurt or ever be unkind to. You are a treasure to my life. For ten years you and I have been best friends and I value you so much, because of the honesty we have. There never has been one lie or one mistrust that I have ever experienced in knowing you the past ten years. You have an amazing knack for reassuring. Knowing my past and the abandonment issues that I have lived through throughout my life, it is amazing that you invite me to go along to the places you go to throughout your life and the journeys that take you where your dreams can become whole. I enjoy every opportunity to reminisce about the reality of our spiritual brotherhood that is eternal, with the best friend that is a man of God, a true Latter-day Saint Christian. I am honored to be your brother and a part of your family. I will always love and honor you and your family.
Your eternal brother – Jordan and Charity

To Todd Christofferson

Thank you for opening my heart and life with your words of wisdom, and extending your kindness of friendship. You are a blessing of respect to remind me that being gay is not the end of

EMBRACED

the world, and that I can overcome many obstacles. I love you and your brother for walking along with me to bring hope and light to all who struggle to prove to the world that God loves gay people and gay people that love God need to be respected, because it is the hardest thing to do, when people in the church bully the gay person as often as the heterosexual men are challenged in our church, with this particular circumstance. I pray their hearts all will be transformed to realize that sin is sin and only he without sin only may cast the first stone. As you have taught me, I will teach them. Thank you for loving me and embracing my transformation. For now, I am embraced.

To my Uncle Bill Bond,

I don't know exactly what it is, but there is something very special about you.

Your wonderful attitude is obviously connected to a warm and loving heart. You are my father's brother and that means everything to me. Your telling me that since my father is no longer around, that you would like to be able to be as a father that Bud would want me to have, if he were still around, still amazes me. It is the little things like this that I value more than anything, Uncle Bill. I pray you never read this book for what I have had to do to make my life survive many dark years, I hesitate to share, but I will go a million miles out of my way to do what is right. The way you are today has helped set the stage for so many beautiful tomorrows. I promise you I am so grateful that you are in my life and I have a biological uncle that loves me and I will be seeing you very soon. I can't wait to share time with you and meet you again. I can't wait to make some very wonderful memories, the joys of two people just being on the same page in each other's history is more valuable than anything else to me.

LVI

It is the little things like this that I value more than anything, Uncle Bill. I pray you never read this book for what I have had to do to make my life survive many dark years, I hesitate to share, but I will go a million miles out of my way to do what is right. The way you are today has helped set the stage for so many beautiful tomorrows. I promise you I am so grateful that you are in my life and I have a biological uncle that loves me and I will be seeing you very soon. I can't wait to share time with you and meet you again. I can't wait to make some very wonderful memories, the joys of two people just being on the same page in each other's history is more valuable than anything else to me.

I want to thank my spiritual family

for believing in me and for teaching me
to walk by faith, to know that our Spiritual Family
is eternal and will last forever.
With all of you in my life this has been
the best ten years of my life.
Thank you for loving me just as I am.
You are the best! Your wonderful qualities have made a lasting impression on me, that I will admire for as long as I live. You all give me so much to be thankful for. You have wisdom that goes beyond your words, a sweetness that goes beyond your smiles, and hearts of pure gold. You all have taken the time to hear my deepest thoughts, my feelings, all my fears. You've dried tears no one else could see. You've helped me find happiness and you've taught me that I really can make some of my dreams come true.

For my adoptive father who raised me,

**I honor you and thank you for carrying me
when I could not walk.
Thank you for being my footprints in the sand.**

JORDAN JANTZ

I'd like to share this thought with you, to tell you that you mean the world to me. Think of something you couldn't live without and multiply it by one hundred. Then, think of what happiness means to you, and add it to the feeling you get on the best days you've ever had on this earth. Now, Dad, I want you to add that all up with your best feelings and take away the rest, and what you are left with is exactly how I feel about you. You matter more to me than you can imagine and more than I'll ever be able to explain.

To the Arlene Schnitzer Concert Hall and Performing Arts Center,

Thank you for thirty years of beautiful performances! I have never been so grateful for this beautiful place for Portlanders to find culture and community in the theatric performances of Broadway productions that tour through Portland throughout the years. To be a part of this brings out my old years in the theater, with the productions and performances, but I admit that I never performed in the most beautiful place in downtown Portland that I have ever seen, like the performances at the Arlene Schnitzer Concert Hall. *Georgia Harrow, you are the light of management* and all that goes on behind the scenes of every production. Incredible artistic abilities you bring to your crew and to Portland Oregon. It is nice to have friends who are real people with the same attractions to the theater and the performances throughout the world. Broadway performances will last til the end of time, just as the friendship I have found with many of you through work for the Arlene Schnitzer concert hall. The professional kindness of the theater has embraced this book, to the lives of many in the theatrical business. Words will never express my gratitude for just how I have been embraced by all of you in the performing arts industry.

To the Christmas Box House,

For opening children's hearts that have lived in desperate hope for finding their voice, you have been just that. Their voice, for those who couldn't speak.
And for some, you are their eyes when they couldn't see, you given so many children the best of what life can be. I have never gotten over the fact that I was sold and I was the *only one* that was sold. I lived with a dream that someday, I could make some sense of why my life was the way it was. For, there is no way to be able to explain the very things that you do not even understand yourself. That is why I am grateful for these the two books, *Out of the Closet, Into the Light,* written by J Adams, and my second book, *Embraced,* because 100% of my portions are donated to the children at the Christmas Box House. You have touched my life and that's the purpose of embraced. May another child sleep safely tonight in the arms of an angel. Thank you for being God's hands, extended. I will support this industry, for I will never let one child go unloved, if I have my way.
'Til the end of time.

To my favorite woman in the world,
my Aunt Marion Lee,

you have saved the best for last.
A little story about you and me.
ME- so lucky to have this special connection.
YOU- the wonderful person I am so thankful for.
ME- someone who means well, but not always just right.
YOU someone who gives smiles and encouragement.
ME- a little insecure, uncertain, a little crazy sometimes.
YOU- a huge help and a calming influence all the time.
YOU- know what is going on inside me better than anyone.
ME- there's nobody else I feel so comfortable turning to.

EMBRACED

YOU- on a scale of 1 to 10, you're at least a 20.
ME- counting my blessings and hearing your name so often!
YOU- a joy to be with, to think of and just to talk to.
ME- so incredibly glad that God made you,
and because God made you,
I have a place where I belong.

To all who operate on a day-to-day basis the Federal Government for the Americans with Disabilities Act and Social Security Administration,

you have given me hope when everyone called it quits. You're appreciated more than words can say. I thank each of you so much and so do my doctors, for taking the time to be there when I need you. Thanks for seeing me through so much medical challenges that were very unexpected. I thank you for taking the hours to help me during moments when family abandoned me. Out of your own precious days and times, the Social Security System worked with me through the most challenging moments and gave me a little more sunlight. Thank you for being a kindness and a beautiful spirit in a world that could use more things just like the social security system. Thanks so much for everything you've done to help me with the disabilities that I am confronted with, and for all that you continue to do for me.

James Lee Bond

LXII

To my Heavenly Father

Thoughts I'd love to share intimately with you are so important to my days, and so essential to the smile within me. I consider the space and time where our lives have overlapped and the place that brings me and you the most understanding, the most peace I've ever had. Understanding of my own self and my own thoughts, these are the nicest memories of You and me, and talking alone with You and my dog, Charity, asking you, Heavenly Father, what Your plan is for my life, and the joy that came into my heart so consistently because You are so important to me. I want your light to shine and I want the world to see Your peace, deep within my soul. <u>Joyfullness</u> is the promise of each new day that I have with You. I have stars to reach, because of you. I have dreams that will come into my life, because of your love for me. And the memories are more beautiful than words can say, because your love for me is the most true love I've ever been able to embrace. **Thank you for not walking out of my life.**

And, God, I forgot I wanted to add, from my heart, honestly, will animals be in heaven?
If there are, I want to thank you for giving me my dog, Charity. My Aunt Frieda found her for me as my service dog.

JORDAN JANTZ

I would never be able to give to the world the way you have taught me, Jesus, unless You made my dog just for me. I named her Charity because that name means "the pure love of Christ" and that's the only kind of love I desire in my life for I have let go of every other kind of love or hope in anyone, after the life I've been given, here on earth. May all of you who ever think of me please know that it was nice to share my heart with you, whether you accepted me as a part of your life or not, I'm not the judge. We all gave it our best, at loving as God would have us do unto one another. So, my love is surrounded by fourteen of years. I've never been in a family or an intimate relationship of any sort as long as I have been with my dog, Charity. Although, I know Jesus is my long-time advocate and will be for all of my life.

I thank you all!

EMBRACED

Oprah, Thank you for the weekend you gave to me with you and your staff. You have been a part of my life for over twenty five years. Thank you for embracing me at your tour in Seattle. You will always have a special place in my life. —Jordan Jantz

Marie, I'm very touched by the way you have taught many to keep going forward in life, and not look back. Your heart is filled with God's love and acceptance of all people. Thank you for never judging me. I have enjoyed the opportunity to see you pay it forward to children in all you do. I will follow in your shoes. Love, Jordan

- By the way I love ALL your shoes.

Donny, I want you to always remember that so often many men look up to you as a role model of a Godly man. When I first met you, I saw the Holy Spirit all around you. You embraced me as God would and even though God doesn't drive in fast sports cars, I love the fact you enjoy heading down the highway to "let it go".

Your friend, Jordan

Ellen, you have opened my heart every day with happiness for the love you tell us to share with one another, and ending your show every day with telling the world to be kind to one another. Sharing these two beautiful statements is what people like myself need to hear for not everyone knows they are loved.

Jordan Jantz

Ty, much happiness you have brought into my life over the years. Learning and watching from you has taught me how valuable it is to not be a respecter of persons. I value our friendship with honesty and integrity.

Love you, Jordan

Celebrating the Christmas Box House for Children with author, Jordan Jantz — 2016. National best selling author, Jewel Adams.

Jewel, you are amazing to me. You went above and beyond the call of duty as my friend and you have taught me so much about myself. I have no words that can describe my gratitude and respect for you. Love, Jordan

-Thank you for supporting *Embraced*.

JORDAN JANTZ

LXXII

Jordan's life-time favorite
Kennedy quote:

"Even though people may be well known, they hold in their hearts the emotions of a simple person for the moments that are the most important of those we know on earth."

Jackie Kennedy 1968

How Your Amazon Purchase Proceeds go directly to The Christmas Box House

Per Amazon, Christmas Box House is Direct-by-Check Sole Royalty Payee.
No Funds Change Hands

This is the only reason for Jordan doing his books and sharing his message and the story of his life.

"If anyone causes one of these little ones--those who believe in me--to stumble, it would be better for them to have a large millstone hung around their neck and to be drowned in the depths of the sea."
Matthew 18:6

Visit the Christmas Box House website today.

http://www.thechristmasboxhouse.org/

PERSONAL INVITATION FROM JORDAN

FIRST EDITION RELEASED ON VALENTINE'S DAY 2016

Every farewell offers an opportunity for a new hello. It does not matter if you are in Chicago, Portland or Utah or anywhere in between. When one road ends, it is time to look ahead in a new direction and remember, as far out as you can see and also out into the universe where we can see even farther than we ever see in our mortal lifetime, what our purpose honestly is for.

That's where I'm heading with this life I've been given. I am nothing without Jesus forgiving me. I want His happiness in what I do in His name. I never want to become someone who leads others away from hope. I want this new book, *Embraced,* to give you all happiness that shows God's love and His embracing joy in this lifetime. Your kindness is a gift to me and I am turning your thoughtfulness for my life around to share what it's like to be loved.

This new book, *Embraced,* goes along with the first book *Out of the Closet, Into the Light.* It is made to be a set that will open the reality that God is the finisher of everyone's life here on earth. This book is done by showing hope and challenges that will make you want to read and reread. It is going to be a classic set that will be treasured by many who walk in light from here to eternity. Reading *Embraced,* you will become a part of a healing journey. You will be introduced to mindful meditation through a gentle approach that opens true feelings, as you are on a quiet and welcoming journey, learning to connect yourself, how to release long-held tension in your body and give yourself permission to breathe, move and relax,

EMBRACED

cultivate internal and external support with the opportunity to be with yourself in a loving and nonjudgmental way. Eventually it will all become a style of relating with yourself and others in even the most stressful times. I want reading the book, *Embraced,* to teach us all how to reduce stress, improve self-esteem, support the process of change to be happier and healthier. The first book and this second book have purposes and reasons and are organized to heal with hope.

I am passionate about sharing practices of hope. I am committed to making my life accessible for everyone to have available. Inquire to Jewel Adams, author of *Out of the Closet, Into the Light,* or Ty Mansfield, President of Voices of Hope and Founding Member and current President of North Star International. These are the finest of organizations that continue to give to my life and many others. So become *embraced* this fall with many programs that are waiting for you. Embrace the change of your life.

A tribute to my missionary who went above and beyond the call of duty: this man mentors me, teaching me God's purpose for creating me and giving meaning to my life and, most important, teaching me to prepare me for eternity.

Jordan and Charity

LXXVIII

CHRONOLOGY

1959 Born, Dec 2, Decatur, Illinois

1964 Sold to family in Compton, California

1966 Adoption contested, resolved

1979 Graduated High School

1996 Suicide Attempt

2008 Baptism to Church of Jesus Christ of Latter-day Saints

2013 *Out of the Closet, Into the Light* published

2014 Jordan's Voice of Hope Videos produced

2015 Beacon of Light Lifetime Achievement Award
    Award presented to Jordan at Gay Pride for same reason

2016 *Embraced* released on Valentine's Day.
    Also on this date: Jordan's grave marker is placed

This publication by
Jordan Jantz Underground 4 Saving the Lives of Children
Office: 1430 SW 12th St. #1709 Portland, Oregon 97201
503-223-3648

BIBLIOGRAPHY

LXXX

LXXXI

VOICES ON AMAZON

Top Customer Reviews, Verified Purchase of *Out of the Closet, Into the Light*, on Amazon.com

5.0 out of 5 stars The dialogue of a survivor
By Baylor on August 24, 2013

While I have been a friend of Jordan's for many years I have never had a clear understanding of his life's experience until reading this book. I know that this book was a massive undertaking because while publicly he lives his life unashamed, he keeps many details and experiences locked deep in his heart. I found this publication to be a raw and gritty view into a very painful part of Jordan's life that few people can even begin to contemplate. My relationship with Jordan leads me to understand that this book is not about religion, being gay, or even the abuse. It is about overcoming tremendous and horrifically painful atrocities humanity brings to bear upon itself. Jordan is a survivor and this story illustrates that in spite of the abuse and grizzly torture he has been exposed to; somehow his heart remained open to receive and then give away the loving kindness he has longed for his entire life.

Out of many, we have the story of one
By Sherry C on June 13, 2013

A straight-forward story of one child, who in fact, represents thousands. This book is open about events but is not graphic. Sincerely and simply written, it is effective without superfluous dressing. It leads the reader through a life that we don't want to acknowledge exists. Now an older adult, Jordan exposes the life that

EMBRACED

Out of the Closet Into the Light

J. Adams

As told by Jordan Jantz

JORDAN JANTZ

too many children still endure. How does a child handle such treatment? What does it do to a soul? Jordan's response is to help other children who suffer. Proceeds from his book are sent to The Christmas Box House International, an organization that provides medical treatment and mental therapy to abused, abandoned and neglected children. Jordan's story is one of kindness rising from abuse and defeating unkindness with love and service to others.

5.0 out of 5 stars eye-opening
By S. Fei on March 3, 2014

I've lived a really sheltered life, and this book opened my eyes to the fact that there is real honest-to-goodness evil in this world. That Jordan could not only survive these experiences, but thrive as a human being, seeking for the light of Christ and blessing those around him, is a testament to the strength and character of his soul. The author did a wonderful job conveying the horrors of abuse matter-of-factly without gory embellishment. Within the chapters and especially at the end, rays of hope shine through. To those who are suspicious of the book, thinking it is anti-gay or pro-reparative therapy, please give it a chance. I have friends across the spectrum of belief on whether God blesses gay unions who found this book to be enlightening and worth the read. It tells of one man's rocky journey that ends with him finding peace and forgiveness. It condemns abuse and judgment while encouraging unconditional love and turning your life over to Christ. It is a very touching book that inspires me to be more compassionate and less judgmental of my fellow human beings.

5.0 out of 5 stars Not one to be missed
By book lover on February 3, 2016

Read this book in one sitting. Once I started, I could not put down.

EMBRACED

It made me sad, yet hopeful. I rooted for Jordan to overcome the horrific abuse he suffered as a result of his upbringing. What a joy to see that he found hope and love in Christ. The author's writing style is one that I find very enjoyable to read. She has a way with words that never disappoints.

5.0 out of 5 stars Jordan Jantz has become a good friend
By Abbey Garfield on February 1, 2015

Jordan Jantz has become a good friend of mine since meeting him at a North Star 2014 convention. *Out of the Closet, Into the Light* is Jordan's heart wrenching life story. I shed tears while reading about my dear friend's hard times and smiled when he found his happiness. I know the man Jordan is today. Reading his book I understand him in a new way, through his past. I have even a more love for him now.. if that possible. This is an inspirational true story of a great man who truly has a deep love for others.

5.0 out of 5 stars
By Willow on January 23, 2015

Jordan has a remarkable story behind such a remarkable being. The pain and suffering he has endured has not made him a cruel or hateful person like it can do to so many. He is loving, compassionate and inspiring. Thank you for lighting the path for others to come forward with their stories. -E.Hugo

5.0 out of 5 stars World AIDS Day
By Abdulrazzaq on December 1, 2014

Happy holidays to Voices of Hope, Ty Mansfield and Jewel Adams

JORDAN JANTZ

for bringing light of Jordan's love for what you all have reached out in love for my friend and you all have done so much to help Portland realize that not just celebrities but people that have a faith in God can love people from all walks of life, like Jordan did on Thanksgiving, giving out baked potatoes to the homeless before he chose to celebrate his Thanksgiving with his family that knows everything like we all do. Also, find value in what my friend Jordan has transformed into. Amen! -With love, People of Portland, OR

5.0 out of 5 stars I recommend this book to those searching for hope
By Lana on November 30, 2014

Jordan's courage to put himself out there, open up and write his courageous story is an inspiration in itself. This is a book about hope, faith and redemption which cannot be measured. Jesus Christ is the source of that hope. Jordan's book is a journey on finding himself, his self-worth and his Savior. This book is Evidence that Heavenly Father loves ALL his children. I recently had the privilege of meeting Jordan, he carries the light of Christ and he shares that light back with whomever he comes in contact with. He is an inspiration to me and my family. The title of this book could not be more appropriately named. "Into the light" this is where this author is in heart, spirit and his physical being. I highly recommend this book to anyone searching for hope, overcoming any obstacles (abuse) and/or meaning in their life, regardless of your sexual identity. This book has brought peace and hope to me, my family and my child who has SSA.

5.0 out of 5 stars God's wonderful Grace
By SANDY on July 23, 2014

The Lord is the everlasting God, the Creator of the ends of the earth.

EMBRACED

He will not grow tired or weary, and His understanding NO one can fathom. He gives strength to the weary and increases the power of the weak. Even youths grow tired and weary, and young men stumble and fall; but those who hope in the Lord will renew their strength. They will soar on wings like eagles, they will run and not grow weary, they will walk and not be faint. Isaiah 40:28-31

5.0 out of 5 stars **Very educational and inspiring**
By geri oyler on March 25, 2014

It is inspiring to know that some people can overcome terrible trials in their lives and come out the victor.

5.0 out of 5 stars **Heartwarming and a must read for everyone!**
By Carolee A. Newgren on March 1, 2014

Jordan shares his life story of being sold as a baby to another family and all the heartaches and abuse he experienced growing up gay. It is an amazing story of the life of a young boy who grows up with so many obstacles in his life and yet keeps on hoping and fighting for the love he so much desires. Eventually, he becomes involved in the gay community. He also recognizes and comes to know that he loves the Savior and chooses to live for Him. He becomes a light to so many and welcomes those friends in the gay community to his baptism and to church services with him. Jordan's example is a bright light to many stumbling in darkness and despair. He knows he is gay, but he accepts the atonement of the Savior and wants to give his life for him. Jordan is a voice of hope for so many people and his story is a blessing to all who hear it.

JORDAN JANTZ

5.0 out of 5 stars Touching in MANY ways
By M. Chamberlain on January 14, 2014

Difficult to read at times, but definitely important to understand how the life of one person can be impacted by 'family' life

LXXXVIII

EMBRACED

5.0 out of 5 stars Into the Light
By mary on November 13, 2013

I read this book in a single day, finding Jordan's story very compelling. Evil exists when an innocent child is subjected to the senseless pain of emotional and physical abuse. I met Jordan before reading his life story, and it now brings me comfort to know he has truly found his way "Into the Light". It took extraordinary courage on his part, and a willingness to move forward through pain and past experience.

Reading about his friend Mark especially touched me because I am an LDS mother of a wonderful gay son. Rejection does not change minds or hearts, nor is it Christ-like. Having differences and seeing the world in different ways can make life challenging, but Jordan's message is one of hope - love truly does conquer all!

5.0 out of 5 stars Sometimes we need to listen from our hearts
By Voges on November 11, 2013

I cry for your youth.
I pray for your adult life.
Hang on - we love you.

Betty Crandall
Ps I read your book three times in the first week I received it.

5.0 out of 5 stars Short, Sweet, Inspiring
By EJK on November 7, 2013

Though the book is not an autobiography in the most technical

EMBRACED

sense, the book flows as a narrative with Jordan's voice clearly evident. Adams did a fantastic job selecting from, editing, and compiling events from whatever else Jordan must have shared with her. The book is short, honest, and matter-of-fact. There is no plea for mercy or outcry for restitution. The book supplies a true account of one man's (unfortunate) upbringing and the surprising and deserved final ending. You will be shocked at the quantity of wrongdoing described in this book. Though descriptive and honest, the author does not step into unnecessary or excessive details. It is a great book to remind us all why we ought to be a little kinder - or a lot kinder - to everyone we meet and see every day. We need more openness, love, and honesty. This book provides all of that. Short read, yet powerful and worth it.

5.0 out of 5 stars Finding your path in life
By S. Nelson on October 1, 2013

This book opens the door of a soul who has made the decision to turn from an early life of dark, self-destructive behavior where his lifestyle is a series of bad choices and makes an astounding turn around in his physical and mental behavior to find meaning and redemption in his life as he seeks the help of the Savior to redefine his direction and purpose in life.

Robert Nelson

5.0 out of 5 stars Heartfelt and Sincere
By Lee Harris on September 21, 2013

I know this author very well and his story has touched the lives of many people. Jordan's message is one of pain and suffering as well as redemption and understanding of Gods pure love for him and all

XCII

his children. Most people would rather avoid hearing these types of stories but to know that we can come back into our Fathers light and love even after experiencing such terrible abuse and heartache is a lesson all can benefit from. I would recommend this book to anyone who struggles with their own worth and understanding of God's love for them.

A descriptive book to know you are not alone
By Jason Thompson on September 16, 2013

Out of the Closet, Into the Light paints a descriptive picture of child abuse and the pain and confusion that follows. Sadly, countless children around the world fall into the hands of sick and demented people and many will end their lives alone and in emotional agony. For those who have experienced this type of pain, reading this book may be the first step in knowing they are not alone. The book is not meant to be written to lead people into theological truth, therapeutic understanding, or even steps to freedom, but rather to help people know they are not alone. As someone who ministers to the sexually and relationally broken at (redacted) my hope is that after reading this book, those who have been wounded will seek a community of people that will love them with the grace and hope of God.

5.0 out of 5 stars
By happycat70 on September 12, 2013

Living in Portland myself, it's not hard to know who Jordan Jantz is, he is a light where ever he goes. Most of this entire book was to the point where I had a hard time putting it down. Honesty brings hope to so many broken people. Touching the hearts of children and giving hope in their life matches my knowledge of Jordan Jantz, who has been a part of the society I belong to. This book opens a life that so many keep hidden for most of their entire life trying to

JORDAN JANTZ

hide what happen to them as children and as adults. Jordan opened up his darkest secrets and some will judge his past, some may judge him today. Some may even judge him tomorrow, but in this very book everyone who has lived a life pleasing the world and knowing how to make other people's dreams come true, Jordan opens up his heart and tells you the truth. He never knew how to find his dream. But Jordan today makes other people's dreams come true.

I know the Lord has a great plan for Jordan; he now has control of his life. I am proud of you.

My friend Jordan's story
By outfor1 on September 5, 2013

First off I have known Jordan for more than two decades now. I knew some of his past because we shared our stories over the years as our friendship grew. I did not realize the depth of what he really suffered and went through until reading the book. I felt his life had been a journey that can bring hope for people in a dark place that have also gone through the trials as Jordan has. I believe God will continue to use Jordan to bring about hope for those who feel there is none. Knowing where Jordan has come from and where he is today is truly a blessing from our Lord and savior. The book is an easy and quick read and I promise you that when you start to read it you won't put it down until you have finished it. I know it was not easy for him to reopen up all the pain from his past, but I believe that is where healing can begin, when we get it out of the closet and in to the light.

Mike

XCV

God's grace is amazing
By Eric on July 30, 2013

I am so proud of my friend Jordan for having the courage share his life with the world. His heart to see the issue of child abuse exposed by sharing from his own life of pain and abuse is truly impressive. My wife and I are honored to be his friends and to be able to see God's amazing grace continue to be at work in Jordan's life as he gives so much of himself for the good of others.

5.0 out of 5 stars A Must Read Book
By Allen Oyler on July 25, 2013

This is a must read book that gives insight into the life of a great man that has faced significant adversity. Jordan's portrayal of his life gives one pause to wonder how s/he would have handled those situations. His honesty about his circumstances is to be applauded. His strength to deal with his circumstances is commendable. The author did an excellent job of telling his story in a way that was honest but not too graphic.

5.0 out of 5 stars Really a great book
By Sweed on July 16, 2013

It is amazing that a person can overcome such tremendous trials and be a contributing member of our community! Jordan is a great person and friend and he has inspired my life in many ways. This book added much to my admiration of him.

5.0 out of 5 stars Jordan's Journey
By skymom81 on June 24, 2013

EMBRACED

Wow, did this book open my eyes. Leading somewhat of a sheltered life in the south, I had no idea this kind of abuse was being perpetrated on innocent victims here in America. Satan is evil, no doubt, and can influence humans to do some unthinkable things to others. This book will open eyes to what some have been through, some we may know. He is an Awesome God and loves all: abused and non-abused. We are the same. Reading this book has helped me understand who Jordan was, and who he is today. Proud to be a sister of his in the family of God.

Trials and challenges result in changes, growth, peace, and strength
By Stephanie Cluff on June 19, 2013

Jordan has shared the ugly parts of his life in a transparent, honest, manner without being too graphic. He has now filled his life with hope and change because of the light and truth in his life. The large print and layout made a difficult book easier to read. I recommend it to survivors, their friends and family...which is nearly everyone.

5.0 out of 5 stars Good read
By Jarrett Henderson on June 13, 2013

I enjoyed reading this book. Understanding and getting along is something that we all need to work on. This is a great book of sharing experiences and hardships in a person's life. I hope all who read have an open mind and realize that this kind of thing still happens. We are not immune to the heart break of abuse. Jordan is brave to share his story and I know some may oppose the book but no one can oppose his life story and experiences. Those are his to own, and I will ever be grateful to him for sharing his life story so that I can be more aware and loving to all mankind. Well done Jordan Jantz and J. Adams.

JORDAN JANTZ

An eye opening account
By Ben on June 12, 2013

Jordan's story is not an easy read, but it is the account of a man who found happiness after a great deal of misery. Child abuse in any of its forms can do lasting and irreparable harm. I feel that the true message of this book is that God loves his children and that there can be hope in spite of cruelty and joy despite great suffering. As other reviews have mentioned it doesn't take long to make your way through the 160 or so pages but I found it a worthwhile use of a few hours and I won't soon forget the story.

5.0 out of 5 stars An amazing story that I highly recommend.
By MickyO on June 11, 2013

This is a well written book about what one child suffered at the hands of those who should have loved and nurtured him. It makes me wonder how many children suffer in silence. The day we received the book from Amazon, I sat down and read it in two hours. I have purchased more books and have been sharing them with family and friends. I highly recommend this book for anyone to read. May the voices of the children be heard and may each of us reach out with an understanding heart to all of God's children.

J. Adams did an excellent job in writing the story of Jordan Jantz.

5.0 out of 5 stars A Must read
By Den Pretlow on June 7, 2013

Abuse, in this country, is a far greater issue than most of us realize. In its varying forms, it is the silent shame in many families and it doesn't survive in isolated incidents but permeates through multiple

EMBRACED

generations within families. Here is a well written story that brings to light a true account of one individual's nightmare. It is a story that had to be written. It is a story that has to be read!

5.0 out of 5 stars Every Mormon needs to read this.
By M on May 23, 2013

I learned about this book from the subject of the book, when controversy arose about its scope. Mormons who have worked hard to find understanding and space in our faith to have same-gender relationships might have felt that a view of a homosexual man who had been abused as a child could contribute to the myth that child sexual abuse causes homosexuality. Those people had good reason to worry about any book that repeats that myth however they can rest their hearts- *this* book does not make such a connection at all. It is an honest book and it wouldn't promote a harmful myth.

I was impressed that this book was able to give a clear view of the inter-workings of families that host abusive dynamics. This is a badly needed skill in the Mormon-world. The average Mormon, for instance, might hold the belief that abusers can be detected because an abuser would be reliably abusive to everyone. In fact, abusers choose victims very carefully, and usually do so inside of family structures that have more to protect than themselves as a way to perpetuate abusive leverage. Abusive family systems can and do happen in every culture including Mormon culture, but because we are so terribly unskilled at recognizing how abusive people exploit family and cultural structures we often miss important clues.

I wish that I could put this book on everyone's doorstep. It took me only an evening to read and I felt that I had walked Jordan's path with him. Reading so much honesty is a pleasure of its own kind. This book inspires compassion. When we walk in each other's shoes (even if we do this through the telepathy of the printed word) we

JORDAN JANTZ

learn to love each other in spite of circumstances.

As a BYU Psych graduate I endorse this book for everyone above age 12. It teaches humans to act humanely.

Charity enjoying the Colorado River

CI

A quick read on overcoming adversity & abuse and finding peace & hope

By JTingey on May 7, 2013

I'm a little biased as I am a friend of the subject of the book. That being said it is an interesting read about Jordan's life and journey to finding peace in himself and with God. This book can be a bit graphic, but it's not obscene. But it does so to bring to light to pain and suffering that many have to endure at the hands of their abusers and the impact it can have on an individual.

There are a few editing and geographical errors in the book, but on the whole it is well-written and has a clear voice. I'd recommend this book for a quick read and also to support the great cause the proceeds of the sale of this book will help support.

"J. Adams did an excellent job in writing the story of Jordan Jantz."

2016

CIII

EPILOGUE FROM THE FIRST BOOK,

OUT OF THE CLOSET, INTO THE LIGHT

(included here by permission of best-selling author, J. Adams)

And Here I Am

How do you piece together a life that was never whole to begin with?

How do you get past experiences and events of such magnitude and start again?

Simply put, you put all in order and let go.

I did eventually see Mama and my biological family again. Surprisingly, Mama moved out east and they no longer lived in the same state. Going back to Illinois, I got to know my father and his sister. That was the only good thing that came of it.

Other than that, neither experience was pleasant. Both brought a new layer of the same old lies, deceits, and hatefulness. My kindness and efforts to reach out were spat back in my face, because none were willing to accept their part in shaping my childhood. So I chose to big those experiences a proper farewell by never thinking on them again. None of it matters now.

EMBRACED

What does matter is nothing can ever be hidden from God, no matter how hard we try to hide it, or how deep we attempt to buy it.

People don't think children can remember things that happen at such a young age, but they do. We all remember things from those young years. And while there are many things that are blocked and hidden in my subconscious, I remember the things that matter.

I remember being told that I was ugly, and in order for people to love me, I needed to be the best little boy in the world.

In order to make it in life and be somebody, I needed to be the best little boy in the world.

In order to be loved enough for someone to stay, I needed to be the best little boy in the world.

I was never taught that, to God, I have always been the best little boy in the world, along with every other little child. I was the best by simply being me, James Lee Bond, then Jimmylee.

That trained mindset stayed with me through my twenties, thirties and forties. I am almost fifty-four now, and I am finally starting to shed the idea that was ingrained in me all those years ago.

So, now I try to focus on where I am at this moment, not where I was. I don't know what will happen tomorrow or in the future. I only know that as long as I stay on the path that has been placed before me, I will be okay. As long as I hold on to my Savior's hand, he will hold on to mine and lever let go. I can honestly say that for the first time in my life, His is truly one hand that has not let go. If He had, I wouldn't be here now.

CVI

Because I had so much support from the gay community, I found it hard to leave that support behind. Once you are part of the life, it is difficult to let go. Many of my dear friends have remained in the community. Unfortunately, many of them have also passed away. They thought they would live forever, but they had been mistaken.

As far gone as I once was, it is truly a miracle that I am still here. Homosexual friends tell me even now, "Jordan, if you can do this, anyone can." I hope and pray that I can in some way help them accomplish the same.

These days I spend my time doing what I can to share God's message with others by sharing my life and the miracles He has wrong in me. I do this by speaking to church congregations and large groups all over Portland. When I can, I take the message outside of Oregon. Like Moses in the Bible, I am not mighty in speaking, and this is definitely the last thing I ever expected to be doing. I never expected to live long enough to accomplish any of the things I have since giving my life to God.

But HE had a plan of His Own for me. And I will be here until my work on this earth is finished.

I have made many new friends in this new life. And there is one friend I will be forever grateful for, because he didn't give up on me. Elder Spencer Wallentine and his family have taken me into their hearts and are some of the dearest people in the world to me. They know the kind of life I once lived, yet there is no judgment. They simply love like a true Christian family should, and my visits with them in Utah, just doing simple everyday things that most people take for granted, are better than any exotic place I've ever been. I will always be thankful to have them in my life.

I am a person who goes all the way or not at all, and I have embraced this new life God has given me with my whole heart. I am

JORDAN JANTZ

still challenged with the residue of my childhood and past-multiple personality and anxiety disorder- and I don't know if those effects will ever go away, but I do know this: when I am feeling afraid and anguished over darkness seeping from under that locked closet door, all I need to do is remind myself that God has seen it all, and my

Savior has born every pain trapped behind it. So I simply throw it open, knowing nothing is hidden, and the small square of darkness is now lit by Christ-like love.

And I never need to be afraid again.

EMBRACED

Pedro and Jimmy in Compton California 1965

JORDAN'S VOICE(S) OF HOPE VIDEOS

Love is all around you, all you have to do is listen!

http://www.ldsvoicesofhope.org/voice.php?v=51#.VrPvoPkrLIU

at

http://www.voiceofhopeinternational.org/

CX

EMBRACED

Jordan's media including these videos from **Voices of Hope (also posted on YouTube)** and the blog, **Jordans-light.blogspot.com** immediately sky-rocked virally with more than 100,000 views within a year!

Amazing material that is used for child-protective services throughout the United States.

PERMISSIONS

wearing my assistant hat,
3 messages

M Wed, Dec 9, 2015 at 7:32 PM
To: Ty Mansfield

I was talking to Jordan about how his book-writing is doing today. He indicated that he really wishes that one of the things that he could include in the beginning of the book, instead of the too-short-and-too-curt material at the front of this second book, is the interview/essay you folks wrote for him to accompany his profile on Voices of Hope, here.

http://www.ldsvoicesofhope.org/essay.php?e=23#.Vmjw5vkrLIU

That would be accompanied by information about Voices of Hope and Jordan's short and long videos.

Jordan asked me if I would drop you a line tonight to see if you could provide the written approval for him to include the material in the link in the "pre" part of the upcoming ebook, Embraced, the part of the book that prepares a reader to read this second book which does *not* start at childhood but is concerned mostly with this last year and only has a *little* background.

I haven't been involved in this, except to help shuttle requests and material back and forth and pick up prints and stuff. Jordan said you would know what he's talking about, so I really hope you do.

I told him I would email you tonight.

best,

Ty Mansfield Wed, Dec 9, 2015 at 7:35 PM
To:

Hi

Yes, Jordan is more than welcome to use that material in any way he wants/needs.

All the best,
Ty

M Wed, Dec 9, 2015 at 7:49 PM
To: Ty Mansfield

Thank you, Ty!

EMBRACED

Jeweladams.com

Hello,

Jordan has spoken with me about your proposed project. I think doing another book about his daily life since the publication of his first story *Out of the Closet Into the Light* is a great idea. I am sure many readers would be interested in learning more about Jordan's present life, how he continues to grow, and the residual effects of all he suffered in the past.

Jordan assured me that this ebook would not contain any content from *Out of the Closet Into the Light*, but he would like people to come away from it with a desire to read his story. I have included an excerpt from *Out of the Closet* that you are welcome to use at the end of the book, sort of a preview to draw new readers and get his story into more hands. If you would rather not use it, that's totally fine, but it is available if you need it.

Sincerely,

Jewel Adams,

Publisher

JORDAN JANTZ

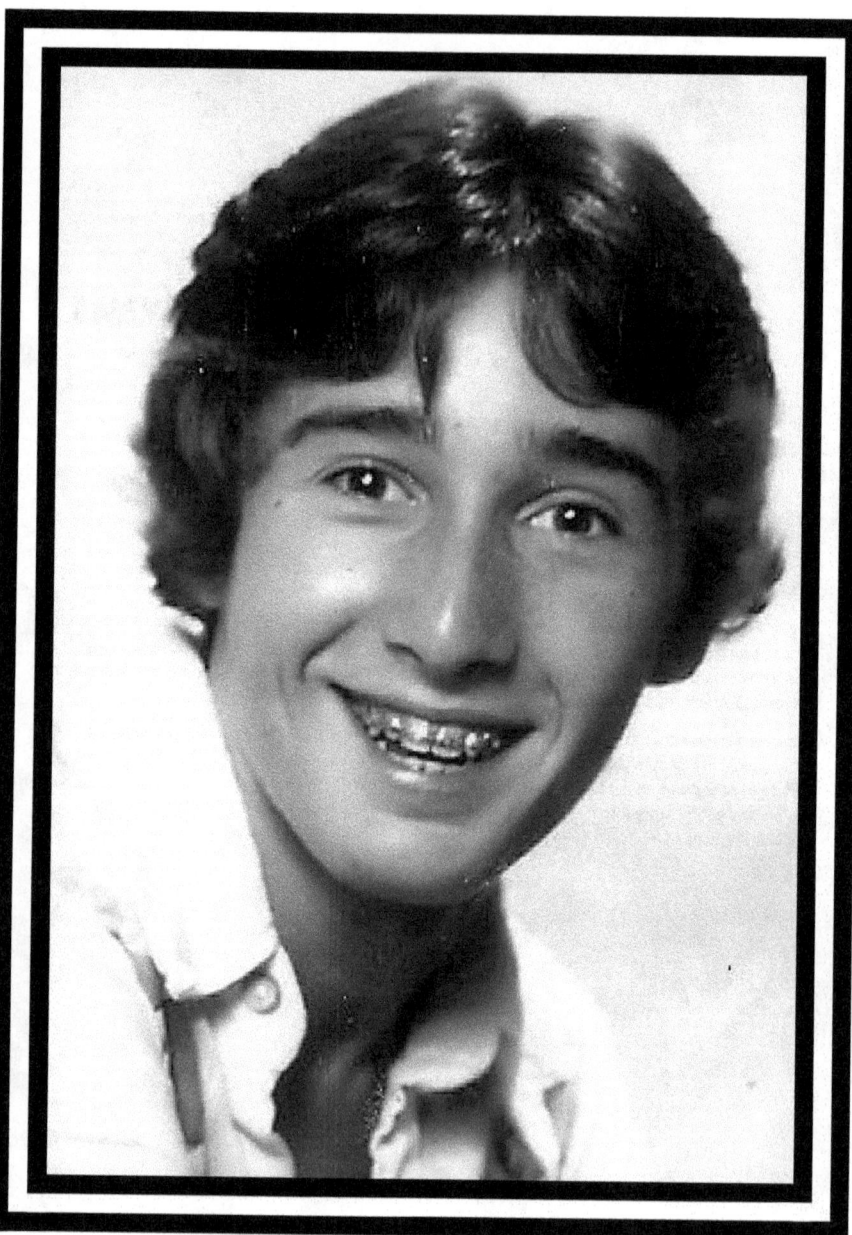

CXIV

EMBRACED
INTERVIEW

This essay was written in connection with Voices of Hope and its production of the video interview that is posted on VoicesofHope.com as well as on YouTube.

Special thanks to Ty Mansfield and his leadership in supporting the special Voices of Hope video with this written interview.

The interview of Jordan Jantz was conducted by phone from Washington, DC.

When I look back on my life, it is a miracle that I made it through all that happened. To this day there are moments when the flashbacks that occur are so strong that I literally lose control of my bodily functions. I see a therapist regularly and take prescribed anxiety medication during the day and sleeping medication at night to function so that I can live some semblance of a normal life.

However, the one thing above that all helps me through each new day is knowledge that no matter how rough it gets or how abandoned I feel at times that God is there and that the Savior is with me. If I hold to the light, I will never be alone again. Now that everything is out in the open, there are no more secrets and no animosity or anger. There is only the sweet peace of healing and knowing that memories of my old life and those burdens are no longer mine. Someone else carries them now, and I can go on.

JORDAN JANTZ

World of Darkness

I had two brothers and a sister and was the middle child. I was very hyper-active and would have been labeled ADD if the term had existed back then. The way that my mother decided to handle my "condition" was to keep me locked in a broom closet, where I lived for two years.

The darkness actually made my hearing acute and that rattling always frightened me because I never knew what to expect, which made me lose it emotionally sometimes. When I turned three, the light that I was thrust into for short periods was for a different kind of bath time. Whenever the man living with my mother bathed me, the water hurt because I was usually sexually and violently abused first. During those times, I cried out for help, but there were no words. There was no rescuer.

Mama yelled at me because I could not use the bathroom like a normal child. She decided the best way to teach me was by inserting a hose in my bottom, filling my rectum with water, and then telling me to hold it until I reached the toilet to release. She did this many times. Every time I would press back into a corner in fear, my body shaking with the rattling of the door, Tina's little fingers were there petting mine, and I made it through. Tina, my little sister, was the only living thing that I trusted, and she worried about what was happening to me. Sometimes I would hear my sister crying for Mama to stop. I wondered if some of the same things were being done to her, which hurt me just as much.
One day after filling me with so much water that I passed out, I awakened in a place filled with light and people around me dressed in white. I had been taken to the hospital by my biological father. He had come back for one of his sparse visits. My father always tried to protect me when he was with us.

EMBRACED

Instead of taking me home, he asked others to watch over me, including my aunt Marian. Mama and Daddy soon told me that I would be going to live with a new mommy and daddy. My new parents were acquiring me through black-market means. Aunt Marian had a sister who wanted to adopt a child and was willing to pay to do it. I didn't want to go and hoped that by doing what Mom and her boyfriends wanted, that I could stay, but that didn't happen.

Mama and Daddy took me to the airport and the planes were so loud, my little body trembled and I wet my pants. This made Mama mad, and she hit me, which felt completely normal. She then grabbed my head, looked down at me and said something to the effect of, "Jimmy, go get on that plane and don't leave your seat until your new mama and daddy come to the plane and get you. Now be a good boy and don't cry. And remember, you are going to have to be the best little boy in the world for someone to love you. You have to do what they tell you to do and listen to what they say."

I cried and held her and pleaded for her to let me stay, but she just pulled my hands away and pushed me forward. As the flight attendant descended the stairs to get me, I looked to my left and gasped. There stood an angel. I had never seen an angel before, but I knew that I was looking at one. He was tall and had wings. To me, he was even bigger than the plane. When he looked at me, I felt like I knew him and he knew me. He smiled and there were tears falling down his face. I immediately stopped crying and was determined not to cry again on the plane. No one would ever have a reason to give me away again because I would be a good boy. No one would ever beat me, hurt me or say that I was bad again. I would be the best.

I smiled at the angel and knew that I would be okay. I knew him and felt that I had always known him and that I would see him again. I also had no idea at the time that I had an additional angel looking out for me. Aunt Marian was sitting in the seat directly behind mine, seeing me safely to my destination.

My New Family

My new parents changed my name to Jimmylee. I would learn that some people use the "children should be neither seen or heard, but be perfect" motto. Daddy wanted to teach me to trust because I really didn't know *how* to trust anyone.

Sometimes Daddy would come home and find me sitting in my closet. It was always Daddy that did the soothing. He would rock me and tell me that everything was going to be all right, but he was always there when I cried.

I was given a pair of tap shoes and enrolled in a tap dancing class with Tina, my *new* sister I was the only boy in the class, but I picked it up immediately. It was like I was born to tap. After many, many classes, my parents had me audition for Disney. Soon we were participating in the Disneyland parades.

As I got to know Mama and Daddy's family, I gravitated more toward Daddy's because they were so kind. They lived in a small Southern Baptist community and were good people. They knew about the life that I'd come from and treated me well and affectionately. They made every effort to show me that I was loved.

Mama's family was different. I didn't enjoy going to see them because they were snobbish and impatient. I was constantly trying to prove myself. At my age and with my mental capabilities, that was pretty hard. The exceptions were Mama's mother and father.

During one of these visits to Mama's parents' home, I met her brother Arthur and, to my young mind, he was Satan incarnate. Knowing what I'd been through before coming to the family, he immediately began to sexually abuse me.

The first day that I met Uncle Arthur, he told me to take a walk with him. He took me out to his father's barn where the chicken pens were. He made me stand in one spot and told me not to move. As I stood trembling, he held one of the large flapping roosters to my face. He threatened me and said, "You see this? If you don't do what I tell you, I will kill your daddy." With an evil smile, he put the rooster back in the pen and pulled me behind the cages and raped me. Soon his friends became involved in rituals with me. The rituals were just another prelude of things to come.

Three years later, Uncle Arthur came to stay with us, and I was told that I had to share my room with him. I begged Mama to not make me share my room, but as usual, I was ignored. So my nights were filled with abuse. Then I was thrust into a completely different world. My uncle started taking me with him to adult bookstores where I was forced to have sex with men in a back room. Sadly, it slowly became normal to me.

I sometimes experienced flashbacks. Doctors didn't know exactly where I was mentally, physically or emotionally. I had such temper tantrums at times that it was hard to know what to do. I was ten with the mentality of a six-year-old, and they thought that I lacked *self-confidence* and complained that I couldn't sit quietly. My constant need to go to the bathroom was also disruptive.

Mama soon joined the PTA and became more involved with the school in order to keep a closer eye on what I was doing. I had begun acting out sexually in school, and this became a problem for them as well.

JORDAN JANTZ

I began going to play pinball at the bowling alley with the other children from school. The man who owned the place said that he would let me play all I wanted for free if I did what he wanted. I soon discovered that the bowling alley was a facade for other things. I was told that if I kept that secret, then I could play all the pinball and other games that I wanted. Since it didn't involve anyone hurting me, the arrangement sounded ideal. This was my introduction into the world of pornography. I had no idea how terribly wrong and sick this all was.

Fed Up

Uncle Arthur was relentless in his taunting and abuse. One day I got so tired of it that I finally told Mama what he was doing to me. I begged her not to tell anyone because he would kill Daddy. Mama was surprised at how well I was now talking. I told her that Uncle Arthur had been teaching me that and many other things. She said that I was making it all up and told me to never say anything to anyone, and that if I did, I would no longer be living with them.

One of my teachers began to notice my growing gravitation toward the boys in my class. She also started noticing bloodstains on the back of my pants. Finally pulling me aside, she asked me about it. I told her that I fell and that I would be in trouble because I wasn't allowed to get my clothes dirty. She asked me about other problems that I'd had, like soiling myself and using bathroom all the time.

I finally told her that I was gay. I also told her about Uncle Arthur and what he was doing to me. She asked for specifics, and I told her everything. I shared how I would pretend that I was James Bond 007, which threw her for a loop because she had no clue how that name connected to my past.

CXXI

Homosexuality was considered a mental illness in the sixties, so my teacher immediately sent me to the principal's office and told him that they needed to call my parents and let them know what was going on. I was afraid. By telling her this, I had done something wrong and would be punished for it.

Mama came to the school, spoke with the teacher and the principal, made excuses, and said that she would take me to the doctor. Of course, this was completely for show. When you are raised in a family with money, anything can be covered up. Money can also buy silence, so the abuse didn't stop. A day dawned when I'd finally had it. Unwilling to deal with Uncle Arthur's manipulation any longer, I learned how to reverse the roles.

I had a little Buddha that I'd gotten from my biological grandmother. "You see this Buddha?" I said, holding it up to him one day. "It's possessed and sees you. It sees everything." Then I placed the statue on the table by my bed and completely freaked him out. Since he was already a psychotic heretic, that wasn't hard to do. That little statue was my ticket to a big change. After months of retaliating with the Buddha threat, Uncle Arthur slowly began to lose his sanity.

Struggling Through

Mama and Uncle Arthur were very deceiving people, and they kept so much from Daddy. Still, he could see how much I was struggling. I became so mentally messed up and finally said to Daddy one day, "Something is wrong with me. I like the boys in school instead of the girls."

"What do you mean?" he asked.

"They say I'm gay because I want to hold hands with boys and kiss

EMBRACED

like you and Mama do. There's something wrong with me."

I could tell this was hard for him to hear, but he didn't get mad or angry. He was such a patient man. He simply said, "We're going to kneel beside the bed and pray."

I will never forget what I felt kneeling beside my dad as he prayed for me. No one had ever done that before. He prayed that God would protect me. Daddy also asked God to help me learn to trust him and know that I could tell him anything. Afterward, he hugged me and told me, "You are a good son and can talk to me about anything that you want to. I promise that I will always listen."

Mama was jealous of my relationship with Daddy because he was always such a happy person and showed me so much love. At the end of that school year, I was tired of being around Mama and did the only thing I knew to do. I ran away. At twelve years old, I hopped on a bus and left for the summer

San Diego

I took a bus to San Diego. These days that kind of thing would be unheard of, not to mention impossible. I had no idea where I was going, I just knew that I was getting away from home and escaping a life of being used for everyone else's gratification.

When I got off the bus, I met Jim, a man who would continue my education in the world of sex and pornography. I got to know him; I shared things about myself, including all the molestation and abuse. I specified that my father had never touched me in that way, and from him I received nothing but a father's love. I refused to ever have anyone think badly of my father.

Before I knew it, he was introducing me to other boys—some my age, some older—and had me shooting videos with them. He had a standing room at the Beverly Wilshire Hotel that was reserved for one purpose: for men to come and photograph young boys in sexual acts. This would be my first paying job and I made great money those two summers. Mama never seemed to care that her young son was caught a bus to San Diego. But, to keep Daddy from worrying, I lied and said that I was working at a drive-in burger place. Since the owner was part of the pornography ring, he had no problem vouching for me working there.

My interactions with Uncle Arthur were getting more intense because I now stood up to him and told him that I would kill him before he killed Daddy. I was no longer afraid, and my threats kind of freaked him out.

My relationship with Tina became strained, not only because I was leaving so much, but also because she thought that I was abandoning her. Mama definitely had something to do with this. I would find out later that she'd been slowing poisoning my sister's thoughts and trying to turn her against me. Tina had no idea what I had gone through for so many years and couldn't understand that the trips were my escape from the hell that I had lived in for so long. I'd leaned on her a great deal and knew that I couldn't anymore. My parents argued almost every day. I knew that it was a matter of time before something happened. I never told Daddy what I endured; he still doesn't know. Through it all, life went on.

New Profession

When I was fifteen, I began working for *California's Finest* at night. Since the jobs were by the hour, I worked a few hours each week in the evenings and managed to keep it from Mama and Daddy. I was never seen by anyone I knew.

Through these friends that I had, I gained connections that led me to work in the adult porn industry. I traveled all over California

CXXV

and Catalina Island making films and escorting. By the time I was a junior in high school, I was a seasoned professional in the adult industry. This is not said with pride or boasting, it was just a fact.

During my senior year, I got a legitimate job as an underwear model for Sears and J.C. Penny in addition to escorting and making movies. Sears and Penny paid nowhere near what the porn industry did. I became disillusioned with *Male Order Brides*, and left the service to do more legitimate modeling because I loved the runway. My appearances on the covers of gay magazines increased.

As far as school went, things were about the same with one exception. I made the cheerleading squad with Tina and was the mascot. Daddy told me that if I was going to do it, that I needed to be the best mascot they'd ever had. I took his words to heart and practiced often. We won the state competition at Pepperdine University. It was a wonderful accomplishment for me, and I'll always treasure that memory.

A week later, Mama told Daddy that she wanted a divorce. I was completely shocked and angry. I wondered how Mama could do that to Daddy. She informed us that she would take Tina and that I would stay with Daddy. Saying nothing, he got up and left. I then turned to her and said, "So, is Daddy a pair of used shoes now, too?" She immediately slapped me, which I expected, but that didn't stop me. "You can break up this family, but you will never come between me and my dad."

She quickly replied, "He never was your dad. You've had many dads, so you don't really have any parents. The best thing you can do is to leave this family and never come back. You have shamed us and are an embarrassment to all of us."

I remembered the angel at the plane again and found myself praying for the angel to help keep my family together because I needed them. As bad as it was, having them together was the only stable thing in my life, even as distorted as my view of stability was.

A Different Kind of Pain

When Daddy remarried, the woman was nice, but I worried that she would take my father away from me. He was the only person that I had left in the world. I couldn't afford to lose him. Daddy did his best to assure me that would never happen. His new wife was nothing but kind to me and showed me more love than Mama ever did. Still, they had a new life of their own, which meant that it was time to be on my own. The problem was, I knew no other life than the one I was living.

I finally moved to Los Angeles and met up with Jonah, a dangerous and affluent Italian man with his own mafia circle. I met Jonah through *Male Order Brides* and was now working for an escort service that he ran. I wasn't really interested in steady companionship, but he was attractive, bought me clothes, took me traveling, and made sure that I had whatever I needed. It was an ideal situation in the beginning.

Our two-year relationship became volatile. Jonah was very controlling and violent. Except for when I was with clients, he was with me. If I even smiled at another man, I was beaten, sometimes so brutally that I ended up in the emergency room.

The Jonah's mother and two sisters feared for my life. They finally pulled me aside one day and said that we were going to leave, or that I would be killed. So in the middle of the night, they helped me escape to Portland, Oregon. I got an apartment and settled in

CXXVIII

the city.

When Jonah dropped me off at the airport, I was so physically battered and out of it that I couldn't even remember the trip. However, this final trip knocked some sense into me, *literally*! And I knew things would have to change.

The Wedding

I went back to Compton for Tina's wedding. She was marrying Dan, a guy we met one night at a dance club and had become good friends with. Dan was nice, and I figured they would be happy together. Though it was great to see Tina, the visit was strained and short. She did not ask me to be in the wedding party nor to be involved, and so I was just a guest like everyone else. That really hurt.

As far as the family was concerned, I cared about no one but myself, and there was nothing that I could do or say to change it. Mama made sure of that.

Mamma said, "Jimmy, I don't know why you came. Nobody wanted you here. That's why Tina didn't ask you to be in the wedding. You're still an embarrassment. I told you before, the best thing you can do for this family is to leave and not come back. Don't tell anyone where you are. Don't write and don't call. Just disappear. We've been fine without you so far, and we'll still be fine without you. Nobody cares about you because nobody wants used shoes. You will always be used shoes. The sooner you learn that, the better. So just leave."

I left. Never had there been a more painful or wasted trip.

Ft. Lauderdale

That next year I left Portland and went to Ft. Lauderdale, Florida, for a few months. I got a job at a gay resort as a pool towel boy, since I wasn't twenty-one yet.

Many of the guests that stayed there were from Hollywood and worked in the adult video industry. They immediately noticed me and I became involved, working on videos seven days a week. I made good money, but the job took a lot out of me. I numbed myself by drinking a lot and by smoking plenty of marijuana. As long as I was sufficiently drugged, I could be whatever they wanted me to be onscreen.

It wasn't long before the hotel was raided and shut down. I didn't get busted, but I was out of a job. It was Mother's Day. I got a sudden urge to call Mama and wish her a good day. I thought it might cheer me up as well. Despite her hatred, I missed having a family and thought of them all the time. So I picked up the phone and called her.

"Hello."

"Hey, Mama, it's your son, Jimmy."

"I'm sorry, but I don't have a son."

What? "Mama, it's me, Jimmylee, James Bond."

"I'm sorry, but you have the wrong number. Please don't call back again." She hung up.

What the hell. I called back and said, "Mama, it's me, Jimmy. I'm calling to wish you a Happy Mother's Day and to let you know that I'm in Ft. Lauderdale, Florida."

CXXXI

JORDAN JANTZ

"I don't have a son." She again hung up. Her shunning affected me worse than it should have. You would think that I would be immune to her hatred, but she was the only mother that I had ever known.

I had too many issues to count. Besides suicidal thoughts, I was constantly worrying about my weight and appearance and suffered from eating disorders. In the adult industry, just like modeling, looks and image are everything, and you are always competing because there are always younger, better looking models, and you have to keep up or get left behind.

Jordan Jantz

Once back in Portland, I eventually hooked up with a few bar owners and started working in underground sex trafficking while I continued to work for the escort service, the runway and Sears, JC Penny and Montgomery Ward catalogs.

The years passed quickly and blurred together because every single day of my life was the same, nothing ever changed. By now I was hitting thirty, and the pattern was set.

It was during this down time that I got to know my neighbor, Greg Jantz. He was a fireman and a staunch Baptist. *And* he liked to party. He said he was a wealth adviser, as well as a spiritual adviser at his Pentecostal church. Greg was very nice to me. There was never anything but friendship between us, but I did set him up with others.

He immediately took me under his wing and became a father figure—which was easy since that was the very thing I starved for—and I became part of their family. His children were very accepting of me, and I grew to care about them a great deal. He got

EMBRACED

re-married, and I became attached to his wife as well. I was involved with this family for years and was very happy.

Then came the day when Greg told me that he and his wife wanted to adopt me and change my name to Jordan Jantz. He chose the name Jordan because it meant 'crossing over.' Greg's pleas went on for years. Something inside me kept fighting to resist his pleas. Worn down by Greg's repeated tearful promise to never abandon me, I finally relented, *holding* him to that promise.

The family had an adoption celebration for me on Christmas Eve. Though a small part of me still felt cautious, I was happy to be loved and accepted for who I was. Greg asked me to call him dad so I did. Since I lost my own father, he sort of filled in, though I knew I could never be as close to him. Still, this was enough.

We vacationed in Hawaii one year where the family was given the opportunity be on a Trinity Broadcast evangelical program. Before it was time to go on, Dad said that he wanted to talk to me about something. He told me that he understood how terrible I had it as a child, and how it led to my present lifestyle, but it was time for things to change. He said that in order for my soul to be saved, I needed to quit my escorting job and stop being gay. I needed to *testify of my new life*.

His request blew me away because it was so unexpected. I told him that I couldn't quit my job or stop what I was doing because I didn't know how to do anything else. I definitely was not going to stand in front of the whole church and lie about my feelings. I couldn't possibly turn it off just like that. There was not a switch that I could simply flip to be someone totally different.

Our friendship was never about loving me; it was about his reputation. Greg Jantz only cared about what adopting me would do for him. With that truth came the renewal of my loneliness. The ache in my heart was excruciating.

Breaking Point

Walking into my apartment in the wee hours of the morning, I grabbed a rope and a couple of weights. Putting the things in a bag, I left and headed to the Burnside Bridge.

Tying the weights to the ends of the rope and wrapping the rope around my neck, I said, "God, I want to leave. I'm tired of the pain and am ready to be with you."

Then I jumped off the bridge into the freezing water and awoke three days later in the hospital psychiatric unit completely confused. The doctor explained that when the paramedics revived me, I was brought to the hospital and was in lockdown to keep me from attempting suicide again. He told me that I was Jordan Jantz.

I spent two weeks there undergoing therapy and was diagnosed as suffering from multiple personality disorder. The doctor explained that I would disassociate with each traumatic experience and was continually splitting to fit every situation.

While I was there, the Jantz family came to see me—everyone but Greg, that is. I was told to keep this information to myself or they wouldn't have anything to do with me. I didn't see that as a major sacrifice since they'd already abandoned me. I would try to contact them several times in the future, but every letter would be returned. We lived in the same city and still do, but to this day, I have no contact with them.

Reunion

EMBRACED

I called Tina to see if she was going to our high school reunion. She was completely shocked to hear from me because my family all thought that I was dead. She sobbed and then explained about Daddy hiring a private detective to look for me. I didn't tell her that the name change was probably the reason he couldn't find me. I was too ashamed to ever tell anyone.

I told her that I would be attending the reunion and asked her not to say anything to Mama or Daddy. She promised that she wouldn't and told me about my two little nephews—I couldn't wait to see them. She then asked me, "Jimmy, why did you leave?"

"Because Mama said [that] I was an embarrassment to the family, that you were ashamed of me all through school. Then she told me the best thing that I could do for the family would be to leave and not come back."

"It wasn't true," she tearfully told me.

Mark

A man named Mark and I soon grew closer and began to spend a lot of time together. I was in a business where I was forced to fake intelligence and was still not functioning well when it came to knowledge of things that others take for granted—and it was nice to be able to be myself with him.

The weeks of friendship grew into something more, and we became involved. Though I had been with a few others regularly in the past, what I had with Mark was entirely different, and I actually felt loved. Not just used, but really loved. It was indescribable.

One day Mark shared something that completely shocked me.

JORDAN JANTZ

"Jordan, I need to tell you something."

"Okay."

"I'm LDS."

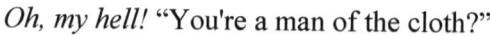

"What is that?"

"I'm Mormon."

Oh, my hell! "You're a man of the cloth?"

He smiled. "I'm a returned missionary."

Thinking about it a moment, I said, "Well, it's okay, but I have to tell you, I'm not into that, so just don't go weird on me, okay?"

"Okay."

Knowing Mark's background brought us closer. I now understood why he was so polite and good. I promised him that what he'd shared with me would stay between us. Because he'd trusted me enough to open himself so fully, I shared the details of my life, including currently making a living not only modeling, but as a paid escort. He told me he loved me and didn't care.

After a couple of years together, Mark introduced me to his Mormon family. Since the day he'd told them he was gay, Mark and his family had grown apart. He only saw them once or twice a year. It hurt to see him sink into bouts of depression about not being close to them. He wasn't the son they thought he should be and would never fit their idea of a perfect man.

He hated hearing this because it was the truth. I told him that I

CXXXVII

would never let religion in my life because I had seen what these so-called Christians did to people. In their eyes, we would never measure up. I don't know if he agreed, but he understood. He understood *me*, and why I felt that way. And that was what mattered.

Mark and I were together for years and never actually lived together, but we saw each other every day. Sometimes it was very hard to be with him because he would read the Book of Mormon and then be intimate with me afterward. I was completely confused by this. How could he choose to live both standards?

Mark asked me one day, "Jordan, would you be willing to let go of the life that you have planned for yourself and embrace the one that is waiting for you?"

It thought that he was trying to change me and was offended. "Never, Mark," I answered. "Not for you or anyone else."

After spending seven years together, Mark's family thought that he was evil and that I was even worse. I wanted out. So one day I told him, "It's my way or the highway." I asked him to leave my life. And he did. I didn't see Mark again for almost two years, but I never stopped thinking about him. I was used to people walking in and out of my life. This fact only served to point out how much my actions had been spurred on by fear—fear that he would one day leave like the rest. So I left him first.

The Test Came Back Positive

I made many more connections through the years working in the adult industry—political figures, Hollywood directors, mafia members—and those connections stayed with me, turning into friends who became important to me.

EMBRACED

One of these particular connections was made when I met a client at a hotel who turned out to be an undercover cop. When I came out of the bathroom prepared to entertain, I was arrested and taken to jail. Needless to say, I was in shock because this had never happened to me before. Many of my clients were on the police force and some worked for the academy. Because of this, I was released from jail and my record was expunged, so I was able to continue working. However, it was during that time that I tested positive for AIDS.

I could no longer work for the escort service, and since I had never held a regular job before, the only income I had was from sparse modeling jobs with companies that I was still under contract with. I also did some table pole dancing in a restaurant just to pay the bills.

I contacted my family to tell them I was sick. Mama still wanted nothing to do with me and even told Daddy I had died.

I eventually did see Daddy again. I admitted that I had AIDS and felt ashamed. Daddy told me more about how he'd hired a private investigator to look for me. He told me many times that he was sorry about how hard my childhood was, and I assured him he had nothing to be sorry for. He was the best father I could ever ask for.

I started getting sick pretty quickly, and for the next few years I was in an AIDS hospice going through blood transfusions and treatments. It was horrifying to discover that my life was no longer mine. I felt like I had lost everything. My priorities started changing in a major way.

I constantly thought of my family and wished that things had been different between us. I also began to think of God a little more. I had always believed in God; I just didn't think He was there for me much. But then again, how could He be, with the way I had lived my life? I knew that what happened in my childhood wasn't my fault, but as I grew older, my choices were my own. Still, I think deep down, there was a small part of me that believed God watched over me, and probably cried over my choices, too.

Lying in my room thinking about life and how much time I had left, I was surprised to see two young men in white shirts and ties standing in my doorway. They asked if they could come in and visit. They looked like insurance salesmen.

Swearing inwardly, I let them in, but I told them up front that I wasn't into whatever they were selling. I then asked them who they were.

One responded, "We are missionaries from The Church of Jesus Christ of Latter-day Saints."

Inside I was freaking out. I couldn't believe it. *Missionaries from the Mormon Church are sitting in my room?* They asked if they could come by and see me that week. I can't say why I did, but I said yes. I only saw these missionaries a couple of times and decided that I didn't want to talk to them again. I told them that I didn't want any more discussions.

Persistence Softens a Heart

Christmas was coming and my health had improved. I was doing a lot better and getting ready to move into an apartment when the second set of missionaries started coming by. One of them, Elder Wallentine, said that they just stopped by to say hello and bring a gift. I thought about Mark and his struggles, and I didn't want to be like that—depressed because of trying to live two lifestyles.

I said to the Elder, "I'll give you a year to be a part of my life. In return, I'll be part of yours. I'll take your lessons and listen to what you have to say. Just don't tell me I'm going to hell because I'm gay."

And they agreed. The following day, Elder Wallentine called and told me how much it meant to them that I had been so open and real. I continued seeing the missionaries, and their messages began to touch something deep inside me.

However, all was not smooth sailing. Sometimes the missionaries would show up and find me drunk or strung out on coke. I was still supporting myself by stripping and pole dancing, and getting high was the only way that I was able to get in front of men and do this.

They never judged me and never gave up. Elder Wallentine assured me repeatedly that they loved me and would be there no matter what.

I'd heard that phrase so many times and was always lied to. But I *actually* believed him. It wasn't their words, but their actions that convinced me. I was a gay man with AIDS, stripping in bars each night and living a terrible life, but they never faltered in their friendship.

Over the next while, I came to experience moments of peace. The feeling was completely foreign because there had never been any peace in my life. Despite my conflicted emotions, I couldn't deny that what I had been taught about the Savior and His love for me was true. I came to believe that God knew me and what I had gone through. God had witnessed my childhood and felt anger in my behalf. He'd also witnessed my choices, and His Son paid for them with His blood.

I felt so ashamed and wished that I could go back and change the

CXLII

things that I'd done. All I could do was let it all go and move on.

Mark and I had started seeing each other again, but our relationship was only one of friendship. When I finally called him and shared about my experiences with the missionaries, he cried and said that he did not want to see me hurt by the Church the way he was. I told him that though I would always love him, I had to do this. I had to make this change. I *needed* to do it.

"If you can't accept this," I finally said, "then there will never be anything between us again." And because he didn't want to lose my friendship, he accepted my choice. I could truly understand why Mark was such a good person. He was raised to be a Christian, became gay, and suddenly his supposed 'Christian' family wanted nothing to do with him.

I'll Never Forget

After a year of taking the discussions from the missionaries, I prayed to God and said, "If you love me and really won't leave me like other people who called themselves Christians, I will be baptized into your church. If you love me, please show me this is all real."

He answered my prayer by giving me a sweet and peaceful confirmation. I made the decision and was baptized.

Mark was very upset, but still came to my baptism to support me, along with many of my gay and straight friends and acquaintances. They were all surprised, but wanted to be there for me. I appreciated that more than I could possibly say.

Not long after that day, things with Mark became more strained. Because he wouldn't accept my decision or friendship, I ended the relationship. It was painful, but I wanted to be a man of God and go to heaven when I died. God needed me to be better, and I wanted to be better. I knew that as hard as it would be, I could never look back. That closet door was closed forever.

It was Christmas Day, and though I was spending it alone, I had a gift for Mark and decided to take it to him.

When I knocked on the door and he didn't answer, I asked the landlord to let me in so that I could leave the gift. I sat on the couch in the living room and waited for him. I wanted to watch him open it and let him know he would always have a place in my heart.

After a short while, I went to use his bathroom. When I opened the bathroom door, the world stopped and everything inside me immediately died. Mark's body was hanging in the shower with his eyes open and glazed over. He had killed himself.

I started crying, screaming, and yelling at the top of my lungs, "Please, God, no! Please no!"

I ran downstairs to the landlord's apartment, banged on the door, and called the police. My emotions were out of control, and I couldn't think. The sight of Mark's body hanging in the shower was branded in my head, and I knew it would never go away.

Over and over I asked God why this happened. That night, I called Mark's parents and told them about his suicide. Their response was, "Well, Mark was a depressed gay man," like it was bound to happen. I couldn't believe it! They then said that because he left the Church and his family, he should be cremated so that he could continue being "a proud gay man."

I responded, "No, you're so wrong. You left your son, but he never

CXLV

left you. He never stopped loving his family, and you did nothing but preach at him and tell him how terrible he was. Love is supposed to be unconditional. He made choices you didn't agree with, but you abandoned him because of them. Who was more wrong?"

They did have him cremated and gave me his ashes. I tearfully sprinkled them into the river at the beach near my home and said an emotional goodbye to my friend. I kept a prayer in my heart that I would one day see him again.

I'll never forget that Christmas or the person that I loved so much. He was the best friend I had ever had. I knew that I would never love anyone like that again. Mark's loss helped me to know with certainty that I needed to hold to my new-found faith and let go of the painful, hurtful things that I had experienced *and* witnessed people do to each other. People don't understand that though a heart may be broken in different ways, it keeps beating just the same. I knew Mark was at peace. He was with God and would never feel rejected again.

And Here I Am

How do you piece together a life that was never whole to begin with and get past experiences and events of such magnitude and start again? Simply put, you put all in order and let go.

In order to make it in life and be somebody, I thought that I needed to be the best little boy in the world. I was the best by simply being me, James Lee Bond, then Jimmylee. That mindset stayed with me through my twenties, thirties and forties. I am finally starting to shed the idea that was ingrained in me all those years ago.

Now I try to focus on where I am at this moment and not where I was. I don't know what will happen tomorrow or in the future. I only know that as long as I stay on the path that has been placed before me, that I will be okay. As long as I hold on to my Savior's hand, He will hold on to mine and never let go. I can honestly say that for the first time in my life, His is truly one hand that has not let go. If He had, I wouldn't be here now.

Because I had so much support from the gay community, I found it hard to leave that support behind. Once you are a part of the life, it is difficult to let go. Many of my dear friends have remained in the community. Unfortunately, many of them have also passed away. They thought they would live forever, but they had been mistaken. It is truly a miracle that I am still here. Homosexual friends tell me even now, "Jordan, if you can do this, anyone can." I hope and pray that I can in some way help them accomplish the same.

These days I spend my time doing what I can to share God's message with others by sharing my life and the miracles that He has wrought in me. I do this by speaking to church congregations and to large groups in Portland. When I can, I take the message outside of Oregon. Like Moses, I am not mighty in speaking, and this is definitely the last thing I ever expected to be doing. I never expected to live long enough to accomplish any of the things I have since giving my life to God.

He had a plan of His own for me, and I will be here until my work on this earth is finished. I have made many new friends in this new life. Elder Spencer Wallentine is one friend that I will be forever grateful for because he didn't give up on me. He and his family have taken me into their hearts and are some of the dearest people in the world to me. They know the kind of life I once lived and do not judge. They simply love like a true Christian family should. The time that I spend in Utah doing simple everyday things that most people take for granted are better than any exotic place I've

JORDAN JANTZ

ever been. I will always be thankful to have them in my life.

I am a person who goes all the way or not at all. I have embraced this new life that God has given me with my whole heart. I am still challenged with the residue of my childhood and past and with multiple personality and anxiety disorder. I don't know if those effects will ever go away. But I know that when I'm feeling afraid and anguished, all I need to do is remind myself that God has seen it all and that my Savior has born every pain trapped behind it. So I simply throw it open, knowing nothing is hidden, and the small square of darkness is now lit by Christ-like love. And I never need to be afraid again.

EMBRACED

EMBRACED SYNOPSIS

the book that changed lives

We are all writing the story of our life. We want to know what it's about. What are its themes and which theme is on the rise? People demand of it something deeper, or richer, even more substantive. People want to know where this book is taking them and where they are headed.

Not to spoil our heart-embracing ending, but I want to ensure that when the ending comes, it won't be shallow. I will have done something life-transforming for others through this book. Honestly, I mean particularly, in this book, Embraced, I will not have squandered everyone's time. This book is about that life-transformation we all want for ourselves. I began this book because I hit that point in my life. I became intrigued by people who had unearthed their truth calling …or those who were at least willing to try.

In this book, *Embraced*, nothing seems braver to me that facing up to one's own identity and filtering out the chatter that tells us to be something we're not. In this book I hit on an incredible well-spring of honesty. Complete strangers opened their lives and their homes to me, confessing honesty and events that had never been revealed to ordinary people. By that I mean they did not have resources or character traits available to them to give them an uncommon advantage in pursuing a better life.

I'm not an expert of any sort. I have not one credential and nothing to speak about in the academic department, just what you all read about from the book produced by author and owner of Jewel of the West Publishing, Jewel Adams, Out of the Closet and Into the Light, and the live video produced by the President of North Star

JORDAN JANTZ

International and Voice(s) of Hope, Ty Mansfield. These are the only things that I did that ever can be considered helpful additions to the human world we share.

I did learn from working on this book, *Embraced,* that it is the hard times that change the course of our lives. In this book I reveal these moments to show my own fallibility. This book is far different from what I originally envisioned. It reflects what I've found not what I predicted.

This book does not follow a conventional outline because as you all know, real life is not conventional. Each experience can become embraced in our life. So this book is to unearth the psychological secrets that haunt us. It is not organized by industry or personality type. It is not a travelogue. It is about misconceptions and fears.

When people heard this book's title, the most common question I got asked was, "So is your book about your life, or about careers?" and I'd laugh and warn them not to get trapped by semantics. I answer, "It's about people who've dared to be honest with themselves." When reading it, I know you will become embraced.

> "An exceptional man living an indescribable life, one filled with trials, triumphs, and courage. Thought provoking and heart-felt writing. Jordan's story will forever inspire, long after the final page."
>
> Jewel Adams's Endorsement of *Embraced*
>
> Best-selling author of inspirational romance and motivational speaker

Surfing was always my favorite sport since growing up in California.

CLI

SPECIAL MESSAGE FROM JORDAN JANTZ

Jordan wants to share a special message with you in the hope that you can know him a little better and understand what drives him:

Hello, my primary and most essential goal in life is to remain connected to the world of God's love and Spirit. Everything else will take care of itself. I'm reminding myself daily, continuously who I am today, a spiritual being having a human experience.

My number one spiritual practice is trying to live in the present moment, to resist projecting into the future, or laminating past mistakes. To feel the real power of now; that, my friends is my secret to living an inspired life for me.

The book Out of the Closet, Into the Light and project of Voices of Hope are for people who want help to heal and the brokenness of people's lives who are walking with the pain of their own personal secrets and shame and lies of their life that others have placed upon them.

There is no age limit on abuse, but I have learned that I have the ability to change the future of others with my truth.

-Jordan and Charity

EMBRACED

JORDAN JANTZ

FROM THE COMPILERS

Many people throughout Jordan Jantz's life support the doctors, the case-managers, the ministers and the many special relationships that have been working for months with Jordan Jantz to transfer his experiences and techniques to survive inhumane activity that others put on him even today and throughout his life into a book form. Jordan Jantz's gift of survival skills will astonish anyone who knows the meaning of forgiveness, because when meeting Jordan Jantz, you can't help but feel humbled by his kindness. He describes with clarity his inborn instincts and observations in this book with no other purpose than to heal and uplift. In fact, 100% of the author's proceeds are sent directly to the Christmas Box House International. Jordan Jantz wouldn't do this book any other way, and he had many offers and requests for a second book to answer the question so many ask, "<u>What has become of your life today?</u>"

Jordan Jantz shares his ability to sustain courage while maintaining vulnerability. **Jordan Jantz is a rock star of honesty**. We all believe the creator of the universe finds in Jordan Jantz today and throughout his life from infancy <u>a willing vessel</u> for his goodness in the world. The ideas in this book will become a memory for each of us, because nobody else exposes shame and embarrassment of truth as found in the set of these two books. Professors at BYU have said that the two books, combined together, will become a good movie for the Church's ministry and outreach for many of the issues we are all confronted with in our daily lives.

Embraced would not have been completed without 100% consistent support of Jordan Jantz's phenomenal medical team and social support system. All forms of professionals in Portland are an incredible force for Jordan Jantz's healing energy that he gives out into the world today. After reading the first book, Out of the Closet, Into the Light by Jewel Adams and when you finish this second book from this set right now in your hands, you will find that you will want to both **pay it forward** and **walk by faith**.

These days, everyone is vulnerable, even the most successful corporate executive. There is no longer any distinction between groups that are immune from invasion of their privacy by the media and groups that are not. No one is immune. Some of the biggest names in business, entertainment and sports have had the harshest reality facing the public with their life. We are grateful that we have changed the names to protect the innocent. As with the first book, Out of the Closet, Into the Light, many names and some specific dates in this book have been changed to protect the innocent and the guilty.

It has been our privilege for each individual volunteer to assist in compiling this book. We hope we have brought it honor. We all hope the readers feel this book is valuable and addresses the issues of today's life ...all of which Jordan Jantz has survived and he has learned there is nothing that can erase the post-traumatic stress disorders and the flashbacks of a life born in drowning darkness which has continued throughout his life.

Jordan, our Moses, has never steered us wrong.

ILLUSTRATIONS

Fig. 1 Personal Art Collection of Jordan Jantz "At Lagoon: The Happiest Day in Jordan's Life" crayon on paper, Stephanie Wallentine, 2016 on PAGE 593

INTRODUCTION

NO BOOK I WRITE IS THE PRODUCT OF MAN'S EFFORT

To me, reading a book should be like exploring a new world. That unknown *something* around the corner always seems to hold possibilities even more fascinating than my present discovery. Perhaps you feel the same way, perhaps you are always pressing on to meet new people, to see new places, to gain new knowledge – and if this is true – you may welcome our journey into the realm of life-transforming books.

For a long time, I didn't want to write a book. I had my reasons.

When I completed my previous edition, I knew that if I were suddenly taken ill and died, I would leave this earth a satisfied man – certainly a fulfilled author. I am not in competition with anyone, even myself. This second edition contains critical material that leaves no room for doubt.

Few things are more enjoyable than a good story as a book or a movie. It makes no difference whether the story is happy or sad or long or short, if it has elements that keep you dangling and opening the heart. When that happens, I succeed as an author.

My life involves the communication of Biblical truths that many cannot imagine in today's world. They work like magic. I have witnessed one well-placed song that I relate to scripture change the mood of my firesides in less than two minutes. Until you've been to one of my firesides, you haven't experienced a real one.

JORDAN JANTZ

Everyone will tell you that. If you have questions, check out the YouTube videos available on the internet. God has opened up the transformation in my life, which amazes me today.

Except for my firesides, I am no longer up on that stage, an untouchable pedestal of fashion. My modeling stories are endless, of course, and each one captures the reality that I have *re-lived* in telling this book, as if I stepped into a time tunnel to where it all began. It became impossible for me to remain aloof while sharing such events, and the events are such that neither can you, the reader, be separate. And that is good. A good author doesn't permit casual observation. I have learned to wrap up the truth and hold on to it, and I won't let go.

So, let yourself go with me. Place yourself in my true story; *be involved.* You will interact with truth on a deep and personal level because you are in the true story, and then the true story is in you. When it is over, you will sit in the embrace of truth, Valentine's Day and every day. From the beginning to the end of a true story, reality resonates in the deepest part of you, and for this moment you are still because it takes some time to get your mind and heart back. After reading my second book, *Embraced,* you are never the same again. That's what the story of my life will do for you.

These scenes actually happened. This whole plot happened to me. This book is not fiction. And here is the truth for all of us: there is no escaping life's calamities.

Throughout the pages of my book, I reiterate the importance of *embracing* truth, and not just hearing it or thinking about it. In this information era it is easy to become fascinating by more and more words (and it is good to be interested in intriguing concepts) but not at the expense of embracing the truth presented.

I have enjoyed spending time with you in the pages of my book. We share emotions as, together, we push aside the clutter of lies and return to the basics of a simple life.

Admittedly, some chapters of my book are direct and pointed. You may even think I am a little too severe. The dimension of God's message of truth is so necessary to my life. Except for Jesus, no one has ever embraced or found me good enough, without expecting something in return. All human beings throughout my life have expected something from the day that I came into this world until Jesus said, "No more." God does not stand aloof from me, pointing or shouting words of condemnation, about me and my life as a man who has same gender attraction. He reaches for me with open arms; He gives His strength in place of my weakness. He desires to help me write this book to rescue children from sinking and to bring them to safety. Jesus knows my heart. It is HIS.

I am fully aware that few facts are more unpopular or more offensive than the words I have just written. Certainly that is true among philosophical types. Nevertheless, Jesus taught me otherwise, and I would be an unfaithful messenger to fail to tell you so. If you really desire a life worth living and the kind of faith I have been writing about in all these pages, you need to start with Jesus.

In reading my book, look closely. Think clearly. Jesus spoke of *checking the fruit* and paying attention to what is being taught – both what is said and what is left unsaid – and how what is said is lived out. What are the results? That is the first place you would look in reading a book that is about transformation, like *Embraced*. In the final analysis there are many who appeal to our senses and many who plead for our loyalty and especially for our money. Discerning the value of the messages of others is not foolish. Be genuine and not counterfeit. Be sincere. Don't be side-tracked by other things as you attempt to discern truth.

Many children who have been where I have been do not live to communicate these memories. God allows me to write about what my transformation means in my daily life and over the decade that I have been committed to saving the lives of children. I did finally succeed in communicating and created a way to help the children. Nothing else has given me as much happiness as coming into close contact with helping the lives of children, children who are as I was, as a child. I have experienced exceptional moments writing *Embraced*.

My book also teaches how to become friendly and even close to people you don't yet know.

This book would never have been possible without my service dog, Charity. This book never would have been written from the beginning to the end without her, for she was *in* the book throughout every word that was written. She is a super-hero. I am grateful that my life has touched so many lives. I have been blessed. I do believe that *some people were born to touch so many lives*.

In my pages of *Embraced*, you will be exposed to dynamic statements about grace. Transparent grace is my power that I receive from God, for myself, without any cost. I sincerely believe that if I take these gifts I've been given and meditate upon change and transformation, God will walk side-by-side in the light of His beautiful sun.

In my past, I have heard a lot of teaching about faith, what faith IS, what it is NOT, and how to operate in it. In spite of all that, to be very honest with you, I am not sure how many believers truly understand faith. If I understood more about faith, I would see more victory in my daily life. It is a way of life, and I must choose to *let go of the past* and *proceed to where I am celebrated and not*

EMBRACED

tolerated. Actually, the grace of God that I have found is not complicating or confusing. It is simple. And that's why many people miss it. There is nothing more powerful than grace. In fact, everything in the Bible/salvation, the infilling of the Holy Spirit/fellowship with God and all victory in my daily life, is based upon it. Without grace, I am nothing, I have nothing, and I can do nothing. If it were not for the grace of God, I would be miserable and hopeless.

You and I are vessels through which God does His own works. We are all partners with the creator. What an awesome privilege! He allows us to share in His glory as long as we remember that apart from Him, we can do nothing. If I really believe that, when God is in complete control of my life none of the things that go wrong will upset or discourage me, because I will know that through it all, God is working out His plan for me. I will not glory in what I am doing for God, but only in what He is doing through me. I must always submit to the commitment that my life belongs to God, trusting myself to Him in everything and for everything, relying not upon my great faith but upon His marvelous love. It is truth that is important to me. But even with faith and truth, when it comes to us with grace, I receive it as a gift that must be shared. Everything in our lives depends, not upon our merits or abilities or works, but upon God's divine willingness to use His infinite power to meet our needs and at no cost to us whatsoever. That is grace.

If you have needs today – and who doesn't have needs? I know I sure do – I urge you to cast them upon the Lord. It is fine to have plans and goals and dreams for your life. It is wonderful to have things that you are believing in God for, but I suggest that you make a commitment to put all that aside for a moment, just for the time it takes to read this book. **FREE yourself from all attempts to achieve anything by your own faith and effort.** Instead, just relax and place yourself in a comfortable position, peacefully and solely upon the Lord. Let go completely of all thoughts and see what

JORDAN JANTZ

dynamic power He will bring to bear in your life as you simply yield yourself to receive His amazing grace through letting Heavenly Father embrace you with this book, *Embraced*. I believe you will see such a change in your entire approach to life that you will never desire to return to old ways.

Enjoy your new life, reading and being transformed.

Enjoy being embraced. You will be happier. I promise you that.

PRELUDE

I have learned that you can change anything and make it a beautiful thing. I heard that is how Jesus lived on earth, transforming people's lives. I have learned to open up my life to do the same and touch the lives of children that came from a life like I did. It is embarrassing being sold and it is embarrassing know that you were the first-born son, that was not-wanted, but kept around until the time was right for me to be move into where I would have opportunities of light being brought into my life.

Normally, change is hard for me. I cannot be rushed. For some people, new beginnings can become like brushing your teeth, a daily habit. With God I can handle the new beginnings that are expected in my life from many people, as well as the expectations they have placed upon my life today. I will remember all of you.

I have one heart, one purpose, to touch the lives of others. I am going for the real gold medal in my life, and that is to change the life of a child that does not have hope and does not have a family.

I will be there with my heart to fix and to mend the broken hearted and I am going with Jesus all the way, where ever you or I are at, we will be together because **friends are friends forever if the Lord is the Lord in them.**

CLXIV

FOREWORD

I'll be home soon, too. I might not have noticed it, but I am closer to home than ever before. Each moment in my life is a step taken. My breath is a page turned. Every day is a mile marked, my personal mountain climbed. I am closer to home than I have ever been and before I know it, my appointed arrival time will be coming.

I'll descend the ramp and enter the city. I will see faces that are waiting for me. I'll hear everyone's names spoken by those who love me and maybe, just maybe, in the back of the crowds – I'll see the one who would rather die than live without me remove his pierced hands from his heavenly robe and applaud a guest.
I have no authority to proceed since the property is not mine.

Dropping to my knees, I say to the Lord, "You have been my guest throughout my life and I have been a host. From now on, I am going to serve. You are going to be the owner and the master."

Running as fast as I can to the strong box, I take out the title deed to my house describing its assets and liabilities, location and situation. I eagerly sign my house over to God alone for all time and eternity, saying, "Here it is, Lord, all that I have and have ever had, You run the house. I'll just remain with you as a servant and friend."

Things are different since Jesus Christ has settled down and made His home in my heart. Embracing what matters most in my life - saving children from abuse, abandonment and bullying - is the legacy I choose. I've written only to bring awareness of the consequences of actions made to individuals who many are not able to speak for themselves. No matter what their disabilities are, everyone can shine. This book is dedicated to all like me, who have been left behind, but have found the courage to journey on.

JORDAN JANTZ

This photo was taken to give a family in California the chance to see what they were buying for a son. In those days, it was called Black-Market Baby-Selling. Today, it is called Child Trafficking. Today, Jordan lives a life transforming hearts for children and is a Voice of Hope and has been awarded the lifetime achievement award as Beacon of Light. Miracles in this man's life could only happen by God Himself. The fact he is, he is still alive today and thriving. This has opened adult protective services honoring Jordan for the truth that so many keep secret and the majority wouldn't even want to talk about. Most people push it under the rug. So sad, that our society say, "Impossible. How can something like this happen?" Jordan's mission has only just begun to live.

EMBRACED

Jordan's final resting place will be: Section 6, Lot 21,Space 4 of Macon County Memorial Park 5700 W. Main Street Decatur, Illinois 62522 217-963-2202 Jordan's death certificate will say *Jordan Jantz*, but the grave marker says *Jimmylee Bond Grubbs*. This is all pre-arranged with Jordan's biological brother, Ronnie, and the cemetery authorities.

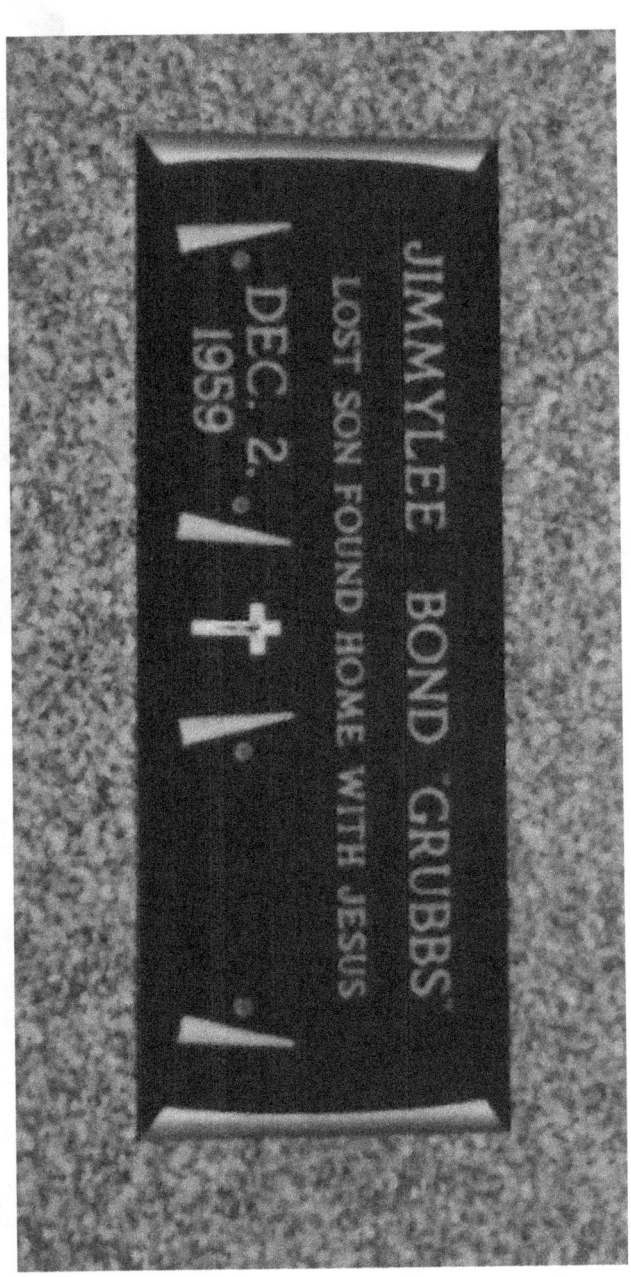

Embraced Valentine
2016

CLXVIII

> For Jordan, it was always that the stage was his pedestal.
>
> When he was up there, he was untouchable.
>
> That was his safe spot.
>
> And today, he is free from the limelight.

THE SPIRIT OF VALENTINE'S DAY

SNUGGLED WITH CHARITY in my red-and-pink-hearts Valentine's sheets and pillows, I lay in pre-dawn red crystal light in my own bedroom. That same sparkle of red light shone on moonlight late nights in Milan, when I was chosen by elite employers who embraced my love of runway and fashion work in which I would bring designer's apparel into the pages of fashion magazines and prints. I worked hard to maintain *the look* for each catcall with diets and make-overs. In Milan, I breathe and glide down the catwalk in cupid angel wings at a very special exclusive show for designers only, who in turn will sell the clothing to buyers who want to sell the clothing I am wearing at this moment in top-line American lingerie boutiques and resorts. I had jumped at the chance and the dollar.

    I drop candy hearts into their glasses as I walk by, drawing the buyers in. I make them kings and queens of the night, as I maintain my smile/etiquette and blow a kiss. I catch their hearts as that is the main requirement of *being* a runway model. Everyone is touched by the uniqueness of my appearance for this work and the confidence of continued years of work in this industry which makes my life very successful in the eyes of the world.

    While I work this Valentine's show I experience the beauty of my favorite holiday. Being exhausted on stage comes with the job. Vanessa Williams herself is performing, relaxed and focused upon a white baby grand piano. She sings her love songs and as the show is ending and we models appear all together on the stage for the last finale of the night, Vanessa Williams sings "Save the best for Last". It brings the house down with confetti falling from the ceiling and flying all over the stage while I model Valentine Pajamas and lingerie given to me (the waist 30"/"Daddy Sizes"). It looks like I'm becoming big, but I've already been through a rehabilitation program for eating disorders. *Thank God* for therapists. **I am *everything* on Valentine's Day.** My joy and my looks are my signature selling points in my industry of eternal beauty, love and fashion.

    Back then I relied on coaches grooming me for the catwalk, a rigorous southern California mentality. I put myself out there as a protégé for bidding with hours conditioning my body inward and outward to appear the *most radiant and marketable* to buyers of clothing lines across America and beyond. I sometimes wondered if my body would give out before I would, because it is hard to make everyone happy. Thank God for this gift of

consistent outward appearance. Even through my 30s and 40s, people continued to choose me and embrace my walk and appearance in magazines on this special day of romance, fashion and good food with top-of-the-line buyers that come (they always came, and with box-seats) for incredible encounters and get-aways. Money was nothing, before or after the show. There was great *joy* in *celebrating love* with other runway models who worked as hard as I did.

My dreams fade for a moment and from my bed I see my sunrise-reddened window-sheers are blown by wind into my room, and then the sheers shift color to a *California* warm orange, shining sparkles of tangerine crystals throughout my room. I snuggle closer to Charity and draw a blanket up to shield my eyes. Valentines-past make me realize how grateful I am to have my little Charity be my Valentine, as I snuggle to her and she snuggles to me, chest to chest. She's in her Valentine pajamas, too.

My dreams are so beautiful it is hard to want to wake. The California colors bring me more memories, memories in which I grab my *Louis Vuitton shoe*s and my man bag to *jet* out the door. My memory is playing as I cruise down Melrose Avenue in southern California. More of my senses join my dream; I smell my favorite fragrance, Acqua Di Gio for men. This has been my signature scent since it was first presented decades ago at a show in New York. At the Beverly Wilshire Hotel I will enjoy a beautifully appointed breakfast. This classy restaurant is one of my favorites. Valentine's Day there can be *overwhelmingly romantic*: chilled Dom Perignon is served at the nearby men's fragrance boutiques to cool clients out for the morning with their lovers. As I am let out of the car to enter the hotel lobby, I converge with my fellow industry workers from all backgrounds in entertainment.

As a group of the physically attractive, we know we are overwhelming (which I was even among the industry workers) and

EMBRACED

we shade our eyes with black sunglasses to cover up the ache of hard work for the quiet morning as we eat.

Such youth-obsessed, superficial judgment ought to be outgrown by twenty-five. I'm still in recovery from the ageless attraction industry. But somehow I carried myself in this career throughout many years, abusing my body and emotions to maintain what I knew to be a success, for a price tag was put on my life as a protégé for others' expectations and pleasures. If this could only be a dream how much happier my life would seem. Years have passed and now the time has come to me and I see what my reality turned out to be.

Back in my home, my alarm clicks on to music which ends my dreams of my life's truth. It is for the best, I think. Also, I don't know how to adjust the alarm clock to snooze, so it really is time to get up. I hold Charity in my arms. I've never had a more faithful Valentine. I say, "Let's go out and do the potty dance! Then Daddy's got to go to men's therapy. Daddy cannot be late!"

The phone rings. I grab it before the second ring. At this hour, I know who it is likely to be. "Good morning, Sister Sophie!" I say. (By the way, Sophie is the wonderful lady who saved me when I was homeless and didn't even know my name. We are prayer-partners every morning and have been for over 15 years). "It is a beautiful morning isn't it?" I say.

"It is, Jordan! Are you ready to pray?" I can hear her gardening equipment in the background.

"I am so glad to pray with you *every* morning, Sophie. Whatever you want to pray about, let's ask Heavenly Father now, because He answers every single prayer that you and I ever prayed. We are going to *bring* it to God in prayer this morning. We *lift* our hands up! Are you lifting your hand, Sophie?"

"I am!" She says. "My hand is up high, reaching for positive energy!"

"This morning, Sophie, YOU are going to be the designer of those flower beds at McMinamins and they will be *beautiful* because you will be guided by the Holy Spirit. I know He is guiding you to ponder and to visualize and respond to the spirits of those who come to those gardens to connect to the beautiful nature that God alone could create. The Holy Spirit is guiding you at this time, financially and physically and He's not letting go. God is consistent and faithful." I love saying this because it is the truth.

"Yes, Jordan, I need this prayer! And what do you need this morning, Jordan?" she invites.

"What do I need?" I repeat and then answer, "I need this prayer for not being consumed with trying to make everyone happy! There are so many deadlines to meet that I need to just accept that I can't make them all happy. I want to have peace that I am doing what God wants and asks me to do, because I do have the experience to create love out into the world which is what I want to do, and that is impossible without Jesus and I know it! So that's what we are going to pray for, for me. I need it now!!"

Now I get ready to claim this through Holy Spirit with her, "Tell me that you are holding the phone with your right hand, and your left hand up and you are raising it *high* to Jesus ("It is!" she says) and we say together now –"Heavenly Father, Lord God, we call upon you this morning- my sister Sophie and I do, and where two or more are gathered in Your name we know that You are in the midst of us- and we ask You through your holy power that You will pour upon us through the blood that dripped from Calvary, to gift us to say to all opposition: "I am a child of God and I deserve to walk as a child of God and we just thank you Lord, for all that you are doing!" Now put the phone on your

shoulder, Sophie, and press your hands together and we know we really embrace hand-in-hand with Jesus for guidance and spiritual knowledge to design flower gardens that are beautiful artwork and to figure out how to make impossible things happen! We ask this through the power of Jesus AMEN! Yes we need it LORD and we CLAIM IT through Jesus's Holy Name, AMEN!!!"

"Amen, Jordan. I claim it!" she says.

"Are you good, Sophie?" I ask.

"I'm good, Jordan, and I hope you have a wonderful day." She says, "I'm off to move the planters. I love you and bless you, honey. Let's talk later on tomorrow after your event tonight,"

I know she will want to hear about my Valentine's Day tomorrow and I want to share it with her.

I say, "Absolutely. We have a plan, Sweet Pea. I'll plan extra time tomorrow morning."

"Alright then," Sophie says. She knows me and that I will keep my promise.

"Bye, Sophie, I love you and Happy Valentine's Day!" I say, to give her encouragement.

She responds, "I love you too, Jordan. Talk to you tomorrow. Bye!" And then we hang up together.

I listen to morning radio. The jockeys know to bring out the love inside music. We are serious about this stuff in Portland.

Talking to my mirror-self through my toothpaste, I say (out loud, for Charity's benefit), "Look, what a devoted man, in therapy seventeen years!" These are important relationships, built over years of consistent therapy. Charity understands devotion and

EMBRACED

commitment. I explain more to her, "The men in this group-therapy are survivors of sexual abuse, dealing with abandonment, just like your daddy still does today." Charity is paying close attention, as always.

I ask her, "Charity, do you think this *abandonment emptiness* will ever go away? Will I ever feel real love? I know you love me, Char-bear. You've been with me longer than any set of parents or boyfriend has ever been. I've never had a little spirit animal or person stay in my life this long and not leave me. You are the most faithful creature God created for my life, and you haven't left me like everyone else has. *How come* you haven't left me, Charity? I know I'm not that good of a person, or I wouldn't be all alone, going to therapy all these years."

I am brushing my teeth and I can't help the tears falling down my face, tears from the reality of all this truth.

I need to switch the subject back to therapy, so I say, "Therapy relationships are gold. *Ain't nothing like the real thing, baby,*" to Charity to cheer us both up again. Charity and I embrace reality, and my reality is that there is a big difference between the glamor of Martha's Vineyard and the healing of Portland's Wellness Center for Men. I have had to let go of control and trust God in this particular group of men. Charity is totally all over it with me. That's what a service animal does.

As I am walking Charity at Portland State University's dog park, I realize that another year I have kept a promise and another year I have taken a chance continuing therapy since childhood. My promise is to let go of the suitcase of my brokenness and to embrace new growth as a *healthy spiritual man*. By my devotion to incredible medical support and walking by faith, I do the best I can daily to balance my brokenness that came of being everything to others while not embracing myself. Some days I want to focus on the harms of grooming and abuse that I still see in the world every day, but I know that I have to take care of myself, because nobody else will, unless they have an agenda.

Charity finishes up her potty dance. I pick up her present carefully and cleanly and dispose of it and then we both head home to prepare for therapy. I am not really excited that therapy is on Valentine's Day, but I am loyal.

I zip up my elevator again to find there are flowers at my door for *me*. Flowers, love, romance!! I had missed the delivery when I was out with Charity. It is my first bouquet of this Valentine's Day. Is it ferns and roses with baby's breath? No it is a tropical floral design, my favorite. And chocolates! I can smell the rich dark chocolate without even tasting it. I bury my nose to breath in the fragrance of bird of paradise flowers. I feel almost tidal-waved again by the dreams I experienced early this morning.

It is decision time: Do I really *need* to do the therapy like I usually do, or is today a *special day* to throw the schedule to the wind? Do I *want* to continue this journey and take several chances of (painful) healing in group therapy, or do I want to take a time out for myself and *do what I want to do on Valentine's Day*? I am a man that has been *extremely* spoiled *rotten* with romance, gourmet dinners to which we flew in small airplanes for romance to be *flaunted* with extravagant people or even just the simple watching of a good movie with someone very special to my heart.

But those days are over now. I look into my life and realize for the first time I get to choose. And I want what is *best* for my whole life including my next life to come. Somewhere, there will be another Valentine's Day waiting for me in another life.

Charity and I leave my apartment and lock the door and go down the elevator again. When I am outside my lobby door, I

board Portland's best kept secret: the excellent public transit trolley. Portland has the best transportation of all types. Charity and I are going to therapy together today.

As I am sitting down on the trolley, I spot a member of my therapy group, Paul, and sit near him.

Paul says, "You always dress that dog up and paint her nails. By the way you treat her, you'd think she was the only thing that you ever loved."

I just smile. I know that everything he just said is so right. Love isn't love until it is given away and received. His statement is the reality of my life and he knows, like everyone else does in Portland, that I was an orphan. He really didn't need to say what he said. But I guess it made him feel good. That's the way life treats some who has been forgotten.

Paul and I are both dressed with Valentines colors and prepared for the day. Paul tells me of his Valentines plans with his husband and his two adopted children for later that night, although he knows I'm no longer with anyone since my boyfriend died at Christmas years ago. Paul is so happy to see me, he tells me that he is planning on going off his HIV medications because the side effects are a challenge. His husband was misdiagnosed with AIDS and had been taking the medication and now he is going to go in for a second series of tests to see if the virus is in his body. It's so scary at times with same gender attraction and the concerns with your immune system, and the many diseases that are undetectable until it is too late. They may even be misdiagnosed as in Paul's husband's case. I guess we take chances. That's why, for me, God is my last chance to have a life and that is why I have the doctors I have, because they are faithful to me being truthful with my life.

We are near our stop and I say, "Paul, I will see you in group, with confidentiality, as always."

EMBRACED

We get off the trolley as if we have never met. That's how confidential my Men's Processing Group is. It is for men that have serious challenges to live with, of all kinds.

Inside the medical plaza and down the elevator toward the therapy room, all it takes is a single visual to make my memory begin to connect: pink, red, flowers, roses, tulips, diamonds, watches, cruises and exotic meetings... and we are all wearing something red or pink. Then I find myself shaking my head. I'm middle aged (and yes, I still have the looks) but honestly my heart is not in it, as in years past. My spirit reaches for restoration and transformation so that I can be a person of love for the many who have walked or still walk in my shoes. I see them all around me today no matter where I go, even while I go to therapy, healing. Win or lose, therapy and healing are the right thing to do. After all, I couldn't let the boys down in the psychiatric healing group.

There are many medical plazas in Portland and I am familiar in all of them. Many offices are specialty medical outreach to the Portland elite community, dealing with emotional and mental abuse from childhood, and many deal with continued abuse in their adult life that started in childhood. I arrive at last in the warm colored offices that give nothing away. Charity, under my arm, is dressed in her pink valentine outfit which of course I'm matching in my black and red tailored coat. I'm still able to rock it, *glory be to God*. Within two minutes my name is called and I am greeted as I cross over the threshold.

We all gather humbly in a circle and sit down on the floor with our mats, legs crossed in an upward extension of our chest in breathing exercises until my guru walks into the room to clear our consciousness. She sits in her space, speaking to each person first as individuals. Addressing individual issues of life and goals, she goes around the circle. She has long beautiful white hair, manicured and tailored African attire. She is very observant and has the ability of transforming lives with those who have been rescued.

Her first peaceful spoken words directed to us all are, "Happy Valentine's Day, gentlemen. Today we are going to explore our hearts and look back at the love we are sharing among our relationships. We will find the beauty of the meaning of Valentine's Day to you, personally, and embrace the meaning of this day."

She hands out a pink paper heart and a pencil to each of us to write a word that expresses Valentine's Day, today, in our own life. We are quiet as we each write down a word and hand back the pencils. She tells us to hold on to our pink hearts until the end of therapy. I put my pink heart in my back pocket so that I don't lose it.

"Gentlemen," she states, "this is where finding meaning and transformation *happen* because this will always be a challenge," and I'm thinking, *it should be simple after all these years*. Everyone here knows my baggage and I know theirs. Throughout this life of mine, my appearance has always been embraced. The beginning of therapy was even harder. Some say that group therapy is like a curtain flirting with light; you can't see the true form until they talk. That isn't quite true with me. I had to learn to read people before I could talk or understand their talk. I had to learn to read spirits and what they wanted. Today this is a gift and also very heavy. A lot of group therapy is respecting what a person is ready to express and embracing that person with safety and kindness.

In the group, a gentleman raises his hand and shares his Valentine-gratitude that he and his partner have survived their recent near death experiences along with their long-challenging anger issues. Another man is grateful that he is able to realize God loves him, born intersex or hermaphrodite. All at the group today experience disabilities *inside* certain experiences. A news broadcaster for Portland TV expresses that he is grateful to be free from his addiction to food and internet sex and pornography.

As I listen, their realities affirm for me the true blessing of being free from the *need* for affirmation through physical intimacy for myself. Looking at us, nobody would understand why any of us would be sitting in this group of broken hearts because so many, like myself, can make the outside so plastic and fantastic that nobody would know what is on inside. Hiding your heart becomes a part of life.

The therapist opens to me, asking "Jordan, what is your happiest idea of Valentine's Day as a middle aged man?"

I say, "Well, honestly, that is exactly what I wrote on my paper valentine." I pull it out of my pocket and open it. It says, *middle aged.*

The others may not feel happy about their advancing ages or they worry about their waning attractiveness. I know I am talking about something they are more than a little anxious about. I say gently, "I have the ability to *not* embrace sex to sooth my feelings. I live in a city that supported the *young me* and actually the city supports the *new me*, too. Portland is so small that everyone remembers everything anyone has ever done and I certainly had to live my life in the *wide* open all these last 35 years. I owe everyone respect that lives here who includes me now just as they included me before. They know who I really am and give me *respect and dignity.*"

Then follow two hours of questions and responses between the group's members.

JORDAN JANTZ

We dismiss with the pact: *What is said in the group, stays in the group.* We commit to return in one week. We wish each other well.

Last, we walk out as if we don't know each other.

I do breathing exercises as I exit the medical lobby, exhaling everyone's energy and I center myself to think of the positive day ahead, especially my lunch appointment that I planned for me on Valentine's Day. This meeting will not be the most romantic, but the most loving.

Just two blocks from this Portland medical plaza there is a quaint Mexican restaurant hidden on the Columbia River before the boardwalk expands on the marina. You can take a boat and go fishing if you want and have quality time, which is what I value most in my life, but fishing is not my plan today.

I see my minister is dressed in a pristine tailored white shirt, charcoal suit and his salute to the holiday is his red tie with matching red socks above his shiny black shoes. He stands to spiritually and physically embrace me as our greeting. This leader knows my opportunities for freedom in my life are because my life purpose today is to emulate the love of God to others, even when they are family and want nothing to do with me because I chose to be real with myself. My minister and I are here to celebrate what we have in common: living as brothers, exploring the love of God for ourselves and in our relationships, and not being embarrassed because of what other people think, especially on Valentine's Day.

He holds me out, "How are you doing today? How is your book selling? How is your health this morning?"

"Well, today is Valentine's Day, you know that." I answer. "This morning I received my favorite tropical bouquet of

EMBRACED

flowers called of Bird of Paradise, and of course chocolates …that I am going to re-gift to *you*, because I can't handle another pound."

He laughs, "So *California* of you."

I present the chocolates box with a flourish for this friend I love. "This is the only day in the entire year I can get away with loving everyone in the way I want to love them, without other people judging me for being in love with the blessing of my life. *Today* I am not eccentric when I embrace the people I love. Isn't that funny?"

He says, "Jesus would do the same thing."

He turns to my little girl, "I know that you are getting Charity ready for her Valentine's Day Doggie Dash. It is going to be a big deal in Portland. I heard it's at the Timberline Lodge. Are you going alone or with friends?"

"Only my usual," I nod to Charity, "my princess."

She always knows when we are talking about her and now she's showing off.

He laughs at her circle-y strut and says, "Are you ready to take her on stage?"

I grin, "You know me don't you. She's already prepared. She has her diamond studs and her nails are fresh. She has a reputation as a show-stopper. You *know* Charity is known for being a *very regal dog* that prances with her head up high."

It is his turn to grin, "She got that from you, and I have NO problem with that." He laughs while Charity swirls around me on her leash, black and white coat glistening like high-polished patent leather shoes.

He says "You two have been together for 14 years. That is longer than some marriages."

I nod, "… and definitely longer than any man has stayed in my life on a continual basis. Charity is the easiest to please on Valentine's Day and every day and that's why she will prove that the catwalk is not just for cats."

"Charity's costume, is it from Vegas?" he asks because he knows I love Vegas costumes.

"No, her outfit today was locally made. In fact, the beading was done by the girls at church." I have been saving telling him that just so I could see his smile. He doesn't disappoint; his face shows his heart is delighted to learn of kindness in our church branch.

My minister says, "Charity's a light show, and I completely support it."

After the meal, we walk out onto boardwalk, passing the moored boats and marine life in downtown Portland.

He says, "Jordan, I can't imagine how challenging *life* is with your past, given your honesty and the difficulty of your mission to improve the lives of children who have been in your shoes."

"I feel it" I agree, and then I say, "I could use a blessing. In fact, right now."

He sits me on a park bench on the marina. He looks at me quietly. "I am honored to give you this blessing of peace."

He places his hands gently on my head, "Jimmylee Jordan Jantz, by the power of the Holy Melchizedek Priesthood that I hold and as your priesthood leader, I place a blessing from your Heavenly Father upon you. You Father blesses you with peace, upon your spirit and body."

JORDAN JANTZ

There is a pause as he searches for the Holy Spirit's guidance to say the words, "Your Heavenly Father is mindful of you and of the hardships of this day, of the memories that can be confusing even as they are healing to process. You are His loved child, *never* abandoned. By God's Holy Spirit, God's love for you can be communicated from you to others, which is the task of angels and those take upon them the work of God. I seal this blessing upon you, and all others that you stand in need of at this time on this Valentine's Day, through the power and authority of Jesus Christ, Amen."

I feel the Holy Spirit and I know he is speaking God's words to me at this time. I thank him for this experience and the gift of our spiritual brotherhood. He is so precious.

With hugs, I depart. Charity circles around me like I am her sun. We have our special walk, and I let her protect me as I pass the handle of the leash around my back and across my front, over and over. Showing me that she wants to protect me by circling around me is a way that she expresses her love for me.

We are soon on the train and I go home to physically refresh and focus on the big event at Mt. Hood this evening in the Timberline Lodge.

On my docket at home, I have to do Charity's last minute costume touch ups (must snip those extra threads) and immediately consider my nutrients. I hydrate and consume some raw coconut and bananas and kosher meat. My friends have brought me fresh foods and juices and I am so grateful to have these nutrients when I have a demanding day.

I play my music: "Oooh child, things are going to get easier. Oooh, things'll get brighter!" I sing along to Charity, "Someday, we will walk in the light of a beautiful sun. Someday things will get brighter!" As the song continues I realize it is a promise from God, if we will embrace it. Things really *have* gotten easier and brighter because of God's love for my health and for giving me the love of professional doctors in all parts of my treatment. I have the finest of Portland's medical services and I am so humbled at how they value my life. What a true and loving Valentine's gift that really is to me.

Also, I rest. I think more of my doctors and my healthcare. I am so blessed as someone that lives through challenges with disabilities. But I still pray so hard that nobody notices the disabilities I've lived with since childhood, and that they don't pick up on them at this year's Doggie Dash. What shame it would be to be so publicly exposed! I think of who I will meet; knowing everyone from Seattle through Idaho will be present for this Pacific Northwest event at Mount Hood's Timberline Lodge. Many will be asking personal questions during the mixer and the evening's event.

I also play my recent therapy-recording-CD which my therapist creates every week to help focus me and do my meditation "Oomm!"

And now, it is time to rock the clock off the Timberline Lodge! I check one last time in the mirror and then Charity and I are out the door.

Charity and I catch the light rail that takes us all the way to the base of Mount Hood as the setting sun glows a Valentine pink on February's mountain snow. We disembark at the gates draped with roses, lit like a wedding, with the smell of cotton candy. All dogs and their owners are chatting during the hors devours, human and canine. There are champagne glasses for the adults and many ice water bowls with treats for the dogs. I've been to so many of

EMBRACED

these upper echelon functions that I no longer get nose bleeds. I know every action and etiquette for politicians to police officers. My cocktail jacket is red and black, a headlining outfit by Versace. On my sleeve are the red hand-stitched letters "Charity".

Pink Martini plays romantic melodies by the fireplace. One of my favorite former Portland mayors spots me and comes over with his dog. We ask the attendant to watch our dogs while we escort ourselves to the veranda to enjoy the immediate, live jazz of this incredible musical group, my appreciation heightened by knowing the members of the jazz band personally.

My colleague, the-former-politician, has been a part of my life for the past thirty years. Throwing benefits to embrace my choices is one of his finest attributes. He attended my transformational spiritual baptism eight years ago that was a highlight in this same community that I am surrounded by tonight. As I look around the room, he's not the only one who was at my life's transformational baptism. It gives me goose bumps, for they all knew I no longer allow the conduct of the past. I think of what they will ask, even while they already know what is most important in my life today.

My friend the former mayor whispers, "When are we going to be throwing a benefit for those children of yours?"

He knows where my heart is, though I can't explain how difficult my events and the speaking engagements really are.

I sigh, "If it wasn't for my doctors and Charity, I would be dead."

He encourages, "Jordan, we are so proud of you in the community. We continue to bless the church for what they have done in embracing your life. And, I am proud of how you have been teaching the church people about unconditional love and authenticity."

This man can see so much. He continues, "I don't know any other church people that have embraced all that about you. So, you keep it up. When I am asked about you, I let my head soar above the clouds. I called you my favorite philanthropist for children, and I called you *Portland's Bridge Over Troubled Waters for Children* at the Make-a-Wish Foundation this year. That event opened a lot of people's eyes to who you really are."

He leans close. "You always smell so good and the smell of your breath is so fresh. That is not just the clean living. Jordan, there is no doubt you opened eyes this year. You walk into a room tonight and all eyes are not on Charity. God is doing more than we ever expected in your life."

I think, *He really gets it. Even though I can't explain it all, he gets it.* The music ends and we walk back to our companions, our beloved animals. Charity dances to me.

As he departs with his Corgis, the dog of the queen of England, I glance down at my Charity, her pedicured sparkly pink nails under her finery that speaks her value to *me* to everyone. Never has a human given me the peace that I have in my relationship with Charity all these 14 years. We are secure with our life together. It was Charity who taught me that I could be more than what I think I can be. God promised it, but Charity – a gift from God to me – convinced me with her ever-present love and trust. Charity is the *pure love of Christ.*

I know I won't be alone for more than a few moments, so I lavish them on Charity. She is my princess tonight. Charity is a Basenji, a bark-less exotic Egyptian breed with ears as pointy as pyramids. Basenjis are the dog of the Pharaohs shown in hieroglyphics. With her silky black and white coat, Charity is an

EMBRACED

aristocrat among dogs. It means so much to me to have someone to dote upon and dress up, choosing, as I do, to not to participate in physically intimate relationships with other men. Charity is my perfect and stunning Valentine, as much a princess as Lady Diana and as queenly as Grace Kelly.

Then, we are surrounded by old friends and new. As clock ticks, the elite of Portland and the Pacific Northwest wouldn't be any other place than at this Valentine's Day evening event with their dates and spouses and their pristine dogs in costumes that declare their value. So many people politely interrupt conversations to find out where I got my dog. We are a team; everybody says this eventually, one way or another. One of the judges smiles, "She will present professionally on the catwalk."

It is time! The Hawaiian version of "Somewhere Over the Rainbow" plays on the speakers while up high on the risers I put on my old style strut – called the pony-walk (which is the hardest but the classiest) - before these oldest of friends. I turn and Charity turns with me. I know Charity's every step will match.

Then, I hear mocking from below, "Oh, it is Jordan! Look at that! That's Jordan Jantz!"

Another voice says, "I hear he's living *the spiritual life* now."

Then speaks the first voice, "Jordan, I haven't seen you since the *mooovies*. You've really come a long way, baby."

I recognize his Maltese before I recognize him, a former client. *Oh, has he aged.* Today, he and his partner (they are both ex-preachers) are commenting out loud near my feet, though I know they can't touch me up here.

JORDAN JANTZ

They continue, "I wonder what it feels like being a part of the Latter-day Saint Church. I hear he calls himself a *Christian* also and a lot of Christians don't like him being a Latter-day Saint and calling himself a Christian. Maybe they are finding out about his past and want the name "Christian" disassociated with him because of what he did for a living."

His partner answers him, "Well, he was good to us and we're all cut from the same cloth. Everybody's had a *piece* of him."

As I walk above there is no place to answer from the stage. I just keep smiling. Charity and I finished to applause, applause, applause.

Back down on the floor level, there is no *avoiding* these men if I want to maintain my manhood among my friends. They approach and I do not retreat. The conversation topic has switched to people who are in the *adult industry* (because they know my past).

I look straight at my former client and his partner and say, "What is it like to be two *preachers* that are rubbing my nose in what I feel liberated from, mocking me and saying that I can just *try* to please God instead of the world? How does that feel to you? Because I can tell you how this really feels to me. The reason I want to talk about God is because I can be here on Valentine's Day and not be embarrassed showing my love to everyone and showing everyone how good God has been to me. And if you have a problem with that," I reach for my glass that is filled with coconut water, not champagne, and now is the time to emphasize that I am choosing differently by lifting up my cup where people can see it, "that's a personal problem. And by the way, I do believe that one of the commandments is to love your neighbor as you love yourself. Gentlemen, I have to be going now." I turn away.

But they aren't done with me and my former client knows where to cut, "Before you go, Jordan, let me ask what's it like not

EMBRACED

having anyone except your God to talk to? Does he really give you the comfort that you've always been looking for? *Everyone* in Portland knows you have no *family*. Everyone knows that your boyfriend was so upset with you because of your *transformation*, that he took his life! He couldn't tolerate knowing that nobody would ever want you. So he took his life!"

They turn with mean smiles and their cocktails held up high. "Enjoy your little dog, because she is all the family you have ever had and ever will have. We are *so sorry* for you. But we see you can still put on that smile, and cover your emptiness up." And they dig in their last shot hard, "How does your *heart* feel now on Valentine's Day, Jordan *Jantz*?

I respond, "Tell all the guys down at the bars hello and that I love them."

My voice is stronger than I feel at the moment because even though I do not let it hurt me, I know that they meant to hurt me. They flounce away -middle aged married men who at one point had each been married to women and have children not thought of tonight.

I figured it out tonight, the reason that I feel sorry for the children. Some people control their children by making them become what *they* had wanted to become in their younger days, and I see the same thing often in some of the people I know who have children. It takes me back to needing to be *the best little boy in the world*. These two men do not interrupt my heart or my spirit, because I know, although I am alone, God loves me, even if He is the only one. And if God is the only one in the world that loves me, I'm fine with that. I see the couple go.

I turn back to talking with kinder friends.

JORDAN JANTZ

A moment later, I pause talking to hear Pink Martini playing their beautiful finale for the conclusion of the evening.

Then, a pleasant tenor on the loud speaker says, "It is time to announce the awards. Here are the winners, though today we are all winners on this holiday of love." Names are called and dogs and owners begin to gather again on the stage. I am so grateful to those who conduct this event so that I can relax and enjoy it fully.

Then, I hear Charity's name. Guests separate for me to walk up on the stage again. The announcer says, "For great presence and grace, Ms. Charity wins Ms. Congeniality, and we present you, Jordan Jantz, with tickets for the Valentine's Midnight Cruise on the Spirit of Portland."

A boat ride! I'm thrilled! Streamers, confetti and balloons fall all over the animals and their owners. We smile to each other and to the hall filled with people, in gratitude for this acknowledgement. "Somewhere Over the Rainbow" plays again and this time with all these people nearby, I remember my boyfriend who killed himself on Christmas Eve. This was our song!

When I go to accept the trophy for Charity, I speak from my joy and my pain, "I want to thank everyone for being so kind to one another this evening, and remembering my life as you all do, knowing that I'm living my life now for the next life to come. And those of you who have given me grace in my transformation, I know God will honor you, when you meet him. And I want to thank all of you for helping me raise up my little Miss Congeniality in giving her this beautiful trophy tonight on

EMBRACED

JORDAN JANTZ

Valentine's Day. I have never loved anything in life that has given me love as Charity has and she's still with me today. Tonight is a miracle for all of us. Thank you for honoring Charity and Happy Valentine's Day to everyone!"

"Somewhere Over the Rainbow" continues while I fight tears and get off the stage. I know my deceased partner is smiling down from heaven at this sweet moment and I am just overwhelmed.

I am *so* ready for the river ride. There is nothing so beautiful as a river trip on a decorated boat at night in the Willamette Valley! Lights brighten every ship. The *Spirit of Portland* is one of the largest ships that ferry the blessed and I know the beauty will fill my heart with joy. The band, Pink Martini, joins us as *all* the winners leave the Mount Timberline Lodge and board the train. After a short ride, the river dock is steps from the train and the short walk is pink-lit with twinkling Valentines lights on the historic downtown waterfront. I can go with the flow with Ms. Congeniality in my arms.

During boarding, I notice many specialty physicians that work with many of the secret challenges within me. I realize that the winners on the boat are the highest names of note in my community. Long ago I had to develop the ability to mingle intimately in charm school for grooming of a gentleman (a course that I had to take. Such lessons were for my work in order to have proper etiquette) and very fortunately this talent has always borne fruit for me. I do pretty well intimately and can carry myself. I even astonish myself with the multiple personalities that so many people have spent time and money for me to become.

The river is all pink and twinkling white lights shining on the boats and homes in the harbor. The water acts like a beautiful,

EMBRACED

perfect mirror. Pink Martini plays peaceful intimate jazz covers. As I lean into the wind toward the lights on the river I think of how grateful people are for the transformation *they* experience in my life. Valentine's Day gave them the opportunity to explain their love for what they have seen and experienced through my life.

I look in the peaceful, cool water. I think of Mark, who was my last boyfriend and a Latter-day Saint, with whom I celebrated my last romantic Valentine's Day. Then, I recall slowly pouring his ashes in the Willamette River that we are all floating upon.

I'm grateful that I experienced what I did today *and* what I experienced before, although the best Valentine I could ever have is not a man but the spirit inside me that leads me and my Charity home to God's peace.

At last I leave all these friends and this beauty and go home with Charity for sleep.

JORDAN JANTZ

EMBRACED

FAR FROM HEAVEN

2

I BECOME HALF AWAKE at 4 am when Portland's Valentine lights are still twinkling.

I have been dreaming. I have always dreamed. Dreaming takes me between moments and places as I can't do in my consciousness. These last months, *vivid* dreams have transported me to a place I do not remember when I am awake. In the dream I'm on an old country road. It is lined with old houses and old trees and old people wandering about. They wave but don't speak to me and Charity as we walk right down the middle of the cracked, bricked street. It is so peaceful. Nobody talks. In the dream nobody knew me from anyone else and I am not a public figure of any sort. In this dreamland everything's very old and safe. Maybe the people are angels in the village that I am in and they have been waiting for me to arrive. It is all very small-town, real and congenial. I can sense that everyone has worked very hard. I can sense the privacy and the restfulness.

This dream tonight has repeated over and over. I even talk to my therapist regularly about this dream and what it means. "Is this a side-effect from medication," I ask my therapist often, "or am I having a post-traumatic stress outlet?" I thank God for the medical people that God has given me, so that I can talk about this intimate activity, playing in my mind throughout many months of sleep.

This night, though, all of Portland is still lit up for Valentines. In the twinkling lights on the quiet streets, I wrap up my little

Valentine girl and take her out of bed in my arms and make her breakfast. I put on her warm coat to protect her from cold wind and rain and then we go down the elevator, ready to visit Portland State's dog park. This park is Charity's favorite property and is across the street from my home. She can meet her girlfriends and have her pre-morning *social*. She does her potty dance and then she jumps up for me to grab her into my arms and take her back home.

On our way home, I remember again my reoccurring dream. Maybe the emptiness of the Portland streets at night is bringing me back to the memory of the country road I dream about. I am honestly thinking that everything is taking me back to where my life began. That is what my soul is telling me. I smell the sea-breeze Portland air. I ask Charity, "When are we going to find out what this dream means? Do you want to go find out where life began for me, Charity?"

As we wait for the crosswalk light my mind is racing, because through many therapy sessions I have learned that anxiety paralyzes a person when that person has no *clarity* to realize what is actually a part of their consciousness. That's what I learned in therapy, for the past seventeen years. My dreams could be telling me something I actually already *know,* inside.

As I enter my home I come to a sudden stop to hold myself up, because I realize that the dreams are leading me to my genealogy, the history of my life. I have been saying *no, thank you* to that idea for years! Am I going through a mid-life crisis or male menopause? The dreams are so intense that male menopause could be result of the reality of my body transforming from one decade to another.

But I know that's not what this is. I'm being given a message that is from God, and with my past behind me, thanking the Lord, I can erase the chalkboard of shame. I was told this by a very special lady who is the most valued woman I have ever met in my life, and

EMBRACED

who I have known since I was 3 years old, my Aunt Marion in Decatur, Illinois. *Oh my,* I'm wondering, as Charity is relaxing. *Lord, honestly, do you hear me? What is this all about?*

I open up my wooden desktop and realize that what is in my hand is my Aunt Marion's personal Bible that she and Uncle Dale brought to me when I was in Milwaukee, Wisconsin, working with an executive at Anheuser-Busch. Aunt Marion and Uncle Dale had come up from Decatur to meet my partner. They came to our home on Lake Michigan in White Fish Bay to stay the weekend and make sure I was being treated well and was having a good life. She was only family member and only person in my life that never wanted me out of her life. She embraced me in every decade and every year that I have been alive on this earth. Nobody has ever remained in my life living with me more than 14 years. Aunt Marion and Uncle Dale don't care what the rest of the world thinks about me because they both have witnessed how far I have come from out of the closet to where I am today, living on my own as an adult. So this Bible I am holding speaks volumes of what I am talking about as this is shows her unconditional love to me.

I know my emotions desire conversation with her and I feel heated and spiritually and mentally in extreme peace as I open the book. It has pink marker in the chapter of Ruth, when Ruth says, *Entreat me not to leave thee, or to return from following after thee: for whither thou goest, I will go; and where thou lodgest, I will lodge: thy people shall be my people, and thy God my God.* And stuck between the pages is picture of her and Uncle Dale. I turn it over and my mouth drops open.

The phone rings for morning prayers and grab it and I say, "Marsha, Marsha, *Marsha*! You are just not going to believe this! I just found a picture of Aunt Marion and her address is on the

back of it! The Spirit has led me to her. I have to mail something to her right now!!"

"Your Aunt Marion who saved your life? How did you ever find her contact? I thought that was a lost needle in a lost haystack!" Sophie says.

"The Spirit led me to it. I have to go and get a letter to her immediately. I have to go and get the cards, find some photos of me and visit the post office as quickly as I can right now, pray with me to get in touch with her!."

We pray and I spend the next two hours preparing mail that almost feels like I put my heart in the package (with my current phone numbers!) and send it off in the mail.

Seven days roll by, I am counting each one.

I have not talked to the family that adopted me since my Aunt Freda picked out Charity and bought her for me from a pet store, about fourteen years ago. This waiting time stretches on but I walk by faith.

Then at last the phone rings as I knew it would "Jimmy! Oh JIMMY!!" I hear before I even say hello. I *knew* that she would immediately respond as she always has in the past in my life.

She showers me with loving questions, "Are you still in Portland??? Are you with anybody? Are you single?" and then, "You know your Aunt Marion loves you no matter what, just like your father. And how is your father?"

As we talk I learn that she is no longer living at the home that I remembered (and the address that I wrote to, which is why the mail had to be forwarded). Her beautiful home had once been the most popular beauty shop in Decatur. Her vision is challenged though she still moves without a wheelchair, but she does need assistance now.

JORDAN JANTZ

She is not in a convalescent home, she states very clearly, but an assisted living center. Uncle Dale had to be transported into a special memory care unit, and Aunt Marion is so upset that Uncle Dale cannot be living with her anymore. She is not given the opportunity to live with her husband and take care of him in their final years. "I can't believe I'm in an Assisted Living Facility, Jimmy. Can you believe your Aunt Marion once had everything and that it would happen to me that I am in an *old folk's home* where people go to *die*? I want you to know, Jimmy, that I learned you can't *take it with you*. And nobody will remember anything of who you were, but they will remember what you did for others."

Aunt Marion and Uncle Dale's children and families (my cousins) are still in the Decatur area.

Aunt Marion says, "If it wasn't for Mark and Robin living here, I would not be able to handle all that I have to live with, with my health and Uncle Dale's health."

My cousins visit her every weekend. I understand that they do all that they can to see that my Aunt Marion and her husband, my Uncle Dale, are in the places that they can get the care they need, though they are *not* in the same facility.

Aunt Marion says, "Jimmy, I feel alone. I feel left! I am grateful that Mark and Robin are in town, but I'm sad that I don't have my husband. The Memory Care Facility is not even on the same block."

I tell her that I love her and have always loved her, every minute. This is the only woman that saw me as a tiny child and found a way to save me. My great grandmother, Ina Agnes McNear, who I called Gram, worked with my biological father, Eldon Roy Bond, to plot the opportunity for Aunt Marion's sister in California to be able to get me out to California and remove me

from circumstances that my biological father and great grandmother wanted me out of. The two of them together with Aunt Marion, the town's beautician and a leader in the community, saved my life. My biological father made sure that I went to another man that would be a father to a little boy that was taken (and sometimes forgotten) from place to place, forgetting which house the little boy had been dropped off at.

As I am sitting on the phone listening to the voice of my Aunt Marion, I think heart-filled thoughts from my spirit, which is filled with emotion of longing to embrace this person who has always been nothing but the good in my life.

She says "You remember, now, that Aunt Marion knows that you have been removed from a family more than once, and your Aunt Marion is telling you to remember that Aunt Marion and Uncle Dale know what this has done to you and your life. I know you love the beach and Portland coastal northwest beauty and that clothing is your favorite beauty, and wearing your favorite brands and modeling the brands. Aunt Marion knows this is important to you. I know what has happened with my sister, but Aunt Marion will wear these things for you, for your life has always been centered on performance and your ability to continue with marketing each season of the new lines of clothes that come out."

My response is, "You know me and that with me, entertainment begins from when you wake up to when you go to bed. And I want to let you know all of this is meaningless to me, Aunt Marion, without God in my life. You have been through every stage of my life with me and you know the pain of not being able to connect the way I want to be connected to your sister who raised me, since the divorce. I think she actually believes that she divorced *me* also, when she took off with my sister while we were seniors in high school, cheerleading together. To this day things have never been the same between us."

EMBRACED

Those heartbreaks are really in the past for me, and I want them to be in the past for Aunt Marion, too. Now that I have found Aunt Marion, I want to honor her and uplift her. I am *alive* because of her!

I know it is right and so the Spirit helps me say, "Aunt Marion, I really want to come out there and show the world how I honor you and how you saved my life and have loved me so perfectly my whole life. I really want to come out for your birthday in May."

"Jimmy, you know I would want that more than anything in the world. But can you really come out just to see *me*? It is so expensive and I know it would be hard. I want to see you so badly, though!" Aunt Marion says.

"Aunt Marion, hush. You are one of the most important women in my life. You know the truth of what I lived through as an infant."

She says, "I should have kept you for myself, me and Dale, but we couldn't."

I know this. I needed to be taken far away to be saved. I say, "It turned out the way it was supposed to turn out, and I'm glad it did. Aunt Marion, I know this is the right thing to do. *I promise you and claim this in the name of Jesus* that this is right and possible and it will be so. I'm going to get off the phone and begin to look for God's miracles because God wants me there for your birthday in May."

In the following days I call and call again.

She calls and calls again.

We talk often and I tell her about how I manage now and how I managed before. Secrecy and my personal fear of men were noticeable since childhood, and Aunt Marion had known it, so she understood that I learned to hold on to my adoptive father (Daddy) as much as I could without him feeling that he had to be there for me, because my adoptive mother (Mama) who told me I was *high maintenance* and that I needed to let my father and his new wife 'become family' to each other. Also, Mama had said, "It would be best that you leave since your sister is engaged, and you know I'm also married now again to a man that has never had children, so the best thing is for all of us to go our own directions."

I told Aunt Marion that I had responded to Mama, "You can divorce your husband but you cannot divorce your children," and that Mama responded to that, "You've been left behind more than once. Don't let the door hit you on the way out. I'm sure there's a man out there waiting for you, somewhere. You don't need to embarrass this family anymore."

I learn from Aunt Marion that nobody in the family knew *any* of this background and that everyone had been under the impression *from Mama* that I had just decided to leave! In Mama's telling, I was the soul-less child who went into another world to find where I belonged.

I think of this and recall the pain of leaving all safety behind and having to start over all alone, being so completely alone had made me feel like I had been in a witness protection program (without the protection), having to go someplace where I have never been and seek another opportunity to hope that I may be found by someone who doesn't want to purchase me for my outward talents.

I tell my Aunt Marion about my feelings at those times and say to her, "Aunt Marion, I want you to know you never expected anything from me and neither did Uncle Dale. I want to thank you for giving me to a father who loved me, but it is true that Mama has said many things that cause my words to be void. After all she said

EMBRACED

to both sides of the family, I do not think this can be changed to this day."

Aunt Marion says, "Well, Jimmy, I never abandoned you, and I never have told anyone anything bad about you. I want you to know that we all have done bad things, Jimmy. All of us. Even I have done things that would embarrass me if my mother knew. Also, I will never hang up the phone on you, Jimmy, or dismiss you, ever."

She adds, "And I want you to know that your biological great grandmother, Ina, also loved you more than anything, too. That's the only reason why she talked to Bud, your biological father, about getting you away. Bud always wanted to protect you and keep you. You were his first born child. And both Bud and Ina did not want you to be abused anymore from your biological mother. Bud wanted you to go to a couple who wanted a little boy more than anything and he trusted your Aunt Marion and came over for Thanksgiving dinner to my house, along with Ina, where you could come in. It was a great challenge to hide you from your biological mother and take you with him to places and lock you in the car so that you would not be around her and be abused."

Phone call after phone call, some for hours a day, we talk and talk about memories of long ago and issues we are dealing with today. With her, I don't have to hide anything.

Very soon, I call her and say, "Aunt Marion, the tickets are bought. I am coming to Decatur!"

"Really, Jimmy? It' okay if it can't happen. You can tell me if it really can't happen." I hear hope in her voice but she is also worried, "I want it so badly, but people say it can't happen and it won't happen. But if you say you are coming, I will tell everyone you *are* coming."

JORDAN JANTZ

"I am coming, Aunt Marion." I tell her about my flights and what minute exactly I will be able to see her, finally, and "I will be there bright and early on your birthday. We will have about two weeks together and I will dote on you as you always dote on me, Aunt Marion."

EMBRACED

WHO DO I BELONG TO?

DAYS SPEED UP. March looks just like February in Portland. I'm glad Charity has good coats for wet weather.

Today I have a social spiritual mixer: my men's bible study at 12 noon at the Portland Art Museum. Its time and location are designed to help gather the businessmen. It promotes community within Portland's downtown. In my city Christian men come together for spirituality. This is my group that I am a part of without leading, just supporting as Jesus calls us together.

Unfortunately, the subject of the week is gay marriage, which everyone had been preparing for the ballot. Oregon would have passed the *Right To Marry* initiative anyway, if it had gone to the ballot box. Most of Portland is jubilant but others in the state are not as happy. Through it all I remain silent because I am over *all* the antics of something that has already taken place. I am letting it all go, while holding close to my little Charity.

About my little old 14-year-old Charity, our routine is good. We return again and again to favorite spots in our neighborhood near Portland State. As I am fixing Charity's brunch today day, I think back to the wonderful pastors throughout the city that I meet, and what it means to have such a beautiful environment and such a beautiful *spirit* among all the men that wish to make Portland *kind*. It is so gratifying to live in a city that connects men and women of all backgrounds who love Jesus Christ and who want to be part of each other's lives. It all excites me. But most importantly, it opens doors for community and truth. With truth there is growth. Where there is growth, I will find healing. Where there is healing, there will be restoration. Where there is restoration, I can be found.

I realize that the things that happen in my life are far too great to come from me and these things could only come from God. Jesus has rescued me and gives me amazing and unimaginable abundance.

Case in point: some of the older people in my church are very excited about genealogy and temple work. This means caring about your extended family, even the dead as they still love us from the other side of the veil. I tell some of these special folks about what it means to me, the *pure miracle,* of hearing Aunt Marion's voice again and that I am exercising faith and saving money hard to go see this woman who saved me as an infant from the frightening place I was in. I share that in my memories of that life before I was rescued, there were other children who I left behind and never saw again.

A special church lady from the Relief Society says right away that she wants to find them for me, so that I could maybe contact them when I am in Decatur visiting Aunt Marion in May. This very special lady from my church dedicates time to genealogical 'detective work,' as she calls it.

Many people have made this suggestion before – to find my blood family - and I have always felt that it was better to not disturb family members who, like me, might have difficulty putting the traumatic past behind them. I was pretty sure I didn't have family to disturb. But if I did, how might it affect them if I return? I give the church lady the information I have, which is not much.

Suddenly that dear church lady gives me a piece of paper with phone numbers for three of my father's other children, all

EMBRACED

living near Decatur. My heart starts racing just *looking* at the phone numbers!

I wonder what the right thing to do might be and put it to prayer. I tell my case manager what I am thinking about and that I will only call <u>if</u> the Spirit leads me to it. From experience with flashbacks myself, I know that just the sound of my voice on their answering machines could bring back the worst kinds of memories that they might not be prepared for at all. Or worse, another choice: they could just say I don't exist. And there I would go again, down an emotional sinkhole.

As it happens, I will be in Decatur for Aunt Marion's birthday on May 22. The trip already includes Memorial Day on May 25th. My Aunt Marion knows where my biological great grandmother, Ina Agnes McNear, and my father, Eldon Roy Bond ("Bud") are buried.

Eldon Roy Bond is my biological father and *also* the father of the three people's names and phone numbers that were put in my hand by the special lady from my church. Ina McNear is my father's grandmother who had raised him. Ina was the person who took me with her when she had her hair done by the best beautician in town, who later became my (family that adopted me) *Aunt* Marion, who I was always told I was named for. Her name is *Marion Lee* so my first name on my adoption became *Jimmylee*.

Between me and Aunt Marion, I know Memorial Day will be wonderful, but the idea of seeing the other blood brothers and sisters, if I actually did, sounds like it could be stressful for us all.

On the other hand, Memorial Day *could* be a totally appropriate day to meet them in a way I might be able to cope. And how cool would that be, if we could meet, and it all be okay?

JORDAN JANTZ

I was the only child sold and the firstborn, but I was kept throughout my infancy and toddler years. It would mean the world to me to visit the graves with my Aunt Marion, who herself has been part of a *YaYa Sisterhood* of special Parker women who conspired with my father and great grandmother to save my life, more than 50 years ago. That Sisterhood worked hard to bring a new chance for me to reality; Aunt Marion's YaYa Sisterhood's mission was to save a little boy's life.

I am pondering all of this and I feel shock all over again about how many hearts I really do touch in my life, and I am so grateful to be going to Decatur to meet the past. As I look back on my first leaving as a small child today, I know they all realized that they were saving a little boy's life. There were vast obstacles but these special people stepped up to the plate and they made miracles happen for my sake.

That's why, I believe, it is the right thing to do to go to Decatur, even though I know that every one of my friends and people who are in my life *now* tell me I have *lost my mind*. Some say that if I go I will be setting myself up for suicide because of the pain of rejection, which is very possible. But from my dream, I know that it is <u>right</u> to find this place and these people and *not* just call or text them from afar. You don't text or call when you owe a person your *life*. No, you find them personally and wash their feet and bless them. That's what I will do for my Aunt Marion and for my brothers and sisters, if they will allow the opportunity of communication and contact.

Now, with my siblings' phone numbers, I think God might have even more in store.

I dial. I find myself listening to living memories in their answering machines.

JORDAN JANTZ

My biological sibling, Ronnie, responds the most quickly. Then, Teresa. Last, I hear from Kevin. Plans are made. I am going to celebrate my aunt's birthday and Memorial Day with my (adoptive) aunt and meet my (biological) siblings.

Now is the time to show consistency with my biological siblings. There is a time for caution and a time for courage and it is courage-time. I am stepping out to the best of my disabilities with my service dog, Charity, under my arm, with God as my compass.

YOU CAN'T PRAY THE GAY AWAY

4

MY LIFE MOVES FAST as the BART in San Francisco.

For me, today is for Penny, a former dance partner from years gone by. She is my sister in the church today and she was my lesbian friend who loved the dancing in the gay bars as much as I did, from Arizona to California to New York. And now, we are both here together in Portland, Oregon, in the latter part of our years. Today we come together in our church that allows us to be honest, but nobody ever understands our friendship, including her family.

Penny had to lie her whole life in the LDS church (my church, the Church of Jesus Christ of Latter-day Saints) about her same-gender attraction. She can at last be honest at the age of 65. She is able to come out of the closet and tell the truth about why she was not able to keep the men in her life, because it was all a façade created to look good in the church and to be accepted as a child of God. She was told her whole life that the only way to be important to a man would be to submit because she was the wife and he was the husband, and the reality is that the lie was killing her identity as a woman. She had to depart and abandon ship and she did just that, to save her life so that she could live in truth.

That's when the LDS church accepted the fact that she could come to church and wasn't possessed at all by the devil

because she has same gender attraction. I'm so excited today to spend time with my friend who has, like every other lesbian friend of mine, been told that God hates lesbians and gay men, and that they shouldn't be allowed in churches.

So today is a day of sharing that heartfelt love that I share with others on Valentine's Day, because every day is Valentine's Day in my heart. For me, I like to always think that way, and Penny is the focus of it today.

One of my priesthood brothers from church picks me up and immediately asks me if I am prepared for the baptism of Penny. He wants to make sure that I have the procedures down. Of course I am ready to go.

Penny's uniform is prepared, a thick-fabric white jumper with a zipper down the front. My white jumper is also laid out for me. The baptismal tank is warm and ready for us both. This is Penny's second time being baptized, after some repenting and asking Heavenly Father to help her with her struggle of same gender attraction. She still has held on to her attraction to women her whole life and is tired of faking it in front of others. She wants to worship and love God authentically.

Before this baptism day, Penny asked me to share truth to the church and its people. I have been praying about it for weeks, and do not know the right thing to say, even now. I will let the Holy Spirit speak instead. People are sitting in the room who want to know what is true, while they are here to witness this baptism of Penny.

Then, words fly out of my mouth and into the hearts of all that are there, letting them all realize that we all are here for forgiveness and repentance. That's what the waters are for.

JORDAN JANTZ

As I round up Penny's baptism I can only pray that if I am to ever baptize another person who is gay or lesbian, that I will not have the fear of baptizing them and wondering if I am doing the right thing. I shouldn't have that fear put upon me. It is pathetic when people of God and leaders of the world use their power to mess with your mind. I have had that experience in my past. Many *ministers* of God have done that to me, in the name of *Jesus Christ*! They said they deliver me over to the world for the destruction of my flesh, so that my soul will be saved, and that is what many of the Christian churches say when you do not walk away from the gay marriage to live your life for God and be in His service in all you do.

A week later I get a letter from my stake president saying that it was a beautiful baptism. He says that many of the other stake presidents and the temple president are looking forward to getting together to hear me speak about what God is doing in the gay and lesbian community. My stake president and I set a date to get together and talk about what we can do as a church to open up the lives to the gay and lesbian people in the church to come out from their fear of others about their true feelings inside, to realize what I feel about Heavenly Father, that He honors and respects those of us who have laid our lifestyle down in order to take up the cross and follow Jesus and live according to what we believe to be God's ways. This is what I try to do at the best of my abilities.

I think about exactly what I want to communicate. The most important thing I want to express to all the stake presidents and the temple president and any other ministries that work with same gender attracted people is that *you cannot pray that* the gay *will ever go away from you*. Many ministries continue to say that if you consider yourself gay, then how can you consider yourself a leader for the savior, because the two can't go hand-in-hand, which belief is not true at all. You *can* have same gender attraction and be a *leader in God's Kingdom*, no matter who you are. If you

follow and believe in the Savior through His Holy Spirit, everything is possible. Not through man, but through the Spirit all people are equal in Savior's eyes.

Many people with same gender attraction who call themselves leaders have told me that I need to be in a Bible-based church and that the LDS church is not Bible-based. I learn from re-baptizing Penny that *I am in a Bible-based church*, the only difference is, I have something called the Priesthood. It is not something that I boast about but it is something that I am grateful for. It is not something to be used or abused. It gives me no authority above any other person. There is only one way a person can ever have eternal life and that is to follow Jesus. That IS God's test and there is no other and *Father forgive them for they do not know what they do* to those who say anything else. I will never turn a brother or sister away as I have been turned away in the House of the Lord and in the homes of my earthly families that call themselves Christian.

And I admit that confusion is deep for people with Same Gender Attraction who are seeking spiritual lives without empty connections, but meaningful and deep covenants. That same-gender-attraction folks stumble and leave the church often is not all *our* issues. How can they stay if they do not know how they fit in? How are we supposed to stay?

God's answer is, "YES this is where you will shine My Light and become the light that others need to see."

And God has said to me, "Don't walk away from church abuse for you have endured much more abuse than most. You can handle this, for the teaching of church leadership and the reward that you receive for going through much abandonment will be embraced when we meet." That comes from the presence of the

Spirit of God's Love for me as a gay man who loves Jesus and wants others to hear: *Don't leave. Please stay.*

As I am sitting here thinking about the present and how I got to the present from the past, I remember how it all started for me with my decisions.

About ten years ago, I was barely alive from physical challenges and exhaustion and I wanted to have true spiritual encounters. I had been in Christian churches before that only wounded me more, which churches (or rather the people) asked me to get up in front of hundreds or thousands of people and proclaim that God had delivered me from the evil spirit of homosexuality in my life. Anywhere else, people would recognize that as shaming abuse, if only because it tells a person that they *are not OK to God*. I knew God would no more "take away" my same gender attraction than he would take away my maleness or any other way in which I identified myself. How can I not identify myself with something I am born with and be honest? How could I have even one spiritual encounter when these people and their forces are so strong?

That understanding was what was already *set* before my new spiritual brother and mentor, Elder Spencer Wallentine, and I made a commitment (each of us) to learn from one another for a year.

The LDS church had an answer, before I even became a member. At the time I was still living the vive le loco, the wild life, I was not able to be very open in many ways because I had been so shamed before in church settings.

Then, a very private group was assembled to meet regularly at the local "stake center" or "big" building that sits among about 15 smaller church units in Beaverton, Oregon. This group of men met in the stake president's "high council" room, or an office with a large table and many comfortable chairs. The same gender attracted men met in the room and talked about their faith, families and struggles of even being heterosexually married *while* actually being same gender attracted.

If those people were finding God I wanted to find God, too. Who better to show me? But these men were also under a great deal of stress, having been raised to be ashamed (while not publicly shamed in church as I was) of their same gender attraction which was in times past associated with sin and predators in the minds of many in the LDS church when according to God *any* intimacy outside of marriage is sin. They just saw it as much worse that I was a man attracted to another man, but I was not about to allow someone to tell me that in order to be able to come to church, I had to become someone else, with expectations and performances attached.

After a few months of group attendance, the Downtown Portland LDS Institute Director, Stewart Weed, asked to meet with me. He said, "I'd like to know how I can support you, because of what you are doing and the challenge you must have of being in the special faith group with those who have same gender attraction while not being a member of the church and having faith that God loves you as you are and not who you can become."

I didn't know him well at that point, but I could start to talk to him. From my point of view, spiritual paths seemed to ravel *and* unravel.

My partner at that time, Mark, was LDS, and I could tell that that part of himself was almost too painful for Mark to talk about, because he had been with women after he got home from his mission because he wanted to get married, but it was a lie to him to marry and not be attracted to his wife sexually. Mark chose to leave the church after his failures and attempts at marriage after

returning home from his mission. Mark's mother and father considered him to not be like the rest of his brothers who were successful in raising families and following the ordinances of a Christian life. Mark's same gender attraction was the most shameful truth for anyone because it cannot be changed so it must not be forgiven. Mark left Utah and came to Portland where I met him at one of the premier runway events. We became introduced after a hard night's work at the mixer where he was with many buyers for the clothing lines I was modeling that weekend. Ever since, Mark and I remained BFFs until I left my sexual life and became celibate and refused to live with him.

I felt I was doing something for myself for the first time in my life, I was making *my own choice* and really at that time I didn't even know how to make a choice without someone telling me how to do it, but I did. Unfortunately, Mark was not able to share in my happiness of becoming a Christian Latter-day Saint, and as told in the first book by J Adams, *Out of the Closet, Into the Light*, he took his life on Christmas Day. But at the time that I sat down for my first talk with Stewart Weed, all of this was just beginning.

One of the feelings that I was dealing with when I spoke to Stewart Weed was that the men in the LDS same gender attraction group that met in the Beaverton, Oregon Stake high council room also treated me as something of a black sheep. I was the one who had done everything they were told not to do. Of course, I told them all that it wasn't worth it for me, but that didn't make me less experienced. Others LDS men were told about the group, men that I had not even known were LDS or heterosexually married because I had met them and their many sexual partners in the bars downtown for years. When they learned that I was in the same gender attraction group that the local church leaders assembled, they had the need to spread suspicion about my ability to tell the truth of what I really did for a living in the gay communities throughout the United States, which was very public.

EMBRACED

People who know the truth about me have known me and are still my intimate friends to this day no matter if I become LDS or not, because of my honesty. These are intelligent true friends who have seen me mature as an adult with many emotional challenges thrown at me with spikes, making it impossible to ever completely stand strong. So, because of what some closeted same gender attracted LDS men did and said, many people in the church shied away from me. To this day my very reliable gaydar meets other same gender attracted men *in church* with their families and they usually decide to try to act invisible, if only because they do not know if they can trust me, even though some *paid* for me, proving that God is not a respecter of persons. We all make mistakes and I forgive them for they did not understand what they were doing anymore more than I myself understood what I was doing, which is understandable, I suppose, but also very lonely. And here I was talking to yet another LDS man named Stewart Weed that I just wasn't sure of.

That's when Stewart Weed made it easier for me to know who he was and how truthful his soul was, because he said, "I would like you to meet my son, Josh, who has same gender attraction, and his wife. You are a lot like my son and I think you'd really get along with him."

So I met Josh and Lolly and immediately loved the two of them, especially Josh. I'd never been around such a *normal* person with same gender attraction. He was so real and lived in reality all the time. In Portland, we have so many Christians who call themselves "set free" and married that it makes me want to vomit, because they *use* their wives and kids to show that they are set free, in whatever church group. But in their interactions, anyone can tell they are not set free. Normal people aren't that anxious, insecure and controlling, as if they are all looking for ground to take back.

JORDAN JANTZ

I explained to the Weed family some of my feelings of being in the LDS same gender attraction group, "I'm the biggest sinner and I have no garments."

Among the LDS men people wearing garments is big *worthiness* issue, and because I didn't have them, I could constantly be treated as less worthy. It shouldn't have been a factor but it was. But just talking with Josh about how ridiculous it was, and his complete and transparent agreement and validation of the feeling I was experiencing healed a lot of that feeling at least on my side. I couldn't affect how other people were going to choose to treat me but I did address my own feelings about it.

Later that same winter I got a glimpse into the real lives of the LDS same gender attracted men in the confidential LDS same gender attraction group, when I met their families and for sure these were the best beards I had ever seen. I was very nervous to meet their families. I had so often been *the secret* for men who were hiding from their Christian families and *not* being hidden was shocking.

A stake president, Lee Harris, and his wife, Lisa, were each under one of my arms as I walked into a building to meet the families at a Christmas party, because they knew how I had been treated by the other men, and I would only go if they would go with me. The other LDS same gender attracted men who held the priesthood wouldn't acknowledge me as a human or even as someone standing in the room, although they follow me out of the corner of their eyes and my panic attacks became overwhelming at times (including sweat attacks, from not knowing how to respond to a Godly man that I had experienced an encounter with, years prior. It is very hard to believe you can change something that is spotted and bruised when you have to go through the hoops to become cleansed from a life of survival. But I did learn because I believed there was a God because of the angel that I saw as a small child going to live in California).

There were so many children at this party. When the children ran off to watch a video and eat popcorn, the married men and their wives stood around the piano singing chorus lines from Broadway productions. It ran all night long. They smiled at one another. It was their moment to be "real" with each other, without their kids nearby to protect from their adult issues. It made me realize why a gay person might want to marry a person of the other gender to begin with. And the music did all the magic that night. Music can do anything to the mind, heart and soul, especially a chorus line.

Then, two years into that group's meeting, I received a phone message stating that the missionaries would no longer be picking me up for the confidential group in the Beaverton stake center that had been in development for so many years. I understood that this was due to its lack of ability to embrace the transformation of leadership in the stake and throughout the church's metropolitan area. The local same gender attracted men or other groups were not in compliance for the group to continue to represent itself publicly to others as of the church. Just like that, it was over.

But not really. It continued and still continues meeting in secret but I am not invited and I have never been called to see how life is for me to this day. I know I have been forgotten again and left behind. Hiding the group meetings like that, I don't want to go.

Several years passed without finding another spiritual support group for people with same gender attraction in Portland.

Last September I received a phone call to ask if I could commit my Tuesday evening to a group of same gender attracted men and women to come together in support of embracing the Savior's love for each of us. The group was only for those who have experienced *taking back ground* at some time in their life. As all communities that work in the same gender attraction community throughout metro Portland, everyone has been exposed to Jordan Jantz in a variety of outreaches in the inner city communities. I was touched to be remembered and included in this special invitation.

When Tuesday came for the first meeting, it was a blessing to be refreshed by experienced and seasoned men and women in the community who want to live their life in healing and wholeness instead of addiction to another human being. We all had so many doors opened that night and embraced each other to see the joy of many from years and decades gone by who were still alive to be able to make a choice to walk in light.

After that night, I walked home over the Burnside Bridge, smelling the river and passing through the coastal haze, which helped me recall the cold evening when I tied weights to my legs and jumped off of this very bridge a couple decades ago. I marveled at where God has brought me. I had hope for this new group that decided to walk on the solid ground. That is what they called the name of the group: Solid Ground.

But as we finished and completed the first year, the second year has started and I was given to understand that again I am not wanted, because, to them, I am not in a Bible based church. I can't serve in any capacity because I identify myself as a Latter-day Saint Christian, who has same gender attraction, and the truth is the truth and I'm not going to hide.

The Solid Ground group told me that there is *no group available for me* and that I could not have any opportunities because

JORDAN JANTZ

I need a Bible-based life with Bible-based friends and if I am not willing to do what they felt was right in regards to being involved in the right kind of church, they have no place for me to serve.

So again, I experience abandonment from a Christian community. Nothing feels worse than feeling like you are excommunicated because of the truth you speak.

"Where is God at?" I asked myself at the time. I will never try to jump or take my life again, because I have doctors and medical people that love me even if a church can't love me, and I have people that God has put in my life whether they are in one church or another church. God's love is *unconditional love*, and I am not receiving that from this Christian group anymore, because I had crossed the line from the gay community and become a Latter-day Saint Christian, and many Christians who were working with believing gays in Portland were about to explode because of my honesty of God loving gay people. I know you can have same gender attraction and tell the truth of what you really are <u>and</u> have the Savior wrap his arms around you, because of His unconditional love. I receive that unconditional love to this day, without this group that I did, for a short time, depend upon, and now I stand on the solid rock as a lighthouse.

The Church of Jesus Christ of Latter-day Saints has allowed me to be open about the truth of my life and being truthful means more to me than anything else as a disciple of Jesus. I am worthy and I am redeemed. The Savior said it all in His message to you and to me. No questions asked; no eligibility or qualifying.

I continue to walk in truth. It isn't easy where I am in my church. Often same gender attracted men in my church find heterosexual relationships to develop in their life and keep themselves busy with their families and associations with the actually heterosexual men. They scurry to develop into the hetero concept of transformation to be a godly man in the church. Praise the Lord for those in transformational relationships that create positive lives, but I am left out, often, because I have chosen not to marry. The reason I have not married is that I feel it would be wrong for me to marry a woman when I cannot fulfill her most intimate needs. I'm content with what God is doing in my life, though. I have to let others do what they feel to do. I have no time to work on self-esteem issues or anything that is going to keep me from my own spiritual transformations which only happen inside light and truth with the God who sent me an angel when I was four. No one can spend their lives pleasing anyone but God, because all else is emptiness. And God is *very* supportive of who I am and how I live.

    Dealing with the others is not as easy. As I am now in my fifties, I no longer let this world dictate shame of my past survival and the disabilities that I manage today and cover up day to day to make others happy. Whether such people are in or out of church, <u>shaming is *never* OK</u>. Christians, especially, should know better.

    Today my life is about happiness and gratitude. Portland black churches, Baptist churches, Catholic churches, Pentecostal churches and the Church of Christ churches - all of these have asked me to share an LDS Fireside, because so many of the gay community that go to these churches have told their friends about the LDS church firesides happening and Jordan Jantz, the one who God is having speak, *can you believe it?* They say, "The last person on earth would ever talk about God or healing, or restoration or sex in front of the cross is Jordan. Nobody would believe that. Jordan would be the last person to trust God for anything after his survival in this life. He's lucky to be alive and to do a fireside."

JORDAN JANTZ

But *you* are lucky to get a seat if Jordan speaks.

EMBRACED

GIANT OF A MAN

~ 5 ~

Spring has jumped upon me with the reality that I need to communicate with my support team for the plans ahead to schedule without conflicts. My first priority is connecting to my biological family in Decatur with what little information I have been given. Also, I must prepare for the opportunity for embracing my favorite woman in the world, Aunt Marion, at her new assisted living facility. All of these details have to be prepared for months in advance in order to have the support to travel and connect, given my disabilities.

I am running out the door for a spiritual group when I pick up the phone and it is my minister and stake president, Allen Oyler, who I adore. "Allen, what is going on, what are you doing?" I ask.

"I am doing very well, Jordan, and how are you?" he asks and I respond to him.

Then he gets to his reason for calling, "I was wondering if you would be interested in going to the North Star International Conference, to be held soon in Provo, Utah? I know many people would enjoy meeting you and seeing you. It would be a beautiful opportunity to introduce you as an author in the community."

Well, I say, "Wow, Allen, I will do it, if you are behind me 100%."

JORDAN JANTZ

He says, "You know I am. And I'm sure there are some other big events that will be taking place, and I believe you will be a strong part of those events also, so look at your schedule and get back to me."

Not even 30 minutes later, I get a phone call from another stake president, in Ogden, Utah, asking me if I would come to the North Star conference with him and that, as a member of my spiritual family, he would pay for my expenses. This has been continuing for the past four years of dedication to this ministry and the transformation of Evergreen International coming together with North Star International for one solid beam of light springing from the ground of Utah, reaching to the world. Because of the leadership of love that is manifested in the message of Voice(s) of Hope, the corporation started by Ty Mansfield, North Star International and Evergreen International joined teams to make a stronger community of believers who want to live a life in the presence of the Holy Spirit.

I'm not saying that doing this makes you be given the blessing of praying the gay away or praying any problem away. No, not at all. It just gives you the peace of knowing that something stronger than your ability can comfort the loss of not having the ability to overcome your own personal circumstance. We all have a thorn in our side, every single human being on earth, is what my therapist and medical support team in Portland have taught me.

In fact, truth spoken, my only reasons for staying in Portland to this day are because of my medical support team and my housing support team, who work for preventive health problems in my future and preventive challenges in my housing, so my life has been consistent with the same physicians and housing specialists who know me personally along with my social security and government communication that supports people confronted with diagnosis of a disability. It would be great if I could consider

EMBRACED

moving to Utah but I really do not have that choice. It is humble pie, when truth is exposed.

On the phone I say, "If I can get away, I will."

He says, "If it is possible, it is very important for you to show up. People are thinking about you and looking for you, Jordan."

I say, "OK, I understand and I will get back with you."

He says, "Jordan, did you ever think your life would be used to touch and help other people overcome things that you survived, and that it all would be opened up to the world in such a vast way?"

I think, *This is just the beginning and hold on to your seat, because I can tell it is going to be a bumpy ride, as Betty Davis said, because we are not going to be able to make everybody happy.*

I say, "I've been down this road of being in the public eye, and people will find fault in loving someone. People look for fault even when faced with truth. Excuses are so easily justified."

He says, "Well, your life is so justified by the way you expose opportunities of hope, giving abundance of affirmation. Many seek but never find people blessed with this gift of sharing this form of encouragement. You have the gift from the Holy Spirit to light up the room with the exposure of truth for others to have a rock to stand on. You turn into that rock for others and show where it all began; it is a great parable to help others understand that things do happen without choices being made."

He continues, "It was nice to have been sent this honorable invitation, and that's why I want you to come and represent Portland and be the light that you are, to others. I'm sure they will be calling you."

It really is so kind that my walk is being supported this way and I say to him, "I am so honored that you are financially continuing to walk with me to get this message about Heavenly Father's love that He has for the LGBT community out there, and the many extensions of my mission that honor what I have to speak about God's love for this community is educating me, because of the love I have been given from my medical team in Portland, gives me abilities to do the same to others with unconditional love. So, I thank you for calling me. You are such a big part of my spiritual life and family and I honor and respect you for wanting me to come out to Utah. I feel so spoiled! You are all so good to me without any expectations!"

He asks me to please think about it, saying that he has talked to my stake president and expressed his hopes, and he knows that many others hope that I will come out.

I say, "Well, thank you," *Why is everyone being so kind?* is the first thing I think, but I sign off with, "I'll get back to you as soon as possible."

He says, "Okay, well, just know that we'll get the tickets and we will set up the accommodations and the transportation. You just need to show up."

I say, "Okay, I'll talk to you later."

Not even 7 minutes later, the phone rings again. I pick up, and it is Ty Mansfield, Founder and President of North Star International and Founder of the Voice(s) of Hope project. Ty is

EMBRACED

asking me if I will be coming to the North Star Conference in Provo, Utah, saying that everyone there is looking forward to seeing me.

That's when he tells me that "the whole North Star worldwide community voted and they would like you to receive the Beacon of Light Award at this year's conference." I am blown away! The Beacon of Light Award is given to the North Star Member who is a living light *unto the world*.

Ty says, "I, as the President, want you to come out to the Conference, if you can. I am inviting you. I am planning this special award ceremony which will be a surprise during the conference."

I say, "Ty, if you are presenting me with this award and it is coming from you into my hands, I would be honored."

He says, "Well, I am the president and you were asked for and picked personally for this honorable award that goes to the one who has a life as a lighthouse, such as yourself. You are becoming a Beacon of Light at North Star's conference and it would be my honor hand this award over to you. And you know, Jordan, being a Beacon of Light speaks of the character of man you are from *within*, not about who you are on the *outside*, because light shines through from the inside out, which is how a beacon of light can be found by the people looking for hope and finding it through you. It is the truth, Jordan. So can I put you in the conference schedule for the award ceremony?"

I'm just listening to him because I'm so touched I can hardly speak.

Ty continues, "What a beautiful surprise this will be, for the many who have read your book and listened to your Voice of Hope message and followed the transformation of your life from childhood to this present time of becoming a Beacon of Light in my fifties. You have shown that anything is possible and that you can drop the luggage of the past and say, *Good bye, God's got plans and I gotta go do what I gotta do.*"

I say, "Well, then. You can absolutely count on me."

I continue, "Have I ever said something and not followed through it with, Ty? So, if you are calling to ask me to be there to accept this award from you and your organization, this baby you have developed, then I will be there to help cradle it and see this baby become successful because God is in your life and my life. That is one of the common grounds you and I share, our key to our success in Christ and His love for people like us is humbling. And for the church to accept same gender attraction and the honesty of *no more lies* is why you and I hit it off from the start. We kept the faith and hold on to it. I'll be out there in a few days for this event and for any other events you would ever need me for."

Ty says, "You never have broken faith with me. Our friendship is loyal. So, I will see you there with the stake presidents?"

I say, "Yes, and what about any of the bishops, will they be coming too?

He says, "I heard many bishops have reserved their seats for the luncheon at the awards ceremony. And we have a special seat just for you, you know. So, we will see you in a few days!' and we say our goodbyes together.

YIKES I have only got a couple of days to plan to leave, and to plan and take my service animal with me, to guide me and keep me from my post-traumatic stress disorder attacks. I hate being rushed! But I embrace this also, because I know I am changing the lives of children because of the way that I live my life. If that were not true, I wouldn't be going out there to receive this award.

My phone calls stop for a moment and I focus myself.

Leaving quickly? I think, *Impossible!* I feel a panic attack coming on. BREATHE, and take some medication. I thank God for my medical support team for knowing how to treat severe panic attacks as these last minute plans of to get ready for this event with Charity, who always travels with me everywhere I go. I couldn't leave my home without her. Utah is always beautiful. Park City and Sundance are my two favorite places to go to for relaxing and people-watching. The altitude and dryness of Utah are definitely out of my comfort zone at times. But the people are worth it, for a short time.

In my final preparing of the itinerary with my family stake president in Ogden, we both agree to not rush but take our time getting to each of the events at this year's conference. We will just enjoy the moment with those who are not plastic-fantastic. This stake president is magical to me. He is a true member of my spiritual family and I love him. He has shown me so many good times, along with other members of my spiritual family who mentor aspects of my life and are significant to my spiritual growth and happiness to this day. This is like a gift from God at this time in my life, when I never expected to be embraced so unconditionally.

"Wow, do I have a lot to think about, Charity!" I talk aloud to my dog on a regular basis. She probably understands me more than anyone. In reality she already knows we are leaving to Utah because she sees the suitcases out and she is sitting *in* them, ready to go.

"What are we going to do, Charity? What does God have planned at this conference for me and for you? You and I both

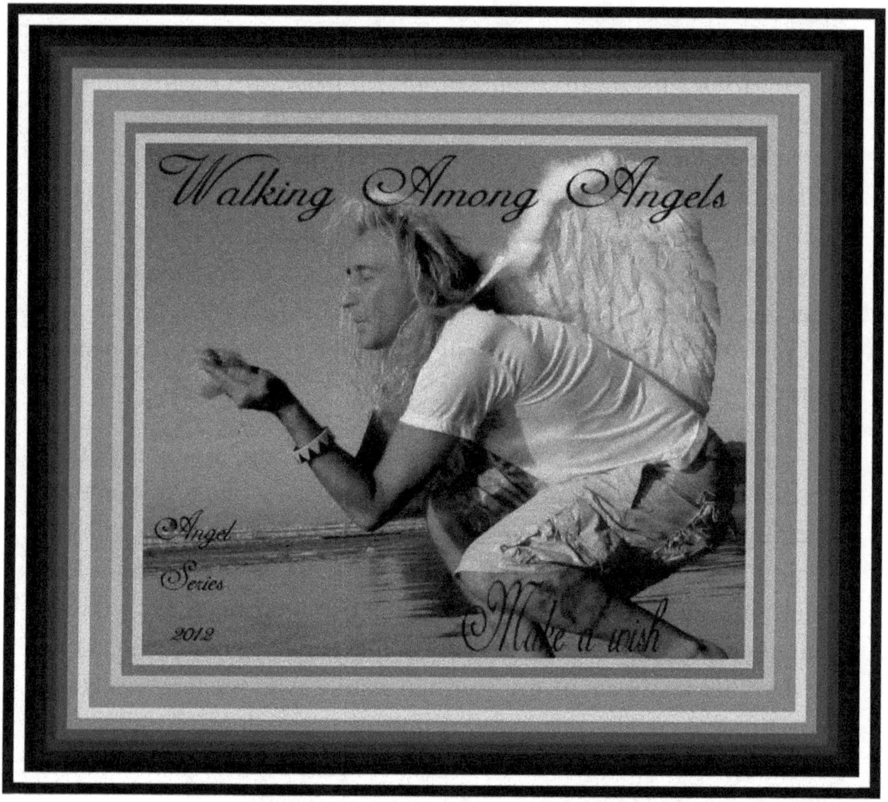
Walking Among Angels
Angel
Series
2012
Make a wish

know that God has always been good to us, since we have decided to ask Him to be first in our life, so we can trust He's not going to abandon us. So, don't worry about getting out of that suitcase. You are going with me. We are going to follow the Spirit and where it leads."

I've been given abundant mercy and grace, that the lifestyle of my past is no longer my lifestyle today. It's a relief! I think of my years of hoping, waiting for God's gift to me to be found, to know now that I belong. The cord of my addiction of pleasing my only family that truly made me feel needed could finally be cut. How fearful to ever think that my gay family throughout the world could be shaken by my faith, which draws me toward a major panic attack of fear of uncertainty and worry about my value that I have been given from 35 years of devotion to this beautiful and colorful community in downtown Portland and the Pacific Northwest. As refreshing as catching a wave on your surfboard, it is smooth sailing when you know you are on the right wave.

That's how I feel about my relationship with Jesus Christ. I know I am on the right wave, leading me to the most refreshing place my mind could ever be. Never feeling stillness or experiencing peace like this in my life before, this trip is not about packing up the products and the hair formulas and the designer clothing to market myself as a godly man, or just putting on the right tie with the right colored suit and, of course, it must be a white shirt, if I'm to fit in with the leadership, but I'm not there to fit in. I'm not being given the award because I fit in. I am being given the award because I have realized that I can identify in truth that yes, I do have same gender attraction and I am gay, but Jesus Christ is the Lord of my life and he is my identity and being gay is just an attraction in my life and no longer my lifestyle, which the gay community is embracing at this very given moment.

JORDAN JANTZ

It seems like just *minutes* later, everyone in downtown Portland and in Seattle has heard that I will be receiving an award in Provo, Utah, for being a Beacon of Light to the world from a group of people called North Star International and a group of people called Voices of Hope, which everyone knows are the most significant spiritual growth group I have in my life. I can look through their eyes in receiving this award and be able to come back to Portland, knowing that I have *taken back ground*, because I *live* on *solid ground*. I now see I have evolved in becoming a true Portland fellow-shipper to all mankind.

Catching my breath, while being touched by the Spirit after receiving these calls today, I cry with deep emotion. I just weep with gratitude at this reality, knowing that many people despise what I am doing. But making others happy today seems to not be of value. I am realizing that I don't have to pack my skin care products, my skin creams, and hair treatments. I don't have to run down to Adam Levine's Skin and Body Care Center where Charlie my BFF works, who can give me free body and seaweed exposures and the most high-end body massages with coconut oil and coconut milk. There is no more praying to *look renewed*. Sun tanning beds with honey all over my skin for the removal of evidence of aging was my friend's gift weekly to *maintain* the youthful glow. What a lot of work I have put into the ability to arrive outwardly flawless, which hid my inward emptiness. But now I flush it down the garbage disposal, and I reflect as I pack my bags on how much garbage has been put in that disposal as I continue to daily lay down my life for the mission I hope will be embraced in receiving this phenomenal Beacon of Light Award.

As I am packing I wonder if any of the people that ever knew me in my life – parents, brothers and sisters, grandparents- I wonder if they were to know what I kind of man God has opened my life up to become, would they embrace me? Or would they still consider me second hand, *used shoes*. Would I still be the son that

EMBRACED

can only support himself through modeling advertisements for clothing lines and through entertainment abilities that were developed from my ability to please professionals who groomed me into a child-protégé from so many aspects of entertainment from childhood throughout adulthood? Even traveling was always actually work with an agenda to become what I was told was my role for the job. I was chosen from the cattle call for the job, whether it was runway photography or personal weekends.

I also entertained many political events throughout elections. That made me realize the value I have as an American, that I do have a choice and I have chosen what I have been taught and living in America I can be a Christian that is same gender attracted or gay *and* love Jesus Christ and have Him in my heart and obey His commandments because He loves me, and when I make mistakes and fall, He is there to pick me up. So I recall the many ministers I know who told me I need to be in a Bible-based church, I think, *I am so free from their judgments on me, and the judgments that I have placed upon my own life by being honest about who I really am and what I stand for.* This trip will be spiritually uplifting because of the gay people that are OUT and love Jesus Chris and follow His standards for their life with same gender attraction. What an honor to be a Beacon of Light to my brothers and sisters like myself and to those who are not like me, a lighthouse.

While my head is visualizing all this, the phone rings again. It is one of my ex-boyfriend, Mark's, employers, the president of Northwest Wear, which is a fashion clothing line for ski-wear with many high end corporations that are buyers. He asks me to work the runway for the season's premier of his new line.

I take a deep breath and let him know that I am out of the business. I have made plans to pursue advocating for children who have been abandoned and abused. I have left the catwalk to become a philanthropist, raising money for the broken.

JORDAN JANTZ

His reply is, "*WHAT* did you do? Did you go into a monastery? Do we need to get together over a bottle of champagne and talk about this? This is one of the biggest clothing lines for the ski season, and are you really telling me you'd rather take a trip to Utah to see a bunch of spiritual gurus?"

My reply is, "I love you dearly and I thank you for remembering me for this ski show, but honestly, my runway and modeling days are over. I would rather go out gracefully and with the blessing of my Heavenly Father, than to be asked to leave or told I am too old."

He says, "What? You want to leave with a blessing from your Heavenly Father in *this* industry? You are *lucky* to be working past age thirty as a male runway model. Jordan, why would you even think of not letting this in your life? You, NOT taking this, could be the END of your memory as a runway model that touched many covers and it is because of people like me. You owe me! And you owe the industry."

"I made a promise and I am going to go accept this award and I am sorry," I say.

He replies, "You know, Mark would have wanted you to be at this event and you know how much he loved snowboarding, and for you to not be there *where he would be at*, with all of the other buyers and fashion coordinators is an embarrassment to the relationship the two of you had."

I say, "That's just it. That is the relationship that I had. But his memory will *live* with me forever. I think of him every Christmas day, the day I found him dead. So don't tell me where I need to be. I love you, and I made millions of dollars for all these companies throughout the years. You all have said *Do This* and *Do That*, and I was at a place where I couldn't even do anything without you telling me what to do. My whole life I've had people telling me

EMBRACED

do it this way, do it that way, look this way, look that way. I couldn't make a decision to do things for myself and this is the first time in my life for *me* to tell *you*, I can't do it anymore. I just can't do it anymore. The lifestyle nearly killed me. So please, my friend, understand, I'm a missionary now, with a new mission. And if you ever did love the money that I made for you and the many companies that you worked with, you will share with everyone my happiness in the change that has taken place in my life."

He says, "Well, I did read your book. And everyone in the industry is asking about a new book. So, I will let them know you have a new venue of what is important in your life."

He pauses a moment and then says, "I can tell you this, Jordan, you were one heck of a dedicated model. You lasted many years longer than expected, and I gotta hand it to you. The agencies are still calling me, looking for *that look* that comes natural to you. It's hard for me to find, so don't throw the baby out with the bathwater. You still have it in you if you want it. You've got everyone's contacts and we'll just leave it at that."

Wow, what a blessing and kindness, I think, after getting off the phone. Thank you, Heavenly Father, you really are watching out for me. You really are turning 2015 into the most incredible year of my life, and really it is just beginning. Another beautiful year and I'm celibate! I just don't know how to say my blessings of gratitude without crying for never experiencing your love or anyone's love like I do today. It is like fresh grapefruit, being massaged all over my body with ice cubes, like they did in Morocco for relieving stress. I can smell and feel the breeze of the ocean and the moments of that modeling event in the Moroccan resort.

I sigh with relief, "I am no longer a protégé having to weigh, look, walk, speak, sit and be what people have paid for me to become, never knowing what the end result will be, except several

JORDAN JANTZ

hefty checks slid into my pants by many coordinators of the events that were planned out each season and the shows that called for the right runway models to walk the catwalk for certain benefits and fundraisers for the fashion and political worlds to help people keep up their image and that's what I was, an image-planner. I helped people's image by my image of expectation from them to be the best, which is what I was always told and recall as a little boy: *you've got to be the best little boy in the whole world* is what my biological mother told me, *in order for anyone to want you*, and it worked. It made my light shine from within but many abused it. Now, I'm packing my bags to go receive an award for what God is doing with my insides. I am receiving this award because of what God has done in my life and my devotion to live in the light.

And I am *so* loving the fact that I don't have to make a list of things to bring to make this event pleasing for everyone else. I can just pack up and *accept this reality* that I have been chosen and not for my outward abilities that bring light to others, but from the abilities of God's love through me, I am able to be a beacon of light.

I can *just* go be with my North Star and Voices of Hope family and the many others throughout the community of churches that believe in this ministry that is touching the world and transforming it. After spending a lot of money for therapy, I have been taught to *let go* of all plastic fantastic events and the many people that expect me to play that role with them as in days past.

FAMILY HOME EVENING IN PORTLAND

6

MONDAY EVENING BEFORE I LEAVE for Utah, I'm making my favorite Thai main dish for this evening's special celebration of my regular *family home evening* devotion that I now enjoy in my life. I usually have my family home evening with Charity and myself on Monday nights. I always have an activity planned around her. She and I do a little doggie dance together as we sing a special song of gratitude to the creator of the universe who gave us this new way of living and teaches me to become the best man that I can be. Charity's favorite song is *To have Faith, Hope and Charity, that's the way to live successfully. How do I know? The Spirit of God teaches me so.* It's a song that my aunt taught me, the one who bought me Charity 14 years ago.

If I am with others for a larger family home evening or leading it outside of my home, I usually involve a spiritual or social discussion for everyone's interaction and ability, giving them comfort in the activity for the evening. Tonight's event will involve some really fine food that I have prepared better than any man on any cooking show. Yes, I am confident in my cooking abilities, especially Thai food.

JORDAN JANTZ

Tonight's Family Home Evening is planned for me to speak and share about my life-story written by Jewel Adams called *Out of the Closet, Into the Light,* and my Voices of Hope video that was produced through Ty Mansfield (who I just talked to yesterday on the phone) and really my whole my journey that started with my missionary who respected me. ANY or each of these three discussions can be exhausting because these are not something that anyone can just share like the food I'm making. Transformation doesn't work like that for me. It is my process and it is deep, serious and sometimes very slow, manifesting difficult transitions that give me fear of acceptance from past realities when judgment of men that call themselves Christians say that I'm unacceptable because I lack goodness and truthfulness of God's identity of manhood and Godly leadership skills and that if I identify as a same gender attracted man, I would be excommunicated from any Christian group *because you cannot be a Christian and still be attracted to other men.*

I say, "It is called being gay" and they say, "that's called *having chosen* the identity of being gay." The truth I speak is that I was born with this attraction and I'm not going to lie that I'm not attracted to other men. Experiencing what I have, many gay community leaders come over to my house on Mondays to share Charity's love on our Family Home Evenings because my message is *God Loves You* and wants you to have the best life. He, God, is the one that transforms your life and transforms our addictions and our embarrassing actions that are hidden because of expectations such as eating a second serving in hiding when you never eat more than one plate of food in front of anyone. But I must admit, I sin a lot and to some Christian eyes I take a second helping of food.

Many gay friends tell me, "This religion of Christianity or the LDS church or any controlling religion they must be watching out for your future as an old man modeling, if they are worried

EMBRACED

about your weight at your age. You are still as skinny as a 25-year-old, Jordan, so don't worry about the sin of gluttony."

Some laugh, "You are just really trying to be a do-gooder, aren't you."

And I say with clarity, "It's time for change. I don't want to be in the public's eye doing what I've been doing anymore. It does not suit my heart and spirit of who I really am."

And they all say, standing around me, "Girlfriend, you really are serious about Jesus. You are the only gay man I know that makes it so very clear to all of us girls at the health club that we can work out as long as we want to, but our bodies are still going to end up aging no matter what cosmetic we use. You are Mr. Truth. You say to us when we are trying to look young, *We're **still** going to get older* and that's why everybody loves you at the men's personal fitness center. Maybe that's why this *glow* is all circled around you, from what everyone in the gym tells each other when you walk in with your towel, ready to get into your moment of enlightenment."

Since tonight's special family home evening is at the Mission President's house, I know I want to show artistic skills by making homemade pot-stickers with stuffed Gouda. And of course, my dog Charity is always decked out in her pink princess outfit with her pink manicure and pedicure. She is ready to attend to our family home evening responsibility, being a part of missionary service to all churches. She watches my preparations from the little red bed that my old boyfriend who passed away, Mark, made for her. It is still her favorite bed and it has his memories on it. He would sure be shocked about tonight. But I know he is looking down from heaven and he loves what he sees, that I am going to an incredible place and sharing incredible

information with some incredible people who want to have the best life possible.

Charity and I are picked up by two missionaries, and of course these missionaries are astounded at Charity's glitter as much as my laid back Jungle style apparel, which could be conceived as a little bit mental since I live in the Pacific Northwest and it is cold and often rainy here especially in spring, but I love the colors of the tropics and the feeling of flips flops.

The missionaries are in their traditional suits and ties, and I know before I leave my home that everyone will be wearing the same style clothing as the missionaries, also. I personally know that when I'm asked to wear attire for matching the event that I am attending it is never a problem, but when I'm not asked, I take advantage of the blessing to enjoy me as Jesus does and I don't worry about pleasing others. I find joy in wearing clothing such as the coat of many colors.

The missionaries are excited because they had heard about me but had never met me. They tell me that there are several more missionary companionships already at the family home evening waiting to meet me and hear me speak. Everyone anticipates hearing about my experiences with the missionary who taught me the Gospel Standards.

While driving to the fireside, I knew I would be asked why I dress so casual. My reply is, "because I value making others feel comfortable if they don't have as nice of clothing as I do." In the car, I expect more questions. I don't expect to be embraced. I don't expect honesty from people, but I choose it.

Common questions are always asked and begin from the missionaries, "Can we ask you, how hard was it for you to accept the church standards, the church standards that they say you must live by, if you want to join the church?" and, "How did you decide to live a life that would cause you have to make changes in the middle of your life?" Everyone is astonished that somebody would actually decide to change in the middle of their life and try to become spiritual. I have heard this from many in my community: Why would you *want* to become spiritual? Everyone's heard and seen the clothing lines you wore and the magazines you represented. Your turning and facing yourself for what you did to get where you are today and still have a heart to heal and change the darkness into light, what is your reason for that, Jordan?

But the missionaries don't think in that direction, really. The missionary says, "Everyone's got candles lit for you so we better get there or people will wonder what happened."

The missionaries are helping me get there, but also asking for me to communicate with them before everyone distracts me, asking, "What made you choose a change?? What was it like, emotionally and mentally? And your missionary, how did he even communicate? We've never met anyone like you before. We've only been told about people like you, and to make sure we stay away from people like you on our mission. So, this is amazing to us that a missionary was able to even do what no other missionary has ever done. Please tell us."

I have much more to talk about, so I don't mind giving them the easy answer, "Well, you guys, I'll tell you honestly, I embraced every standard when I made the choice accept the gospel, because I knew the life that I came out of would *never be nothing again* but somewhere over the rainbow, never to return again, never to be desired again. After the addictions to desiring sex and many formalities that are hidden in the culture of the gay community that are also underground at times in certain communities, it is impossible at times to be accepted when everyone's competing, unless you've been blessed with abilities that you are born with, meaning outward appearances that will take you places others cannot go. Unfortunately, this is very sad to me but it is the only thing I've ever experienced. That's why communication is the most developed skill I learned that is the most valuable to all people. If you can't communicate, you won't make it in any business, especially a profession that is demanding on the body, on your appearance, your weight, and your ability to speak. Roll it all up in one, and you have a ball that has a signature of communication. If you can't communicate what you are wearing, what you are doing, what you have to offer, no one is going to buy you or anything you are wearing. So I learned to communicate at a very young age.

And I am grateful to communicate tonight, about the opportunities all of you have in touching the lives of people that are just waiting for light to come in and dispel the darkness that torments so many people all over the world, whether they are gay or straight. No matter what age they may be, we are susceptible human beings to dangerous circumstances and *silence, I have learned, equals death*. So that's the only reason why I share my life-story, like I am tonight." And telling them that, as I sit among these young men talking with me just before we arrive at this family home evening, I realize how critical my journey has become to young people. I also realize the many lies that people in my life told me, because they never believed that any spirituality or godliness that could exist in my presence.

In my past I was told over and over that God *would* not be a part of my life. I sometimes feel hurt by this and one person explained it, "You just have had a life and it is hard for people to understand because it is not normal so they can't imagine it, ….and you speak *as if* your former lifestyle and the abuse you experienced as a child are only a disability that leads to a challenge and hope." They say this because they don't understand that it is true. All those things became a disability and they now are my challenge *and* HOPE.

JORDAN JANTZ

92

now how to do presentations. The missionaries and I ring the doorbell and wait. I will stand to talk to them as I was taught when I was a child, holding my arms down at my sides.

I say to them, "I hope you guys will all be prepared for tonight's challenge of learning that we all come to this earth with different challenges, different disabilities, different emotions and our Heavenly Father made each one of us to be in this situation of facing the challenge. Are we willing to face the challenge? That's what tonight will be about, young men."

The door opens. I am ready to do this with these young people. The missionaries reach for Charity to pick her up in her lovely sporty missionary outfit with white shirt and sparkly bow tie. You can tell she is a missionary in training. The Mission President's house is lit up with white lights; we are greeted with a warm welcome.

The downstairs furniture has been removed and the whole downstairs of the house is converted into a sanctuary. The sofas have disappeared for the night and additional chairs are set up in rows with aisles.

I do my equipment set-up. I am shocked to see so many of the presidency and other leadership in the temple. Throughout the room I see many missionaries from other countries. I know the Lord is ready to touch the hearts of these people with the message of hope for people who struggle with same gender attraction or any sexual addiction, whether they are gay or straight. I greet each individual with a card introducing my next book to be released, and many are excited and urge me to begin. I reply that I will find my seat now, and whisper to the Mission President to please announce that the evening's discussion is about to begin and to ask everyone to find their seats.

I know that Charity is all situated in the other room. My mind is centered.

I can feel the Holy Spirit as everyone moves forward to hear my message.

I ask everyone, "How many of us want to be in place in our relationships and life where we are celebrated and not tolerated?"

I say, "Can you imagine how the Savior felt, never being in a place where he was celebrated, he was only tolerated?

Then, "I would like to open up this evening with prayer.

I start to pray with everyone, "Heavenly Father in Jesus Name, I pray over all the missionaries here tonight, from all over the Portland's downtown mission zone, for the opportunity to have these missionaries throughout the downtown sharing light and hope to many who are just waiting for the gospel. Thank you for using me as a light from the gay community that has been my family since I came out of the closet and realized that I had same gender attraction and I thank you, Heavenly Father, that you do not condemn me for having same gender attraction but you embrace me and love me, just as I am. That is why I am here tonight because I am *living* who I know I am and what I say I am, and that is a Latter-day Saint Christian that has same gender attraction which means I believe in God and you cannot pray the gay away because I have tried. I thank you for teaching me that I could never have prayed the gay away. It is not my fault, in Jesus Name, we thank You for this evening, and what you will do tonight through your Holy Spirit in the hearts of everyone here, in Jesus name, amen."

I continue, "None of our relationships can have excuse in them for discrimination. To be the man that I am today I had a true relationship with my missionary and my leadership who didn't just

EMBRACED

walk the walk, but walk the whole *journey*. My missionary is still walking it with me to this day.

I say clearly, "You have the opportunity to pull the thorn out of your brother's side without excuse or judgment and *but only by love.*

I announce how we are going to learn new things, "Tonight we will each pick a slip of paper out of this basket. It will ask you to do something that is different from your ordinary life this week. You have to find this within your spirit and meditation – to step out of your comfort zone as missionaries."

As they draw paper slips, the room is quiet.

When we speak, it is hours of opening hearts directly to each other.

I close, "Thank you all for supporting Voices of Hope and *Out of the Closet, Into the Light.* Good night."

I walk to the back to give Charity assurance that I am aware of her. The missionary that brought me to the meeting approaches to ask me when I would like to go home. I say, "I believe now is the best time. Let's let the Spirit do the rest." I depart early.

JORDAN JANTZ

LIFETIME ACHIEVEMENT AWARD

7

THE NORTH STAR CONFERENCE IN UTAH is three days, packed for me between two five-day round-trip flights. My notice was short and I have no information packet, so I need to throw together something nice to wear and get prepared for time with my spiritual brother, Paul. He is the uncle of my missionary that taught me the gospel and is the family's stake president in Ogden, and he also desires to help with the transformation of hearts in the church for people who live with same gender attraction and want to go to church and serve Jesus Christ but they are told, some by their families, that they are unworthy to serve Jesus Christ because of their same gender attraction, which is far from the truth.

The LDS church **does not** teach *"You cannot be gay and believe that the savior loves you and walks with you with your same gender attraction that you live with."*

When people say that, my response is, "You are so far from the truth, because I feel the spirit of the almighty creator of the universe in my life today, working through my doctors and my therapists and my case-managers that want the best for me, and that is God's way of telling me that he is taking care of me in every aspect, by giving me the things I need as a gay man that believes in Jesus Christ as his Savior. I did not ever choose this

attraction and really I ran from it until I realized its ability to compensate my inadequacies that I was raised with when I had to be the best at all events. There was no placing *second*. My congeniality came from the sorrow I saw in other people's hearts so I overcompensated with happiness to balance out the sadness within that existed as an empty hole since I had been sold by my biological mother. And sometimes people that are that *told* God doesn't love them because of the challenges they live with feel that hole can never be filled, which brings feelings of emptiness.

Jesus fills that empty hole that people made in my life, this void that was printed upon me as an infant, which was not my choice. The consequences are that abused children who become adults live with the PTSD that many adults to this day carry around with them, expressed as control issues or addictions or abusiveness to others. It is sad how child abuse can break any human …especially when they are told that they were the firstborn and the first and only child to be sold. It doesn't give a man that much self-esteem when he finds this out as an adult. It makes you wonder if I was just a hidden mistake, waiting to be embraced somehow.

Right off the plane in Utah and the moment I lay eyes on my spiritual brother, Paul, I feel joy! He and I don't talk lightly but passionately and we both love North Star, Voices of Hope and how God uses our disabilities in our lives to become abilities to touch the lives of others.

"It is miracle that you are alive," he states often for at many times I am challenged just getting from point A to Z. Airplane trips are huge challenges.

"God's grace and *medical support* is the foundation of daily living," I answer back, with a smile.

JORDAN JANTZ

"Jordan, no one looks as good as you. Look at you! You know how to pull it off! And you have a spiritual family that just adores you," Paul says.

Paul and his nephew, *my missionary*, Spencer, and I cherish our hours together, spending them on a morning ride up Ogden canyon on horseback, while I tell them about my medical team back in Portland. I talk about the best pharmacist in the state and the best group of women and men that know about my life and my lifestyle and my past and that I can be totally transparent and they embrace me with good health.

I tell them I have the best housing management anyone could want at the Rose Schnitzer Towers. I prayed and I prayed and everyone prayed for me to be able to have the ability to spend my last days of my life at the Rose Schnitzer Towers. Then a very special housing expert worked with her team to make this very special opportunity for a healthier environment for me as I grow into my years. Because of my housing there, I also have the convenience of getting the best transportation at my front door. And I really do have the best because I have been given a lot of grace through God and the people that God put in my life today. The past is a chalkboard I can erase it but some memories and events will always be a Polaroid picture in my mind. That's why I remember exact situations since the age of two.

I say, "As we are riding up the canyon, I want you all to know right now, that I would never allow myself on a horse unless I was being paid to model horse-wear or to model a horse on the runway, which I have seen many do and I have been offered the same but I declined for the fear that I have of horses, but I'm doing this with you guys even though the last time I was with a horse, it was traumatic."

They are a little surprised because I get along just fine with the horse, a beautiful stallion. Paul observes this and says, "Spencer always said you always have a way of making people feel comfortable even when you don't know anything about them."

Riding side-by-side with Paul and Spencer, my missionary, up through Ogden's winding hills on the most beautiful horses, we watch the sun come up and it is like looking into heaven.

Spencer says he felt that meeting me and having me become a part of his life and his spiritual family was one of the reasons that he was sent to our mission. It is not common for a missionary to bring *home* a person to be a permanent part of the family, as a spiritual member of the family so this is very special.

Paul says, "These things happen for a reason and a purpose."

I say, "I hope that everyone will feel that way at the convention tomorrow." I know I am going to need rest because the horse is making my rear end sore and I feel bow-legged already.

Time to suggest some rest, "So what do you cowboys say we go down and get some breakfast, since we all got up so early for this *men's spiritual morning awakening*." These encounters mesmerize me but they also exhaust me. I don't have the strength they do.

So we eat. Everything is right-there-on-the-farm homemade from the pigs that he grew to the chickens that laid the eggs, and that is countrified to me. I am exploring the cowboy spirit I didn't know existed in me. As we talk about heading out to North Star and receiving the award soon, I know I will be bringing my spiritual family who wants to walk my life journey with me into the light, too. I hope we are all ready for that.

JORDAN JANTZ

Many medical facilities that contribute to my life support system are grateful for the medications that help me manage emotions of gratitude and thankfulness and I feel intensity of their support during this incredible event at which this award is being presented to me through North Star International and Voices of Hope. My doctors never knew that I was involved in an international church, but to see peace instead of shame and confusion, this award has touched every community I've been a part of because of my honesty and openness of life's reality in sharing the story of my life with the world. The only way that the story can be revealed and understood is through each *reality of experience*. All who have maintained their commitment to my mission and transformation on this earth participate with me to hopefully teach the message that we can manage our disabilities and turn them into abilities with the right support system, in which spirituality is the main ingredient for providing peace along-side my medical support team that has walked beside me over 17 years consistently and into the truthful light of my life today.

The next morning at 6:30 am we start driving from Ogden to Provo, bringing us to the conference in downtown Provo by 8 am. This conference center is near where the second temple in Provo is being built today. My dear Janet and Richard, my missionary's aunt and uncle (and so also in this sense, more spiritual family to me) are side-by-side with me, experiencing a whole new level of church mentality. Never before have they seen members of the church that belong to the LGBT community. I am so proud of my spiritual family, to see that they are able to understand that a lot of people are born different from one another.

As members of the church gather around, I can see my spiritual family open their eyes for the first time to <u>*not understanding*</u> why men or women are born with these differences that run so deep to where they met many people who were born with both sexes.

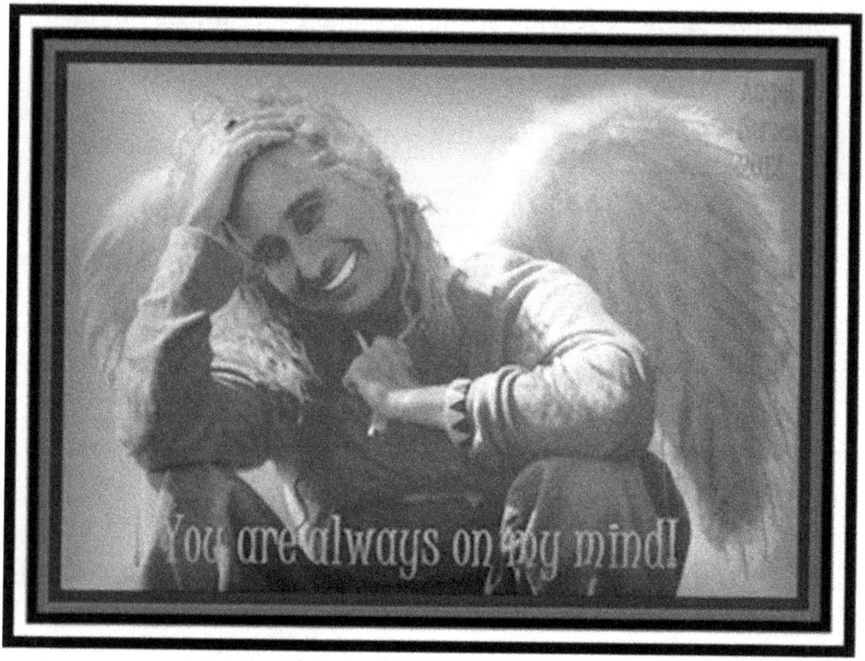
You are always on my mind!

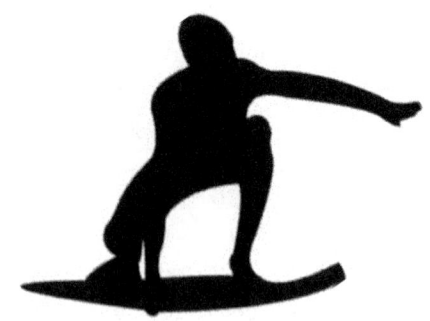

They ask "What do you call them?"

I reply, "Hermaphrodites" but another important word to understand is 'transgender'. Transgender is when a person is called one gender at birth but transitions to the other gender."

"And what is gay or lesbian, is it part of that?"

"No, that is what I deal with – *same* gender attraction."

If there are more questions in the future, I will make sure to get every single one answered.

Many people follow us, wanting to talk and wanting to listen in, and even while that was happening, we knew <u>we</u> were there to listen and to embrace the moment of North Star's conference in Provo. With my spiritual family by my side I am very at home and everyone knows it.

Ty Mansfield starts off the ceremonies. The speakers are incredible and my friend, Stewart Weed, who for many years ran the Institute of Religion in Portland *and* who baptized me is there before us as a guest speaker. Stewart and his married son, Josh, and Josh's wife, Lolly, who have together participated in firesides with me in the almost nine years of me being a member of the church, are also here. I am so proud to see them!

Nobody can take a picture of what I am feeling: the *love* that people within the church that are here have for those with these many identity and sexual challenges, including me. Some of my disabilities that I was born with seem to be easier to me now, because I know that I've let go of trying to be in control and appear to hold it perfectly together when all that is needed is perfected, in fact.

When we break into the next session, my dear spiritual family member, Janet, and I go on our own side-journey to another group and it is a blast. You see, my spiritual family is not just a family, it is a spiritual bond that we have all made and that is different than blood family. It is spiritual and it is the closest thing that I've ever had to what a consistent love may really be like. I could not really tell you for sure.

Aunt Janet continues to look over the information being taught in the discussion, when we both realize what the title meant - that we are in a group that is for people that are transforming their *gender*. It comes to our understanding that all who are attended this session are *already* in the middle of their transforming as a man or as a woman, as we all greet each other. Their voices, Adam's apple, and little cosmetic procedures are still in process and have not yet been completed for their transformation. We were the *only* two in the room that are not transgender and *boy, do we learn a lot*. We laugh so hard because we realize that we are where we are so that we can learn the most, and we now have a better understanding for men and women who transgender into who they feel they are supposed to be, which understanding we never would have had any other way. We get it practically firsthand in the best way.

You see, we *learn* as a spiritual family, *going together*. The truth is that asking real questions about each other's life is the only way to be real in a relationship with anyone, instead of getting off a plane and having a "fun time" for me, or going alone and isolated to see the sights for someone else. What a waste of time it would be for me to not have the relationships that focus on growth for all of us.

And no, I'm not an animal in a zoo for people to pay money to look at, which is sometimes a real and valid feeling for some who are different at church._ When you aren't in a <u>real</u>

relationship with people who commit and follow through and who are there to grow with you, you absolutely can feel like a Guinea pig in a labeled container, alone and hopeless.

So ends the first day at the North Star Conference. We drive all the way back to up to Ogden, stopping only to have dinner at a Mexican restaurant. My spiritual family knows that Mexican food is my favorite. When my body is this challenged, eating is all about feeding my body the nutrients it must have for these long, transforming days.

The next day we do it again. The event schedule has a forum that is like meeting *all* the people in the church that are dealing with identity or same gender attraction issues. That took a lot of planning to make that happen and my hat is off to North Star.

My spiritual family asks me what seminar I want to participate with next, and I decide that I want to go to a seminar that deals with the church's view on youth and LGBT.

I knew this seminar could be heartbreaking. I see so many youths that are broken by the actions of their parents, even though I also see some parents on the panel, sharing the truth of their adoring feelings about their gay or lesbian child. Many youths are sitting right next to me in tears, sharing with me how they have heard their parents say how *ashamed* their parents are to have anyone outside know that their family has anyone in it that has same gender attraction or is not living the standards of the church. Many of these men were born into the church and then became married with children. Many are missionaries that I have personally met in the state of Oregon that were called to go do their mission and I was blessed to get to know them and let them know that when they finish their mission, I would like them to contact my friend, Ty Mansfield at North Star and Voices of Hope for they along with Evergreen International are the three religious communities that have not

EMBRACED

walked out of my life or delivered me to the world for the destruction of my flesh so that my soul would be saved, because of my identity as a Latter-day Saint Christian who was born with same gender attraction. I sit and listen as I embrace the hearts of many parents who are broken from not knowing how to respond to their children or other family members with same gender attraction and their children who are broken from being emotionally abandoned.

During and after this seminar, people ask me personal questions about my views with the hope of hearing the *right answer* and I know that I couldn't give them the right answer for each of us is different, but the true answer is that Jesus loves all of His children and I have experienced that intimately and deeply for my nine years of commitment with the Church of Jesus Christ of Latter-day Saints, that WILL NOT let go and abandon me but instead pursue my growth in establishing the characteristics that I never knew I had to be of interest to the world, let alone my life being anything of value to anybody.

How wrong it is to listen to others who have their own opinion with the ability of controlling many people's heart, spirit and soul and I will never allow anyone to control my life ever again but the Savior. My spiritual family has given me this gift of insight that nobody could ever have made sense of the freedom I have been given through following the traditions of living a good life and believing that there is a Savior in the world today that knows me before I ever came to be. Shame on many churches today that create fear in the lives of others. God is not about instilling fear but instilling faith, hope and charity and above all these the greatest that he has instilled in my life, is charity. I see the fruits of this gift throughout the past nine years of following Jesus Christ as my Lord and Savior and in the support I have received to become the best man God has created within me to

share with the world that He created for me to live in, until I meet him again someday.

I know none of this is possible for my life without the support of the multicultural medical support team that I'm surrounded with only because my life is now so open for the healing and restoration of others. My primary care physician always tells me *silence equals death*. Disabilities can become abilities, I know, if I continue to seek out removing the shame that has been placed throughout my life history. Maybe that's what being *born again* is really all about. I guess you could even say that I am a Born Again Latter Day Saint Christian. In fact, I know I am, and so does my spiritual family.

How grateful I am to be able to soon go home to Portland Oregon, knowing the respect that is always received from Social Security and Disability agencies throughout Portland that embrace many adults that have severely been abused emotionally, mentally and physically. Some do therapy groups with me and some do men's therapy groups. They ask me to share my reasons for joy during the most empty times of my life when they have all watched long-term intimate relationships walk away from me, whether they are adopted family, bought and paid for family or spiritual family or community family. Many embrace the challenges that I also have, and we support each other throughout this time, I realize that they have all embraced one very important thing about my life and that is my faith that I now walk in, which is to live by and try to express the kindness of what it would be like to walk into my doctor's appointment side by side with Jesus Christ at my side. How would He want me to express faith, hope and charity in the circumstances of life that I have been dealt? To make abandonment issues become abilities and the light of hope, that reward comes through giving yourself the ability to share kindness with the person next to you.

JORDAN JANTZ

My mind runs with gratitude for God exposing His love for me to many communities that endorse the ability of making life become as healthy and healing as I've ever been offered. Sadly, I've rarely been given a choice or offered control of anything in my life. It has always been told to me what I will wear and how I will look and how I will make my money this weekend, doing this or that. The freedom my medical teams see in me now is freedom from the fear that I will never be what I'm supposed to be. I used to fear that I could never become equal to the other men, because I have an identity of a human being that has same gender attraction and *if I hold on to that identity that is a slap in the face to God*, which I have been told by many ministers throughout my life.

But they all are wrong. I have searched many places in life for healing, places I never should have gone, but one place shared the truth with me and that is the Church of Jesus Christ of Latter-day Saints, letting me know that same gender attraction is not a sin *and* you cannot pray the gay away. You can do everything possible, whether it be getting married, praying, fasting to have your life changed but the reality is the first seven years of anyone's life are the most significant years on earth and what is developed is developed and there is no pill you can take to transform your same gender attraction, period. That is why I have the best with my medical support team and the disability services that have been provided in my life, so I can continue to live and share that it is not too late to find where you belong and become found. When I was found and embraced by Jesus, pain fell off me as though Jesus was washing sores off of my skin. This is the best analogy of this experience I can explain.

As the conference day comes to an end, people ask how I feel personally after all that I have experienced at North Star. They had read my first book, *Out of the Closet, into the Light*, and some say that it opened their spirit to become honest about who they really are. The pain that I feel in this group makes my spirit

EMBRACED

exhausted, as if I am carrying their loads as well, which, because I love them, maybe is a little true. This is because I remember what it is like to be in their shoes, praying for an answer and someone to bring me hope.

I'm SO looking forward to seeing my colleagues a little later and catching up after they've completed some of their favorite events throughout this conference. As the day is nearly over we attend the *Meet & Greet* (a mixer) to embrace the many authors and leadership that are deeply rooted in my church. I am able to encounter conversations with leadership that only God could set up. Many have read the story of my life and I am now sharing with them the coming forth of new dimensions in relationships in my life with my biological family in Decatur coming up soon, which they are excited to see. They feel I'm teaching what they know in their heads (that we really follow and glorify the savior) <u>to</u> those who should have known the Savior all their lives. I explain that those who have been rescued by Jesus need and know him most and we all have been rescued. I sign a few books and embrace a few colleagues and immediately head out to be driven back to Ogden with my spiritual family.

That evening, Janet and Richard talk about how much they love North Star and Voices of Hope and how the LDS LGBT people are just so friendly and loving, and to have them in our church and be so honest and desperate, they all are kind of looking for hope and healing.

Janet says, "They are looking for a life of peace and they are looking for the opportunity to have a faith in the Savior and Jordan, you are letting them all know that just because you are same gender attracted does not mean you cannot have any of this in your life."

"The truth is, you can have it all," I tell them.

EMBRACED

Richard says, "We've never heard people be so honest, anywhere. Jordan, your honesty about your challenges put other at ease and we see this. This is one of the reasons so many want help from you. You have put your life on the table to be able to save the lives of others from experiencing unthinkable circumstances. We are so proud of your honesty."

After these words of encouragement from my spiritual family, I embrace them and thank them for opening their hearts to a lifestyle none of them ever knew about, but only heard about and I'm so proud to be with people who celebrate my life instead of tolerate it. I have never experienced family that has stayed with me as long as my spiritual family has that continues to celebrate my disabilities that I have been working on to become abilities so I can fit in this world and not be abandoned or left behind.

The family reminds me that I must get to bed very early because I am receiving a very big award tomorrow from Ty Mansfield and the North Star and Voices of Hope communities. No problem for me, it is still daylight and I am exhausted. I know I have to be up. I fall asleep the instant I touch my pillow.

The next morning, I pack up everything as I will have to go directly from the conference to the airport. On the drive down to Provo, I think I don't really wake up for the whole trip.

Then, as I am standing with my priesthood leadership I know that I am about to encounter something very special in my life. I am about to be able to explain the experience that I have, that this church family throughout the country really does do what they say they do and they do it to explain the love of Christ to others the best way they can. That is the most important thing to me: that someone tries their best at following the Savior and that is exactly what the Church of Jesus Christ of Latter-day Saints tries to do. I say this from my experience. I say this only because have

JORDAN JANTZ

EMBRACED

been told this continuously that I should not have same gender attraction *still* after following the Savior and living for the Savior. They say, same gender attraction should be *gone* if you have truly committed your life to the savior.

As I turn my head to remember all of this, I am about to be presented with an amazing momentous moment, I become very nauseated and experience flashbacks of many 'spiritual' men and women throughout my life that have told me that I will *never* see the Kingdom of God because I still have same gender attraction, when I should have been set free. How sad I think to myself, that I ever believed all that. *HOW SAD* it is to know many are excommunicated from churches for having same gender attraction. How sad it is that when they come forth and share the truth of their life, many ministers today condemn and burn people with words and actions, stating that their life is unacceptable because of their attractions and choices so they will not enter the kingdom of God, but "You cannot pray the gay away." I respond to all of them in this manner.

Today I'm resented for being here at the North Star conference by many men and women who believe in Jesus Christ but were told that *they are not accepted because of having same gender attraction.* This breaks my heart. I have seen children take their own lives because of this very issue. I acted out in the same manner when told there is no heaven waiting for anyone like me and there will be no God waiting to share an eternal place of peace because *there is no room* for homosexuals in the kingdom of God. While remembering the decade I spent with my boyfriend who took his life at Christmas because he wasn't able to become what he was told he needed to become in order to be a man who walks with God and lives with same gender attraction,

I really feel how sad it is that he can't be here with me for this moment in my life, to see how embraced I am as a man that was born with same gender attraction and is honest about his medical challenges and my desire to help other children that also have been abandoned and abused. My heart remembering these intricate precipices of my life brings me to where I meet the actions of my transformation of hope and really becoming the man that I want to become: a Beacon of Light, a Lighthouse of safety for those who are broken and have been forgotten. That's why I am here in Utah today with my family, but I'm remembering moments of pain just when my mind should only associate God with mercy and joy. Mark would never have hung himself on Christmas Day if his family had embraced him instead of *pouring shame* upon him.

An announcement comes over the speaker system. The lights dim in the convention hall. The stage lights up. An introduction of the finale of the conference is about to encompass the hearts of every person who has come from all over the United States for this beautiful weekend created for all who walk in this world to a different beat. The stage has been set. All of the leadership surrounds the President of North Star and Founding Member, Ty Mansfield, who speaks about his book, *Voice(s) of Hope*, and then about one individual that has inspired many people all over the world by his voice of hope and his message of transformation.

Then he says, "to a person who has opened doors with Oprah Winfrey, who enkindled the true-hearted spirits of brother and sister, Donny and Marie. This person who receives this award that has been voted by the North Star international membership and that is Jordan Jantz, a Beacon of Light to the world." And that's when I walk up and my friend, Ty, dotes over me, because we are friends and colleagues who have much integrity for one another even since the moment we met.

EMBRACED

As I embrace him giving me the award, I am also embracing the love of my brothers and sisters who voted for award to even happen. So, so much gratitude, showcasing the efforts of many.

When I walk off the stage, many people give me standing ovation. I tell my family that I will meet them out by the car, for that would be the only proper way to dismiss myself from such a moment and such a conference, after receiving such an award.

My family soon comes to the car. They drop Charity and me off at the airport to fly back to Portland on their way home back to Ogden. I get through airport security on spiritual energy only, I think.

On the flight, the stewardess asks me if I am Mormon, and I tell her I am not a person who considers himself a Mormon exactly, I consider myself to be a Latter-day Saint Christian.

"Oh! I like that better," She says and then, "Are you really the gentleman that has that book, *Out of the Closet into the Light*, who survived all those *experiences*?"

I confirm that I am.

She says, "I read the book."

I ask, "Did you respond on the website?"

She says, "No, I didn't, but I would like to."

I suggest, "You know, you could write it as SKY MOM, since that is your job."

She says, "That is so clever! I never dreamed that I would meet you."

I say, "It was for a purpose with a very strong reason, for your life and for someone else. That's how that goes."

There will be someone in her life that will need love and understanding to choose a spiritual life with relationships of truth. I am pulling out my bag and the flight attendant asks me if I need anything.

I say, "Yes, I would so appreciate some water to help me take my medication."

She says, "For you, an honor!"

She asks me where my little service dog is, that she read about in the book. I say, "Oh, she's right here under my arm. You just couldn't see because blends in. She is so attached to me! She'll be fifteen years old in 2016."

"Well," the stewardess says, "I can understand her feelings. She's all you've got if I understand correctly, after reading your book. You've taken care of her as well as I have taken care of my own child."

"Sure do!" I say.

She offers Charity some water in a bowl and offers another blanket to comfort her. She'll look for the airliner kiddie wings if she can find them, for Charity's leash.

I am deliriously tired. I think back to Valentine's Day, just a couple months ago and I am so glad that I can look back at Valentine's Day of years past with understanding, logic and reason, for it would be so wrong to judge my friends that don't believe what I believe. I love my friends, and I am so grateful that even though our beliefs are different these same friends still have enormous love for my life as a person. I can see how much the

EMBRACED

church desires to transform to operate in a non-judging way and instead to embrace each person with consistency, because that's the only way that relationships of truth can be formed, I have learned.

When my plane is descending into Portland, I realize that I'm grateful that I can be open regarding my medical challenges and disabilities and that I receive the care I do in Portland, Oregon, better than any other city that I know. We touch down on the runway and the bouncing inside the plane pushes me to think of *when* I am, Portland time. I think about my doctor's appointment tomorrow and what an honor it is to have the finest healthcare and the finest home environment and the finest public transportation in any city in the US.

As I depart the airport to go to my apartment with another friend that sustains a relationship of truth, I know that this is all a part of the purpose of me being alive on this earth. This is what keeps me moving: faith, hope and charity. Those are the three things that are simple enough to embrace and understand. I am home and I am so blessed.

At my door, there is a bouquet of pink roses, welcoming me home. This is from my doctors and my case-managers. The card says, "From one industry to the next industry, we are proud of that you are living in the light. See you tomorrow!"

JORDAN JANTZ

GOING THE EXTRA MILE

(HELLO, ARE YOU THERE?)

NORTH STAR'S MOMENT LINGERS with me. I don't know what to do with my trophy. It is beautiful! I want to put it out for the whole world to see. I've never before received an award on my integrity or character. And the fact that it has nothing to do with my physical appearance makes me intense about my trophy, for it is **the most** that I have ever accomplished in my history of my life about responding to the hearts of others and not my own.

I've never had the opportunity to make a true difference in the lives of others out from behind private doors! I dance with my trophy. I am glowing that *no money* has been attached to receiving this award, nor did I have to do anything or become someone else for it! I am living the right life in the right way for the first time! Never have I experienced such a high-precipice-moment when all that I have lived for has been enfolded to me. *This feels so good!* I can dance now in the rain when the next storm comes, because of the choices I am making in life today!

But I also know that if I was to display my award in my home, people will focus on it and instead of being happy for me they may feel jealous or competitive, and I'm not talking about my friends outside of the church, but my friends inside of churches including my church.

I have similar feelings, that I am so unworthy to represent the savior. They have actually said, "You don't have a degree," You don't have the experience," "You don't have the knowledge of what the Holy Spirit is even about," "How could you stand up and say all that you do, and people believe what you say is true, when you are still holding on to your identity as a same gender attracted man and you *go to church* with *that identity on you*?" "How can you do that to God and feel comfortable?" "You are really comfortable with letting people know your truth, your life? "You should be ashamed to even sit in church, because of what you came from and what you did to make a living," "We hope you aren't tithing on any of the money you made in the past, because it is dirty, sinful money."

These feelings I have are only because I've been told continuously and repeatedly that I am NOT okay the way that I am. People have said all those things to me repeatedly.

But I am not OK with *them* choosing my value anymore.

I can tell some close friends about my trip in Utah. I can share the trophy with them and discuss my feelings with them over brunch. The truth is, I have my trophy sitting right in front of me with friends, but I can't share it with everyone.

I am sending letters often to Decatur to show consistency to my blood relatives. I feel so hopeful and anxious about what I am doing. I try so very hard to communicate with my biological family which is difficult to do while keeping my heart open. I know that truth and vulnerability are required to give us all a chance.

EMBRACED

Every communication with people in the east feels like nearly panic attack: What in the world am I getting myself into? My Aunt Marion is easy to communicate with, though. She taught me young that there is really only one thing to do: the right thing. So every day I am choosing the right thing and following (exposing, actually) my heart and life, really, for I know most people can't keep secrets to themselves.

I write to my siblings and to my entire community as I prepare for this incredible, once-in- a-lifetime opportunity. I never dreamed I would have the opportunity of going back to my birthplace, I never even dreamed I would *want* to, after all I have been told and remember being exposed to now, after many years of therapy of learning to maintain and heal from heinous early parenting.

This meet-some-birth-family-thing has come about so *fast*, too, through my special friend at church who worked on my life history. I could never have done that. I trusted her to look into my family history.

And boy, did I hit the jackpot.

"I have never heard of a family tree like yours" I hear over and over. My great grandmother Ina Agnes McNear was a Mott, an applesauce Mott. Her family history is in a book in the national library. I had always heard growing up that Johnny Appleseed is all about me. Ina was also a real estate tycoon, too. She went to church, in spite of her challenging careers. She chose to become not only the grandparent but the parent that raised my biological father, who went by the name of Bud, instead of Eldon Roy Bond. Bud's mother also left my father when he was a little boy the same age that I was later released to Grubb family. Through all the genealogy, it was found that my blood relatives trace back to the second century after Jesus!

And if that is not enough, WOW, what an amazing miracle it is that so many of them who remember me are still be *alive* at really advanced ages! That we will have the opportunity to unite at this time in our life gives each one a choice to really make something magical happen in opening the vulnerability of our life to embrace.

I'm not going to allow my disabilities to shame me away from experiencing what promises to be life-transforming. You see, that is the problem with a medical, emotional or mental challenge. People can become very mean and judgmental when you have challenges and disabilities. I've been able to cover it up throughout my whole life with my appearance; the same challenges that I chose to put aside until this time, God is ready to use for his glory. So that's how I am able to follow through with my trip and experience of this journey, as I prepare my suitcases and ready myself for what will be occurring in my life. My disabilities could become the opportunity-moment of God's miracle to communicate love and acceptance.

As the days go by, phone calls are consistent between me and Aunt Marion. I find such peace knowing in my heart I'm doing the right thing no matter how uncomfortable I may feel. I also feel strong negative pressure from many who have said that this is the craziest thing I could ever open my life to. Torn between what others think, I realize that I would not have received the Beacon of Light award just last month if I didn't have the ability to make proper choices. The choice I made to go to Decatur is still the right choice.

Giving grace and mercy to people and circumstances that I do not understand is my best approach to my own spiritual growth. Spiritual growth is the true reason for opening the closet doors in Decatur, Illinois that have been hidden and closed for five decades. So many biological family members appear to be elated for my coming to Decatur, letting me know that I am on their meet-

EMBRACED

important-people "bucket" list. I know that many must have had some kind of information about my life. Maybe I was like ghost story or legend told to children – the little boy that was sold. I know that secrets were exchanged and misrepresentation has been discussed but the truth is the truth and nobody can exchange the truth for a lie. Fifty years seems like enough time that truth can come out fully.

WHERE IS THE LOVE AND WHERE DID IT GO?

9

IN EARLY MAY, I AM deep in preparation, paying bills and coordinating with my doctors.

Then, everything is in order.

Thank God for my social worker. She is able to keep much confusion and disorientation in proper perspective. I have so much to look forward to in this once-in-a-lifetime event. Contemplating the fact that it is even happening, and that I *am* even speaking and conversing as a person who survived abuse but is dedicated to functioning and health, has opened my heart to the question of what it has been like for all of *them* in Decatur to have been kept together while I was taken away. I wonder what they honestly feel about me being the only one that was sent away. Maybe they imagine me as traumatized as I was when I was small, now grown into, you know, the *Rainman*. Or maybe they think of me as someone who is only a family myth. All I know is that I'm going and I will be a better man because of doing the right thing and making contact. It is easier to turn away from the truth than walk towards it, but that is not right. What I am choosing is right.

The evening before I am to embark on my journey to Decatur, I receive a blessing. Comfort and spiritual company is what I need before I board the plane. My social worker and case manager

EMBRACED

already made sure that all details are in order for me to travel. These two women are such a team. I have always wondered if they are partners and they just weren't telling me, because they agree so well in how they care about me so much. What a nice feeling it is to have such meaningful medical attention. I do not take this devotion for granted or what I receive from it: all that I am about to experience in Decatur.

Traveling is *sixteen hours* with layovers and puddle jumpers. If it were not for the Americans with Disabilities Act, I would have never have made it, for travel is way out of my comfort zone. I always have an agent with me throughout my journey. Traveler's Aid in Chicago O'Hare is right on track with me every minute.

Charity and I finally land in Decatur, and I am surprised at the size of the airport! It is the length of a football field and framed by corn and soybeans fields that you can't see from the plane's doorway but you can smell in air immediately the moment they open the door.

It is very late, but the moment I am ready, my hotel driver arrives to pick me up at the curb. He is willing to help me gather some fresh flowers and items that I want to put in my Aunt Marion's arms on her birthday morning.

The hotel is perfect in every way. I picked this hotel for it is the only hotel directly across from Aunt Marion's assisted living center. *Right now I am anticipating seeing Aunt Marion for the first time in decades in just a few hours!!!*

I plan to wake up in the morning and celebrate her astonishing life and heart, just as I promised. I sit on the bed...

AUNT MARION'S BOY SINCE AGE THREE

~ 10 ~

GOODNESS GRACIOUS, am I in Kansas? I open up hotel drapes and it looks like I'm in Oz! I see cornfields and I see fields in all directions. I realize as I get out of bed and take my dog out for her potty dance that this is the very moment that my life is going to change. It is May 22nd and it is *just perfectly beautiful* outside. I couldn't have ordered better weather.

I can't wait to take the birthday gifts to my Aunt Marion and put my fresh purple bouquet into her arms. After my long, exhausting trip, the fresh morning air feels out of the loop in a good way. I call the front desk and they say they've already made arrangements to drive me over. I am so excited to see my dear Aunt Marion! I get Charity all decked out in her purple sparkly outfit to greet her Aunt Marion and pick up my Aunt's favorite pie that I brought with me on the plane from Portland, a pecan pie made from Tiffany's, the finest pie shop in the Pacific Northwest. The driver helps me load into the hotel limo with my pecan pie and gifts and my service dog, Charity.

And right there, sitting on the bench right out in front of the building is my Aunt Marion, just waiting right outside in the bright, shining sun for me to arrive. *Talk about faith!*

EMBRACED

She pops up in her walker and embraces me with tears, saying, *"I can't believe you came all this way to see your Aunt Marion!"*

She grabs my face and looks deep into my eyes, "You are still the little boy I have always known, oh those beautiful brown eyes! So here, let's go on inside and I'll show you where I live."

I thank the driver for helping me with moving the birthday gifts and the pecan pie and of course, Charity. This was the beginning of a true fairy tale. I can't believe I am walking into the adult assisted living center with this angel that has been so kind throughout the history of my life, who actually knew me as a baby and has loved me through my whole adulthood, *win or lose*, and she has never judged my life. *She is private and confidential, for many years she was the only soul I could trust with even a word.*

This makes me even more grateful that time has not changed our bond, even though were apart. We have always had a very special relationship that most nephews only dream of.

In her person, she always reminded me of "I Dream of Jeannie" actress, Barbara Eden. And, Aunt Marion's husband, my Uncle Dale, always reminded me of Major Healy, the person who rescued "Jeannie" from her bottle. As I tell Aunt Marion this, she giggles.

She and I go down the street to see my Uncle Dale at the Memory Care Facility. It is very different because the people inside of his facility have different needs, and I am so glad that my dear little Aunt Marion has all these people to help her husband, my Uncle Dale. She has always loved Uncle Dale and treated him with love and respect and he has treated her with respect, but I can see that he is very confused now.

JORDAN JANTZ

Amazingly, he recognizes me. I did not expect that! I suppose it is because he remembers me as a child and from the past he is able to remember me today, because with Alzheimer's, they say that it is the short term memory that they forget, not the memory of the distant past. They remember you if you were significant to them long ago. We walk with Uncle Dale in the front yard of his memory care facility. We sit in the sun and chat. When he gets tired we return him and Aunt Marion cuddles him in a way that he feels loved.

Soon it is time to mosey down to the dining hall and have lunch with Aunt Marion in her adult assisted living home. I am impressed with the architectural design of this special senior center, and the order with which they operate their dining room. I feel very much at peace with the environment that my aunt is in. I am so happy to sit with her and her girlfriends and have lunch. I see my aunt has laughter in her voice, sharing her memories of me with her girlfriends around the table. They love every story. I hear the stories differently now, though, as I am older and can sense what she might really have been like in her day - someone like my aunt, who was in politics in the state of Illinois and who held many offices in the town of Decatur. I would say she was the first forefront woman in politics in Decatur, Illinois. She talks and talks with barely a breath and shows me so many beautiful memories that we both know on this first day, we will *not* be able to get it all in!

I feel we need to go out for her birthday dinner. She says she would love pizza from Monical's, the Italian Restaurant just across the way. I fetch us a complete soup, salad, pizza and dessert special and we watch the Cubs baseball team in her room. The Cubs have always been her favorite baseball team and she has kept collectible memorabilia of all the Cubs players throughout her years. I knew about that, but it is still eye-opening to me to see her happiness and excitement just watching a baseball sports program. I will cherish this moment of her birthday forever.

EMBRACED

The game ends, and we talk 'til well after midnight. I tell her she needs to get to bed and I do, too.

I say, "We aren't in a rush – we have two weeks to be together, so let's embrace this miracle."

She says, "Jimmy, it is so good to see you in front of my face! You're the only one that would come all the way out here just to visit me for my birthday. I can't believe that you *would come* to me for my birthday and even bring all these gifts, why are you so kind like this?? You've always been so good to me," she cries, and I hide the tears back, too, because I know she is so happy.

She says, "Oh, this is one of the best times of my *old* life! I never thought you would really come see me. Breakfast is early in the morning, so you just call me and we will have breakfast ready for you."

I give her a hug goodnight and Charity and I walk across the street into the hotel. What a blessing from God for only He could bring a moment like this in my life. I look around and I am pinching myself because this is the city I was *born* in. This is where my whole life started! I feel as if God himself is zooming down upon me with binoculars, personally watching every move. *Goosebumps!* What an exciting feeling to experience this reality – this gift - between me and God. I know that His plans for my life were never my plans, and that He has something big in store and really I am just clueless.

I walk into the hotel. I realize that I could *only* walk by faith because anything else would be impossible for me. I walk to my room hiding my tears, from this monumental moment in my life history that I am experiencing. I am realizing that the story of my life was written once but I never thought that I would be faced with it all over *again* after it had been written. Really it is just something out of the twilight zone. This is an experience you just can't even understand when a book is written about you and then you go and

JORDAN JANTZ

re-live what is in the book, talk about *reality*. You can't help but know God is in the center of your life and obviously I'm where I am supposed to be with God.

BROTHERS FOREVER WITH EMBRACED LOVE

11

FIRST THING THE NEXT MORNING, I call my biological brother, Ronnie, to let him know that I have landed just fine and am at the hotel, so that all the family can make plans, excluding my biological mother. I am gently leaving the door open for more of my siblings to connect, asking the Spirit to lead me in the right direction. I am careful to not allow anything damaging to operate in a misleading way. My biological family always knew *something* about me, at least as a figure, but I never knew anything about them. I am out of my safety and comfort zone meeting all of them for the first time.

I then talk with my Aunt Marion. She is on my side in all of my decisions to open to my siblings. We talk through my feelings during breakfast and an early lunch.

Soon, my biological sister, Teresa, picks me up. She rises out of the car and gives me a hug. We talk for a moment about the Decatur weather.

When we are in the car, she tells me that this kind of meeting is definitely a bucket list event for her. She has always heard about me, throughout her whole life.

She says, "People always wondered what happened to you, if you were alive or what," and she smiles.

She tells me that she had been told that my biological mother was very abusive to me, and that our dad would take me away from the biological mother all the time, and Teresa heard about all the stuff I had to live through, but Teresa didn't *know* everything, Teresa was just *told* that she had a brother that had been sold.

I was able to be calm because of therapy. My therapist continues to work with me today through deep trauma of heinous child abuse.

As we are driving, she is sharing about what she remembers or had been told about my life, and it makes me realize that I must have been someone special to have been discussed so much after being sold, so I must have some form of value with my biological sister. I choose to value her and respect her for who she is and that is my biological sister. I honor what God is opening up in my life.

Although soon, I am shaking inside with complete fear of the reality she is discussing. I also wonder if she *knows* what I *know* and if she experienced or survived similar events. I was in enormous fear that she would even bring it up and I wouldn't know what to say because I only talk about it to my therapist. I did learn with my therapist that I'm able to help somebody that has been abused because I can talk about the reality of abuse with another person who has experienced the same thing. That's the only reason why the first book was published about my life, because of the reality *that I'm not the only one in the world that is sold or put up*. Child trafficking happens all over the world and is the number one biggest money underground activity taking place today, and also not talked about. Back in the fifties it wasn't called Child Trafficking, it was call Black Market Babies, and it happens when parents sell their children or gave them away for benefits in the exchange of their child. The short drive to the restaurant is *surreal*.

EMBRACED

We pull in the parking lot. I observe that my brother, Ronnie, and his wife picked a beautiful restaurant. Teresa and I are escorted to our table. The restaurant has a peaceful Italian ambiance, lit with red candles.

When I see my brother sitting at the table with his family, I know him immediately. When our eyes meet for the first time, I realize that we have the same eyes, and other physical similarities and characteristics. When he gets up and walks towards me and gives me a hug, I can see his body immediately as like my own. His wife and kids come forward and give a hug. My adrenalin is about ready to make me pass out.

Ronnie set all this up. He really has a lot of dignity to step up to the plate like this. I respect people like my brother, for he has the ability to follow through with plans and that speaks about his being able to follow-through with people and commitments. In my past, I only had the ability to follow through with pleasing others and being a protégé for the benefit of some other person's life. It is so refreshing to see this great ability to commit and follow through in my brother, Ronnie.

I am seated between my brother, Ronnie, and my sister, Teresa. I understand that other siblings through my father had other obligations. Ronnie's countenance is calm as he asks everyone at the table what they would like to order, and he says that we should not worry about what it costs; we may order what we want. I can tell that it is a strain somehow for family to get together for this event and it would be difficult for conversation about that to continue. I can't quite explain that.

Our food comes and it is beautiful. I notice more characteristics in Ronnie that are like me and I am just speechless. Even the way that he uses his knife and fork with the pizza. I also know right off the bat from experiences of my past that this man sitting next to me is definitely a hipster and knows what is going on in the world, even though we are in a very little small town in the middle of corn fields and soybeans. I am astonished at Ronnie's etiquette and I know from many people that I have encountered that he is sincere. I can read him and I know he is being real, not plastic fantastic, but totally true blue.

His wife, Lisa, also makes an instant connection to me. We just click from the start. I don't know how to explain it, but I guess it is just a God thing, because she can also read me like a book and I know I can trust her. That understanding is the safest thing at the table for me to hold on to. So, while eating dinner that is what I held.

I open up and ask, "So, what have you all been doing since Dad passed away? And what do you do now that you are parents with children graduating from high school? That is a big transformation."

"Well," Lisa, my sister-in-law says, "I work a lot at church and I also work as a nurse. Your brother, Ronnie, works in the medical field, also. We keep our two kids pretty busy: Zach is just finishing high school and received the Prom King crown, and Hannah is finishing her last year at Milliken University in Decatur."

Those two, sitting right there, are beaming with light. They are as excited about a meeting their father's brother as I am to meet them.

Teresa says, "I show exotic chickens at chicken shows." I know she has children but she came to this dinner with just her husband. No one mentions anything about her children so I don't say anything. Kevin is not at this dinner and he is not mentioned.

I ask "Do you all get together for events often? And what about the rest of the family?"

EMBRACED

It turns out that this is one of the worst things anyone could have said. I sure put my foot in my mouth. I am given to understand that *this* dinner is the first time that the family has even seen one another since the death of their mother. I didn't know that so I really feel like I turned on a light bulb that never wanted to be turned on.

Partially to help recover the conversation, I start to embrace my niece, Hannah, and nephew, Zach, by learning more about the two of them. As they speak I learn how much love they have been given. That is an indication of what kind of father my brother is and what kind of mother my brother's wife is. I love hearing the two children call me 'Uncle Jimmy.' I have never been called uncle before in my lifetime. I have never had this embracement from any man before, and to see my brother's concern and to see his wife reach out to show me that she cares… it brings me an unexpected and indescribable feeling.

I went on this dinner not expecting, but I can tell that my brother is going to make the most our time together. He has a purpose and a reason and he is going to open his heart for real. I know while I am sitting here at the table that he and I have much in common. Even the tone of his voice matches mine. Our choices of words are also so exact. I can tell that he also has had to learn to use particular, carefully chosen words when he communicates with people, because of the clarity that he and his wife practice with one another.

My sister, Teresa, and I try to embrace but I can tell it is very hard for her. I know it is strange that the other brother, Kevin, has not been seen by either sibling since the funeral of their mother. This time, I don't bring it up. I *want* this to be my Wizard of Oz story – *there is no place like home* – and it can't be if I open a can of worms by asking questions, even though anybody that was removed from their family and sold at the age of five would want to ask some questions. My fear of the table blowing up with the pizza on it says it is too chancy. I feel that I will have other opportunities ahead to find out my family's reality, more peacefully and slowly.

And for *real* we are not in Kansas, we are in Illinois; same crops, different state. I can tell there is turbulence in the air that might be bumpy if proper words are not chosen, and offenses could be made and taken wrongly if the words are not measured again before spoken out loud. This is how sensitive it is, the first evening we all meet.

I must respect the fact that my brother, Ronnie, and my sister, Teresa, decided to come together for the first time since their mother had passed away, all in order to make me feel comfortable as their brother. I honor that. I can see that it wasn't an easy decision to make.

After dinner, my nephew and my brother drop me off at the hotel. My brother says he will call me in the morning, before work. He says he hopes that I enjoyed the family gathering together this evening. I tell him thank you, and I look forward to talking to him in the morning. I notice I am wearing a black shirt and he's wearing a black shirt. I'm wearing nice jeans; he's wearing nice jeans. I'm wearing nice black shoes and he's wearing nice black shoes. We both have an olive complexion and same eyes and lips, and our voices are very much the same in our tones. It all blows me away to just to hear him talk.

I go into the room and pick up Charity off the bed and take her outside to go potty.

Staring up at the stars, I just say right out loud, "LORD is this for REAL?

I wail, "Lord, I know you see me. *What* do you have planned!??"

EMBRACED

"I am in my fifties, Lord, and I am challenged here on *what* you would want me to do! You know my anxiety levels and you know my sleeping patterns and my emotions throughout my life so I need to know: *what do I DO?*"

And that is my question, right out in the open sky. If it is an emergency, all I'd have to do is call my doctors, because I have a strong support system. That eases everything.

I get into bed and am out immediately out from mental overload.

WASHING THE FEET OF THOSE YOU LOVE

~12~

IT IS MY THIRD MORNING in Decatur. The phone rings, and I know it is Aunt Marion calling to give me my morning wake up call, which is the best way to wake up in Decatur, Illinois.

I hear Aunt Marion's happy voice saying, "Good morning, Jimmy, Jimmy, are you going to come over and tell me how it went with your biological family?? I already ordered you a Denver omelet, so make sure you come over, and make sure you bring Charity, also, and her food, so you can spend the day. I can't wait to hear what your biological family was like for you! such a big event after all these years. Your Aunt Marion was so worried all night long, because I knew you were just finding out things for the first time! I wanted you to call me when you got in, but I didn't hear from you, so I stayed up worrying, whether or not things were okay with you and your family! So come on over. I've got breakfast together, and let's talk about how it went!"

So I jump out of bed and throw myself together and walk out of my hotel room with Charity to go P-O-T-T-Y and prepare to feed her and say good morning to the wonderful people in this environment in this beautiful little country town called Decatur. As we finish up Charity's potty dance in the middle of the soybean and corn fields surrounding us, we both know this is going to be a beautiful, beautiful day with Aunt Marion.

EMBRACED

As I am just walking across the street to Aunt Marion's Adult Assisted Living Center, I realize the majority of the people here do not wear color, and I have a lot of color on me. So, I go back again into my room. I put on a pair of "proper" jeans and a classic black t-shirt and a classic pair of black shoes. I also feel I need to take Charity's lovely outfit off of her and choose something more demure because it is uncomfortable to be out of place in Decatur. I gather together the bag of Charity's goodies (because we are likely stay the whole day again talking with my Aunt Marion) as we watch Golden Girls and all of the oldies-but-goodies on the Hallmark Channel on her TV. Unfortunately, I didn't pack finger nail polish remover so Charity's nails are going to have to stay sparkly pink this whole trip. Thinking about that, I have an idea…

At Aunt Marion's breakfast spread with Charity, Aunt Marion is dressed in her pretty pink outfit that matches Charity's nails, and she says she just *loves* the color of Charity's nails.

I say, "Well, I can paint your nails the same color. Or even red. We could do red *or* pink, whatever you want!"

Aunt Marion says, "First, go ahead and let's have you eat your breakfast while it is warm." We say our morning breakfast prayer and I eat the fresh, healthy food Aunt Marion has arranged for me.

Then I say, "Now, I'm going to give you a manicure and a pedicure and tell you all about dinner last night with my brother and my sister!"

She says, "Jimmy, did they all show up?

I say, "No, and it was kind of different because actually they hadn't come together for anything since their mother passed away a few years ago and, Aunt Marion, I could tell that was unresolved and so I didn't want to pry."

JORDAN JANTZ

She asks, "Are you going to be getting together with them again, Jimmy?"

I answer carefully between bites, "They did not make commitments. This was our first meeting and I don't know if they like me, or what. I don't know if they want anything to do with me. This really is the hardest thing in the world but at least I'm finding out the truth, that my dad did have other biological children besides me. And Aunt Marion, I was always told growing up that I was born illegitimate and that my mom and dad did not get married, but they *did* get married on Valentine's Day of 1959. Then I was born December 2nd of that same year, so that means I was conceived on Valentine's Day so that makes me a real Valentine Baby!"

I wrap up the breakfast tray and wash up the food area. I grab the mani-pedi case and get set to give her the full works, with all the bells and whistles. I begin with massage and moisturizing. There is no reason at all to rush this. As I am doing this, I recall a moment when I was very young, when "Gram" -Ina McNear- had called me *her valentine baby* and this makes me grin, to really understand that, finally. Then I smile again, because Valentine's Day really has always been my favorite holiday. I explain to Aunt Marion, "Now to know that I really am Gram's Valentine Baby because I was conceived on that day makes me elated today. And, it is clear from other things spoken last night that there are uncles out there, too, and aunts and cousins. Oh, Aunt Marion, this is so exciting."

I gloss her toenails with a beautiful watermelon color and say, "Thank you so much for staying in my life and not ever abandoning me, Aunt Marion! I don't know if my biological family will stay in my life or not, but at least I know that *God knows* my heart and I am giving everything I can to do what is right and to be the man that my biological dad would have wanted me to be to the rest of my brothers and sisters. No matter what their response is after

EMBRACED

this point, I know I am doing what my biological dad would have wanted me to do in the way that I am responding. That is something he would honor in my life today, if he were alive."

Aunt Marion agrees with that and says, "Jimmy, you are doing the right thing. That's what matters."

I am doing her fingernails to match her toenails, and add a high clear gloss on the top.

I say, "I'm reaching out to them, Aunt Marion, and also respecting my biological family whether or not they choose to accept and respect the truth of the choices that were made for me without my consent. Maybe then they will realize that child trafficking has been around for thousands of years and really, they have the ultimate choice of whether to accept or reject me," Aunt Marion is taking it all in with me.

I say, "It takes my breath away because I have never been in control of what someone else chooses to feel or respond to me."

She says, "I understand you, Jimmy. That is true."

She is so happy to see her beautiful nails and toenails popping out as they do. "Oh Jimmy, would you believe this is the first time in my life that I have ever *received* a pedicure or a manicure, though I gave them to so many others all throughout my career. This is such a joy to me, Jimmy," says the angel who was once Decatur's leading beautician.

She can't thank me enough. She asks questions that I don't know how to respond to, because of not knowing my biological family the way that I know my aunt. My aunt has been in my life since diapers. I am transparent with this precious aunt for she is so non-judgmental that the truth is safe.

She says again, "Jimmy, we all have done things. I would die if my mother or father ever knew that I did some things. Don't ever think that you have done anything that Aunt Marion would be angry at you for. I've known you longer than anyone and <u>I know you</u>, Jimmy. Remember this. Always remember that you can't do anything that will turn me away from loving you."

As she says this again, I think, *how many children have never heard anything like this in their lives*? How many people go through their whole life never hearing this Godly reality about real love that comes from a committed family relationship? My aunt has broken the mold on what it means to be an aunt.

So, we open up our hearts to each other emotionally. She's crying and I'm in tears, for she knows what I survived as a child, never knowing who my mother really was, because I called everyone mama. Even while my dad was married to my mother my dad had another girlfriend, Carrie, that I called mother. Carrie's mother, also, I called mama, as she was very kind and very good to me and greeted me with happiness and always would make sure that I was safe and away from my biological mom for as long as she could. My dad eventually did end up marrying Carrie. Carrie was so kind to me and good to me.

So many memories are Polaroid pictures for me because abuse is the darkest experience for children to be exposed to, and when a kind act is given to such a child, lights appear for the first time. I experienced that with my biological father's girlfriend, Carrie, who became his wife during my toddler years when my dad would take me to safety from the heinous abuse he found happening. He would arrive at where I was staying until I would be picked up and taken to the next place, and a next place. There never was an end to next places. My dad would track me, trying to find where I'd been left at and then park with me at Ina McNear's home in the car with the doors locked and I would sleep with my dad all night long.

EMBRACED

Sometimes, my great grandmother would come out to the car and get me and take me in and feed me and my dad would stay in the car asleep. Little memories like this are valuable to me. I loved the mandarin oranges that Ina McNear would open up in the can and put in a bowl for me to eat. I learned so much of smells and tastes that I never dreamed existed. To this day, I still have an eating challenge with certain foods, but mandarin oranges are like rose petals from heaven.

My Aunt Marion and I talk over how what happened to me as a child during my formative years which affects my many emotional and mental challenges that have been put upon my life to this day. I was without precious committed family for most of my life. Aunt Marion wants me to take this opportunity while I am in Decatur to really get to know my biological family. She says she does not want me to grow old by myself.

With her, I open to explain that I cannot judge the fact that my biological siblings do not communicate. I also cannot expect kindness or love or respect or integrity just because they are my biological family. I realize that I do not know what they went through as children, they have not shared their personal life with me, but I do realize they know all about my infant years. They were told how hard my life was from birth to five years old, and they knew that my biological mother extorted money repeatedly, wanting more and more money to be able "release" her five-year-old son and sell him. This all happened, though it was illegal, and that's why the courts had to intervene when I was age seven. I had to come back to Decatur for a legal adoption.

My siblings knew about these things but none of this is ever talked about or even mentioned directly. It is all memories to them; I have been "discussed" since I had been removed as a child from the presence of aunts, uncles, brothers and sisters, and other family members. I was someone that had just disappeared and many never really knew exactly if I was alive or if I had died. They didn't know what had ever happened because it was never mentioned on an open level though everybody recalled exact moments of my years and they certainly recalled me as my biological dad's son. In fact, Aunt Marion knew that my biological dad was very proud of me and would take me to the bars with him. I would sit out in the car and wait for him and he would bring people out to the car to meet me. He was so proud to show people his son. He would also go drinking to get away from the reality of the abusive acts that left me hospitalized. He was helping me by hiding me but couldn't hide me enough.

Then, Aunt Marion asks me if she could share Memorial Day *with* my biological siblings and I say, "I would not have it any other way." Her manicure and pedicure are done and she sits like a white dove on a perch, waiting to dry.

Feeling the moment, I call my brother Ronnie to ask him about Memorial Day. He states that he has taught his two children to always remember the family that has passed away and that they usually go together and put flowers on the graves of the people in the family. He and his family are looking forward to celebrating this very special Memorial Day with me and, after going to our particular family graves and seeing the historic graveyards of Decatur, he hopes to take me out to a special dinner. If I agree, he would be happy to pick me up on Memorial Day morning.

I ask, "And, Aunt Marion will be with me?..."

He says, "I already planned to include her this holiday."

All I can say is, "Right on! You are so <u>on it</u> and I love it. I like the way you plan your events, Ronnie. I'm sticking with you. I can tell that already after just these first days of meeting you. I like to know where I am going and what I am doing, and you communicate that way. So Aunt Marion and I look forward to

EMBRACED

tomorrow, celebrating with you and Lisa and the kids. See ya at 9 am after breakfast!" We say our goodbyes.

This is perfect!

Aunt Marion prompts, "We're going *where* tomorrow?"

I say, "*We* are going to put flowers on the graves for *all* the sides of the family at the graveyards in Decatur, and we'll visit your future grave plot, too, and everything! We'll all be together!"

She says, "Well that will be nice! And how nice of your brother to invite me!" she smiles and looks down again and adds, "I am going to look *really nice* with my nails and hair all finished, Jimmy, thank you again, *so much*, for making your Aunt Marion look *so* pretty. I wish you *lived* here. There are things that Aunt Marion just can't do any more. But wait 'til you meet your cousins again, Mark and Robin. They help me so much! They are always there when I need them. You know they come every weekend."

We go downstairs for the meal with it seems like *everyone* in the building. We share a nice brunch with her friends and enjoy the hospitality of Aunt Marion's beautiful assisted living facility.

That night she and I watch episodes of the Golden Girls and we laugh our heads off. We stay up past midnight again and she says, "You've only been here two nights and each night you've been up past midnight. You're not going to make it the two weeks!"

I am so happy just to see how alert her memory is. She is so amazing and so *together* and the fact that she can get her little self all around the way she can, this is a gift. She asks me if I would let Charity, who is curled up with her on her lap, actually spend the night with her. Aunt Marion says that she would love to take her out to go potty, too. I say that Charity doesn't normally like to spend the night with other people, but I am sure that Charity would like to spend the night with Aunt Marion.

It is well after midnight as I walk across the street to the hotel, leaving Charity with Aunt Marion, hoping all will be wonderful.

As I get in my room, I see that there are messages from my brother, Ronnie (He *did* call, just like he promised! But we had talked at Aunt Marion's, instead.) but not from Kevin or Teresa or any of the other members of the family. I can see that a big issue, a big lump, is swept under the carpet with the passing of their mother or maybe even the passing of our father years before that, but I am not about to ask about it. I just read the expressions from everyone. The expressions communicate to me that really these people are getting together just for me and that they do not get together just because it is a holiday or family event that is shared.

This touches my heart but also makes me sad to think that my own flesh and blood siblings are not able to talk. This is something that I have to pray about, when I am less tired. I do know that I am not about to allow anyone to interrupt God's plans, for His plans for my life are not the plans that I set for my life, His plans are greater than my plans can be or will be. This is something that I learned from the father who raised me.

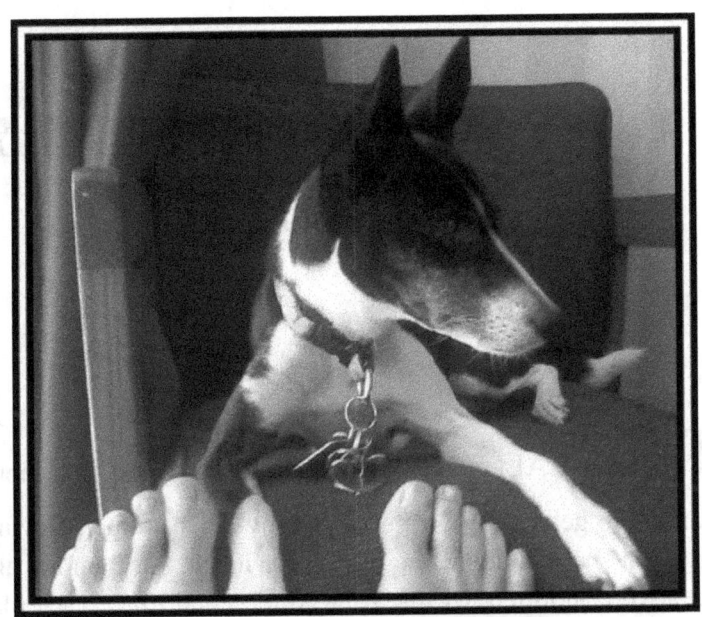

Look at all our beautiful nails!

JORDAN JANTZ

WHY WAS I THE ONLY ONE SOLD?

13

TERESA CALLS ME UP FIRST THING the next morning, wanting to get together with me and my other brother, Kevin. She says that she will be picking me up for lunch, but I am not able to get a word in to tell her that Aunt Marion and I had made plans. I call Aunt Marion up quickly and Aunt Marion says she would so happy to babysit Charity the whole day and that she *wants* me to go and enjoy every bit of meeting the rest of my biological family, as much as I can. Bless Aunt Marion for her kindness!

So I get ready to meet my sister at 10 am to go to her house for a barbeque lunch. I know this will be a long car ride, about forty minutes. That will sure give us time to talk.

In the car, she lets me know how *much* this means to have the day with me, as spending a day with me has long been part of her bucket list. She takes me to her home. My biological brother, Kevin, shows up. Kevin brings with him his pre-teen daughter and introduces her to me. I know that my sister Teresa also has children but they do not emerge from their rooms.

We visit and walk mostly outside in the backyard. I am so impressed by all her exotic chickens. They are very beautiful, even stunning. Her street is pretty with no sidewalks, just lots of trees and

EMBRACED

the smell of country. I sit between my sister and my brother at the table to talk. It is just so nice to have this opportunity. However, I also see that this is something different that I can't quite understand, yet. Kevin and Teresa explain how *together* they are, and I understand and respect that. I ask a few questions because I'm not sure who is who among the faces and voices that I remember as a child.

The person that I do remember from my time in my biological mother's house was the little girl who loved me and cared for me more than any of the others, my sister who slid the mandarin orange slices and other food to me through the space beneath the closet door to the closet in where I was kept most of the time. Teresa is *younger* than I am, so she couldn't be that little girl, so I ask Teresa if she knows.

It turns out that Teresa does know. That little girl – now a woman – was never able to separate from our biological mother, and so she still lives with my biological mother and is to this day challenged from her upbringing. That little girl does remember me and my biological father, but she is not in fact the daughter of *my* biological father. She is the child of my biological mother and some other man that my biological mother knew before she married my biological father. This all came to light in 2006 when this girl asked for a memento to remember my father's kindness to her after my biological father's death, but it was determined that our father was not *her* father and so she did not receive any mementos of my biological father.

I think about this for a moment and I don't know how to feel. Growing up, I had been told that my parents were unmarried. I had had only a short period of time to think about the marriage that did happen, since the day my special church detective in the Relief Society showed me the proof. When I saw that, right away I wondered if the reason that my biological father had legally married my mother, a single mother already, was *because* of that little girl who did not have a father present. So how would my biological father feel about keeping mementos *away* from this person who knew him as perhaps the only kind man of her childhood and adulthood? I can't think of any way to phrase that kind of idea to my sister and my brother.

Then, there at the table on the patio, they give me what I have always wished for: pictures of my father. Teresa and Kevin could have been selfish but they are not. I now have pictures of my biological father and everyone tells me that we look so alike; we could have been twins at birth. I am overjoyed to have his childhood pictures!

My sister and my brother also give me another thing from my biological father that is very special: his coat. I remember he wore it a lot. She has had it dry cleaned for me to be able to take something of his back to Portland, Oregon, with me, forever, to keep me near my father.

What a shock it is to put the coat on for a moment and mentally register the fact that his upper body was truly me-to-a-T: collar size, sleeve size, waist size, we are a perfect match. I have, though, been told that he was a bit shorter than me. I have very long legs and I have very long arms and now I realize why I'm the only one that has these long arms and legs, and still I'm grateful because I would not have been able to have done the professional modeling and fashion runway work *successfully* without these inborn-attributes that were handed down to me from my parents, and obviously so much from my father, because I look just like him. I just wonder if his personality was like mine. I wish that somebody will feel comfortable during my stay in Decatur to express desire to belong to me as real family, just as I so truly fit into my father's coat. It is a dream, but my dreams seem to become broken or removed, so, no, I will have no expectations from anyone in this

EMBRACED

journey here in Decatur. Still, I can literally feel the shape of my father in this coat, and that it is my *own* shape.

There are so many things that my sister talks about that I don't know how to accept, but to accept her. She tells me that she is able to hear spirits and that she is something called a Reiki master, and that in the clouds there have been signs that tell my sister that I must return to the family to heal by forgiving our father. I treat all that she shares with me with deep respect though I am unable to really comprehend it then or since. Kevin is mostly quiet.

My sister's husband is very kind. When he understands that I like pepperoncinis, he runs out to the local grocery to get me some to go with my hamburger. When that happens, I just think it is the kindest thing that I have experienced in Decatur, and I think, *This man isn't my biological relative, but he's married to my sister and he is treating me so kindly like this. I hope this is reality and I'm not dreaming because I am used to crass kindness that isn't real but is actually plastic fantastic from the industry that I survived. I'm retired from magazine ads and hard core weekends of catwalks and being emptied of the Spirit afterwards. So I hope this is not going to be a let-down of any sort because I am so afraid of them asking me what I did for a living in my life. I am all about the truth, but do these people deserve to know* how *I managed my challenges to become abilities so that I could live? I don't know if they have the ability to embrace what it is like to be a protégé in someone's pocket. I'm afraid to just open up with them when they are not opening up with me or with each other. I realize that they cannot communicate with one another, so why would I communicate such deep intimate realities of the history I have had to live?* And that's what I'm thinking while we continue to chat. The preparations and smell of barbeque fit so perfectly into the neighborhood, between the houses and corn rows.

JORDAN JANTZ

After eating Teresa invites me to take a walk in the neighborhood. I wonder if I am looking for the reoccurring dream, but I realize that during this lunch with my sister, Teresa, and my brother, Kevin, I could not feel what I was hoping for. In my dream, Charity and I walked down the cookie cutter houses and no one talked to us. Is that what is happening here? I can't understand why my spirit feels so shut down, even as I walk between the old homes with character that look like actual pictures, cut out and popped up for me.

It is a treat and yet it seems as though my presence is challenging for Teresa and Kevin, and that they both are very connected to each other without room for me. They share with me about how hard their lives were but how easy others' lives were, because of other members in the family. They have gone on and live their own lives now because of actions that were inappropriately done. This is what they communicated and how *they* felt about their biological mom and our biological father. I know that a lot was unsaid but they said enough to give their reasons why life is the way it is, for them, as brother and sister, and I know that I embraced them because I felt that I may not be ever see them again, because I did not show approval of what I was experiencing about the dissention between my siblings.

I didn't want to show approval for that kind of thing. I want to talk about embracing, forgiving love. From where they are, I realize I really am just a bucket list opportunity to see our biological father's first born son. I felt like an animal in the humane society because there was no communication from the heart. All the communication was about achievements. I am very familiar with achievements. They didn't know I am so grateful to be in the Midwest cornfields, where *nobody* would even know anything about me or anything about what I had become and what I had developed in my work in the fashion industry.

EMBRACED

Teresa says, "I was so amazed to hear the story that you were returning to Decatur to visit with your Aunt Marion."

I say, "Oh, it is so much more than that! This is a birthday celebration of her life. My Aunt Marion saved me. Don't you know she saved me? What realities do you know about my life, Teresa?"

She says, "I just know you were sold. That's all I know. And that your mom was really crazy, that's what my mom told me. And, that my mom would help take care of you at times."

I say, "That's 100% true. I remember her." Teresa looks doubtful so I continue, "She reminded me of *that girl* with the hairstyle like the lady on Bewitched, and she was very short and petite."

Teresa's face shows a little shock, "*YOU DO* remember my mom don't you! How can you remember that?"

I say, "When you are very small and someone is kind to you, and hands you a mandarin orange that is so cold and fresh, you remember those hands that gave you something that wasn't slid under the door, but given straight to you with love. I remember your mom."

Teresa responds, "That's what Dad said. He said Mom took care of Jimmy a lot, when he could find Jimmy. And Dad would get upset."

I say, "Yes, tomorrow on Memorial Day I will see the grave of our father and great grandmother. I am so humbled to have this experience!"

Teresa says, "You are a wonderful nephew to do those things for your Aunt Marion. I have never had anyone celebrate my birthday that way. I hope you remember this all, and especially that

I have felt the spirits say that your return is necessary for you. Please, please, I beseech you, please promise me that this is not the last time I will see you, and that you will come back again to Decatur."

I look into her eyes and respond, "I promise you, I will return." I embrace both her and Kevin with a hug.

I say, "It means so much to have you, Kevin and Ronnie, in my life."

She says, "Well, we are not all able to rise above all things. Ronnie did some terrible things regarding our father and he still hasn't made them right."

The ride back is quiet, as it would be after great moments. Really, though, I feel that I am causing difficulty for her just by being there. I am glad to let her have more relief when I get out of the car because I am so ready to take the back seat when it comes to Kevin and Teresa or anybody with this type of mentality. I will take the back seat if it is going to make the Bonds a happier, reunited family, because that is what it is all about for me, reuniting people together. That is my purpose in life. I guess that is part of my mission of finding my family and maybe bringing them all back together. Maybe that is what Jesus would have me do through this experience that he is guiding me through.

I know I do not have to understand to love her.

Late that night, I am struggling to find the energy to move, when my father's coat beckons to me.

I put it on and look in the hotel's mirror. I'm shocked. For a moment I see my father. It is not to meet him, just to feel him. I am given understanding that I am very much part of this man's life, then and always. This knowledge comes through the Spirit into my

EMBRACED

bones, changing me forever. It eases my heart as tears fall down my face and I just start weeping as if he is in the room with me, seeing me try on his coat. He would have been so proud that his son knows how to wear fashion, I think to myself. The way I sport the coat, he would have just probably been so happy to know that I overcame the criminal activities that I had been exposed to and from which he had rescued me so often. I know he would have been smiling if he could have just seen me in his coat. I must say, it is very attractive.

JORDAN JANTZ

A MAGICAL MEMORIAL DAY WITH A GIFT OF LOVE

14

THE MORNING SUNLIGHT IS BRIGHT when I get a phone call from Aunt Marion, "Good morning, Sugar! I have breakfast all ready and your sweet Charity is ready to see you! Are you ready to celebrate Memorial Day? I'm dressing up in my patriotic outfit and I'm looking forward to seeing your brother who is so nice to you and your sister-in-law. I just like the fact they've reached out to you and have done the right thing. You know he always was a good kid, Jimmy. We're going to have a beautiful day. We've got to go across the street and get flowers."

With the heat rising fast, I am headed toward Aunt Marion's home before seven.

Aunt Marion is decked out like *royalty* in her red, white and blue holiday outfit, with beautiful twinkling nails highlighting her chic dress, and she is sitting right outside the assisted living home with a little Memorial Day American flag in her hand. She could teach the sun how to shine!

Charity is right in her lap, communicating to me that last night was one of the best night's sleep she has had in a long time. I can tell that Charity had gotten right up underneath the covers and

EMBRACED

snuggled my little Aunt Marion just the way Aunt Marion's own dogs used to do, when Aunt Marion said, "She made me feel that she needed me."

I say, "She *does* need you, Aunt Marion, that's why she's so at peace right now. You make her feel at peace."

She says, "I'm glad I can make someone feel at peace today, on Memorial Day."

After breakfast (with flag-ribbons on the tables) we go back out to the carport area, which is an outdoor flower shop today. I purchase the prettiest, the red sparkly roses with hearts, while she counts up the graves to visit. I pile the bouquets on her lap in the sun. Charity is coming with us today, and I can tell that she is excited.

My brother, Ronnie, and his wife, Lisa, and his son, Zach, pull up in their car to pick up Aunt Marion and me. Ronnie sees the bouquets of flowers and everything that Aunt Marion and I got to put on the family graves *–all* the graves that we could think of, that are related to Aunt Marion *and* also the family that I was sold to. Ronnie is so classy about this. He takes Aunt Marion and opens up the door for her and lets her in the *front seat of honor.* As he shuts the door, he tells her how pretty she is.

My sister-in-law sits in the backseat on the hump of the car and Zach and I sat on the sides. It is so wonderful being squeezed in with family! We go for a drive to celebrate this beautiful day together, that each of us took out of our lives to spend with one another and to remember people that have touched our life in a positive way. To see my brother respect that makes me realize how much he must value where he is today in his life, which I can't help but compare to my experience of Kevin and Teresa. I think I share more of the character of my brother, Ronnie, than I do of the other siblings in almost every aspect.

JORDAN JANTZ

I can see that Kevin and Teresa had not communicated with Ronnie, and that makes me realize that the family has serious communication challenges. I think first, right off the bat, how grateful I am to have therapy. Because of therapy, I'm able to learn to live with my challenges instead of run from them, so I am feeling at this moment that somehow I am the lucky one after all, to the degree that it is better to be lonely and empty than it is to be in a room filled with people that know you but can't embrace you, if that makes sense.

That *push-away* is not what Ronnie is about. And I am not that kind of a person. I don't believe that this characteristic is in the genes of my family but instead that it is a choice. I see the *choice* that Teresa and Kevin and other family members choose to disassociate about *whether* they have family. We all have a choice to share love and come together or to distance ourselves from the reality and the truth and live a life that is filled with plastic fantastic *impressions* of having it all together. That is a false contentment.

I know Ronnie has figured this out. He makes his own destiny and he achieves it. He's as punctual as I am. *It has got to be done right, obviously*, and I like that about him. I'm noticing so many characteristics that are similar between us, but I don't want to embarrass myself by letting anyone know that I see characteristics inside myself in him. It makes my adrenalin heightened that I feel this, because I've never met anyone like him. We even sound the same when listening from in another room. Aunt Marion told me that.

We are all cozy in the car and headed the cemetery, when we decide that we should probably stop and eat something first. Soon, I'm helping my aunt out of the car while Ronnie gets her walker for her from the trunk.

EMBRACED

I'm just so proud of Ronnie I'm beaming and then he says, "Order whatever you guys want" and Aunt Marion is just touched by his kindness.

Aunt Marion whispers to me, "You can tell he's proud of you."

And I say, "Well, I'm proud of him!"

Aunt Marion has a wonderful chicken pot pie and salad I choose the same. It is really nice to sit next to my sister-in-law while Ronnie sits next to my aunt and carries on a conversation. My nephew, Zach, is quite intelligent and I enjoy hearing my nephew talk about graduating from high school, and how cool it is to find out *that Dad had a brother that had been missing.*

Zach says, "That's like something you read in a book or hear in a movie." And, "I'm so glad we found you, Uncle Jimmy." I am very impressed to hear such a person who is a biological relative speak with such kindness. I can tell that my nephew was raised to be very polite to people and that speaks a lot about my brother and my sister-in-law.

This encourages me that my siblings are not all plastic fantastic and that is a relief, after my experience of feeling so empty after Teresa dropped me off when I knew I was just an "event" on a "bucket list" to her and to Kevin. I suppose I will be nothing but a memory, because I can read between the lines on people's integrity and see what people say and if it is followed by actions. It felt so painful in the car with Teresa, kind of like the feelings from the lady who gave life to me. To Teresa, I am only worth what she can get from me or out of me.

Sitting at the table, I realize that I have just got to let these emotions go, because I am not of value to Teresa and Kevin. I have to *face this as reality.* How must it feel for my brother, Ronnie, to *live* near this and what is it like for my niece and nephew and sister-in-law? I know I've got to let this go, these feelings from Teresa and Kevin.

I want to focus on this beautiful encounter. While we are sitting there eating we hear the Memorial Day Parade go by. Aunt Marion starts talking about it and remembering her days when she used to come down and watch the parade, and how special it is that it is still going on. We hear about my nephew's plans to attend the community college right after high school. Aunt Marion is very happy to get out of the adult assisted living and we are all were excited to go and put our flowers down on the graves. I'm excited to just *see* my biological family's graves.

When we finish, Ronnie helps Aunt Marion, which she thinks is so polite, and which really is. We all proceed to the cemetery to see the graves of my biological great grandmother, Ina Agnes McNear, and my biological father, Eldon Roy Bond. These graves are in a beautiful cemetery called The Garden of Memories of the Macon County Cemetery in Decatur, Illinois.

Next thing I know, I am looking at my own father's grave, feeling him so close as we were when we slept in the car together. I feel nothing of darkness, only of light and truth.

Then, Ronnie asks me if I would be *open* to something. I say, *what*?

He says, "Well, there I something I want to tell you. It is only right to tell you this. You see, this is what Dad would want. Dad would want you to be buried next to him, to have the plot right next to him. He wanted that if we ever found you, to ask you to please take this plot next to Dad. I know it might be hard to understand, but just because he let you go, doesn't mean that he didn't regret what he felt he had to do. So, all along the years these two plots were saved next to Gram, one for Dad, and the other one

EMBRACED

for you, if you would accept, if we could find you, and ask you, and tell you that Dad wished so much for that."

My face is covered by tears. I tell him I'll have to think about it. I am thinking that I am blown over by this incredible gift, a gift that no one could ever give but it is happening. And I am thinking about how kind my brother is, to pass this to me this way. His wife Lisa is nearby and she is just like a sister, very protective and I like that, because that makes me realize that I can trust her. I am thinking that I have even more than I ever thought I did. The rest of the family is just missing out, but that will not be my choice at all.

The cemetery has many people in it, but I am shocked to see Kevin and Teresa, far off. They are watching me and I do not draw attention to them which seems like the way to err on the side of safety, but it is baffling. They turn and walk away. I let the mystery go this time.

Next, we drive to see my niece for a few moments. Then, we drive on to see the mausoleum where my Aunt Marion's brother is kept. We walk in and find that Aunt Marion has her spot all picked out and ready, and it is by the door and on the top, so she can hear the music from the chapel. I sit in the chapel with Charity, who has been having a wonderful time all this day. My brother is so good to my dog and treats her just right like a little human. It makes me respect my brother even more because he knows that I value my little dog, and the way that he treats her shows his respect for me.

We cruise around the Lake Decatur Country Club. I have been teased by many that am like a tourist, wanting to take pictures of everything in America, which is true, I sure do. One of the pictures that I take is later chosen as the art for the cover of this book, *Embraced*.

EMBRACED

Every time I look at that picture I hear Aunt Marion saying again, *"How many pictures of that bench are you going to take! Come just get in the car, again, Jimmy! You're like a Japanese tourist!"* That picture makes me smile every time I see it.

Ronnie says, "Actually I understand why he's taking the pictures. This is where his life began and having the picture is like proof." I just appreciate how Ronnie is able to understand me.

It is getting late. Aunt Marion has been going all day long, running all over, and she is well into her senior moments.

When we get back to Aunt Marion's assisted living facility, Aunt Marion asks, "Can Charity spend the night again? She *needs* to be with her Aunt Marion, and you need to get your rest!"

My brother Ronnie says that he will go upstairs with me to get Aunt Marion and Charity settled to her room, and then he will drop me off at the hotel so that I do not have to walk, because he

does not want me to walk home alone after the holiday and sharing spirit in my new family that day. I'm just undone by that.

When at last I am alone in my room, I call Aunt Marion and she says, "Can you believe what we are experiencing together? Did you ever think that this would happen? Can you *believe* that your brother loves you the way that he does? And that *he knelt down* at your dad's grave and said that the grave next to it is the grave for you, Jimmy, if you want it? He said your dad and Ina would want you to have it, and I know that, too, Jimmy. And that's what it is for! It just breaks my heart that Ina is gone because I have so many happy memories with her, and I know that I wouldn't have *you* if it wasn't for her and your father. I really like your brother and the way he treats and responds to you."

I'm overwhelmed, "Aunt Marion, I feel the exact things you do; all that at once. All of it."

"This will be a day for you to always remember, being at your father's grave, putting flowers on it and your great grandmother's grave, and then to be offered the grave next to them in the *very next moment*! That is something that most people never hear or receive, and your brother did it in his own special way. Just for you. So you have a lot to think about, my nephew. So good night, we're going to bed! Happy Memorial Day."

"This has been the best Memorial Day of my life," is my honest answer.

EMBRACED

I HEAR YOU ARE GAY, AND I WAS TOLD YOU HAVE AIDS

15

THE NEXT MORNING, I get an early ring from Teresa. She says that she, Kevin and I should meet at nine.

They sit in the hotel lobby. She starts, "I wanted to know, did you accept the gift?"

So they knew about the offer of the grave plot. I had wondered why she and Kevin had been there, but then had left when I looked up. I had not known at the time if I was meant to see them, or if she would have wanted me to call her over, or what. Did I do right by erring on the safe side? Why were they even there at the cemetery, if they were going to leave like that, without communicating with anyone? It's confusing.

But I am happy to answer this question, "Oh Teresa, I cannot even express what that gift means to me. I have been thinking of nothing else since that happened. I am overjoyed to think of laying my body forever by my father and great grandmother."

She says, "I am very glad to hear that, Jimmy. This is as I said, so important for you to heal and forgive our father." I don't know what to make of her statement. Kevin gets up to go outside for a cigarette.

She continues, "There is something that I need to ask you. I have talked to your birth mother and she says that you are gay and have AIDS. Is this true?"

I am dumbstruck. First, that she had talked to my biological mother, who should know nothing about me, and that somehow my biological mother told my sister all this? I am flabbergasted by the extraordinary disregard of personal boundaries. I think how to respond to Teresa.

I say, "Teresa, asking questions like that is not …the way that I was taught."

She continues to expect a response.

I say, "Teresa, I would never ask you if you have ever had an abortion. I would never ask if you ever had sex out of marriage, or a child out of wedlock. You just don't ask people a question like that, or ask if they are gay or straight or who they are having sex with, or if they have a disease. It is just not proper etiquette and I don't respond to questions like that either. Everyone needs to have the full and only decision about what to share and not to share. Sexuality and health issues are private issues."

"I wanted to see if you would tell me the truth," she says.

I say, "Teresa, I am your brother. I am Kevin's brother, too. I never meant to meet you just as someone on your bucket list, though I am very humbled that you feel that way about me."

Teresa apparently had said what she wanted to, and I said things that were important to me. I worry that this could possibly be the last time I see my brother, Kevin, and maybe even my sister,

EMBRACED

Teresa, because I can see they do not have joy in living and they don't really want to participate in my joy of being found. I think they are experiencing pain near me; a truthful spirit opens up wounds that have not been healed yet.

Maybe their safe place is within their own life and mind frame. I think I truly am someone on their bucket list, someone to meet before they die. I accept their lifestyle wishes.

Less than an hour has passed since we sat down.

We go out to Kevin. Kevin is nice. Then, they say it was really nice to get to meet me and they leave.

I had met Teresa and Kevin but after eating lunch at Teresa's I realized the 'love' that I saw in them, is the same thing I had seen before in the eyes of a mother who had no love for a motherless child.

I've got to let it go, let it go, let it go. I am my brother's and that is it.

And that is my decision.

That afternoon Ronnie picks me up and we go back to the cemetery to meet with Jeff and Jamie Burch, the lovely people who care for the grounds of Macon County Memorial Park Cemetery, Garden of Memories. It takes almost no time to obtain the right documents and make our wishes known. Jeff and Jamie are so perfect in how they do their work.

JORDAN JANTZ

LAKE DECATUR

16

WAKE UP CALL, "Sunshine, it is your Aunt Marion! It is another bright sun-shiny day in Decatur! Breakfast is ready and waiting for you!"

I say, "Aunt Marion you are *too much for color TV.*" Her devotion to me just feeds my soul with sweetness, "You are better than fresh cold milk, Aunt Marion. I will be over in a moment."

I brush my teeth and head out the door with Charity all ready for a lovely day with my Aunt Marion on Lake Decatur and then later, for an excursion together with my aunt and my brother and my sister-in-law. What a beautiful experience I am prepared for.

By cab, I take Aunt Marion out for a drive along Lake Decatur while Aunt Marion tells me the story of how her father swam across that lake when it was first made. Lots of people don't remember it, but Lake Decatur is a man-made lake, built near the turn of the century. I just love the lake. It is so beautiful. We walk along it and I sat down on the bench and take more pictures of the lake, the river and the bridges, the posh Country Club of Decatur. It is just such a perfect and beautiful place. I meditate for a moment and focus on my feelings because it feels like such a peaceful and safe spot, a place that I could sit down and say everything I have ever thought of.

EMBRACED

I get my aunt back in the cab and we poke about the city a little bit. We are enamored with hanging out together. Every minute my Aunt and I want to do mani's and pedi's, eat ice cream bars and talk about life. There isn't anything positive that we don't want to share. In honor of her years doing hair as a beautician, she gave me pair of her hair-cutting scissors, her very first set from when she went to beauty school. I have them in my handbag as we go around the city.

She directs the cab to the house that she owned before going to assisted living, that both she and Uncle Dale lived in. As we pull up, the people who live there are in the front yard and they let us come into the home. They show my aunt around her former home and she just cries and cries and the people were so kind.

She says to them, "I always loved sitting out here on the back porch with the fan going and watching all the flowers and the trees around the back-patio, here in this covered porch. This was my favorite room in the house."

I just hold her and hug her and tell her that I love her and it will be okay, that this is a part of life. Unfortunately. As we get into the car to go to her home at the adult assisted living center she says, "Getting old, Jimmy, is the hardest thing. Everything your Aunt Marion's ever worked for is gone. Remember, you cannot take it with you." She says that she really is so glad that I was there with her. Me, just being there, means so much to her and that nobody has taken the time to come and stay and celebrate her birthday like this before.

She says, "You always were appreciative. And you should have been mine. I should never have let my sister have you. I wanted you to have a sister to grow up with. And I was too old, we thought."

I say, "Aunt Marion, you did the best you could do, and I love you. Everything has turned out the way God has planned and it is a miracle that we are all still alive today. It is just a miracle."

Back at the assisted living center, we both rest until Ronnie and Lisa pull up. I'm helping Aunt Marion get ready when I see their car.

Ronnie takes us to more sights that interest me very much. I ask to just get out of the car and walk down the street and take pictures, because it is just like a movie set. I embrace the moment of reality that this *could* have been my life. I feel peace seeing the smiles and laughter of so many people leading very humble lives. My camera clicks and clicks.

I hear the car honking and Aunt Marion saying, "ENOUGH with the pictures, Jimmy, honey, come on let's get going. Aunt Marion wants to go to the bathroom!"

My aunt teases again that I will take pictures of anything. I am proving her right, by getting the right angle on the stop sign outside of the hospital in which I was born. Aunt Marion pokes a bit and says, "Craving Japanese food today? Because you take pictures like a tourist."

But it is very hard for me to stop. I have borrowed a digital camera and I am so hungry for it all!

"Oh now, Lord have mercy, there he goes again with the camera, documenting his life!" Aunt Marion isn't really angry just amused.

I hear her say to Ronnie, "At least now he's finding out the truth of it all. I can't believe I'm alive for him to face the truth of where he's come from and that he has family still alive."

EMBRACED

I hear Ronnie's answer, "I can understand why he's doing it. After all, this is where he was born. We want him to know that he is wanted here, and we want him to come back and be buried next to Dad and Ina. That plot was not just sitting there for anybody. It was meant for Jimmy to be next to Dad and the family he never got to know until this trip."

As I keep taking pictures, Ronnie says, "I think the hardest thing for Jimmy to understand is that he is loved the way he is, with no expectations. He struggles to feel the love I'm trying to give him. He must have not felt that love was secure without having to perform. What do you think, Aunt Marion?"

She says, "He's always been a good, kind hearted kid. He would give his shirt off his back for any other kid in the neighborhood. He never went without. But he never felt like he was loved."

Having driven all over the city, we park ourselves at a Dairy Queen. Aunt Marion gets a strawberry shortcake blizzard and I get the same.

Aunt Marion's comments put us all in stitches. Everything she says is true and real and that makes it all so dear. She says, "Jimmy, I just can't believe after all these years I'm as old as I am, sitting at this table with you and your brother." She was beginning to get a little emotional, "I really wanted to keep Jimmy, but I promised Ina and Bud that Jimmy would go to California."

I reach over and put my arm around her and tell her, "Aunt Marion, you are giving me the best, right now, right here. I am spending two weeks here for your birthday with Ronnie and Lisa their whole family. This is the sweetest moment. I have no question that if it weren't for you, Aunt Marion, really for *you* and Dad and Ina, *all* of us wouldn't be here right now. None of us. I wouldn't be alive. Ronnie wouldn't be alive. I'm so grateful, Aunt Marion.

JORDAN JANTZ

There were so many oppositions, but God created this day and this sweet, sweet moment just for you and me and Ronnie and Lisa at Dairy Queen today."

For the first time I see a light in my heart where all was darkened by questions that were never answered. I'm excited that Ronnie has the ability to be able to see inside of me, and that he understands my feelings of distrust. Being together like this, I realize that someday we will walk in the light of a beautiful sun, and that someday life is going to get brighter; someday we'll all be together.

One of the best men who assisted me in Decatur.

EMBRACED

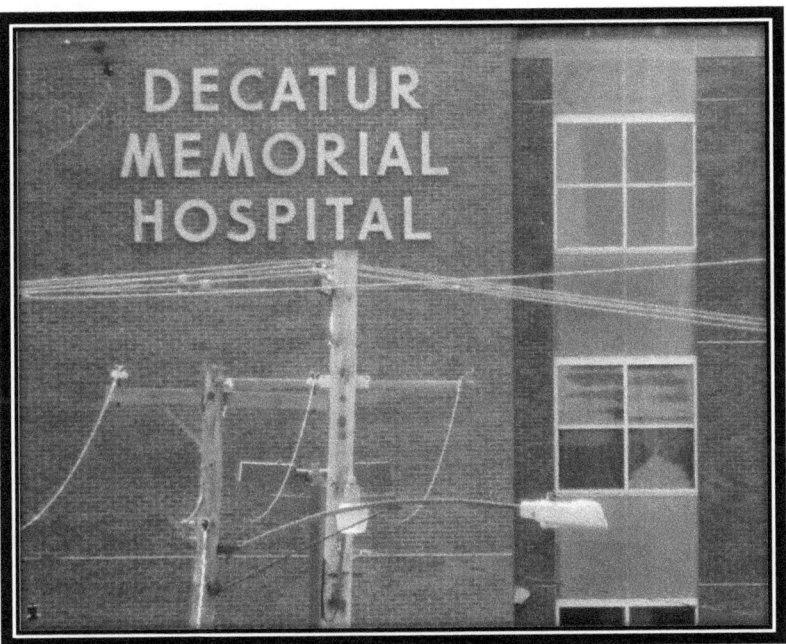

So much to see! I was born in this hospital.

What do you think of my post-card art?

JORDAN JANTZ

CORNFIELDS AND SOYBEANS FOREVER AND EVER, OH MY

17

As WE ALL DRIVE AWAY after saying goodbye to Aunt Marion at the adult assisted living center, I realize what a wonderful time we all shared at the Dairy Queen. I hope that Aunt Marion's blood sugar doesn't pop up too high.

It is so peaceful to drive out to the country where my brother's property just *surprises* me, even though he had talked about it a little bit at Dairy Queen. He did talk about *acres* but I don't understand that. The property is many BLOCKS wide and deep. Ronnie's driveway leads to a grassy land with a beautiful oak tree that is huge with a giant swing in front of it. It is a beautiful home with a patio that my brother built.

It is just so surprising to see that home, right in the middle of nowhere. It is nice to be able to walk inside of his real home and feel the peace that my brother lives in. Country living, I never dreamed it would be something I ever valued, but I can see why my brother values living out in the country. It is different and unlike anything I've ever been exposed to.

I see a piece of pork that my brother has marinating. I am really impressed at his culinary skills. The dinner smells so rich with

EMBRACED

wonderful with seasonings and toasted bread, dipped in olive oil. I love that. The dinner couldn't be more right for me.

Later, the heat moves us out to the shade of the enormous tree. We have a peaceful time sitting the porch, visiting and looking at pictures that he wants to give me of my father and my grandfather and everyone.

"You know, you are the first family member that I've had out to my house since Dad died," Ronnie says.

I can feel in my heart that Ronnie has emotions similar to me. Ronnie honors other people. So I respond in our discussion that I love and acknowledge the simplicity of living out here. I never dreamed I would be out here in Decatur like this, in your home. It was so nice even just to be given the ability, thanks to familyhistory.com *(and my special friend in the Relief Society)* to share this time with you at your home. I still can hardly believe it! You are amazing. I never knew I had *family* in my blood. It is nice to know!

My brother accepts my gratitude graciously and he lets me know that there are no hidden secrets or angels or guides to instruct him or reiki masters or signs in the clouds to worry about. And Ronnie says, "You know, Jimmy, what Lisa said before? Well, I want to say again, there are no conditions on that. There are no secrets or angels or guides to instruct but Jesus. No masters or writing in the clouds." He definitely understood how Teresa had communicated to me.

Ronnie says, "We are very happy about what we see in your heart, and learning about you is not at all offending us. You are showing love, even if it isn't possible to be received by everyone. You are still showing God's love."

I say, "My life can't work without God in it."

He nods, then smiles, "And one more thing, we think it is just adorable how you have held on to your relationship with your Aunt Marion. She's a *sight*, in her nineties, just doting all over you. Anyone can tell that she has doted on you her whole life. It's sweet to see."

We talk all night, and when Ronnie drives me home, we talk the whole ride in.

At my hotel, he says, "There is so much more to say, but I have to get up early in the morning. I'm glad we have a few more days before you leave. We'll talk soon, okay?"

I say, "Absolutely, yes, Ronnie. And thank you again, for everything."

He puts the car in park and gets out of the car when I do and walks around and gives me a hug. It is *awesome* to be hugged by your brother! I notice that we are both wearing the same color in our outfits – black shirts and tan colored pants and black shoes. It is a kind of note that it not important, it is just *sweet*.

The sincere hug gives me the most emotional affirmation. I guess hugs can do that, when they are received with a true heart, open to honesty and vulnerability with my brother. I realize all over that he accepts me and loves me the way I am and expects me to be nothing but me. It is out of this world. The only other person like that as far as a man goes is my father that raised me.

What a sweet time this is, to be with my brother and experience what it is like to be with real family that expects nothing except truth and honesty and respect.

EMBRACED

FAMILY HOME EVENING IN DECATUR

~18~

It is morning, so of course I get a phone call, "Your Aunt Marion just wants to make sure that you made it home alright from Ronnie's last night, and come on over when you are ready, Honey!"

I had not called her when I returned because I arrived back so very, very late after being with Ronnie at his home for dinner.

My body is filled with energy and happiness! I have so much to tell Aunt Marion! And, I still have some presents I for her. Boy, do we need to *visit* and I need to see my little dog, Charity, because I know Aunt Marion loves Charity and Charity loves Aunt Marion, but I do need to come over there and relieve her of the obligation.

It is Saturday and my (adopted) cousins are coming over for their weekly visit with Aunt Marion. They are two just purely wonderful people. They have heard about my expanding visiting-relationships here and do not want in any way impede my availability to open myself to the important opportunities with my biological siblings, yet they want to communicate to me their desires, also, if I have some free time to come visit them at their home.

JORDAN JANTZ

It is so nice to see my cousins! Aunt Marion tells the story (I still can hardly express) about how my biological family saved me a burial plot right next to my biological father, Roy Eldon Bond, and my biological great grandmother, Ina Agnes McNear, in the Macon County Cemetery called the Garden of Memories.

"Can you believe this?" Aunt Marion says to my cousins (her son and his wife) who are dumbfounded at the whole heart-opening, yet morbid invitation to lay with my blood. It means so much to me I can't talk. The cousins can tell I'm sensitive to the reality of my grave being next to the man that gave me life.

"What is it like, experiencing this … *re-unite-ment!* How do you feel about it?" my cousin Mark asks.

I say, "Just the fact that Aunt Marion has made it into her late nineties is *my* number one miracle. I know by the Spirit that I am supposed to be here doing what I am doing, giving my love to this angel who transformed my life more than anybody else possibly could. She found me a place to belong in a world that had no home for me. And now," I start crying, "I am with my biological family, too, and wanted forever…"

Mark sees I'm beyond expression, "Well, I just want you to know that I'm glad you are here, Jimmy. We want you to come out to the house sometime. You can come see my bees! I collect the finest grade of honey in Decatur." I think *Fried Green Tomatoes*. I smile and wipe my face with tissues.

I tell Aunt Marion that a plan has been made for this evening with my sister-in-law, Lisa, and my nephew, Zach. We are going to the movies after dinner, which dinner I would like to have with my Aunt Marion. Aunt Marion is thrilled that I will have more time to love my biological family (especially Zach because she just *adores* Zach) and for dinner she will like to go downstairs and show

EMBRACED

off her pretty new sparkling birthday outfit that I brought to her from Portland, Oregon.

So I fix her hair and give her a new nail polish. We do a knock-out make-over and prepare ourselves for the evening festivities and socializing over gospel music at the assisted living center.

We go downstairs to the sound of music, a local church playing gospel music full of the spirit for the residents who are dining. The Spirit is moving; all of the seniors' expressions light up as if they are being sung to by angels. It is a feast in the same cafeteria they eat in each day.

We decide to end our evening with butterscotch sundaes with lots of nuts. I take Aunt Marion back up to her room as the music fades. We hug and I thank her so much for watching over my Charity and spending time with her.

She says, "Oh Jimmy I *love* this little dog. You just remember that *she* knows she's really *mine*. I will take care of her any time, you just know that and you don't even need to ask it, just know it."

Well, Aunt Marion is so sweet. I realize all over that I am so blessed to have this opportunity to see and hear her and devote a part of my life to her, especially with her transitions that are taking place in her senior moments. And yes, Charity will be in the best hands tonight.

I return to my hotel room to prepare for my movie night with Lisa and Zach. The movie theater is also just across the street from my hotel.

It is darker and the hotel staff is happy to drive me right to the door. Again, I am so blessed.

JORDAN JANTZ

    One life you have certain things to help you get by. Friends, adult beverages, and when you have nobody, you've got the bar and the disco. Unless you are fortunate enough to have a mixture of love, peace and happiness besides your evenings of entertainment. This was my home away from home, at one point.

    When I needed to have a break from everyone, I could run away to the bar where all my relationships would be waiting for me to join in on the festivities with the ability to socialize with people at were also same gender attracted. This was my bar.

EMBRACED

My church that I now have social relationships that I feel are eternal and my life has become somewhat 100% different in so many ways as I have matured into a spiritual being, I have found for myself that there is no room for plastic fantastic in my life. I've chosen true intimacy over acquaintances.

I've chosen to be a philanthropist that goes to bat for emotional, mentally and physically damaged and abused children and adults throughout my life.

JORDAN JANTZ

At the ticket counter, I buy three tickets for *Tomorrowland*, a Walt Disney production. I am sure it will be no stress for me, because it *is* a Disney movie, after all, so it would *have* to be kid-friendly. I don't know if Ronnie's children watch PG or R movies and I didn't want to be inappropriate in picking and buying the tickets.

When Lisa and Zach get there, Lisa is astounded that I would pay for the movies but I tell her, "Come on! This is Family Home Evening, and we get the opportunity to share this evening, doing something good. This is what families do on Family Home Evening."

We go in and sit down for the movie, me between Lisa and Zach, which is such an honor I am hardly able to think about the movie. I am so tired from the full day and the almost gospel music *evening ball* at Aunt Marion's, all on top of the incredible day and long evening just the day before with my biological brother that I fall asleep. I am so embarrassed because I think I started I started to snore, from exhaustion. I still don't know to this day if they heard me or what. They sure are being very polite about it.

We part with hugs. She says, "We'll talk to you this week" and I understand from her that she has a big work-load this coming week and is working on important projects with time requirements, but she says she will create time for another family get-together and, "Yes, you can invite Teresa and Kevin, if you want to, or not, if you don't."

She sees my face, "I guess they are doing what they feel they can do in communication, Jimmy. Ronnie and I want you to know – to completely understand - that this communication that you might be experiencing has always been this way with his side of the family. You didn't bring this upon yourself or cause whatever you are thinking about, in the family. We've been living with challenges forever. So, please hear me as I say, *Let it go*. It is what it is. Whatever way you approach things to make peace with things that don't feel good, please do it now and just realize it is not up to *you* to bring *them* into your life. They know you've spent your time and your finances to able to experience this moment of time. There is no control here that works, so just let it be whatever it is. As for us, WE hope to see you tomorrow but if not, then this week for sure. I LOVE you, Jimmy."

That night when I get into bed, I am so happy to have spent two hours sitting with people I love.

I promised at dinner to call Aunt Marion after the movie. I sit down and call her number and she answers immediately. I tell her how it went. I wish I could tell her about the movie, but I can tell her about the fun and relaxed time that Lisa and Zach shared with me.

"Get some sleep and rest! Sleep in, why don't you! Let Charity spend the night again with me and come over for Sunday brunch and church in the morning, ok!"

I *am* tired, "Okay, Aunt Marion. I'll pick her up tomorrow but she can't stay over there all the time or you'll get in trouble."

She says, "I just love Charity and I won't get in trouble. She's potty trained. She's a service dog. You are lucky to have a dog like her. She just *minds* you."

HOLY GHOST REVIVAL ELEVATED TO HEAVEN

19

When I finally wake up, I meet with the fantastic housekeeping department of the peaceful Hawthorn Suites, every one of them bustling through the hallways for turnovers. They are truly just so good to me and my service dog, Charity. They watch over my peace and safety, they take me over to my aunt's for the day or bring me where we need to go, and give me so much of their limited flexible time. I am glad to have the moment with them all together to express to them how grateful I am for a hotel that has people operating it with such deep and true hospitality within them.

My time in Decatur is winding down. I will be flying out in less than 48 hours.

I was so happy to come to my Aunt Marion. I savor yesterday's memory of her stunning evening all dressed and shining, swaying to the gospel music, just as she did when I was younger. She was always the most beautiful woman.

This morning, she asks for a nail-polish change, and I sure do give her a nail-polish change. We spend the afternoon talking about my life and my time in Decatur and …how much she is going to miss me.

EMBRACED

Aunt Marion says, "I am looking forward to going and seeing Uncle Dale today. I'm so grateful that you were here to go every day with me and to take Uncle Dale out. If you were not here, I could not have been able to take him out of his memory care facility at all. Jimmy, I would not have been able to have done this – this beautiful time with my husband this summer - without you."

I say, "Aunt Marion, you have done for me things that I could not have done without you. You have made things happen for me that I could not have had without your help."

She saved my life. I don't know how to express that over and over again, but it means everything to me.

We hug each other, hold hands and I say grace over our brunch. Having her hands in mine, I rub her beautiful hands that once were without spot and now blemishes of aging have set in as a part of life to remind us about what is most precious. We all age. I encounter through the Spirit her accepting and embracing of this during my prayer with Aunt Marion, as we start the morning that will lead to our last evening together. We both know it could be our last evening together, truly.

She even gets teary-eyed and says, "I'm going to miss you. I have not enjoyed my life for many years. It has just been awful, the way I was removed and put into a place. You know you are going to die in here. We all know it. But it is a part of life. Remember, now, I do not want you *ever* feeling like you can't tell me anything, because we all have done things, even I have, that I would embarrassed for my mother or father to ever find out, that I did that. You and I can talk about anything. And you can trust me."

That has always been true but she has never said it before. I think it is because it often comes before, "...I will take it to my grave," and I realize again how serious that reality is for her.

She says, "You have done so much for me. Your cousins, Mark and Robin, have done so much here in Decatur for me, as well. I am so blessed. I just wish that you didn't have to leave Monday. It is going to be different without you here."

I say, "I feel the same. It is almost like I'm going back to different life now, too."

She says, "I think it is really nice that your brother, Ronnie, *knelt down* at the grave and showed you where you could be buried at, if you choose to take that grave. What do you think about it, Jimmy? Did you answer him yet?"

I say, "I have prayed about it, and I'm all about it. It is the right thing to do." As I say that last bit, I smile because I now realize that when I say that, I am saying something that Ronnie also says. "So, I'm going to let him know before I leave how much I respect the fact that Ina had purchased something to hand down to me if I returned, something that would be a permanent part of my eternal life even into the next life." I feel as though God had this planned all along and was saving the best for last.

Aunt Marion and I sit in the living room, she in her big recliner with Charity on top of her legs, and me on her couch, just resting.

Aunt Marion lays back in her chair. She opens up her spirit and heart to when she first met me. I had never quite heard this story this way. She says "I will never forget what I felt when I hugged you."

And I say, "Don't tell me I'm going to need a box of Kleenex, now!"

She says, "I want to share a little bit about this with you, just a little for something special for you and for me. I'm very glad you have somebody in your life that wants you the way that you are, which is how your brother Ronnie and his wife want you. Jimmy, this is the way love is supposed to be. Love is not putting on your tap dance shoes" she smiles at me, "though you sure could tap. There is a difference though, in expressing the value you feel of others through your talents, compared to what they asked you to create and become your personality, to earn approval. I'm not trying to have a hard talk, I just want to express what I felt and knew when I first met you and what I experienced by knowing you your whole life."

Aunt Marion cuddles Charity. Charity doesn't let just anyone do that with her. Aunt Marion says, "This sweet girl, for instance, brings you *love*. She loves you all the time without condition or expectation."

I say, "Charity has been a better partner than any man *ever* in my life, but God. I haven't had another partner since I got Charity, in fact. That is fourteen years."

I say, "Aunt Marion, what an amazing two weeks it has been, celebrating your life on your birthday, celebrating Memorial Day with you and meeting my biological family. It is all, every part, so valuable. I have absolutely loved every minute of my time with you, and seeing your life here. I loved getting to go take you to the places you used to live at, seeing your many old beauty shops. *You* have touched so many lives! I enjoyed watching so many old and new friends reach out and embrace you with respect and kindness. I loved when we had Uncle Dale with us on little trips. He is even more heartfelt than I remember. I am astonished that he remembers that he taught me how to swim! The mind is incredible and he remembers me as a little boy and growing up. I have no idea how I stuck in there like that but it is a gift to me and to him to experience this joy. I see the beauty in Uncle Dale, the miracle."

I am hearing my own beating heart as I say, "I'm so grateful to see that the human being that one person may throw away, another person may find and cherish." She looks me in the eye and knows what I'm talking about.

She asks me to open the table drawer. In it, she says, is an envelope with her thoughts regarding her funeral. She has been writing the words she hopes she has chosen to live, for her eulogy.

We spend hours as she instructs me about what is important to her, concerning her death. I promise her that as long as I am living I will make certain that her instructions are carried out exactly as she hopes.

That evening we watch the Hallmark Channel. Aunt Marion and I eat ice cream bars all night. She wants to savor the peace.

Aunt Marion asks, "Is there anything that you wish could have gone different?"

I think and say, "I wish I could have gotten to really know my biological brother, Kevin, and his family, instead of just meet them. I would like to get to really know all my biological family, and would like them to know me, but maybe they don't want that, after I go home to Portland. They just have not let me know yet what they want from me in their life, going forward. But I would like more. I would like them to have the opportunity to at least know me and I could know them, as you know me, Aunt Marion."

When I get to my room that night, I call and let her know that I am in my room with Charity and I will see her in the morning for church. She begins to weep that I am leaving. I tell her that tomorrow we will create a beautiful ending of this miracle to remember forever.

This is the first night since my arrival that I have enough energy to journal a bit: *I am in my fifties, and yet the expectations that I live with were often placed into my life by others. They have wanted me to be beautiful and desirable. But I have wanted to be found, to be invited, to share. Especially, I have wanted to be normal. I was misled with expectations of what people wanted out of my life since I was born, while also wanting things that I shouldn't have tried to be or do. These things have prevented happiness for me in the past and have also prevented some of the happiness and light I could bring into the world and to others.*

I envision tomorrow and my encounter with God. I realize that I always had the thing that is the most important of all things to share: me. I put my journal down and realize it is time to let the peace enter my body.

I have always trusted God because God will not ever use me. I am definitely fallible but I know that since I have chosen God, my faith is grounded because I know what I feel in my heart I can live 'out' in my life through honesty of following the Holy Spirit and communicating through the Spirit to others, whether it be dreams, hopes or endeavors. God will transform the unmanageable or painful by giving clarity. God surely was with me as a tiny child when I was flying to California to become another little boy with a new name, which was my first transformation.

I cuddle my Charity. Charity has been given to me by God for my comfort through this often painful and frightening journey to truth and wholeness. Charity means the pure love of Christ.

EMBRACED

AUNT MARION'S LIFE-LONG PROTECTION OF ME

20

SUNDAY MORNING DAWNS: my last full day in Decatur. When I call Aunt Marion to let her know that Charity and I are on our way over for breakfast and church, I can tell her that Ronnie just called and he and Lisa and the kids want to take us out for lunch after church. Aunt Marion's excited!

Church services are brought to the residents of the assisted living center every Sunday. It is simple and Christian. We take sacrament together. I open her juice lid for her and we partake of the sacrament emblems, lifting our cups and bread to Jesus in gratitude. We sing music and listen to the preacher with joy in our hearts. She sings and she reminds me of her eulogy. I promise her again, quietly, that I will make sure her funeral will happen as she directs as long as I'm alive. She holds on to my hand and tells me again that she is so glad that we are in church together, and that she is enjoying every minute inside this day. After church, I escort her back to her room. I tell her to stop talking about her death.

At 2 o'clock my brother, Ronnie, and his lovely wife, Lisa, and their children arrive, ready to take Aunt Marion and me out for late lunch and for a Sunday drive.

EMBRACED

We mosey down through Decatur downtown. Aunt Marion talks about all the streets that she lived or worked on when she was a little girl, young woman, and mature years. I love each of her neighborhoods. My favorite is called Merchant Street and has all types of boutiques, very artistic and colorful. I love hearing my nephew and my niece talk about their lives and what they hope to do or see. They are each graduating to new schools or activities, transforming. My Aunt Marion is just in love with my nephew and my niece; she thinks Zach is the sweetest young man and a lot like my brother (and me) in some ways. I have loved watching the two of them interact during my stay.

I value our time over lunch and I value the heartfelt gift of my grave-plot. It still blows me out of the water. It also shows me what kind of heart my brother really does have. I am embarrassed to say this, but of all the energy put out on this two-week journey (this definitely was not a vacation) and getting to Decatur from Portland, I see that my sister-in-law supported my brother's choices. As I met the niece and nephew with integrity and respect, and I compare this to how other brothers and sisters caused me to feel like a foreigner or a bucket list item to check off. I tried so hard to share my open heart because I knew that if I didn't they would never have the chance to know who I really am. They chose to not call me or respond to me or say goodbye. How in the world does a person get on the plane in Decatur, Illinois, and leave knowing that they were a *bucket list item* to a brother that didn't even care to pick the phone up and say good bye, or "I was glad to see you." I received nothing except empty memories of what I had hoped for and prayed for from some, but maybe what I prayed for was all I received; being with my brother Ronnie, who made up and then some, when others turned and walked away.

My brother and sister-in-law need to drop off my niece for school (it was finals week for my niece, who shows me the value that she gifted upon her Uncle Jimmy, to take that extra-precious time for me. *Wow!*) It still feels incredible to be an *Uncle Jimmy*. This is the first time that I have felt fully accepted by family as an adult. I have never had anyone value my time and energy the way that they did.

Next we drop of my Aunt Marion. I tell my Aunt Marion I will see my brother, sister-in-law and nephew off and call her again before I go to bed.

As we are driving in to my hotel parking lot, I ask them if they would like to come into my room and say goodbye together and say a little prayer, if it was comfortable for them.

My brother and sister in law say, "Absolutely, we would enjoy that!" My nephew jumps on the idea, also.

As we walk in to my room, I have golf balls in my throat. The others look no better. We know the value of what we have had these past two weeks and we are thankful to have experienced real honest family love. I think they knew I had not experienced this family love or affirmation without also facing reality that was never spoken, that I was also once abandoned. And now, I am not. And all is open.

We hold hands in a circle. My brother asks me if I want to say the prayer and I say that would be great.

We all bow our heads and I just *open up* and thank Heavenly Father for the miracle of love, the miracle that my biological father Eldon Roy Bond and great grandmother Ina Agnes McNear and my aunt Marion Lee came together to find me a home. I thank God for giving me the blessing of having a brother who has gone above and beyond the call of a brother. "I thank you, Jesus, for Ronnie and ask you to bless our brotherhood and bless my sister-in-law with love in her heart always from me. And help my niece and nephew become the people You have created them to be. You will

EMBRACED

open their hearts and eyes to all the beauty and meaning of these past two weeks, because we have gone out of our way to meet and become family to each other, a family that loves God, for we are thankful for what YOU have done with the miracle of Decatur!"

I just pour myself out to God who always hears my prayers. I close with *amen* and gratitude.

They repeat *amen* with me, firmly. Ronnie says again the incredible words he has said, "You will be loved and I will be your brother in this family forever. There is nothing that you can ever do to erase the truth that I am not only a biological blood brother and I am also your friend. You can always count on me as long as you don't run away or disappear."

I think, *he reminds me of me with his honesty and transparency. Maybe blood is thicker than water.* This is the first time I've ever experienced a brother validating his love for me. This is not just biological; it goes deeper than that. Because of meeting me these past two weeks, they say, they can tell that I am a direct and honest man.

I find myself saying, "You've managed to carry yourself very well, with integrity. It shows when you speak and in the way that you respond to others, when asked a question."

Lisa's response is a big hug, "I love you, Jimmy. You are family. Ronnie is my family and you fit inside here, too."

It just breaks my heart, that anyone could ever feel that way about me. We sob and hug each other, and say goodbye.

As I stand there, watching family load into the car, I know that we had been visited by the Holy Spirit, for as I spoke He gave me so much comfort, letting me know that this is not the last time for me with my brother.

JORDAN JANTZ

There is no stopping such happy tears.

Then, the *hotel staff* also comes out to watch Ronnie and Lisa and Zach drive away. They <u>all</u> know that my brother's family has gone out of their way to spend time meeting me, hoping to have enough time to get to really know me.

But how can anyone, honestly, know somebody enough in two weeks? But God is in control. Everyone I know in Decatur is out waving goodbye. I thank everyone at the hotel for being a part of this miracle that most people never get the opportunity to embrace. I feel to say that this has been possible because of God and because of God's teaching to let go of the fear in order to create the opportunity to embrace.

Evening is falling, so I stop by one more time to surprise Aunt Marion with a goodbye hug and a goodbye kiss and to pick up Charity. She says she is surprised because she really had thought that I was going to spend the night with my brother and his family because of her having Charity and Charity is doing just fine and, "Charity wants to stay with her Aunt Marion," Aunt Marion says to me. I tell her that Ronnie and his family just left and what I experienced with my brother Ronnie and his family. I tell her about the beautiful prayer in my hotel room.

Aunt Marion says, "That's a *true brother*. I am glad you got to finally meet. I am also glad that you got to meet your niece and nephew and your sister-in-law. And of course, the rest of your brothers and sisters, as they could come. Do you feel a lot happier and more at peace now, after all these years, from being removed at an age that I know you can remember a lot, that was never talked about? You can talk to me and ask me anything you want," Aunt Marion says.

I say, "I've always been able to talk to you about anything and everything. We've always put everything on the table, Aunt

EMBRACED

Marion. And, with Ronnie, he showed me actions backed up with desire to open up his life and his family life to me. He showed true gratitude that we found one another after fifty years. *You* are a miracle and if it wasn't for you, none of this would be happening. You are going to live to be more than ninety and I will be here for your next birthday, I promise you.

She says, "Oh, I hope I live another year!"

I say, "Now, I'd better get going because I have to get up early to catch the plane, and Travelers Aid will be there for me in O'Hare to get me to my connections that will get me back home.

So, we hug and she kisses Charity goodbye and it is very precious to be able to experience true, genuine love that has *always* been there from the moment Aunt Marion saw me when I was three years old. This is proof that God sends people like Aunt Marion into a child's life for a purpose. There is also purpose for me being in her life, when Aunt Marion's turns a year older. What a blessing it is to leave and know the truth has set me free from my own judgments and other people's judgments of my life.

As I tell this to Aunt Marion, she tells me, "You have always been a joy to my life. You have always thanked me and called me to show me how much you care. You have always been very special to me and to your Uncle Dale. Jimmy, don't you think there was a *purpose* that we went and drove all the way across the country to Milwaukee to meet you and the boyfriend that you had at the time and Aunt Marion wanted to make sure that *you were okay* and that he was good to you? Uncle Dale and I drove out there to your home and stayed the weekend with you for a reason."

"I remember," I say, "It was wonderful to have you come to my home, Aunt Marion. That meant so much to me that you would take the time to let me know that I could be so open with you and so honest with you about my being same gender attracted. You know where my heart is at today, and how much it means to me to have a spiritual connection to the creator of the universe, more than anything else in my life. And I am so grateful that I had the blessing of being raised in a home with *opportunity* to be free. The truth is, there are things here in Decatur that I don't know if I could have handled as well as Ronnie, because if I would have grown up with my brother, Ronnie, I would not have tolerated if anyone had mistreated him. I would have been protective of his heart and if anyone mistreated him, I don't know what I would have done. I feel just the same for Ronnie as I feel about the sister that I grew up with, Aunt Marion. I guess it is in some blood, this feeling to protect. I want to thank you for protecting me and getting me out of the closet and into the light. I'm forever grateful for what we shared. I will call you in the morning before I leave."

Aunt Marion and I embrace each other again and say goodbye. As I close her door she has tears coming out of her eyes as she sinks back down in her little recliner.

When I am back in the room, right across the street from Aunt Marion's assisted living center, I am thinking about my life and what an incredible journey it has been on. I'm thinking about why I came Decatur and what the purpose is. Charity is with me on the bed. *This story of where my life began.* Lying on the bed, I remember how it seemed like *everybody* felt that going to be Decatur would be something I needed to protect myself *from*. They thought that my brothers and sisters couldn't handle the reality that I would be alive. Remembering all the stories that they were all told from many relatives and people that had known me *as a secret*, I can only imagine what it would was like for them. I wonder how it was for them growing up. For me, it comes together finally. This was the moment that I had been given to gather up my past and to make sense of it at last. This is the greatest moment of them all.

EMBRACED

Snuggling up to Charity, I think about how the smallest thing can change your life. In the blink of an eye something happens by chance - when you least expect it- and sets your course onto another path into a future you never imagined. Where will it take you? That's the journey of our life. Sometimes, finding the light means you must pass through the deepest darkness. At least, that's how it has been for me.

I have been misrepresented by many, whether they are family that is biological or adopted, because a lot of people are challenged with ability to embrace reality. Lying in bed and thinking of this all, it just touches my heart, that my brother embraces what I do and believes in me, and is so happy that I have a relationship with him and his wife. We are brothers forever. That this was not just something for the moment. And that I'm going to need to trust that.

Ronnie can tell that a lot of trust in my life has been broken. Ronnie also said that he is really glad that I have my dog, Charity, as my service dog "for she is experienced, you can tell, in paying attention to your needs. She is faithful and is the best friend that can give you the most support in your life, Jimmy, she has made your spirit shine and has stayed with you for so many years, she'll be turning fifteen years old and that is a miracle, my brother. She makes life complete for you. I can't believe you found her in a pet shop. I'm grateful that Charity has the capability to get through the thick skin of your heart, because you grew that skin to protect yourself. But I will always be your brother and I will not leave you and I will not abandon you, and neither will my wife or my two children."

JORDAN JANTZ

A Devoted Spiritual Family for all time and eternity.

My little brother that I love and thank God for finding him today. Better late than never! It is amazing when love touches your life. It can touch you one time and change your life forever.

And Ronnie also said, "Dad is looking down upon us right now. Don't ever think Dad forgot you. He never did, ever. And you have an Uncle Bill and an Uncle James and you have cousins that all remember you and you have found me and my wife and your niece and nephew after fifty years. Your Aunt Marion is the one that helped Dad rescue you from your biological mother, that is all true."

I lay in bed and tears fall through my heart because I finally have received truth.

Some people tell me God is in control of my spirit and heart and that I am the one that has the choice to give him control of my actions. I have found many malfunctions in my life. I remember especially my emotions of self-consciousness with shame that I was plagued with, guilt that I did something bad to have been sold and a child, which led to my careers and the industries of utilizing physical attributes, not knowing the value of anything else. The difference between shame and humiliation is that I don't feel like I deserve my humiliation of being sold and not wanted. I know I am not alone for there are other children out there.

As I lay and think of my life, I think of my cousin Mark and his wife, and I think of my other cousin Sandy in Florida, and my other cousin, Bruce, in Texas and I just hope they know how much their mother, my Aunt Marion, means to me and how she has changed my life.

Aunt Marion told me that she had recalled something very important that happened before my biological father passed away, who she cared about very much. In 2005 my biological dad was admitted to the hospital and she got a phone call and went to go see my biological dad. He had severe cancer that was spread throughout his body.

EMBRACED

Aunt Marion said, "Your dad was never able to send you a letter. He said he should have found a way to tell you years ago about how he remembered you on December 2, your birthday, and every day."

I remember now that there had been private investigators involved at one time, or I had been told so. I think about *other* fathers, including the Jantzes.

When opportunities came my way, Mr. Jantz would remind me that I was a part of the Jantz family, the Christian family. He would remind me that I need to be with people of importance. He knew I had nobody else. I had prayed, God, please let this Jantz family be removed and their religion be wiped out of my life, because their actions were for the moment and if God's love is forever, why wouldn't their love be forever?

As I finalize my questions with God in my journal in Decatur I know as I look back that Mr. Jantz had my character in control and had my life always questioned because of my same gender attraction and my honesty that I showed with him. I realized that if a father loves a son like he should, he should do what is best for his son, and that is what my adoptive dad did for me, and my biological dad, too. By giving me up they are both two separate men who have reasons for doing what they did to make my life better. **That is what a true father does.**

Often I feel today as I journal that I've removed being the one running in circles around what's at stake. But now the time's come for my feet to stand still in one place. Is it here in Decatur? Am I supposed to stay with my brother? I embrace him and he honestly wants a brother. I don't think he'll ever understand what it has been to be looking and searching for something so important that you would give the last red cent in your pocket to know you were never forgotten and that I was loved.

JORDAN JANTZ

Aunt Marion is the one who told me this precious information about my father's last days that nobody else could ever reveal. I respect her for going to see my biological father at his bedside, for stopping by as a friend would. I respect her for inviting him over for Thanksgiving; I respect her for inviting him over for Christmas. I respect her for letting me know how alone my dad really was, even when he had people around him. But Aunt Marion did let me know that everyone loved him, and he was a man that made everybody feel important.

Aunt Marion was right when she said, "I knew you would find me. Before I died, I knew you would come." Aunt Marion has always fascinated me in the way that she communicates. I sense that Aunt Marion and I can call out for one another and that is why I am here. Aunt Marion had the heart to cry out for me, and I was crying out to be able to say how much I love her. The world tried to knock it out of me and keep her from telling me the truth of my life. Love is all around me as I leave Decatur. All I have to do is listen to the Spirit.

Aunt Marion tells me my words back to me, "Jimmy, when you get on that plane tomorrow, just remember that someday we'll be together again. And I want you to make sure that you start letting yourself be happy."

I am not meant to stagnate. I know that is why I am here in Decatur, because facing the truth develops change. My goal is figuring out while I am here in Decatur and how I can use my new certainty of my life to my advantage when I get to Portland.

I realize after meeting my family, that *Embraced* is the significant name of the book. I will modify, transform, and refashion my life for being able to embrace this book that I will write, that I am *inspired* to write, because I am saving the best for last. Aunt Marion's the only woman that continually shows love,

EMBRACED

Labor Day Picnic, Dancing to Kidd Kaddilac and the Continentals. What a day it was to dance with my Aunt Marion! She was always the dancer of my life and inspiration for me to dance and let it all go! And that's what we shared together on the dance floor – letting it all go as we held each other up to reach the sky and say, "Oh, my my, what a beautiful day together forever."

JORDAN JANTZ

EMBRACED

*This season
Save the Children at the
Christmas Box Internatial
You're a beacon of Light!!!*

WITH A VOICE OF HOPE

YOU WILL NEVER BE ALONE IN LIFE
IF YOUR HEART IS OPEN TO THE REALITY
OF YOUR PURPOSE ON THIS PLANET

love, love. And when I think there is no more love she will remind me, there is love.

As I lay in bed for the last few moments, I realize a *book* will mean I have to dedicate myself again to doing something to change the lives of others. Do I have it in me, to make this promise? Do I have it in me to tell the painful journey? I will follow and I will go and do what I can do because God has called me out of darkness and into the light. This book is now the purpose of my returning to Portland.

My bags are being loaded into the hotel shuttle to go to the tiny Decatur Airport. The hotel manager, Kevin, asks me, "Did you relive some great childhood memories? I hope you did. On behalf of the staff, we have determined that we hope this is not your last time to Decatur. We enjoyed every moment assisting you while you embraced the life you once had, when born here in Decatur. Thank you for staying with us, and we will get you right to the airport, Jimmy."

I asked the driver to stop by Aunt Marion's one last time before I head to the airport. Charity and I pop through the door and surprise her, just to give her a last hug and kiss goodbye. We both shed some tears, but I promise her that I will come back and be with her, and that I will never forget her or let her out of my heart. She is the most important woman that has been consistent in my life, showing me how important I really am. I am valuable to her as a nephew and she is very proud of how I have become the person I am today. I kiss her again and say, "I will call you when I get back to Portland!"

She says, "Be good to that little dog. She's the best service dog I've ever seen and Aunt Marion loves her!"

At the airport I realize that I have not been misrepresented in any way with my Aunt Marion. She has not lost one memory cell and has not forgotten anything about our life. And she will always be the reason why I believe in miracles.

I sit looking out at the runway in the airport wondering if I will ever be able to share about the first book, *Out of the Closet, Into the Light*, with my family. I want so hard to share that with Aunt Marion, but she is too old to have complicated new things, but not my brother. Trust is the hardest thing. What do you do when you find you are in your fifties and you desire *solace*? Where does it come from? Helping children has been my mission. Many people overlook children and their lives today. But I know that this is a mission *from God*. And it gave me the opportunity to have safety in growing up as a man, surviving my multiple personalities that helped me cope and function without others ever even knowing, and be successful in the one thing that I was capable of achieving in my lifetime.

This is the kind of airport where you do all your own walking. I wonder if I would have shared the book with Ronnie, if it would make everything I do to cope more clear to Ronnie. The truth is that I was modeling and doing runway shows for buyers who bought clothing at high end prices and I had to be prepared for these events at all times and look and be the best in order to make a living. I did *anything* and *everything* to become all things to all people. If you have the goods, they say in the business, you better use them while you got them. I was born to be able to pull off this gig, I used to think. And I realize at the airport I was also deceived, so, so deceived that my gifts or talents or abilities were utilized for making a living, how wrong I was. I would have been dead long ago without being born attractive with the ability to make a living. This is not spoken out of being confident in my appearance, but being truthful of what it is really about in the industry that I survived. And yes, it is embarrassing to say, but I am glad I'm out because being attractive is not the most important thing in life and I realize it is so important to hold on to the value of one's soul and eternal life. And

JORDAN JANTZ

I to this day *have to say* that I was the best little boy in the whole world and that I never had anything but everything that I asked for, as long as I did what was right and expected.

I can feel the plane moving. I'm not supposed to, but I make a last quick call to Aunt Marion.

She just says "I love you."

I say "Love you back, Peaches." Peaches is the name that my Uncle Dale called her all the time, so I called her Peaches.

She just laughs and tells me to call her when I get home.

The plane gets loud and I take my medication to make sure that I am continuing to be in a stable mind-frame.

Soon I am looking down at Lake Michigan, and I realize this area of the country is where I was born. I never expected to face it in my lifetime. The plane descends over the lake for the runways of Chicago's O'Hare airport. My Traveler's Aid volunteer picks me right up. "Cakes" assists me and Charity, just as promised. It is so nice to travel when you can count on airlines and special agencies to assist those with challenges. I don't take the federal government for granted because it is a government that I believe in. It is a government that is based on truth and based on the idea that equal acts of kindness should be shared with everyone.

After Cakes takes such good care of me and I say goodbye to her in Chicago, I felt so much exhaustion that my senses turn off in sleep.

The rest of my trip to Portland is like a dream, all the way through my apartment door in Portland. It is like I waited my whole life to find the answers and connect the dots of my life and they are all working. I really am wondering where I belong, after this

EMBRACED

experience. Do I belong in Portland or Decatur? I don't know, but I am grateful for *this reality*, after learning the truth. What a blessing. I fall asleep, embraced by my little dog.

Time can only be my friend. All I want is to have a faith that there will be a tomorrow for me. I am amazed that I even *made* a trip like I did. I would have been stuck wondering about my life 'til the day I died if I had not had the guts to face my own destiny. *It is okay to listen to your heart.* I know it is risky, but take that leap of faith.

I remember telling Aunt Marion that I had made many mistakes in my life, but going to Decatur and being with her was not one of them. Some people dwell on the many things we can't control like earthquakes and floods rather than the things we can, like forgiveness and love. Love in any of its forms is life-giving because love gives us hope.

JORDAN JANTZ

FOLLOW THE YELLOW BRICK ROAD

~ 21 ~

It took the whole entire day to make the complete journey back to my life in Portland.

When I wake, I think of everyone who supports and believes in my mission and I'm overwhelmed at just thinking about explaining all of the truths of my trip to even *one* person, and so *many* feel like part of this journey with me.

Sharing with others is priority, as so many have shared with me. My friend who is a chaplain at the hospital shared his own rosary blessed with holy water that I could put on my father's grave, since my father was Catholic. That's just one person to stay current with. I know what I'm going to be doing for a while.

And, I also know what I am *not* going to be doing. I value growing older and want to respect myself with the dignity of becoming a senior, just as I experienced those who are seniors who practice kindness and respect. After seeing Aunt Marion and having transparency with her and experiencing her day to day life, she has given me the greatest gift of all. Being with her is more important than going on a trip around the world. I know I want to write about this. And I know people want to hear about this, too.

EMBRACED

I know that what I experienced will become embraced, if I am guided by the Spirit and I know the Spirit wants this done. I don't understand how this book even has the ability to be published, but all of the children that I know who have been abandoned have dealt with emotional challenges and physical and sexual abuse know why *I cannot let go.*

I realize my experiences with psychiatrists and mental health workers and physicians show every day the ability to work with people like myself and they *want* to have the opportunity to give broken children an emotional and spiritual life and not a life for only this moment on earth, but for a lifetime. I am being exposed to the finest class of medical staff that has *given me a life with a purpose* and I have that here with every single doctor in Portland, Oregon. I have nothing but the best and I am grateful. From my pharmacist all the way up to my home practitioner, from my case manager to my home health care specialist. This is a story that must be told for everyone's sake.

On the day after I return from Decatur, I throw my suit together and rush down to see my minister and then make it to Bible Study. I realize that everyone is waiting for me to share all this news with them at the Bible Study in downtown Portland at the Art Museum. They always ask why I stay in the LDS church and why I am a Latter-day Saint Born Again Christian. With many men from all walks of life and cultures from African American to Chinese, all are believers in the same God but with extensions of different faith.

So my heart realizes how I am going to have to speak from the Spirit, because I have no clue of what I would say unless it was from my heart. I am only remembering *now* that I was even to talk the men's downtown Bible study on this particular Wednesday, the day after my return. I totally am lost for words.

EMBRACED

But they have a tape recorder and I was able to have what I said on record. They gave me the tape afterwards so I know what I shared:

Good afternoon, gentlemen. Brothers, we are here today to open our hearts up for the mission and inspiration of the Savior, Jesus Christ. Many of you have asked why I am here. What is my purpose? What are my reasons for sharing the gospel of Jesus Christ and coming to such a place in my life where I am free of all judgments? For my only judge is Jesus Christ.

But today, I would like to share the reason for me to continue my life mission and my inspiration is that I must continue my journey and my mission statement. I have been given, through the Church of Jesus Christ of Latter-day Saints, something no other church has ever offered. No other same gender attraction ministry to those who struggle ever felt that someone like me a had any potential, coming from being such an open and honest book about everything and from being an orphan and kept away and hidden until sold to a family that had no inclination of the severity of ritual abuse as an infant that caused hideous repercussions throughout my growing into my adulthood and the fear of trusting love.

Today I have no capacity to embrace another person shamingly. This is because shame has broken me so I can't extend my heart with sincerity of trust, and this disgusts me. How can I extend my trust when it is already betrayed and removed at infancy? I am not a pawn or a protégé for the fulfillment of others, anymore. That goes for any other church in my life again.

JORDAN JANTZ

I know that my Heavenly Father gave me my life of hope and the ability to see ludicrous actions that are tormenting families all over the world. I see actions of violence, tormenting nights when fights occur with many families I know throughout households, dismissing anybody that would ever bring attention to this reality that families are so vulnerable and weaker in this manner of being able to lift their own family up. When openness could heal, the opposite takes place in life today with children in many families.

I pray for every little child I see today, and when I hear of the cries of children wanting help, I can be open and everyone knows I have the ability to give them love and satisfy the child's plea for help, and not dismiss his or her being taken advantage of by the people the child trusted the most, the child's family. This is why I am piecing my team together to start immediately on this expedition called Embraced.

I want to write this book for those that I have seen that have been hurt at some point in a very deep way, and I want to rescue them. That's what the book has opened my heart for, more than any other reason, except to help children. The Church of Jesus Christ of Latter-day Saints opens more doors than any other church for me for my mission. I am told on a regular basis from many friends throughout the country that they will not want involvement in my life until I get myself into a Bible Believing church, and that the Church of Jesus Christ of Latter-day Saints is not one of these churches that are Bible-based. People say my church has re-written the Bible and, "it is a shame to think you would feel comfortable in a church like that." But, my friends tell me, I cannot participate in their same gender programs because I do not have "any Bible truth and knowledge of the Word in my life today" so I am told that I am the only one looking for help to continue to live a celibate life and follow in the actions of a man after God's own heart, and they are so sorry.

EMBRACED

Of course, I accept all their apologies and realize after walking away from their events right after just being home from this incredible moment in my life in Decatur, that I never dreamed I am going to leave the ninety-nine of the fold and be the one who wants to follow the other lost sheep.

I still wonder why I have been considered unworthy because of the church that I attend by the gay people in this same gender attraction group that I was going to that evening. But, I was told from Born Again Baptists, Lutherans, Catholics, and Assembling of God congregations where I have taken many people from the LDS church while I have been asked to do firesides or just come visit the church, that even though this is not our church, God still loves these people and God is a part of this church. It has been incredible to see other churches embrace the Church of Jesus Christ of Latter-day Saints and the doctrine of God's love for all churches here in Portland.

My life is transformed into Christianity but many will never forget what I did to become successful at surviving with what I have had to work with. A house can be beautiful on the outside, just like a human can be lovely on the outside; I have lived this in my life, when my inside doors and walls have been eaten away from hidden unspeakable truths and my years finding out if there really is a God that could ever love a man with same gender attraction, who has lived like me. God is not invested in our exterior, and grace is not needed by the good. Those who have been rescued love the Savior the most.

I see that many spiritual bridges are presented to me, including from my medical and support teams here in Portland, Oregon, because of their love for me and my mission touching the lives of other children severely affected and needing healing and my life of trust, because I'm so happy to face my reality now. When love is all around, healing and receiving reality is possible.

JORDAN JANTZ

I have been misrepresented by many spiritual and religious people that want to utilize opportunities of my life for their own selfish reasons. I know that I can talk to my minister and he will come and be there for me. I know I also have a true friend that is a Pentecostal preacher that has always been there for me, and he is my friend to this day. We get together every month for lunch and talk about what God is doing with me, because of my leaving my life that has been so focused on appearances. And he knows I have overcome and the Church of Jesus Christ of Latter-day Saints sees and uplifts God's gifts that others don't.

Thinking about writing my book, I realize that I am so tired and it hasn't even been 24 hours yet, but I know in my heart that the children at the Christmas Box House need me and need financial help, and I cannot *let* any more children on this earth cry. I would rather go without a dollar a day to keep one child a day from crying. If I could only give them a dollar a day. It will be very hard to do, since I have no great fortune and no great income. But I do have a good name with a respected character and the reputation of a man who is a Beacon of Light. That's living proof in writing all over the country, about what kind of man I am in dealing with my medical challenges and transformation of healing.

I am also asked that evening to speak at the Liberation Church. I have made a promise to open up the Church of Jesus Christ of Latter-day Saints to other churches through opening my heart to *show* God's love is everywhere. This church, though, asked me to talk about one of the issues in *Out of the Closet, Into the Light*, and that is <u>homelessness</u>.

It was the most shaming experience of my life to need to belong and want to be found. The hardest time in my life and the most hurt for me than any other was when I had to face the fact I was breaking down. It is as if your friends are the leaves that fall off the trees, they were there but then they are nowhere. Oh, the pain

EMBRACED

to see the last leaf fall off the tree made me realize that the only true friend I have is my dog, lying next to me in my sleeping bag underneath the Burnside Bridge, the same bridge that I had jumped from a few years earlier with weights tied around my ankles. Life then for me was filled with appearances, appearances that were sought-out change results in not being able to maintain what is expected.

I tried to just not breathe so heavily under the bridge. I froze and caught pneumonia. I survived by my friend from South Dakota bringing me food and letting me shower at his home once a week. And, he wouldn't let the public find out about what happened to me, because he knew what I did for a living and my reputation. He felt I was having a breakdown. A woman who was almost a stranger to me opened up her home, letting me live underneath her house in her basement. I knew in my heart that if any of my families that I ever have been given to ever knew of my homelessness they wouldn't believe what happened to their California star. They would think, "He must have fallen off the side of the earth, to become this way."

But nobody realizes anyone *can become homeless.* Anyone.

I continued to sleep in a basement on the cement floor at my new friend's house. I had met her before and she was considered a friend, but here were acts of true kindness. It was cold and she brought me a pillow. Nobody ever chooses to be homeless. To be homeless on Christmas and Thanksgiving and New Year's Eve is the saddest and emptiest, to think of all the people I met when everyone around me was celebrating and that I was under the bridge with my little dog and nobody really cared. It felt like just holding something warm in my hands was the most important thing to me. Nobody ever chooses to become homeless. I know I didn't.

The hardest moment for me living under the bridge, was listening to the children cry at night because of the cold and the

JORDAN JANTZ

hunger they also were experiencing. I also definitely had the opportunity of another homeless camp called Dignity Village.

But in the end, the benevolence of my medical team in Portland came to my aid. Knowing that homelessness is never a choice, knowing that I never thought it could happen to me but it did, and knowing how it broke my heart, I am the person that hands out hot potatoes in tin foil to the homeless so that they can be warm. I am the person with a wheelbarrow of potatoes. In fact, the homeless count on this potato run in Portland and I have a reputation to my brothers and sisters who live in the streets of downtown. Caring for the poor is about humility and honesty. If you have those, <u>you care for the poor</u>. They are feelings that can be exposed with God in my life.

I need to go home and really get some rest.

EMBRACED

GROUP THERAPY

~22~

It is beautiful in Portland today, waking up, in June and seeing such *beauty* of sunshine glistening over the rivers and knowing that the Spirit is with me to protect my life, my mind and the creative thought of helping children from my experiences that have come back as though they were my best friend today.

I realize that I do need to catch up on my group therapy and make the call and get in as soon as possible to share and get advice on my journey with my group of men. And, I am so blessed, because they were thinking the same thing. I got a call that within that five minutes of waking up, wanting to know if I will show up for group therapy today.

"Of course I will," I say, "I can't wait, I've missed you guys!"

The leader of the group says, "You have been *so missed* Jordan, and we are so proud of you with the challenges of facing the pain of being with all of your brothers and sisters that were not sold. Everybody is on the edge of their seat with questions for you. You'll be surprised when you arrive. But it is best that you don't bring Charity today, because we're not having service animals in the meeting today. Will you be able to get here? Or will someone need to pick you up, since you are not bringing Charity?"

JORDAN JANTZ

I let her know that I definitely need to be picked up, since I can't bring my service dog. Thank the Lord for what these animals actually do to a person's life. It is the smartest thing the federal government could do for people living with disabilities. And I thank God for making these incredible little animals.

As I am picked up and riding to the men's community center, I realize that many of the therapists are packed with patients and I am so grateful that I have had the same therapist and this *same* group therapy for seventeen years. To have a group of men who know me, what a blessing it is to have the quality that is available when you live your life in the light of truth and be real, because God opens up the door for others to come in and help ease the pain. Even when you don't have family in your city that you live in, you still can make it with acts of kindness with relationships who are not family.

As we all go into the group therapy room and sit in a circle, we remember the cardinal rule *no embracing* or *showing affection*, just greeting and we sit down. We listen to our guru come out and she speaks words of wisdom with stretching exercises and movements throughout the body, letting our bodies flow with the energy of positive light and hope that she is calling upon for us to embody and embrace as we begin our session.

She speaks, "Does anyone here have a burning desire? Do you feel a burning desire in your heart, and if you do, share it."

One person stands up and shares that they are free, now that their partner has finally passed away and they no longer have to carry the responsibility of caring and providing for the love of someone who doesn't recall one memory in life. Hearing that, I just put my hands together with my palms touching one another, and I lean down and bow down in gratitude for being alive, and the blessing to hear honesty being spoken. How rare men are so

EMBRACED

vulnerable with their masculinity. Another man steps forward and says, "My cat just passed away. I don't know why she just passed away. She was lying in the bathtub like she was getting water out of the bathtub and she just passed away. When I got up this morning, I found her."

I think to myself, *LORD, death! These people need light. What can I do? I'll just embrace them and give them hope and encouragement because I know they all already know about my experience with my ex-boyfriend, hanging himself on Christmas day a few years back. These men, I will support with kindness!*

The other gentleman on the right hand side of me stands up, and he says that he and his wife are getting back together after being divorced for 12 years. The fact that they are now getting back together after the kids have finished college is a miracle for him, because he's bisexual and his wife is lesbian. And I'm amazed at what true love can do when you erase physical attraction. I never thought that was possible until now, being here in this group.

As I sit and watch, I meditate on the guru that I respect and adore, as she continues to place her hands up in the air letting the light come down, she says to me, "Jordan, how is Jimmylee? How is James?"

I answer, "Jordan is taking care of communicating with Jimmylee and Jimmylee is taking care of Jordan and James."

And she says, "Are you Jordan, right now?"

And I say, "Of course, I'm Jordan. I'm just dealing with what I know to be true. I'm not wanting to switch here in group, because I'm focusing."

She asks, "What are you focusing on?"

JORDAN JANTZ

I say, "I'm focusing on the fact that I know that I am in the middle of my life, full circle and that I have just experienced the greatest moment of them all. I have to decide what is right and what is wrong for my life and I need your help because maybe there are some children that need help and that is what my heart is telling me to do with the rest of this year to help these children. And not to be talking about anything, but transforming broken children and starting websites and *get this* and *that* going for the lives of these children, and to hope and raise money for these children. I know I have challenges and live with them, but *I know I can make a difference in the life of a child while I am still alive.*"

I wish more than anything that I could have my Aunt Marion with me today right now, because she did exactly what I am doing today. And I am able to do what I am doing today is because of her. I say, "I am writing a new book and it is going to be called *Embraced* and be about finding out the truth and that I can finally speak the truth of who I am today. I am free, gentlemen, I am free, I am free at last. I am free. I have brothers, I have sisters, I have a brother in prison. I have all kinds of crazy stuff, as you all know me and know the truth, because the truth does what? It sets me free."

They all stand up and embrace me and tell me they have prepared my favorite, a very big bowl of mandarin oranges and sponge cake and ice cream. And they tease me and say, *Now get in the closet and we'll slide them under the door!*

And I just look at them and laugh and say, "Been there, done that, wore out that t-shirt!"

I'm glad that this therapy group can laugh and we can have humor and we can embrace the pain of each other through good times and the bad times.

I'm glad I have the support I do for I know I would not be who I am today without it. I do believe in angels that walk the earth

EMBRACED

today, as doctors or as therapists, I know they are in my life today. As I catch a ride back home from therapy, I realize that it is soon to be Portland's Pride Festival (Father's Day) and then in July I'll be seeing the father who raised me. *What in the world* and *how time has flown!* As long as I'm walking in the light, I'm walking in truth. And when I walk in truth, the world works for me, as it is to this day.

After a long eventful afternoon and a long week of traveling and speaking, I think of my aunt and my brother and my sister and my other brother and my brother in prison and many others and I hope that they know that they were all with me at one of the most greatest moments in time in my life, which was to be back in the hometown where I was born where all my biological family would be with me.

And, God made it happen. And I know, deep down inside, if I follow what He wants me to do through his Spirit for children, there is so much more he wants to reveal about my life. Not only for myself but for others, too.

How weird this sounds to me, I think, who else would care except me? It doesn't matter what others think. What matters most is what I think. But I do realize the position God has put me in to be an example with a purpose and with a reason and with a light that shines so bright. No one can put it out but God and he won't let that happen. So I will start tomorrow with producing the new book, *Embraced*. What an incredible week. And what a blessing to come home with clarity on what to do with my life after experiencing the most momentous moment of my life *where I gathered up my past and I made some sense at last*. When I look back on Decatur I will recall this was the greatest moment of them all. I am embraced.

MOTHER'S BISTRO

23

Father's day is coming up fast, which means another year that many people who are disconnected with their fathers can come together with the community that does embrace the son who doesn't have a father. These people experience a deep intense loss during Father's Day. So Father's Day has become the international Gay Pride kick-off date for many communities in the Pacific Northwest and around the world.

I am looking forward to another Gay Pride filled with rainbows and eccentric celebrations of life. We celebrate the significant men in our lives, people who have been *as* fathers to us, and the abundance today of the things hoped for decades, that we can be treated like any other man or woman who desires to become married. Many celebrate and unite on Father's Day weekend for other positive occasions and celebrations that are personal to them in Portland, Oregon, and this is what I have endorsed since the age of nineteen when I first moved here.

Back then, I was checking out the difference between southern California's gay community and the gay community of the coast in the Pacific Northwest. Before I made my decision I met with the agencies and manufacturers that I would representing, which was all a part of the arts community and the professional theaters that would end up being significant to my career. In so many ways, these communities are a lifeline for those of us who are disconnected from our families and loved ones.

EMBRACED

Jordan's favorite place to eat with good service and favorite place for breakfast.

Jordan's early morning view from his balcony

These dynamics and symbolism show up especially on Father's Day in *my* life. There was never anything stronger for me than the relationship of father and son. I still feel this way today. I have always been part of my community's annual celebration except for occasions of physical exhaustion. These holidays we embrace each other and celebrate the joy and goodness of our lives and friendships.

I come from a community of those who so often have lost everything. I've lost two families in my life, because I am same gender attracted. So, we come together to *give* everything. International Gay Pride celebrations save lives and transform communities and have done so since the days of Harvey Milk. Harvey Milk's political involvement in the 70s led up to his murder. He was murdered for standing up for gay rights.

I recall meeting Harvey; he spoke about recruitment. Not recruitment to be gay, but to recruitment to acknowledge the human value of a gay person, which made me realize that I am human and my feelings are valid and just because the DSM-III Medical Encyclopedia said that gay people had mental illness, which didn't make it correct at all. In 1979 the DSM-III Medical Encyclopedia removed the assertion that gay people are mentally ill. That was horrific when that was in force and after, because people don't change on a dime.

So many of us young men in High School were gay and *afraid* to ever be tagged. But I never could keep truth silenced. I still can't today. Truth is truth and if I live by the truth I know I am set free from other people's judgments and my own judgments, for yesterday, today and always.

This works for me because Harvey showed me that I don't need the approval of others for me to accept my life. I am living and breathing on earth today and I am grateful. Harvey and I never

EMBRACED

exchanged words on God or what comes after this life; we basically touched in a moment in time. I loved my time with him in San Francisco and because of his memory I respect human beings that want all people to have respect and the ability to go to church and worship God even if they are searching for him and for who God is. They have the right like anyone else.

So did Harvey Milk, who was murdered by government officials. I am so grateful that not all government officials treat me in that format. I have seen times change and I *like* the promise of a new and better tomorrow. That's what I hope to give to others – a promise of a new day.

For years I have supported the community on many awareness campaigns and AIDS fundraisers. The annual AIDS Walk recognizes those of us who are no longer with us and reminds us to cherish every day as a gift, and to call up those you love and say, "I am just calling to say that I am so glad you are here today, so glad that you are in my life," because we do not always get extra time, no not at all.

Since my first book, *Out of the Closet, Into the Light,* I have felt that my true mission is to support children of abuse, neglect and abandonment. Many people speak to me about health and friendship. Many never face the truth that those who have been broken as children often do not even survive childhood or cannot communicate or ever develop into adulthood. As a child of abuse, I can communicate reality to many who have been just like me at one point, locked up and waiting to come out as a wrecking ball if there is no support system to guide the hidden brokenness and disabilities that block communication.

I will bring more understanding and more assistance with a fund-raising organization that supports children's lives. Children who survive abuse need deep understanding and loving assistance,

People Pleaser

more than any other group I have met. This is my mission now, and I do respect the true love of the embracing gay community today and every day in my life, and for the way I have transformed with their deep celebration of my life.

I feel gratitude that I have never been tolerated by any of the gay community throughout the country. My brothers and sisters and I walk this journey together of becoming the best that we can become in the world today. I am grateful that I can be an example now to many of my gay and lesbian brothers and sisters and I DO love and celebrate them, and appreciate their commitment to loving me.

I receive a phone call from Portland's Pride Festival team, a friend, who I annually assisted at all LGBT events in the Pacific Northwest, "The team is letting me know that everyone has heard about what my passion is and why I appear to be always happy and upbeat, and that everyone wants to support my new mission and help the community support my focus on changing the lives of children, saying "Everyone wants to join you and share this joy that you bring to all families and honor you at Portland's Pride because of your expression of commitment to your church and its commitment to you."

My friend acknowledges that the children of abuse should absolutely continue to be my focus because these children need help, and the Gay Community and North Star can honor the same good thing. "You received the Beacon of Light for how you are conducting yourself and how you are focused on saving children and the gay community can do no less."

Incredible to me, to receive another award from my old community pertaining to my new community of enlightenment as a beacon of light, which is being endorsed at Gay Pride for the love my life has poured into the lives of children and my church

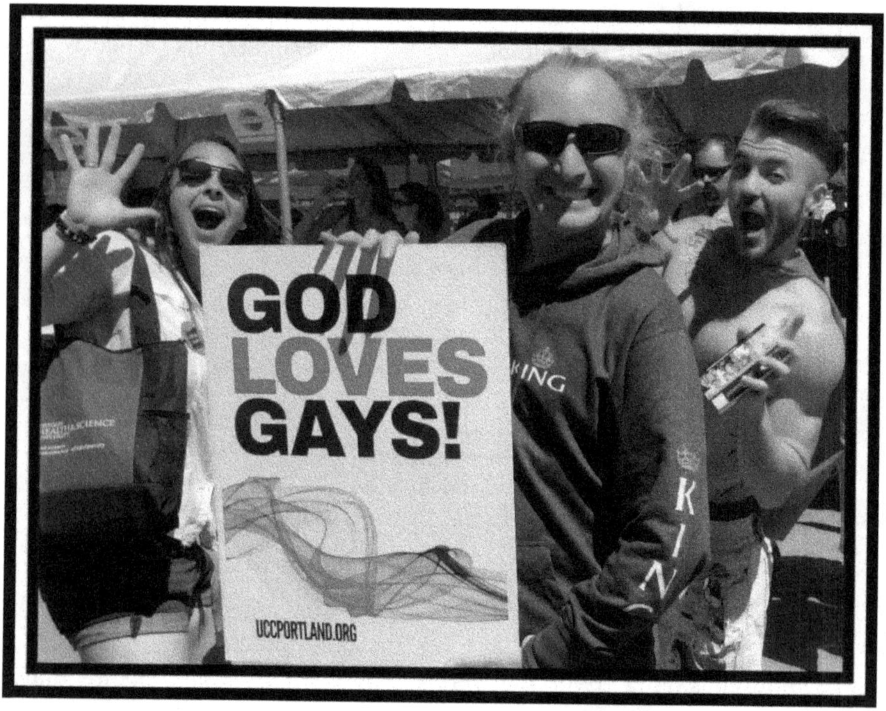
GOD
LOVES
GAYS!
UCCPORTLAND.ORG
KING

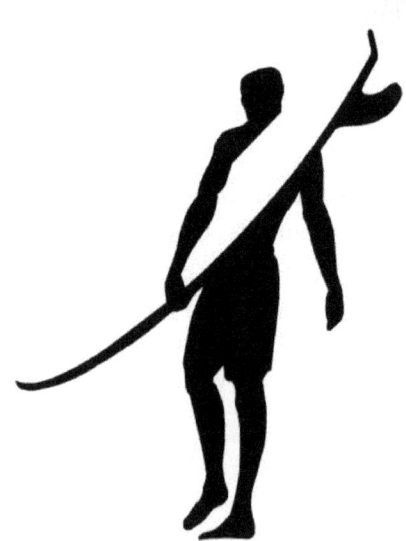

and that the gay community can embrace this also, that gives ability to touch many lives.

I'm stunned! I am willing, especially because I would like to talk to everyone more about the life I am leading with God this day, and what it means to make a difference in the life of a child. I am also so humbled to be honored during this time when many of these brothers and sisters throughout the LGBT community see each other *only* on Pride Festival every year, so every hour of time during that weekend is *precious*.

Immediately I am contacted by my personal friend and mentor who is connected to all of downtown Portland and its metropolitan communities. Samuel states, "Jordan, on the morning we go to Mother's Bistro for breakfast, I won't be late. I'll bring a couple of Portland's LGBT police officers who will be joining this award ceremony. They will be riding their Clydesdale horses, honoring you with your name as a banner on the horses that will say Team Jordan, to prove that Portland's police support what you do, with your open and transparent life.

The town is coming together WITH YOU to celebrate the lives of children, because you share such encouragement to step outside of the box, as you sure did in your first book by Jewel Adams, *Out of the Closet, Into the Light*. And now they all anticipate the second book with 100% of the proceeds going to help neglected, abused and abandoned children find peace and hope. How can any human from any background dispute the character of your heart and your spirit?

As far as the police go, don't be embarrassed if you receive a lot of emotional love including hugs and I know you do not like being hugged personally because of your abuse, so I as your friend will step up and receive the hugs on your behalf. You know I keep a low profile, but I believe in your mission and your advocating

for the *right* support for children that have been abused. The two police officers read your first book and they can't wait to meet you, because of the man child-trafficking rings that Portland encounters on its ships coming up the Columbia River gorge from the ocean. You'll love these guys, Jordan. They will love you. As all of us do.

You're definitely the beacon of light messenger, as if from heaven, to those of us that are joining your journey to follow and support the children that are being saved. Only you would get an award that I would show up at, for another life-changing moment for Portland's gay community through my friend who became a Latter-day Saint Christian who is gay and is *following the Savior* with every beat of passion you can muster up. It is not easy for you and we all know that.

We pray, also, for your church and the people in it that they will see what we have been given in our life from you and your non-plastic fantastic life-style, because you are so transparent and honest about everything and have been, ever since you came to Portland. Even when you were a fashion guru and adult entertainer you were humble and truthful about your survival throughout the years of abandonment. The gay community vowed that would never happen to you again, so we all showed up at your baptism with joy for your new life. And, at this event we remember the vow you made to God and we honor God for what he has done for us in giving us the ability to have a gay Latter-day Saint Christian man teaching and speaking of this reality: we all can change the life of child."

I thank my friend, from my heart.

The Breakfast of Honor will be held at Mother's Bistro, my very favorite place to have breakfast in all of Portland and I think the entire world. Every detail speaks of care and honor, gracious

appreciation of the client as well as love for those who work there. Everyone there is valuable and difference is cherished, says each unique chandelier and ornate tablecloth. The tables are set with fine plates and silverware. Every server is a beautiful ornament on their own, and that continues into affirmation of each patron. It is a unique, gracious, and oh, did I say *delicious?* place to *eat*.

I'm the lucky one because I am known at Mother's Bistro as a regular. They know what I will want to eat the moment when I arrive. They named that dish the Yaya Brotherhood breakfast just for me and Charlie, my best friend of 35 years here in Portland, Oregon. Charlie takes me there weekly as we have had generations of friendship and brotherhood as two gay men that love Jesus Christ very much and value what He is doing for children that have survived similar tormenting, very dark abuse.

The calls continue to roll in. Many individuals in downtown Portland in the medical industry who have worked with me medically throughout my adult life are coming to the event to speak of highlights of our relationship and what I've done for the community through my participation in the religious community.

On the day, the morning dawns and I am up early, as always, for prayers.

Charlie calls and lets me know that he has to be at work and will miss my award, but we will do the YaYa brotherhood omelet next week at Mother's, too, and he asks if he can come on over for a moment, because he wants to bring me a gift from the ocean.

When Charlie is buzzed up to my door, he says, "I want to let you know how proud I am of you. You have finally found your voice to stand up and speak with the ability to change and transform lives. Jordan, you've found your voice and I am so proud of you, and your life is so much better off, now that many

Jordan and Lead Pastor of Elevation Church, Clearfield, Utah

*Thank you, for the testimony and book set that you responded to.
Thank you for opening your church to me.*

Brothers and sisters who go to the Elevation Church and promoted the honest Voice of Hope.

people chose to leave you because of your decision to change and to work very hard to become what we all know you to be today. Over the past 9 years you have been committed to the Church of Jesus Christ of Latter-day Saints *and* the gay communities throughout the United States and nobody will ever look down upon the man that you have become today, because nothing's hidden, you're known as a walking true story of grace and mercy from a God that most of us really don't understand but we see it is real through looking at your life and into your eyes. You have changed and I am proud to be your BFF for the past thirty-five years of sharing life. And by the way, I do know that God is the most important thing because you encouraged me to talk with him and to remember that he knew me before I ever was born and what kind of person I would come to this earth and share of my life to others," he places a collection of sea shells in my arms, colors that he knows I love.

He picks through the box while he talks, showing me the beautiful shells that I know he personally chose for me, and continues, "Your deep desire to live in the next life with Jesus puts emotions of love into the coldest hearts that are waiting to be found. Where are you able to come up with such deep differences that turn communities together, I'll never know, but you sure did it when bringing the hearts of Portland and Seattle's gay community together with Oprah, Donnie and Marie, Clay Aiken, Elton John, Liz Taylor, Katie Perry and now your heart is embracing Ellen DeGeneres and how she has touched your life with sharing love the way she chooses to do on her show, by ending it with telling everyone to be kind to one another and to love one another.

He says, "Every time you say Ellen's words, all I can think of is the day you were fag-bashed and put in a coma for three days. The bullying you have survived throughout your existence on this earth is heinous. Only a guardian angel could protect you from the environment you were born into."

Jordan with Stewart Weed, who baptized Jordan.

JORDAN JANTZ

His voice shakes a little, "As your BFF, I want to let you know that I am so proud of your medical doctors and therapists that support you becoming the beacon of light that you are in the medical community and in the gay community and in the church community and in a world that someday hopefully we *will* all share together, and that's the world that you tell us all about, our Eternal Life that is waiting for all of us at some point. You really make people think, Jordan, you really do, and that's why the political side of this world and the business side of this world continue to seek you out today. Have fun at your party, and I'll see you at the ceremonies of the Pride Parade."

I thank my friend with my whole heart. We are both in tears when Charlie leaves.

I have only 15 minutes to throw on my cowboy boots and my cowboy hat and my big huge cowboy belt with the buckle the size of book. My boots are Tony Lamas and I am dressed like the Fourth of July, all American. Charity is dressed in her 4th of July outfit, too. The gay community expects me to appear in many different formats of attire as I have throughout the history of sharing life with my friends that are gay and lesbian. At my curb I am met by a petite limo sent for Charity and me. It is Bashful Pink!

While riding to Mother's Bistro, out of the clear blue the song comes on the radio "Like a Bridge Over Troubled Water" by Simon and Garfunkel. Immediately I respond to the driver, "Oldies but Goodies?"

He says, "It is just on the Greatest Hits throughout the decades. I like to listen to the Greatest Hits. Do you like this song?"

I say, "YES it is the story of my life and what I do for others in the world today. I wish to be a bridge over the troubled waters for

EMBRACED

many in this world that need love, faith, hope and charity, and I'm that man who will be their bridge, for God to use in His way for a new life."

I show him that in fact I have a copy of the lyrics here with me, "because I will be receiving an award for my firesides that I have put on in the Pacific Northwest. I would be happy to give you a copy of it. And thank you so much for picking us up in this beautiful limo. It is my favorite color in limos and I just love the pink with your white interior. It is SO appropriate for the festival weekend."

He says, "Thank you for the lyrics and thank you for sharing your life. You must be really proud to be receiving a lighthouse award from your community for loving God and treating others with the spirit that I see, because I see this just in meeting you, in driving you to this event. You do not need to tip me for bringing you here. It is a gift in itself in talking to you."

So, I invite him in to share the experience of how open and truthful some people can be and how vulnerable you must be to succeed on this earth. I say, "Honesty is the road to eternal hope and peace for all who choose life."

He says, "I would love to share this event. I've never been to any event in the city honoring the lives of people that come from a different walk."

So, when we arrive, I sit him down with my friend, Samuel, the former mayor of Portland, who embraces anyone that is valuable to my life, because that's what friends are for. Samuel orders the limo driver breakfast and a cup of coffee.

We all sit for the ceremony to begin. I am so overwhelmed to get a second trophy in such a short time, for the same thing. Mother's has partitioned off a special room that is packed with

JORDAN JANTZ

EMBRACED

those who have loved and worked with me for thirty-five years. In the outer room, brunch continues to be served in the beautiful restaurant that for decades has been the best breakfast place in Downtown Portland.

As many of us receive our breakfast, coffees, teas, milks and juices, the ceremonies are ready to begin with an opening prayer. I am ready when called to come forward to pray, to share the value of God loving us that are same gender attracted and giving us the grace to be able to be with Him and follow Him as our Heavenly Father and creator of the universe with no expectations put on anyone.

As I pray I am subconsciously aware that I never want to ever share the love of God as though it is given on a condition. My life was conditional from the day I came into this world. That is not of God. I know that the people in this room are open to God as a father at this moment during this Father's Day weekend, and some know about the father who raised me, who is the godliest man I have ever experienced because of the love he has. I express *that love* in this prayer.

So I ask right now, Heavenly Father, that you will put your spirit upon all the men and the fathers here today who are supporting the life of their child, whether they agree with them or not, because they are showing LOVE, just the way you did for me in exposing your love for me to many communities that embrace my life. I am honored to have all of you in my life, but none of this would be possible without the two men who gave me the character that I own today. That is my biological dad, and my adoptive dad. May we all be able to be able to be fathers to the fatherless today at Gay Pride on this Father's Day, amen.

I receive this second award on behalf of the church, actually, to honor me *and* the church for encouraging us to be more kind to one another. We all know that not everyone in any church lives that, but they know that my relationships in the church are real, those in Utah and with North Star and in Portland, because I won't have it any other way. The church is teaching me good things because the community experiences miracles in my life with me, and I am teaching the church good things because the community can see the church learning to celebrate rather than tolerate. They can see the difference and it means a lot to them. These developments are a breath of fresh air. I am named the Peaceful Warrior.

As we all part, many are in tears, embracing their fathers for being with them, for standing up for them many times in their life that they were bullied by family, by the truth that they would never be like their brother or their sister or their aunt or uncle, but they did have something different inside that simply has been misunderstood by many of us in life today.

I receive kisses and hugs, little gifts of samples of soaps and nutrients for my mind, body and soul because they know I only take in healthy foods and drinks. I begin to respond by borrowing back the copy of the lyrics to the song, and read to the best of my disability:

> When you're weary
> Feeling small
> When tears are in your eyes
> I will dry them all
>
> I'm on your side
>
> When times get rough
> And friends just can't be found
> Like a bridge over troubled water
> I will lay me down
> Like a bridge over troubled water

EMBRACED

I will lay me down

When you're down and out
When you're on the street
When evening falls so hard
I will comfort you

I'll take your part
When darkness comes
And pain is all around
Like a bridge over troubled water
I will lay me down
Like a bridge over troubled water
I will lay me down

Sail on Silver Girl,
Sail on by
Your time has come to shine
All your dreams are on their way

See how they shine
If you need a friend
I'm sailing right behind
Like a bridge over troubled water
I will ease your mind
Like a bridge over troubled water
I will ease your mind

Before I depart, they ask me how it is that God hears my prayers, as they see He does all the time, and I say, **"When you are serious about God, He is serious about you."**

JORDAN JANTZ

EMBRACED

MY FATHER WHO PAID THE PRICE

~ 24 ~

With all the excitement, I concentrate on staying in the moment and not letting the adrenalin override my emotions, for what I'm living today is piercing my center being back together through my years of post-traumatic stress throughout my life.

I will hold fast for I must stay connected to my therapist that meets with me weekly on a one-to-one basis, making CD's that are life-transforming each week. I stay connected to my health care team and homecare team. If I didn't have the embraced support that I have here in Portland, Oregon, with my housing, and my medical team that work hand-in-hand together, that is the reason only that I have had consistency of the finest most peaceful team that has complemented my challenges completely and beaten down all of the delirious fear of being forgotten about, for I have integrity for those who keep commitments to me as my doctors and home healthcare and case-management for housing have done in my life for the past 18 years. I guess it is true that a life that has been beaten down the most needs Jesus and angels on the earth the most.

As I approach my home I realize that I'm so embraced by what *was* abandoned and lost and has all now (all of me) made it where I see myself being found and *not* being lost.

JORDAN JANTZ

Coming up, I am about to spend time with the father who raised me. Time with him is always most peaceful and relaxing, with an environment of serenity. This can be emotionally centering and healing after so much stretching.

Again, through means that are absolutely beyond me, this visit and travel is possible. I'm also blessed to have many Indian medical physicians that work with Indian medicine. It is all natural herbs that I have tried that do not mess with the medications that I take today. They only enhance my immune system and make my life more healthy and vibrant.

The father who raised me is my super-hero and always has been. He is the most enjoyable man that I have ever embraced and trusted in all my years. In his youth he worked very hard, and physical labor was a big part of his life. He taught me how to maintain my appearance and how to be congenial in the toughest of times.

I would say that much of my enjoyment, adoration of art and plants comes from my father and his ability to make a yard look like something out of Better Homes and Garden. I don't mind it one bit to share this trait from my father because just thinking about him gives me peace that in the next life he and I will have even a better relationship because of all he has sacrificed in saving my life and never complaining about the challenge of raising a little boy into a man that was so severely mentally, physically and sexually abused before he ever even bought me, and he did not even know what he was paying for, and choosing to embrace my brokenness of trusting anything was definitely going to be the expedition of his life, and a challenge, that he did not even have knowledge about.

There is happiness in being at peace, practicing honesty and the reality that life just opens up when you let go of controlling the handles on the doors that are locked.

EMBRACED

My service dog, Charity, and I are going to be continuing some therapy and meditation in the next group therapy session at which I can bring my animal and we can all do group therapy with our service animals at our side, for I wish to see in the world and fully receive the excitement of the celebration of my father's life that is coming up.

Never has any man shown more mercy and compassion for me than my father who raised me. Maybe he became compassionate for me because his father was disabled and in a wheelchair.

My dad's father loved me very much. I remember the three of us going fishing at Lake Elsinore. I would bait my grandfather's hook and my father had so much patience with me and the fear I had of touching the worms.

My father said, "SHOW Jimmy, Dad, how to do it instead of telling him. If you show him he can learn to put the worm on the hook. But if you tell him, he doesn't understand what you are trying to tell him to do. Now show your grandson how to bait the hook and catch a fish."

Grandpa looked up at my dad, "I'll never forget this. You really are a good father. And I am amazed at all the work you have done for helping Jimmy learn to trust."

And grandpa grabbed me and put me on his lap and showed me how to bait the worm on the hook.

My dad said, "Now, you are going to catch the biggest fish out there!"

Grandpa said to my dad, "Thanks for helping me be able to help Jimmy."

JORDAN JANTZ

I was so proud that I learned how to bait a hook and fish with my grandpa and my father. It was so nice to be away from all the women and all the craziness of being a child protégé.

I did love to play GI Joes and with my sister's Barbie's and all their clothing. I was able to dress them up and play with something I really enjoyed, and that was playing with the dolls, when I got tired of fishing. No, I wasn't the type that loved to dig with trucks. I didn't like digging in the sand, but I liked playing in the sand with GI Joe and Ken and Barbie. In fact, I am reminded that I did think I could grow up to become a Ken Doll, someday, if I continue doing what I'm doing. And I was excited because I wanted to be a Ken doll. At photoshoots, we would dress up as Ken and Barbie. Recalling back to my hard work for clothing designers I can understand now why I did so well on the catwalk because of *all* my experiences throughout my years, I felt an escape from pressure in my life by playing with Barbie and Ken and GI Joe.

But boy, that day with my dad and grandpa, I learned how to bait a hook really good and enjoyed fishing with them and I still to this day enjoy fishing more than anything else, only because it reminds me of these moments that I can never get back, so I realize to this day how important it is at this time of my transformation in my life to embrace the memories of the past that were positive and realize they cannot be repeated or come back. It is a *happiness* that I must carry and embrace, as I have the *opportunities to recall* the day I learned to bait a fishing pole and catch a fish, which we cooked up that night, and it was delicious and, yes, we all three caught fish and took them back to my grandma's home and she cooked them up for the four of us. I loved it more than anything else, getting away and just being with my dad and my grandpa and my grandma made the best chocolate cake I had ever had.

My dad's family loved me and treated me better than any boy could ever be treated. And my grandpa loved it when I pushed

EMBRACED

him in his wheelchair and I would ride on the back of it, up and down the sidewalk, until we had to leave and go back home. What a memory this is.

It breaks my heart at times to know I will never have a child of my own in this lifetime, knowing that I am on the way to becoming older. I cannot go back to a lifestyle that offers relationships that are bonds for life with those who choose to embrace the gay community. There are fantastic and plastic fantastic people in every community from church to New Age to Muslim to Christianity. It comes down to it being a matter of the heart.

My dad loved to take me on boat rides up and down the river. We enjoyed watching airplanes land because my father used to love to fly airplanes. This was his favorite escape when he was younger, getting to fly free as a bird, away from it all, which I can totally understand.

When I fly, I just have panic attacks and anxiety, so I need a little medication to keep me in the place of being able to enjoy his life's simple pleasures, like spending time with my father.

Always, the accommodations are taken care of by my support team. I am so thankful for what God can do and continues to do for me through challenges I live with. The reality is that I've come out of my closet and I'm in the light.

I am not where I'm tolerated but where I'm celebrated. That's the way it is when I'm with my father who raised me. I do not share or talk about challenges or misfortunes or hardships with

my father. I speak of positive kindness and random acts of love. Charity and the father who raised me have been celebrating their birthdays together in early July. Fireworks are perfect to express the joy I feel in these two loving souls in my life.

JORDAN JANTZ

EMBRACED

My therapist calls me up before I leave to the airport to let me know to call her if there ever is anything I need. This is how it always is, wherever I go, I keep in contact with all of my physicians and people that are wanting to know how to help me with the challenges of so many things pulling at my heart inside my life. I am a living miracle. I know it's all because of God's plan and His giving me the finest professional people to operate with me and help make appropriate choices based on my lifestyle and needs. And they all, each individually, know who they are, if they are reading this book. You are my guardian angels, every one of you from every program, federal to county, psychiatrist to dentist. And that is the only reason that I am able to expand in my life the way that I am doing today: my doctors' confidence that I can become the change I wish to see in the world for others to learn from my life.

What an encouragement as I leave, for I know when I come back my therapy will be all about this incredible encounter of the man who worked with my biological father to get me and have me as his son to raise. Oh, how I wish I could just be with my father right now to talk about my brother, Ronnie, and my other siblings, Kevin and Teresa, and the other brothers and sisters that were not able to meet me, but it's overwhelming to know that my father who bought me also was deceived in so many ways like I was, but he is the kind of man that would say, "Let it go, just let it go."

So until I know if this all is permanent with my biological family, I will not expose any shame or hurt upon anyone in my life. That is not what I want to be remembered for. And when you have emotions that fly up and down and across the world like I do, being in *one* safe place is worth a million dollars and my safe place is with sharing the celebration of my dad's life. I know this as I board the plane.

The flight prepares to take off with Charity cuddled to me, dressed in her swimsuit outfit. Oh, I can't wait to feel some warm sunshine on my middle-aged body, being retired from modeling so many brands and keeping the weight so low where my blood pressure wasn't even able to catch a pulse sometimes, I realize that I am so glad to be away from all of it, and just be free from having to switch fast to protect myself from the expectations put upon me. I'm so glad that James and Jimmylee and Jordan have the doctors to keep them together with the medications, I can make this event of my father's life successful for him.

Spending time with my dad is therapy itself because wisdom will refine and define my many dreams and his many dreams that he has prayed for me throughout my life as his son.

Most exciting of all is the discovery my Indian Medicine Man named Yellow Hammer, who has the gift of being a healer and a leader in his tribe for over many decades. So, when I visit my father I also receive a healing for my immune system and my life. Yellow Hammer is very real and healing and I even asked him if he believes in Jesus Christ, and he said, *100%!*

I said to him, "Then you can do your Indian healing powers that come from God on me. I trust you, or God would not have brought you into my life and I will always make this an event that is very significant for this time in my life and healing of so many things." I also say to Yellow Hammer, the Medicine Man that "it matters to me that you believe in God and know that Healing comes from the great healing power of the creator of this universe." I'm sure not going to miss the chance of a healing blessing out in the middle of the desert before I have to go home. I'm not going to take the chance! This is a part of my healing support team.

All people from all walks of life with different religions have the ability to give healing opportunities. They are not only behind one door, or one doctor's office, or at one hospital. God's healing is through many opportunities if I choose to embrace them.

EMBRACED

That's why I am on the plane right now with my dog headed for the desert.

As we are ready to descend and I am waking up from my travel, I realize that I have been thinking and dreaming about so many things, my father and my biological family, SO much it makes me realize that what I really want to do, I think, is to relax and go up to the room and take my medications and take a nap before I meet with my father after flying from Portland, Oregon, to the Africa-hot desert oasis. I do just that.

And it is 115 degrees! Dogs must pray because Charity got what she wanted. She's such a desert dog. We lay down together in the hotel room bed.

Soon, the phone rings next to my bed. It is my father, telling me he is down in the restaurant and is waiting for me to tell him what all has been going on this past year in my life, and before I begin talking about anything else, I am like, "'Dad, are you serious? It is time to celebration *your* life!"

He says, "*My* life starts by hearing about what's going on in *your* life, and how happy you are or how sad you may be, I need to know."

So, I meet him in the restaurant and he and I embrace and he is so happy. He asks where Charity is and I say, "She is sleeping-in in the bed, but I will take you to see her before you leave today for she will be so happy to see you, Dad."

Then he says, "Well tell me, what's been going on with all the things you are doing for children? I want to know."

I cannot contain my smile, "Okay, Dad, I will just tell you it all."

JORDAN JANTZ

We sit down and eat together. I am able to talk and share the enjoyment of my life about the Christmas Box House and what I do when I have opportunity and am not shut down mentally or emotionally. I find great joy helping children that have been abandoned and abused find hope and contentment. I tell him, also, about an award that I was given at church, for being the Beacon of Light. He wants to know more about the details of the award's purpose and I explain it was because of the opportunity that was given to me from Oprah Winfrey and being able to meet her November 7th and 8th at the Key Arena in Seattle.

For a moment I am taken aback at my dad's questions about *what I was doing in the LDS church*. I tell him that my church helps me help out the Christmas Box House and accepts me as a believer in Jesus Christ. It is the LDS Church and his statement is, "Those are Mormons!"

I say, "Yes Dad, but they are Christians, they are not Mormons. Mormon is a nick name."

He is upset, and says, "I don't want to talk about it. They went and wrote their own Bible."

I tell him, "Okay we won't talk about it and I'm sorry." I will not mention another word. I am just grateful that he doesn't realize many churches don't accept men and women with same gender attraction in their church. They want to serve Jesus Christ, but are turned away. I respect the fact that this is my reality and I have no animosity toward the churches or the people that treat me or others this way. I have no hate in my heart or sorrow in my life for their actions because I know that Jesus Christ is my Savior and my Heavenly Father and my earthly father are embracing me right now, here, in the middle of this desert oasis and I remove the negative thoughts of many church people and their attitude of thinking that the church hates gays when the church does not hate

EMBRACED

gay people, it is what the church has been *told* about gay people, there is misinformation for many. I am protecting my father and the people that would love to see and destroy something good that I have in my life as I protect the things I value the most. That's why I have peace with my father and take the time to embrace his life and let him know he is so valued. I am grateful he is my father, no matter what.

As I sit here with my father and eat share his birthday with him, I realize there are many circumstances that I have never chosen personally to open up to my father about. Specifically, my choices and misfortunes and the choices of challenging events I endured throughout my life that don't need to be spoken to senior citizens that are so at peace in their life today. Why would anyone choose to hurt someone who has loved and protected them? I love my father and don't want him hurt and the world's issues have nothing to do with him or me, anyway. All it would do is create doubt and pain and any human being that wants to try to implement that activity will never be let in to my life again. There are very personal things that I have done that I would never want him to know, that I have chosen to protect.

You see, I went years alone. Nobody was with me throughout my adult life, because I had to do what I only know how to do, and that was what my biological mother told me, to be the best little boy in the world for anyone to ever want you. I recall her making money from selling me and extorting money from the family that bought me that my Aunt Marion set up which everyone, including my biological father is grateful for, so am I. I just don't want to hurt him and he doesn't need to know what name is what and what dad is what.

He just needs to know he is loved no matter what, to the day he dies and I am *Jimmylee Grubbs* and that is who I am to him. He does not understand that I have developed multiple personalities, though I'm sure he knew something of it as he controlled many dramatic breakdowns throughout the years of my life that he was involved in. He was my protector.

Just having the name *Jordan Jantz* is itself is a sign every day to me and it hurts more than anything I will ever experience. I regret the choice of allowing the Jantz name to enter my life. I was so manipulated, so deceived by the word "Christian" that I thought, "Oh, it must be good if it is Christian," but I realize now today I was a protégé in their pocket, also. Thank God everyone knows that if something was to happen to me and no one can find me, they can run immediately to what everyone knows to be true in the Pacific Northwest: these people would rather see me six feet under than for me to continue to live with the knowledge of what they have done to me in my life. They know it was not the right thing to do. But denial is not a river in Jordan.

So I pray that my father never finds out about the books, the specific work that I have done to protect other children that have also been through criminal heinous activity implemented upon them as infants and young children today, which abuse continues. And that reality is why I know that I want to be able to make the change I wish to see in the lives of children.

But I cannot talk about this to my father, so I embrace him with love, because I want him to be prepared to see me in the next life where all that I have been through on earth will be forgotten and removed. This brings me peace and comfort to know my father can pass on with peace and love from a son he is proud of and not ashamed of. He deserves that, after all of the love he has shown to me. I was young and very manipulated, believing another family wanted me again as their forever-son to share their name by taking it on Christmas Eve up at the family's home on Mount Hood, where we celebrated life transformation, when the family came together to ask if I would like to please take their name and become a member

EMBRACED

of their family. What a Christmas! I could never share this history with my father. The shame of being so *needy,* the shame of *needing to be loved,* that filled my life with daily emptiness for all I had at the time was a pretty shell, filled with broken glass. That's how I saw my life and how I felt others saw it too. I was nothing but a platinum card for others to make their fortune.

    I am overwhelmed eating and talking to my father on his birthday and he respects me because he knows life has continued to *conditionally* put me in a position to be in the light, and yet to still feel so dark from knowing that the darkness that I struggle with is *the memories of my life* is hard. I let it go.

    I see my father across the table; I realize that *this* is the most important mission: to show my gratitude to the ones who walk the walk and not talk the talk. My father is very proud that I help children that are starving on the Indian reservations in the desert and that I would even want to go out and give to the children the way that I do. But Yellow Hammer, the medicine man, has opened up my life in a positive way and I see because of my past what I could do to change the future for myself with the ability I receive from my doctors in Portland.

    Dad decides to get up order a bowl of ice cream and we enjoy the coldness and freshness of the vanilla ice cream, which is his favorite, and as for the pecan pie that he wanted for his birthday, I made sure he *got* it. He tells me, "Jimmy you are the only one that continually comes out here regularly to show me how much I mean to you and you don't have time to take off from being in Portland, I know, and I'm worried that your health is not always as good as it should be, because you have always under-eaten and been undernourished because of your modeling and because of the stress of having to always look the way others want you to look. I just don't know how you have your own identity. I know there are things you haven't told me, and I know that you and I are together because we love each other and I am committed, but you need to tell me what I can do because I know there are some things that I don't know about, and if I do have the ability to help I will help. But I want you to be happy and that is the most important thing. You need to let all of the people go in your life that have made broken promises and used you. Everyone."

My father continues, "Jimmy. I know you can't think like you should because of your circumstances that you endured as an infant, and you're not as capable as some of the others and that's why I had to hold you back in the fourth grade to repeat it, because of the traumatic experiences you were born into. I don't ever want you to have to face those nightmares and the post-traumatic stress disorders that you grew up with ever again. The doctors told me when you were in second grade that the memories of your life that you experienced will never be able to be removed. And that there is not a pill anyone can give you to make you forget what you endured. The fact I'm sitting across the table from you right now and we are celebrating my eighty-something birthday shows you and I have stayed together. I know that I have made a lot of mistakes, Jimmy, in my life and a lot of family members have walked out of our life because of their reasonings that they have, but I want you to know, of all the mistakes I've made, you were not one of them. Always remember that. Now I'm going to go up there for my birthday and give my little grand-daughter a hug. And you get to bed, so we can go see Yellow Hammer tomorrow and you can get a healing blessing on those bones of yours. You know, they say once you get older it is a little bit harder to bounce back."

I reply to that, "I've never been able to bounce back from anything. It is just the reality that I've starved myself my whole life to be able to do magazine ads and Dad you know that is my reality because you grew up with me and you know I would throw up my food and take a laxative and diet pills just to be able to continue to

EMBRACED

have that *California glow* that all the buyers wanted for their covers and their advertisements. At least, Dad, you showed me a way that I would be able to make an honest living and that was an honest living, because I sure worked long days and long weekends traveling all over for every photo shoot to make the clothing lines perfected. Thank you for giving me the opportunity to know that I was gifted at something, Dad, always made me feel special, that I had a gift of some sort, even if it was called *being photogenic.*

My father replies, "You were photogenic the day we saw your picture in that sailor suit before we ever got you through your Aunt Marion in Decatur, Illinois. So, I don't think I had everything to do with it. Part of it is in your genes. The way that you carry yourself is what you were taught, but your appearance came from your genetics. Now, God blessed you, Jimmy. I'm ready for bed and you've been traveling all day long to get here, so I want to thank you and see that baby of yours. I'm glad those doctors of yours take such good care of you, and I am very proud you have learned how to manage to the best of your ability to manage your disabilities and let them become abilities. And, I could talk to you all night long but I have to get to bed because your daddy is an old, *old* man. I waited all day for you to get from Portland to here in the desert with me, so I'm going to walk you up to your room and see that little Charity and I will see you for breakfast in the morning, how's that?"

I say, "That will be great Dad, that will be just perfect." I am sitting there just feeling the adrenalin running through my veins knowing that I was able to concentrate on not saying the wrong words or opening up and spilling out about the books or about meeting my biological family and all that, right off the bat. I even don't know what to think of it all myself yet. I don't even know if the biological family really want me as family. It has only been four weeks, but I sure want them. I want all of them. Deep down inside, I think my brother, Ronnie, and I are more alike than any other siblings in the family. As I think of my brother, walking with my

EMBRACED

father to my room, I wish my brother could meet my father who bought me because I know my brother Ronnie would love my dad. Everyone loves my dad. He is a protector and he is very quiet and a respectable man with integrity.

I'm opening the door to Charity in my room, as I think about the integrity of my *two* fathers. Who would do for a little boy like what these two men did together to get me to California? My biological dad and my father that raised me, who got me from Decatur, Illinois did something amazing. Boy, I'm glad my thoughts cannot be read, and I'm glad my thoughts are not verbally spoken. It just puts pressure as I need to take some medication for I am exhausted with anxiety.

I hug my father and say, "This is another year that we've made a promise together, a commitment to celebrate our life and I have never shared anything about this with the family because I value having your love more than anything in the world. It is the most consistent thing in my life even if it is from my commitment to celebrating your life, Dad. That's why I'm here. If you need me, you just call me, no matter where you are and no matter how far," and I give him a hug as he puts Charity down and says that he wants me to get a lot of rest and enjoy my life while I am with him, "because it is not every day that a father and a son get to share moments that are valued like you value me."

As he departs I say, "Thank you, and this was a wonderful birthday dinner, and now do you realize I'm never letting go? I just want you to know that I'm not leaving you, Daddy."

The only reason I ever *did* leave is because I was told I had to leave the family completely because I was an embarrassment, from what Mom had told me, because she wanted me to know that it was time to go find my own place in life. I realize, as I lay in the bed, how lucky I am today.

JORDAN JANTZ

In the morning I am woken up by another call from my father who raised me. "I am having breakfast, come join me downstairs" he says.

One thing he has says surprises me a bit, because he knows that I am not active in the gay community as I was for many years, still he feels to try to uplift my spirits by letting me know that I could always adopt a child, now that gay people can adopt children and it is legal for gay people to be married. I didn't know if he was serious or if he was just saying this to see how I might respond to him, and either way, I am not going to respond in a negative way. I would swallow glass before I would allow him to feel like I would say anything to hurt or disrespect him. His life is more valuable to me than my life. He doesn't know it, and he never has known it, because like I say, those that have been rescued by the Lord need the Lord just to make it through. My dad knows that I'm one of those people that can't make it without the Lord. I am not the man that I used to be. And if any man ever could say this and know it, it would be my dad, because he knows the secrets of my hell, but those secrets will forever be floating down the river, not so important as I am important to my father.

So I say, "I'm too old now, Dad. I enjoy helping children who were like I was, before you got me. That's what I enjoy doing."

Later that day, as we are sitting in a darkened movie theater, he whispers, "I just don't know why you think it is so hard for people to love you, and why you don't open up your life to letting others love you the way *you* deserve."

I realize, I'm the lucky one. I am so much the lucky one. I want to be able to have my father know that I will be there for him, although he is so independent. What matters most to me is love and that he knows he has that from me. That's the way I live my life as Jimmylee, because Jimmylee is the best son in the world and he was

EMBRACED

also the best little boy in the world. Mr. Grubbs got Jimmylee at four years old. I never want anyone to hurt the man who rescued me and helped me grow into my manhood. My father is the only one that can make me cry. That's the reason why I could not talk to him about finding my brother, because I wanted to pray for the *right* answer, whereas the man I was before would do what *I wanted* to do without considering what anyone else thought, as long as it would allow me the opportunity to make everyone happy and take away everyone's pain. Answers through prayer bring me so much peace.

In the theater I answer, "Dad, I want to tell you something, I think about the next life a lot. What will it really be like? I pray that my life will take me to wherever Jesus Christ is at, because that is where my father on earth will be, meaning you, Dad, and I know my biological dad will be there, too, because of the kind act that he did in selling me to you. That was a real act of Godliness to let go of a child that you have had for five years. Only Jesus could continue the journey with me and He is still with me, Dad, today. I would like to have my earthly father who raised me, and my biological father who saved me by sending me away, and my heavenly father standing on the other side of Jesus. So many fathers."

I will take pictures of that, I think.

Watching the movie stars, I realize that dad always was very proud of the way I took care of my body and my appearance. He smiled often when he saw photographs and would laugh at say, "That's my son!" because many others never had the opportunities that I had, and those opportunities came to me naturally, just from walking out into environments that were very Hollywood/southern-California/yacht-style events. In those venues I learned many qualities and mannerisms that would prosper my future. Etiquette and starvation gave me everything as I walked the runway *like a Clydesdale,* perfecting the pony-walk. One thing about being on

JORDAN JANTZ

stage is that nobody can touch you. You are safe, as long as you are up there. These memories begin at an early age; the good times of seeing my father smiling with joy. It is the same smile that he always has had and I know that he is looking forward to another year of fireworks and today I can't see a firework in the sky without thinking about my father. We have made history and broken all the records.

I also realize how empty it felt to not talk to my brother, Ronnie, by phone while I was visiting my father. It hurt me because I couldn't find time to catch him at home or at work. And I know he doesn't like to check his messages. I'm going to have to just *tell* him the truth that his messages mean more to me than a hundred-dollar bill being given to me, because that is the only way I can communicate.

EMBRACED

I give it to the Lord to touch Ronnie's heart that he will realize that when he sees that his brother Jimmy has called him (or his wife, Lisa, shares with him that it is me calling) they will respect me enough with integrity to answer the phone because I *didn't tell* them about my challenges of texting and the disabilities that I grew up with while I was in Decatur, because I was afraid that Teresa and Kevin and Ronnie and Lisa and the other brother and sisters would abandon me if they realize "there is beauty, and no brains" for that was what I was told. What a way to have a first day of kindergarten. I'll never forget these memories. How could I?

And *no*, I'm not going to go out looking for children to adopt, and *no* I'm not going to go out and try to change the whole world, but I will continue to get my life prepared to reach out and transform the life of a child who has been abandoned or broken.

This causes me to consider if my actual, current efforts are *truly effective*? Has my portion of the proceeds of the book, *Out of the Closet, Into the Light*, done any good in the lives of children being helped by The Christmas Box House? I guess it is just one of those questions I will never have a perfect answer to. But I do know that the first time I saw the children, I knew God did something with the book *Out of the Closet, Into the Light*. To have children surround you and you be able to give them little gifts and love has given me the most precious gift of all gifts, and that is to be able to be of value in the life of a child.

It is almost time to head back home. I will remember these memories and embrace them. The ability of communication with my father is impeccable.

As my father and I are sitting together waiting for the shuttle to arrive, I am thinking of asking my father if ever I embarrassed him, being a model. I tell him that modeling was all I knew how to do.

JORDAN JANTZ

He says, "There is nothing dishonoring in being a runway male model. There is nothing dishonoring about modeling clothes and doing advertisements, when the reality is, some people touch so many lives in many gifted ways, and I as your father realized that there is a gift that I never knew God gifted you with, the ability of communicating on film and on camera."

As he says this, I realize that my Dad always has been very proud of the way I took care of my finances and was independent.

The shuttle pulls up and another year has gone by that I must say goodbye until we meet again. I know in my heart I will forever cry for the days that have gone by that I got to share this time of my life with the man who chose to share his life with me.

As I take my seat in the shuttle and my dad is standing there, I reach out and hold my hands in a heart shape to him and he does it back to me.

The driver of the shuttle says, "Jimmylee, it has been a pleasure to see the growth in you. I want you to know that my son is gay and I love him so much, and YOU are someone that is always talked about, and how much you love your father, that you come out to see him and be with him and celebrate his life. We talk about all the things you've been through and the respect you have for him, of not wanting him to know the shame of your past. I read your book and your life makes sense to me at last. I understand *my son* better from reading your book and I am able to love him more for all the things he has to go through to be able to come to the place he is today, an honest man. My son read your book, too. I think you are very wise in not letting your father know about the books, or any of the challenges of your past because it would break his heart, I can see that. Every time I come and pick you up, your relationship gives me something to hope for with my son. You have helped me and my

EMBRACED

son because of your book and I will always look forward to bringing you to your father's for his birthday."

On the way to the airport, tears come out of my driver's eyes. He says that he wishes his gay son could love him and forgive him, because he didn't know how to love another person that was different from him even though he was his own biological son.

I tell him, "It is hard to find the love for another person, especially when they are not like you, unless you see them through the eyes of Jesus. That's the only way true love for anybody can come into one's heart. It has taken me all these years to figure out the true meaning of love. I'm glad I searched and I found out what it really means, that God so loved the world that he gave his only begotten son, that whosoever believes in him shall not perish but have everlasting life. That is in John 3:16, and I want you to know that that is what my father told me on his birthday to remember, 'that is the most important thing in life, to get us into the next life, where we will be together as father and son. And you will not be alone, anymore, Jimmy." And he is just showing me that I am never too old to listen to my Dad."

As I share this with the driver, he asks me to remember all this because someday I'll be sharing this with other people. There is all the opportunity in front of him, I say, "Forgiveness, second chances, love in any of its forms gives us hope for never feeling abandoned but embraced."

I know that someday the father that raised me and I will be together again. Whenever I see the sky light up in fireworks, I think of nothing but times spent with my father, because he has the ability to let his colors burst out so beautifully.

JORDAN JANTZ

EMBRACED

CHRISTMAS BOX HOUSE *PAY IT FORWARD*

~25~

WHILE IN THE PLANE from the desert back to Portland with my service dog, my mind realizes my commitment at the Christmas Box House, in Utah in just two weeks.

I know in my heart I must show up and *show face*. I know I need to experience the safety that has to exist if any healing is to take place for even a single child, in order to know I am really helping the children I hope to help.

My author and friend, Jewel Adams, will be with me to embrace the experience of inside the doors of the Christmas Box House.

I had left a message for them weeks ago. Then, when the staff called me, I was asked what my *reason* is for wanting to see the Christmas Box House.

I said, "I am Jordan Jantz and I'm a supporter of the Christmas Box House in every aspect. I have one of my books dedicated to you with the proceeds that would go to me, going to you. Now, I am writing my own book and *all* of the proceeds 100% go directly to the Christmas Box House. This is my purpose in life to be able to help one child not cry that day. My mission statement is to help relieve the wounds placed upon innocent lives. I was an orphan when I was sold at five years old and had to go to court at the age of seven, because my biological mother wanted more money for me after selling me, choosing to extort finances from the family in California that she had sold me to.

This is why I embrace broken-hearted people and broken-hearted children. I have been there. I'm embarrassed that it has taken me so long to face my reality that I was unwanted.

So, I can only imagine what many of these children feel in child protective services and agencies that protect children like the Christmas Box House. It is my honor to have my life story published for the dream of *no more tears for these children* that have been exploited through their life and left at the Christmas Box House. It is my honor to help pick up the pieces for these kids.

I only want to experience the *environment* of the Christmas Box House, the spirit of it, as a child would experience it when arriving. It will help me understand the Christmas Box House International in a way that will be productive for the charity I am producing through my new book, *Embraced*, coming out February 14th."

They were delighted when I told them that, and wished me luck on the new book and gave me the address and said they will order more copies of the old book, *Out of the Closet, Into the Light*, and, "We hope you experience what you hope for when you arrive."

On the day in Utah, Jewel Adams, author of the first book, *Out of the Closet, and Into the Light,* comes to pick me up. We know this is something special and we immediately take off. We feel so much joy to be able to see this special, special Neverland for children, a special place that they can be *safe*. The Christmas Box House is where many lives are transformed, like an estate of angels for children.

EMBRACED

As we pull in and see it up close, goosebumps raise my hair up. I have a lump in my throat, knowing what's inside and what it is all about. It takes me back to when I, too, was abandoned and forgotten and I feel vulnerable. I smell pine, the scents of Christmas.

Approaching the inside, I see it is *surrounded* with trees and two fireplaces and tall ceilings that have stars hanging down from the ceilings with lights all over as if it is Disneyland or the Salt Lake Temple at Christmas Time, the beauty embrace me. I see toys under the trees, dolls for the little girls and trucks for the little boys, and little tin soldiers and little ballerinas, teddy bears, surround the baseboards of the home. In every shape and every color, the lights continue to twinkle further and further in. There have be more than a dozen, maybe twenty Christmas trees of every color in the rainbow, the most beautiful Christmas trees I have ever seen in my entire life. The place is filled with rainbow Christmas trees of every color and shape. Peaceful children's music plays in the background, and I am embraced by the beauty of hearing a child sing. It just touches my heart because that is something I never knew how to do until I was sold.

I walk over and pick up a teddy bear, and I can feel the presence of my infant years in Decatur, Illinois. The rage of yelling, the sadness of sleeping in a car, the fear of no one finding out where I was left at, and would I be found again? Sure enough, Gram or my Aunt Marion or my biological dad would come find me two or three days later, and I begged them to never leave me again. I promised I would be the best little boy in the world, but I don't feel that my father had a good life as a little boy. When his mother left him and took off to Texas, he never got over it. It hurt him so much. I totally know what he felt and it makes me sad to know that my father did to me what was done to him, but my father did it because he didn't want me to experience the things that he had to experience. I have to tell myself positive things, because when you are an orphan and being given to people you don't even know, a child doesn't know what to expect. A child thinks people will forget where the child is dropped off, and that means, you don't get to eat or drink *anything* until you are found. As I sit on the couch I flash back and realize *this* is why I am doing what I am doing.

As my friend, Jewel Adams, walks around and meditates on the beauty and the presence of this sacred charity that I have proven the desire to lay down my life for and become a spokesperson to even advocate for people with my challenges from abuse, I know I do have a voice of hope with a message that will bring a beacon of light to the children in the Christmas Box House, all gifted to me by my leaders in my church in Salt Lake City and in Provo, Utah. Being awarded a Beacon of Light, I pray I do bring the light into the hearts of these children.

You see, I want to tell you one thing right now, while reading this new book that has been released on Valentine's Day. This is not about me, not about you, but about what we *together* can do. You are reading right now something that gives you the opportunity to change a child, one that is broken, one that has disabilities, one that has challenges, one that might be emotional, one that might be living in fear, one that may have never even met their family and even some that are put up to be sold or given away. I have lived my life since infancy to survive and still be alive today but now I have the best, most successful life I possibly could have, without dwelling always on the consequences of my past. The pain I lived through paid the price and the torture shed my blood for sadistic pleasure in the most dark events a mother could perform.

EMBRACED

I never look for beauty from the outside of a person, like I did before. Because I've learned that appearances are deceiving, but what comes through the camera lens and on to magazines reveals what's within your mind, body, soul and spirit; all comes out on your photoshoots of who and what you really are inside.

JORDAN JANTZ

My dream before my life is over, is to encourage others to connect their spiritual lives and experience the potential and passion that many in life long for. People are simply searching to belong, wanting to share life with honesty and truthfulness, never condemned for their mistakes or misfortunes. My dream is to share love and build solid ground relationships that give renewal.

EMBRACED

Jordan, on the road, working cross country for Ocean Pacific.

JORDAN JANTZ

EMBRACED

Maybe that's why she went to prison. I don't know. I know there are a few people in the biological family that are in prison and no one wants to talk about what they did. But hopefully my sister, Teresa, will reach out in love and my brother, Kevin, will reach out in love, for they sure have made me feel like they both have known me my whole life and have heard about the many sick things that I endured, which information they got from their mother who was dating my biological father at the same time he was married to my biological mother, who was the meanest, most awful human being to my father and to me. To this day, I don't know if I'll ever be able to see a female and believe she could really love me. It hurts too badly to even think of the women that have walked out of my life.

The staff at the Christmas Box House is very kind and welcoming. They say, "Thank you for your phone call ahead of time. We've been looking forward to this. Please walk around and meditate and feel the energy of what the kids feel when they come in. The children are in the back, now, sleeping, so you can walk around." I experience their professional spirit and understanding. That is what I was looking for.

Jewel enjoys the value of the Christmas Box House and its charity. Her presence here with me makes our visit to the Christmas Box House (that receives donations through *Out of the Closet, Into the Light*) complete.

I also want to see how far agencies have come toward meeting the needs of children at risk. When I was small, there were no agencies to speak of. I had to be taken to the Children's Shriners Hospital when I had been beaten or severely abused. They always took care of me and my dad would come or my great grandmother would come and sit with me and promise that they would get me away from my biological mother and the closet. As I sit on the sofa of the Christmas Box House holding a purple teddy bear, I want so badly to go back to the closet.

JORDAN JANTZ

I think about children and what a gift they really are. I am so grateful to be in the Church of Jesus Christ of Latter-day Saints. I will be a lighthouse. I will have this book produced for the children. *They WILL receive 100% directly of the proceeds of this book.* This book will help stop bullying. I was bullied and many other children that are orphans or don't fit in or might have same gender attraction are bullied.

It is time to realize all this and Stop Sexual Child Abuse, End Homelessness for Children, and Stop Child Trafficking (which is the same as black-market-baby-selling, what it was called when I was young). **I'm just ready to say that this is my life-mission; to make it possible for ONE child not to cry that day, by my actions and what I can do.** I will do it because God has made it that I can be alive although I am physically weak and mentally insecure because as these children have had demands placed upon them, just as I also had to be the leader in every show performance, activity and produce what I was *told* to produce. I don't ever want this to happen to a child again.

Tears roll down my cheeks. I sit with Jewel Adams and whisper to her, "Thank you so much for writing my book." At my age, I am able to transform hearts and spirits and souls only because I have been taught by the most elite and most down to earth faith believing Christian Latter-day Saints who accept me being gay and love me and embrace me and know that I no longer have that relationship activity taking place. I am embraced by a great authentic multi-cultured group of medical physicians that handle the child abuse that I live with today, which causes the disabilities that I live with and now I have just totally outed myself, I have just opened up the door, for the world to see that YES I was not born in the Brady Bunch family, or the Partridge family. I tried to get in, but they were full. So, I realized I could only watch them on TV and dream of what could be.

EMBRACED

Jewel can see I'm emotional. We look at the plaques on the wall. One says:

**To the world you might just be one person,
But to one person, you might be the world.**

People need to help people, because people can only heal *with people*.

One idea that is not on the wall but in my heart at the moment is:

**Confess your sins to one another
And pray for one another
so that you will be healed.**

The Bible says this, not because all our pain is from sin, but because all our pain *feels* like sin, as if we did something really wrong. Pain can create sickness in the body, in the mind, and in the spirit. Sitting there, I remember that my biological sister, Teresa, had said that she had *never in her life* had a family member throw her a birthday party, as I had celebrated Aunt Marion on Marion's day.

A light clicks on in my brain: celebrating a person is *something I can do*. I can celebrate Teresa! I can keep a promise that every child should experience. I can put up a *kind* of Christmas tree for Teresa, something special for her birthday since she told me that she has never had a celebration on her birthday with her brothers. It was never a big issue to them, she had said.

I feel in my heart, that what is inside me at this time is a truth. With God - the God that loves truth - all things are possible, *this is possible*. I sit there cuddling the teddy bears a little longer. I think more ideas that I have been gifted with, that my biological siblings likely never have felt.

The Christmas Box House guide asks, "Would you like to have a more time alone, to reflect?"

I say, "Thank you, yes."

My siblings, like all people, need people to heal, specifically people who comprehend and do not deny. I need to express to my biological siblings that I surely do not know what they individually may have gone through, but I believe them. I know the truth of what they experienced, I embrace them and accept them where they are at without expectations.

How can I come up with time and money? How can I make this happen? It is all much more than I can do alone. What is needed is enough time to *embrace* them, emotionally, and hold them, these precious people who share my blood. How can I discover characteristics of my two sisters and my three brothers, especially hard given their fear and coping strategies? My brother, Ronnie, has the most similar characteristics and that is very hopeful.

I think about all, hugging silky Christmas Box House bears, cuddled in a garden of pink trees and big cushions. I decide that my fifties is not too old to have a family. I can be found. We can find *each other*. My *Peter Pan Return* has more than fairy tale value. I see that I can bring more to this now than I ever could at any other time in my life, in these days when I am embraced by medical professionals, supported in group therapy and processing groups, aware of my needs and my impact on others and covenanted to God and authorized by Him to bless those around me.

The Spirit is giving me the choice. When I left Decatur as a child I had no power and no choices. This time, the choices are mine. This inspires my spirit to listen to the ideas of my church branch

EMBRACED

president, my church stake president, my therapist and doctors who realize that this can do nothing but heal wounded emotions of being sold. All the children in my biological family have carried weight, and children become our world. What happens to them and what they feel are not their responsibility for they are infants and children. This is the truth of my life's story. As I sit here and experience flashbacks of my past and think of the children who are walking behind me, I know I am where God wants me to be at this moment.

2016

FALSE TRUTHS COST A FORTUNE

~ 26 ~

Arriving back home in Portland, my case-manager picks me and Charity up from the airport. We pick up my suitcases of home-grown organic vegetables that I love so much that are gifted to me from my spiritual family and head home.

My case manager tells me that my physicians and therapists are going to my therapy group with me tomorrow, and that they all value my desire to help others that have come from my background, whether that is modeling or touching the lives of children or any of the past film industries that brought me to where I am in my life.

My case manager says, "Everything is possible for you now. Your relationships have been brought into your life for a purpose and that is what we will talk about tomorrow. So, get some rest. We are all happy to see your heart glow the way it is today, for your life was filled with such sadness from what the world took away, but I believe you're right, God is going to give back to you what the world took away from you. And I don't talk like this to any of my clients, but you know and I know, all things are possible with God, and we'll leave it at that."

I thank him and I tell him, that he is one of the greatest case managers a man could ever have, especially a person like me who is challenged with trusting that love could ever be real in my life.

EMBRACED

As I get into my apartment (that I am so grateful for because my doctors and housing support team have opened up for me) I sit down and thank God that I am in my beautiful space that I call home. Yes, I have a home, *my own* home, which I have been blessed with. I prayed for many years to be independent and not have to rely on my outside attributes to survive in this world, for it gives me peace to know that there are some people that can see my heart instead of my body. Although I thank God for the gift of putting me in the body he created for me, most people never look or take the time to see what's inside the man but only look at the attributes of the appearance of the outside, which gave me credibility. But that is past and I am grateful for that past to be my past and no longer is my present. Also, it is God who I answer to. It is God who gave me my home and God who gave me this moment in my life today. I am humbled at what I have been given. I am immersed with love for the people that opened their hearts to connect with me.

I decide immediately that I need to call my Aunt Marion, because she would want to know how I am doing. I can't express what it is like to say that someone wants to know how I am doing and that someone would even care to know. My mother who bought me said I am *used shoes*. But that label has been removed by my Aunt Marion, her sister. It will never be placed on me again.

As I call her and thank her. She is the first to hear my new decision as I tell her that I am coming back to see her and that I will be there to celebrate life a second time.

Aunt Marion is just *in emotion* and says, "Nobody has come out of their way at such a faraway distance like you have. You are a very, very wonderful person, Jimmy! Why do you let people put a label on you that is not true? It is not wrong that you have the attraction to men. It is the way you were born, Jimmy. But what matters is what you do with it today, and forget about the past, because you never had a choice. You were always the best little boy and don't forget it. You are, in my eyes, *my* son that I should have taken, but I couldn't because I had two kids already and I was working full time and didn't have the heart to tell my sister that she couldn't have you and that I wanted you. *You have been on my heart* and I have been thinking about what it meant to you, for I don't want to ever see you sad with tears in your eyes again over being told what an embarrassment you are to your family. I don't want to hear that ever again that you chose your own lifestyle to be gay. You're a good Christian man that has same gender attraction whatever you choose to call it, gay or whatever; my message is "let it *end*." <u>Stop this!</u> I want to confirm and commit to you that I will communicate with understanding and walk with you 'til I am taken home into the next life."

Aunt Marion can tell that I am elated and broken with emotion and surprised at her ability of love, to nourish my heart with her words and immediately express to me the value of her commitment to me as my aunt, no matter what special needs I may have had to live with.

Aunt Marion says, "Your past was torn and broken by others and you are picking the pieces of it up with your doctors and that makes your Aunt Marion very happy and I cannot wait for you to come to Decatur! And I do hope that your sister, Teresa, and your brothers, Kevin and also Ronnie, and all of your other brothers and sister embrace you, also, the way you should be embraced if they truly do know God. God makes it very clear He will not ever let go of orphans or widows, that His Spirit is with them, and His Spirit is with you, Jimmy. He is inside of you and I saw that when you came to be with me for my birthday. As I said, nobody has come to visit like you have. And you continue to do, a second time. And I know you don't have the finances to make this possible. *But I am surprised at your ability to let God take control and make things happen that you can't. Obviously, your church and your friends and the people in your life are good people and I'm glad to know that*

EMBRACED

you have doctors that not only care for you as your physicians, but love you as a friend."

I say, "All things are possible with God, Aunt Marion. Miracles, even."

Next, I pray to speak to Teresa and open her heart to this connection. I get her voicemail.

I say, "Teresa, you have been on my heart. I have been thinking about what it meant when you said that no one had celebrated you and your birthday, in the family. I have experience with what it can mean to not be held as precious on such a day. The path is open for me to keep this commitment, this gift that family gives to each other. I have just decided to make arrangements to come back to Decatur to honor you on your birthday and celebrate with our brothers and be there for you, but I need to know, are you serious about wanting to celebrate your birthday? Because it is very expensive for me to make arrangements if they are not that important to you. Don't take this personally, but I do know that since we are in our fifties you may not want that today, even though you have never experienced a brother throwing you a birthday party, as you stated to me before. Please call me as soon as you get this message."

It is noon and I am not surprised to get voicemails for Ronnie, Teresa and my cousins.

After the phone calls, I unpack and lay down with my little Charity after her little walk in Portland's rainy weather which keeps the air fresh. And I am grateful to be back where the altitude is not high and challenging on a person with beach-starved mentality. I love the sea level life that I have had in Portland, Oregon for the past thirty-five years. I guess this *is* home. At least for now, until God takes me home with him.

JORDAN JANTZ

LOVE MOVED MOUNTAINS; A MUSTARD SEED OF FAITH

~ 27 ~

PREPARATIONS CONTINUE and weeks go by and conversation with Teresa is becoming less frequent. She told me that she wants me to come for her birthday and I and my case managers and medical support team make therapeutic plans for another healing opportunity in my life. But my letters to her go unanswered.

Everyone who knows anything about me knows that I have thrown myself into this cave and I will be *eaten by shame* if I'm not acknowledged. By not communicating at all, Teresa is shaming me before almost *every* single person in my life. I am boarding a plane that will throw me out to my destruction, I know it. She hasn't *embraced* one phone call, knowing that I am coming.

I am so ashamed for Aunt Marion to even know this reality about my biological sister. I am so ashamed that my biological brother Kevin has also chosen not to call or respond. Did I not please them, because I am connected to my brother Ronnie and his wife and my Aunt Marion? Did they expect me to stay with them, away from others? I don't know the circumstances and I guess that's reality when people don't communicate. I guess that is why people

EMBRACED

text, instead of talk, these days. I don't know, because I don't text. I choose to communicate with my heart, soul and spirit, *with my words*. That seems to work best for me, but I realize all people are different and I accept that, hoping that they will accept the way I try my best to show my love and communication, the way that I do and the way I can.

Ronnie and Lisa do respond on a Sunday afternoon. Ronnie calls me. He says has not experienced this kind of communication and acknowledgement in life before, and he says he will learn because I'm worth it. He also says that he will not allow anything to happen to me or to Charity. Ronnie tells me that I have the most support from him and his wife and to remember that none of his other brothers or sister or family has been to his home except our biological father. He reminds me that there has been always communication breakdown: "It is *not you* and don't let them put it on you. You need to be loved and that is why I am here to let you know that Lisa and I will not let this happen again to you. For coming all the way out to Decatur from Portland, Oregon, to celebrate your sister's birthday, and for her to not even call, or respond, or thank you, but turn her back on you, is wrong. It is the wrong thing to do, Jimmy."

I just say the cold truth.

Ronnie responds, "The truth, Jimmy, cleanses your wounds. It cleanses what you have been through, never knowing that you had brothers and sisters, never knowing that you were of significance or value. For Teresa and Kevin to respond to you that way makes me sad, and I see why I have had the problems and challenges I have had with them, also. You do not deserve this."

During my lay-over in Chicago in the care of the wonderful Traveler's Aid volunteers, my sister-in-law, Lisa says on the phone, "Jimmy, this won't happen again."

Ronnie also says, "I am sorry. I don't know what will happen when you come, but please know that you are wanted in *my home and in my family.*"

Ronnie concludes that he wants me to feel comfortable in his home at any time, and that I am welcome. Ronnie says, "You are my brother, you have family, and don't feel awkward to call in the mornings for we will be there and make up for what you had expected from Teresa, and make this a wonderful time, and we are so sorry that Teresa did all this, leading you on to make you believe that she wanted you."

"And as far as Kevin goes," Ronnie says to me on the phone, "he and I haven't corresponded for many years. In fact, Memorial Day was one of the first times that we all came together on Memorial Day, and we couldn't even come together for that. Teresa and Kevin had walk away and go and do their *own* Memorial Day thing because you were with us, and they chose to do that to you, and put the guilt on you, because you chose to come with us, you and your Aunt Marion. I've dealt with this my whole life."

I realized right then, my brother Ronnie and I are a lot alike, and I love him so much and my sister- in- law, too. I just want to hug them so much. Isn't that weird, I think, for a man in his fifties to want to embrace his brother and sister-in-law? That I am needy for love after all the work I've done to show and embrace my life for others? I'm still feeling this emptiness? I think I just really want to love somebody that is real and somebody that is true. This feels so right. It is what I have prayed for all my life, that the pieces and the puzzle of my life would come together.

I know what to do. I must *let go completely* of expectations that I have for this second time in Decatur.

EMBRACED

It does not help that everyone I have talked to is expecting a miracle, just as the miracle that brought me back to Decatur the first time. Miracles happen every day, but aren't embraced by all.

Every person who was part of the story in Decatur before is now part of the great legacy that will forever be remembered, long after I am gone.

All of the sudden the tiny plane drops like a rock into Decatur at midnight and I realize that I've been in deep thoughts and deep meditation of praying for positive healing and love to abound in my brother Ronnie and in my sister-in-law, Lisa, and my nephew and niece, Zach and Hannah, and my Aunt Marion. That's what it is all about, *so forget the rest*, as Ronnie said, and Ronnie's been dealing with this his whole life. At least I know he is an honest man.

The little tiny plane makes a tight turn into Decatur as I hold on to my little service dog. The plane bumps on the runway, and the pilot lands the plane safely …and what a tiny little airport! I am a little shocked every time I see it. I grin, seeing the hotel staffer again at the airport with the hotel shuttle, waiting to pick Charity and me and take us to my room. In the Decatur air, cornfields are now towering past the stop signs on the road. I believe my body changes as I am dipped in *Midwest climate*.

As I unlock the door to my room, I see a bouquet of flowers sitting on the table with a card that says, "Have a safe journey. Love, your medical team," and I start to cry because I realize that they have been my family when nobody else was there. They've been there for me. They gave me what nobody else would give me – unconditional transparency and honesty, and I realize that I am not here alone. I have my medical support team with me and my service dog.

Those are true friends that most people never experience. I don't do plastic fantastic. I never could. False fronts are not in my

JORDAN JANTZ

life. I've always been up front on who I am, what I am, and what I would like to be, if given the opportunity to be able to become that man I dream to be. I smell the flowers and I thank my therapist in my heart as I say a prayer before I go to bed with gratitude for this momentous moment in my life.

EMBRACED

BE WHERE YOU ARE CELEBRATED NOT WHERE YOU ARE TOLERATED

~ 28 ~

I WAKE UP TO Aunt Marion's phone call, asking, "Are you awake yet? I can't wait to see you! I bet you are just exhausted. Did they assist you at the airport with your bags and your service dog? Did they help you get around to where you needed to be?"

I reassure her that *yes,* I have been in the best hands.

Then she says, "I can't wait to see you and give you a hug! I've waited for you to come for so long. I am so happy this is happening a second time that you can be with me!"

I answer, "Thank God, Aunt Marion, they sure did help me. And I didn't even have a panic attack in the airport which is a miracle, so yes; I am here, Thank you, Jesus!"

She says, "As soon as you can, get on over here! I'll have breakfast ready for you. How about a Denver omelet?"

"That's just what my immune system needs," I say, "and some orange juice! Thank you so much, Aunt Marion!"

JORDAN JANTZ

I get my service dog out and across the street to Aunt Marion's adult assisted living center. Today she is not in front but is waiting for me in her rooms with an enormous fresh hot breakfast spread that she has all laid out for me. We embrace the journey together over breakfast.

I tell Aunt Marion I brought presents wrapped for my biological sister's birthday and she says, "That is so sweet of you to think of her." I share with Aunt Marion that I brought Teresa a beautiful black and white dress with a classy matching handbag so that she can wear it out and about, or even to my funeral, if that be her choice.

Aunt Marion says, "Well, you are not going to be going anywhere soon. You are here with me, and there's no funeral, but we are going to go see your grave marker design, right? You and your brother are designing your marker so I can see what it will look like? I am just amazed how after fifty years this could even have taken place. I feel so relieved that I have no secrets with you and me, Jimmy."

And I think, *I am so grateful that Aunt Marion has kept confidentiality and kindness of my embarrassing and shameful moments that I was able to climb out of, thanks to my doctors and medical support team.* As I feel the presence of gratitude for them for this moment that would not be possible if it wasn't for the medical support I have. I tell my Aunt Marion about that and let her know I am so grateful to have people that know how to help me manage my health in a proper manner.

I say, "It is a little challenging, Aunt Marion, when you are alone and have to rely on your own God-given abilities to take care of all the needs to stay on track and stay alive."

She responds, "I'm so happy to know you are taking as good of care of yourself. You are just beautiful inside and out. And

EMBRACED

Aunt Marion prays to God that nothing will ever take you away from your purpose until God is ready for you to come home. I just want you to feel that you have some love in your life. And I am so happy that you have that from your doctors – love and support. You couldn't get that anywhere else. You must have really good doctors."

And I tell her, "They are the highest quality of doctors, absolutely, and they love me and I love them and everyone knows it. And I brought gifts for you, and for my brother and my sister-in-law, and my niece and nephew, also."

Even as I say all this, deep inside I know that some members of my biological family most likely are not emotionally capable of responding to my arrival. Teresa's rejection has broken my spirit for any interest of opening and connecting my life with hers. She broke that connection and disconnected me from her promises and led me to believe that she wanted me to celebrate with her and her family. I jumped at the opportunity to be able to give back. I never thought she would do what others have done to me before. I was feeling so taken advantage of by what she has done with giving me the impression that she had love and a connection for me, her brother.

How plastic fantastic! I should have spotted it from the beginning and talked to my brother, Ronnie, *before* I talked to my support team and I worked on making Teresa's dream come true, which never was a dream to begin with. She had no plans of a birthday party or me even being with her. It was all a lie. Again, from a woman that reminded me of my biological mother. All this is something my biological mother would have done.

I also realize after all Teresa had implied on my first trip about the biological family and how messed up situations were, that she wanted me *to be careful* of how close I get or open up to my brother *Ronnie*. Teresa warned me that I should *read everything* or have it be explained to me before I *sign anything*, if Ronnie were to give me something, as Ronnie actually *did* on Memorial Day, the grave-plot next to my biological father and my biological great grandmother! That was just because Ronnie was the one who handled everything about my dad's funeral and his mother's funeral. But Teresa, my sister, made it sound like I needed to protect myself, *"just a little note for a head's up,"* she had said. I could vomit!

    I just realize I have been thrown under the bus with another person that cannot connect but only disconnect and dissociate from the truth. I do not let Aunt Marion know the details of this shameful, embarrassing experience with my biological sister and her birthday and let it just be left quiet, because it would hurt Aunt Marion for me to be exposed to any more pain from another woman like my biological mother. I thank God for the Holy Spirit and the discernment to realize I will not allow anybody to mess with my emotions I share with my brother Ronnie and his wife, Lisa, and their two children. And if Kevin, my other brother, chooses to follow suit and not respond, just as he has not responded to even one of my phone calls, I will just have to realize that I have to chalk it up to *birds of a feather flock together*. And that is what I am experiencing with my biological brother Kevin and my biological sister, Teresa. Shame on them for leading me to believe they have loved me and looked and wondered *whatever happened to their brother, James Bond?* I believe from my experience it is another case of plastic fantastic circumstances.

    With Aunt Marion, I only keep these ideas in the back of my mind. I want to listen instead to Aunt Marion tell me what has been happening at the assisted living center. It is soothing to hear her talk about her life.

    Aunt Marion says, "I'm just happy you are here with me in my home. I just can't believe you came a second time to see *me* and to get to really know your biological family. I know you will share

EMBRACED

your love; you so deserve love from them and they so deserve love from you. You have been giving and pleasing everyone the entire time of your life. What happened in taking you away when you were young was because it *had* to happen,"

Aunt Marion emphasizes, "And I don't want you to feel empty anymore. I have faith that this was all meant to be and I know that your biological dad loved you very, very much for him to do what he did because the same thing happened to him, Jimmy, when he was four years old and his mother left him, too. There are things that you'll find out more as you learn about your dad and about your family. Your dad was very good to me and came over to my home for Thanksgiving and Christmas at times with your great grandma, Ina McNear who was one of my best friends. They both loved you very much and wanted your life to be protected."

And soon we talk of happier things, and Aunt Marion says, "I just love that nephew of yours more than anything. I hope I see Zach again. He's so sweet."

I say, "He is such a good kid! He's only eighteen. I can't believe I'm an uncle! I have never gotten to be an uncle before, in all my life. I don't even know if I can do it. But I will do whatever it takes to be the best uncle to these two children. And I know they are adults and all that, but they are really still children. I am truly elated to be embraced as an uncle and as a brother."

Just thinking of Zach and Hannah makes me smile. Zach has a soft, gentle spirit like I do and it is deeply moving to see characteristics that my brother, Ronnie, and I both share that are very similar.

Aunt Marion says, "And, by the way, put this on your calendar while you are here: Your cousin, Mark, wants to show you his bees and make you some honey, because he knows it will be really good for your health and it is the purest form of honey ever.

JORDAN JANTZ

You will just love it! And your cousin, Sandy, in Florida, says to tell you hello and she sends her love and happiness for you in what you have found in your life. We all are amazed that after fifty years you would ever find out the truth of your life."

Then she says, "And, OH, don't let me forget! oh, you will just love this, Jimmy! Guess what! The Kidd Kaddalacs are coming *here* for Labor Day!"

She moves to her desk area and searches in the papers, "*You will be here for this celebration with me! They were here last year when I first moved here and all of my life's possessions were removed and I was so down! That's what happens when you get old. You can't take it with you*, you remember that."

She looks up from hunting and says, "Your Aunt Marion has had to learn to adjust to a new way of life, and not having your Uncle Dale here with me is hard, Jimmy. We are both alive and have loved each other for so long, but he's over there and I'm over here. I'm so happy you can be with me to go see him, for he remembers things from the past very good but has a hard time remembering what happened that day. Your Uncle Dale knows you are coming and he said to me, "*I remember teaching Jimmy how to swim! He's coming here to see us?*" is just what he said, Jimmy. He really is so happy, but I'm sure he forgot because he has a hard time remembering, you know. He does remember you, a little boy he *loved*. You have always been so lovable. And don't you forget *that*."

She hugs me and kisses me firmly on the forehead, "I don't care how old you are now, you should have been mine! But I've told you that over and over."

And then she says, "Found it!"

Aunt Marion shows me the paper flier listing the Labor Day festivities, with a nice big font.

EMBRACED

She says, "It is so nice, we won't have to go *anywhere* since the Labor Day celebration is being brought here, and we'll have a barbecue. We'll have so much fun together. This is the best and funnest entertainment here at the senior adult living center, Jimmy. You just make sure you hold me up and we'll have some fun dancin'. You know the Kidd Kaddilacs play the fifties and the sixties music! *You'll just love 'em!*"

Later that day when she's settled down a bit, laying in her recliner, she says, "I remember how you always loved to tap dance, and you were the best. It was like Dancing with the Stars when you would dance. You and your sister would get out there and just tear up the floor, whether you were tap dancing or cheer leading, you always stood out. You are so cute and handsome! I can't believe it is fifty years later and this has happened for you a second time in one year! You must have some really good doctors that want to see you healed in your heart because on the outside you *still* look like a model. But on the inside, I want to make sure it's taken care of while you are here with your Aunt Marion."

She pops out with, "And I forgot to tell you, I have some of your pictures and magazines that you gave me from your modeling fashion covers! You know, it was not bad to see you enjoy modeling and dancing and performing the way you did. It made everyone so happy and we were all surprised at the talent that you were born with. I'm still amazed at your ability to even work in the fashion industry and keep *the appearance.* You were just like a little Shirley Temple to so many people, a little boy who could perform so well in a little outfits … and that just built up more in your teens and young adult years. It would have made your dad and your great grandmother just drop their jaw. I know Bud and I know Ina. They are so happy right now, looking down from heaven and seeing what is happening with their little boy who became a man and that makes me know I did the right thing for Bud and for Ina. And I want you to know that your Aunt Marion understands the pain that women have put upon you."

She looks sharp, "I felt it inside of you last time you were here, your pain. You will *let that go,* and hold on to what you have with me, for I couldn't possibly be around that many more years in my nineties, Jimmy. You showed everyone the integrity to come and show me how much it meant to you that I found you a home. That just breaks my heart. *I wish that my sister would not have treated you the way you were treated.* But that is past!! On Labor Day, I'm absolutely going to dance with you as long as you will hold me up!"

Then Aunt Marion says as always, "Is everything is okay, Jimmy? Are you okay?"

I say, "Aunt Marion, I'm just fine. I'm just a slow eater and, I'm just so tired still."

"Well," she says, "you sit right here by me and rest on the couch and we'll talk and watch the Golden Girls like we did last time. You can lay down, and I'll hold Charity!"

Charity just *loves* her Aunt Marion. Charity embraced Aunt Marion the moment we arrived to Aunt Marion's room, getting right up in the chair with her and laying on Aunt Marion's lap while we enjoyed planning our time together. Aunt Marion is the only person that has known me since I turned three that I can count on to love me in this life and in the next life.

I let my eyes close and listen to her sweet voice telling me all the things we're going to do. I end up falling asleep with the Golden Girls in the background and the sound of Aunt Marion's soothing, peaceful voice.

EMBRACED

It's different, you know, when life brings the past back into your life. You have a choice to either accept or reject it. I choose to embrace it, for that is where I know growth will be and healing begins. I know it sounds crazy for a man my age to desire healing, but when your life has been ripped and shredded with tormented lies of never knowing the truth of where you belong or who you are, you break down and deal with getting by and hold on to what you know for that may be all you have to hold on to and survive. I learned that when I was sold. I was told by my biological mother that in order for anyone to ever want me, let alone keep me, I would have to be the best little boy in the world.

I hear Aunt Marion in the bathroom, getting ready to take Charity outside for another potty-dance, she asks me "How was your nap? I can tell you were laying there not just sleeping but also thinking of something. You know you can tell Aunt Marion anything, no matter what."

I just tell her, "Aunt Marion, I just love you, and I am so exhausted of trying to reach out to people that have given the impression to me that they love me and want me, but it is all false impressions from them, for their benefit and for their glory, and they end up benefitting for some reason from my being. I don't know why that is, unless it is them wanting attention because of my life and my life's circumstances and situations that have occurred. Only God knows, Aunt Marion."

Aunt Marion and I take Charity out together. We see some of the ladies that she has made friends with in her new home and they all are very excited to see me again and amazed that Marion Lee has a nephew that comes from Portland, Oregon, to see her and everyone's *elated that I show up,* for Aunt Marion was telling them that her nephew was coming all the way from Portland a *second time.*

I smile and say, "I look forward to this wonderful time with all of you, and I am grateful to be back in my hometown where I was born."

Charity does her potty dance and every one of Aunt Marion's friends dote over the beauty of my special dog, Charity, because of the way basenjis prance like horses in a show, and she is so much a *show dog*. It's so cute to see her show off and prance like she does, for my Aunt Marion's friends.

We head back in to Aunt Marion's home after her potty dance. We tell residents that we will see them all later and to have a beautiful day, and they all wave and say, "We are so happy you are here, Jimmy! And your aunt Marion has been waiting for you and has been talking about you all the time. And you are going to get to see your cousins and your biological family and we are so wanting to hear all about it. From what your Aunt Marion tells us, this is something she never dreamed would happen. And if you would have told her this, she would have never have believed it, she said to all of us, that Jimmy would find the truth and have the opportunity to be a part of his biological family."

Aunt Marion tells them, "I just love the way his one brother, Ronnie, and his wife, Lisa, treat my Jimmy. I think Jimmy and Ronnie are exactly alike. And it makes me so happy to know I get to see all of this at this time in my life, that I have been given this opportunity with Jimmy. And he's got to get going with me girls, but you know he'll be here for the Kidd Kaddalacs so *all you girls get ready to dance!*"

As I look back and see the little senior ladies, and think that they all are here for the ending of their lives, it just touches my heart. I face reality that life is so short and what time we have in being able to embrace one another only comes around sometimes, because very few embrace the opportunity or care to take the

EMBRACED

opportunity to step outside their comfort zone and share anything of themselves or what they can do to change the life of another person.

I think, *I'm so happy that I have this here with you, Aunt Marion, and with my brother and my sister-in-law. I'm not going to worry about whether or not Kevin or Teresa will come and embrace my life, or my other brother that is in prison. The brother that is in prison is a twin and I* want *to find out how he is doing or if he needs help of any sort, but nobody responds to him or wants me to know anything, even how to contact him. So I have no opportunity to connect with some of my biological siblings because of so much secrecy of the family dynamics. I* do not take this personally, *after so many years of therapy. I'm not going to worry anymore. Life is short!*

As we get back into Aunt Marion's home we decide to make plans to watch her favorite baseball team, the Chicago Cubs. She loves the Chicago Cubs and she loves the Chicago Bulls. Those are her teams and I'm all about it, with her. I embrace that moment and we spend the day watching the Chicago Cubs play. I just fall asleep next to her and Charity falls asleep on her lap, all the way until dinner time.

Aunt Marion nudges me and says, "Jimmy, you've been sleeping ever since we brought Charity in from her potty dance. It is time for supper already."

For me, it seems like I just had breakfast.

Aunt Marion coaxes, "Everybody's waiting, Jimmy!" and we head down for dinner, making sure Aunt Marion has her keys (I lock the door for her). Charity is very at peace within Aunt Marion's home as we share a lovely evening down in the dining room of the adult assisted living center.

JORDAN JANTZ

I sit at the table with Aunt Marion and her girlfriends that she has made and they all ask questions and more questions and say they've never had a nephew "that would do what you have done for your Aunt Marion."

And I say, "You don't know what Aunt Marion has done for me! Aunt Marion does not have pride in what she does for others; she doesn't have a boastful spirit. She does what she does from her heart. And that's what she did as a friend to my biological father and biological grandmother. They were all three friends and acquaintances. So I owe her the gratitude of letting me find out before it is too late, if I have family that wants to be a part of my life or not. But, that's the reason why I'm here and you are here, to face the truth and be with the ones that love you and celebrate life's honest reality. Some things come back around, even fifty years later, for a purpose."

And the girls reply, "We are all glued to this event. It is like Marion is telling us a story of a book that she read or a movie that she has seen. Your life is like a movie or a book and we can't believe all you have lived through and what your Aunt Marion and your dad and your great grandma did to save your life from your biological mother, and the fact that your Aunt Marion's sister doesn't tell you today affirmation of the truth of your life has really hurt your Aunt Marion, for she did everything she could to give her sister the little boy that she always wanted and dreamed of. But let us girls tell you, your Aunt Marion says, she should have just kept you and told your dad that she wanted you to keep you here in Decatur with her and her two children. But she is so kind that she felt her sister needed her little boy that she was waiting for in California."

I say, "I know, girls, I know. I'm just surprised that you, Aunt Marion, shared this with the ladies, but it is all good, I have no problem with it because it is all true. You are *all that*, Aunt Marion, and much more. Are you girls enjoying your chocolate pudding?" I ask them.

And I ask Aunt Marion, "How is your pecan pie?" (that is my Aunt Marion's favorite pie, pecan pie) and I love to see her just *enjoy eating* with these little old ladies. I realize how short life is and that I have been given the blessing to be here and I know I may never pass this way again.

After dinner we return to her home to talk and relax and I tell her that I'd better get to bed early because Ronnie is coming over tomorrow and I would like to be ready for this brother. I don't know what he's got planned. Maybe he'll come over and just sit in the room and visit. That would be fabulous. Charity gets up off Aunt Marion's lap and comes and puts her little coat on and we head home and Aunt Marion goes to her window as we did on my first visit, and she watches me get across the street and home safely and then I call her to let her know I am safely back in the room.

On the phone I tell her goodnight and thank you so much, this was the *best first day* of this miracle that I am even here a second time and, "I have to go to bed and I will talk to you tomorrow, *I promise.*"

She says, "I love you and goodnight, Jimmy. I watched you all the way from my window as you walked across the street, and I'm so glad you are here. I can't tell you that enough, Jimmy, so goodnight and you get some sleep and you take your vitamins and make sure you get rest. I don't want you getting sick. In fact, sleep in tomorrow."

And I say, "I am so glad you said that. Thank you! I need at least eight more hours of sleep because my muscles in my arms and in my legs hurt so badly just from just getting from here to there. So, goodnight, and I'll call you in the morning."

JORDAN JANTZ

She laughs and tells me, "Well, I'm putting on my muscle cream before I go to bed so that I don't have to ache all night."

I say, "Lord have mercy, Aunt Marion, we're both getting up there in our years. I can't believe it. I'm in my fifties and it is just amazing to still be alive. But I'm going to bed, so goodnight, sleep tight, and don't let the bedbugs bite."

She laughs and says, "There are *no* bed bugs in my home!"

I say, "There had better *not* be!" and we both laugh and I hang up the phone.

I lay there for a minute reminiscing about her transparent love and how she doesn't hold back from expressing it. She and I are a lot alike when it comes to expressing truth, feelings, and what is right. She knows what is right and she did the right thing. I thank God for her as I fall asleep, and I thank God for letting her find me.

Ronnie's Corn

KITCHEN TABLE: THE NIGHT MY WORLD CHANGED

29

I WAKE UP THE NEXT DAY and see the clock say, "Oh my goodness, it is 11:30!"

The phone has been ringing so I know I have messages and I didn't even hear it!

I get up and go to the front desk to get my messages and have myself some juice and milk and take my medication to prepare me for a calm and peaceful day. Yes, I am open and honest, you can see, I as I write this book, about medications and everything. So, you as the reader open up your heart and your eyes to what this truth is about for people living with challenges.

The messages are from my brother, Ronnie, who wants me to call him as soon as I can, and the another message is from Lisa, my sister-in-law, wanting to make sure that I am doing well and that I had a good time with Aunt Marion. Lisa says she can't wait to see me. She hopes that she and I can go do some bonding together, just her and me, and that she will take time off from work for we love going to antique stores (she knows I love antiques). We both love restoring and creating art projects (me, to the best of my ability).

I immediately call them both and touch base. My brother tells me he wants to pick me up tonight to take me to his home for a dinner that he is going to prepare for me. And he asks, "Do you want me to pick you up or do you want my nephew or my wife or my daughter to pick you up?"

I say, "Whatever works best, I will be ready."

And he says, "Okay, my wife wants to pick you up, while I finish making the food and preparing the table for you. I am making you something special. Would you like to come around 5 o'clock and have dinner at 6? Or would you like to be picked up earlier than that?"

I say, "Of course I would love to spend the day with you, but I know and you that Aunt Marion will want me for some time today, so I think it will be best if we just plan for the late afternoon. How would you like that, Ronnie?"

He says, "Jimmy, you are so considerate. Lisa and Hannah will be there to pick you up. They both want to come and pick you up."

"Tell them I can't wait," I say.

I have the opportunity now to prepare to get my gifts together for my niece and nephew and get the special birthday balloons together for my niece's birthday and her birthday presents: I bought her a diary for her years in college at Milliken University and several other little gifts that I hope she will like as she is into entomology. I'm scared to death because I have always screamed when I saw bugs and I still do, to this day. But if that's what she wants to do, I'm all for it.

I will go the distance to show her and Zach, my nephew, the value they are to me, even though I didn't get to see them as infants

EMBRACED

and teenagers. I'm grateful for the blessing to be with Zach as he graduates his senior year in high school, and Hannah's first few years of college. I truly have been given a second chance, a chance to forgive the past and renew the future of my life, and do what is right with my biological brother and his family.

Dinner is fabulous! We all sit around the table. Hannah opens up her presents and loves her blue balloons. I didn't get her pink, I got her blue, because I know my niece doesn't like the girly things from what her mother and father told me- and Hannah just loves them! She is so surprised! This was one of the first gifts that she has been given from her uncle and to have her give me a hug made me so overwhelmed with emotion, I almost start to cry, but I hold it back.

Zach opens up his present, also, an Oregon Ducks bathrobe. He just loves it! I just hope it fit him, because he's so kind he wouldn't tell me if he didn't like it or if he did. I *know* he wouldn't tell me. *My brother and my sister-in-law raised two wonderful children.*

The two children leave the dinner table for their personal tasks and agendas for the evening. Ronnie and Lisa and I talk and share the truth about what we want and expect from this trip, to receive from our second time together.

Ronnie tells me, "Jimmy, I have spent more time with you on the phone than I have other members of the family. I have enjoyed every minute of it, because I see through you and into your heart and your life. You have had to be a people pleaser," he states, as the hair raises up on my head again, because that is so true.

I say, "How did you know?"

He says, "By the way you listened to Teresa and wanted to make her happy on her birthday, to come out here and you brought all those presents for her. Don't worry about it, Jimmy, that she doesn't answer the phone. She has chosen her fate with you. She has always been like this with the family and we all have dealt with this, with her, in some degree. And with Kevin, I don't know what to tell you. It is an on again/off again mentality with him. So, you'll have to decide. I am very sorry and Lisa is very sorry that you were given an impression and came out here with gifts to celebrate your sister's birthday when she had no intention at all and didn't express it. It is just wrong."

"Are you okay about all this?" my sister-in-law asks, concern for me in her voice.

I can only reply, "This isn't the first broken promise from my biological family. I had broken promises the first five years of my life, from my biological mother. With Teresa saying the biological mother contacted her and told Teresa that I am gay and that I had personal medical issues that I have. Teresa said my biological mother thought Teresa needed to know this," I feel tightness as I explain this.

I say, "Ronnie, I won't tolerate that.

Their faces show support.

I say, "And after what Teresa did with this trip, my expenses, my time and knowing *after* talking to my biological mother…(however in the world she ever found out about my personal life just blows me out of the water) it makes me realize *loose lips* will *sink my ship* and that ship *means my life!"*

I am just broken again at the table as I tell all this to my sister-in-law and my brother. They can tell that it has emotionally thrown me in the cornfields.

Then I ask them, "Do you guys want to know the truth?"

EMBRACED

They look concerned. I realize that I am going to release *the truth* of what my third adoption was like that they don't know anything about *Jordan Jantz*.

I open up my soul at the dinner table and I say again, "You both want to know some reality here? Can you keep this confidential? Will you make a pact with me to *never repeat* this to anyone or show what you are about to experience to anyone? Because of the mistakes and the manipulation that I have allowed to trust others with, I need you both to realize that this trip is about getting to know one another and not meeting one another."

I say to them both, "This is the only reason why I am here, *because I want to know you. I want to be with you.* I have never had anyone in my adult life that wanted to be with me without any *conditions or control*. What do you think, am I asking too much, do you want to know the truth? And can you handle making a vow?"

They are not withdrawing. They are open to me.

I say, "If you can, put your hand on the table, over mine."

I place my hand flat on the table. Ronnie immediately places his hand on top of mine. Lisa places hers on top of her husband's. They both agree that they will never tell anyone or show anyone any of this, and that I can trust them and that they want me to learn how to trust.

Lisa, my brother's wife, says, "I can tell you've never had anyone you can trust."

I couldn't even respond to that, because I have a lump in my throat that my sister-in-law can read me so well.

So, I say, "Do you have a laptop or a computer here?"

They say, "Of course," and they go and get it and bring it to the kitchen table.

I tell them, "OK we made the pact, made the commitment, and made the promise. That means the three of us here are eternal family."

I explain how strict this is, "My niece and nephew are out of the house right now and that is important because they cannot ever know what their uncle has endured for I am ashamed for anyone to realize the criminal activity that has been done in my life to me. And, I am ashamed that nobody defended me. And, it is my fault because I was afraid that I would be given or sold so I became everything that the world wanted. So are you ready for this?"

They nod and say, "*Yes.*"

I say, "Okay, Ronnie, punch *Jordan Jantz* into the computer."

He asks, "Who's Jordan Jantz?"

I say, "Just punch in the words, *Jordan Jantz*."

He says, "Well, you do it."

I am so embarrassed because I am computer-illiterate and I have a lot of challenges that most people my age would not have.

I tell Ronnie the truth with shame in my heart, "I don't know how to do it, Ronnie, I just don't know how."

And he says, "It's okay, Jimmy, it is okay. Dad didn't know how to do this either. Dad was illiterate and had a hard time reading, writing and spelling,"

I begin to emotionally feel a break in my heart for I realize how he had to have felt for I have felt so ashamed that I have a block that can't connect the dots of what to do academically. It is a peaceful moment at the table for understanding the challenge that I have worked so hard to overcome and have never known *why* it has been so hard.

I immediately say, "Thank you, Ronnie, for telling me the truth, because the truth can set me free from my own judgments for not accomplishing what the average human lives with the abilities to do, that they can do and perform in life. But I have other abilities that I used by learning from people who groomed me to become capable of developing an income that I am not proud of. And it almost killed me."

Ronnie has punched the name into the computer.

Ronnie looks as reads, "Jordan Jantz. It's got *your* picture here. Are *you* Jordan Jantz? "

I say, "Yeah, there are <u>three</u> different names that I have had in my life, unfortunately, and I am dealing with *three* suitcases of luggage that I have been carrying around that need to be let go of. And I need you to promise that what you are about to watch, you will not ever let go. I can't tell you enough how much I need to hear the words, *"I promise through the end of my life, I will not expose this and neither will my family, to anyone. You don't have to worry about your Aunt Marion, or anyone that you love and don't want them to be hurt because you did whatever you are about to show me to survive."*

They repeat what I need to hear and Lisa says, "It just breaks my heart. *Three* different names that you've had to go by, with three different *families*?"

I say, "This is the truth. And I'm embarrassed, but you are my blood brother and you are my sister-in-law."

JORDAN JANTZ

They click on the Voices of Hope and see the website and watch the ten-minute version of what North Star and my church family have created for my mission to stop child abuse and child trafficking today.

My brother says, "It's as if you are trying to stop what happened to you, being sold."

I answer immediately, "I am so grateful you know the truth."

Ronnie says, "I've always known the truth, just from what I was told, that your mother sold you. Dad knew that, and we all knew that, but he did the best he could to help you and I don't know how you handled what you experienced. Selling a child affects you throughout your life. It is a memory that can't be just dissolved, Jimmy, so don't be so hard on yourself."

They watch the internet and check out all the realities of where I am at, and who I am today, receiving knowledge of what got me to where I am at today, by reading the history of my life right there on the public internet.

He says, "YOU HAVE A BOOK!"

I say, "I do, and I brought a copy of it for you, if you want it, but you've got to promise to put it away and only you and Lisa have knowledge of it. I do not trust anyone else with the knowledge of what is inside the book, for I know my life would be in danger because I had to change the names in the book to protect the innocent and the guilty."

Ronnie says to me, "I can't wait to read it!"

Lisa has tears in her eyes as she grabs my hand and lets me know, "You will always be my brother-in-law, and I am very happy that you are in my home. And, we are also Christians and reading here shows that you are a Christian living for a new way of life and looking for a new way of life after many years."

Lisa says, "We will not let go." I give her a hug and thank her.

My brother gives me a hug and tells me, "I can't believe all this stuff that you have lived through, and how you are turning it around to help children that come out of the life that you have lived. Jimmy, I know and can see how the damage of broken promises and delusions of truth were kept in your life, spoon-feeding you to keep you doing what was expected with control. You don't have to worry about that here. *Not here.* Leave that behind. When you are with me, I don't care what you did in the past in the adult industry or as a professional runway model to support yourself in the fashion industry. Modeling is something to be proud of. You did that, because that is all you were taught. Your value was placed on you when you were sold at five years old. So your mentality of thinking *was if you were paid high money in the industry, it gave you the value of what you were worth.* You were reminded throughout your life how much you cost as a child. And continued to have that imprint in your heart that opened up doors through your entertainment of tap dancing and performing and as you said, *being the best little boy in the world,* turning that into the best man in the world, by receiving high end dollars for the adult industry that you were opened and put into from your modeling. One door just leads to the next when you are in the public eye, as you were. And don't worry about it. We are not going to bring it up or hold it against you."

To hear this from him was better than any therapy session I have ever had, for it made me realize that he was telling me the *same thing* that my therapist has been telling me, back home in Portland, for decades.

JORDAN JANTZ

I just tell him, "Ronnie, it has been so hard to keep track of who I am. Am I Jimmylee Grubbs, am I Jimmylee Bond, or am I Jordan Jantz? And who am I really? Does God even know my name? It has been changed so much."

Ronnie looks pained *with* me.

I continue, 'This has been quite an emotional moment for me, because I have never done this, and I'm exhausted. But I'm so glad to have you both, and I want you to protect yourself. And not ever let anyone take what we have away. I do not trust Teresa or Kevin, Ronnie. I do not hang out with people or associate with people anymore that want to lie to me, and call themselves family. I do not let any of the 3 families that have been involved in my life to come close to my heart anymore because of the deceit. Certain members I embrace, such as cousins, and aunts, and uncles and then there are some that I must let go, because I cannot *afford* to have them in my life, although my dream on this trip was to find a sister that would bond with me and we would be connected. I'm realizing this trip is also about letting go."

"That is so wise," my brother says. His face and body communicate peace.

I get up from the table feeling weightless and I say, "Thank you so much for a wonderful meal, my brother, you are a good cook, and I love to cook also. I think you and I have a lot of things in common. WE should cook together sometime."

He says, "Of course we will and that "sometime" will be soon, Jimmy. You are my brother and you are honest and you want my family in your life and we want you in our life. And don't worry about what my sister Teresa and my brother Kevin think about their brother, Jimmy, because they haven't had anything to do with me or my family for years. Our kids have had Lisa's brothers as uncles.

EMBRACED

I step right up to the plate and say, "But not anymore! They also have an uncle that is a Bond, who has their blood and has their heart. Now that I know where my family is and I know the truth that there are other brothers and sisters that are alive and out in this town, I will not let go. I'm not like that, and it is not in me, so we are going to make the most of this trip and embrace the moment no matter what Teresa chooses to do on her birthday, that is her choice. I'm *letting go* of *abandonment*, once and for all."

And I say just to Ronnie, "And I am so sad that they speak the way that they do and I am so sad that they have chosen to respond to my niece and nephew and my sister-in-law and you the way that they have. For them to speak of you taking advantage of their mother and their father and doing all of the burials and real estate makes me want to vomit."

I pray Teresa and Kevin do not involve me in any of that drama, for I will run from them as fast as I can to the airport because I will not tolerate bullies.

I continue, "It was wrong what they did to Aunt Marion and to me last Memorial Day when we were all at the cemetery to honor our father and they chose to go their own way and dissociate from me and you. I don't call that a true sister. I don't call that a true brother. And please watch your back because I've been down the road, Ronnie, where every corner I turn is a broken promise, coming from the people that you think would love you the most."

We have talked deep into the night and I say, "So, here are your keys and I'm exhausted and I have to get back to my room and take my little dog out."

Ronnie asks, "Can we *both* take you back to the hotel?"

And that's what they do. It was incredible evening at my brother's home that will always be remembered of when I opened up my life for the first time. For the first time, I have to trust Jesus that my brother and his family are walking side-by-side with me. It is a matter of walking by faith.

Lisa, pulling some ears of corn out just for me.

PHONE THERAPY: HELLO, ARE YOU THERE? CAN YOU HEAR ME?

~30~

B<small>ACK</small> AT THE HOTEL, as my brother and sister-in-law drop me off. As I get out of the car, I also open up Lisa's door to let her in the front of the car. I think, *What a kind soul. She made sure I sat in the front seat with my brother.* It just touches my heart.

Lisa gives me a hug and says, "Tonight was wonderful, and I'm glad that you came over for dinner and you did something you never did, to open up as you did at the table. Please trust me and my husband. He is your brother and he loves you. You have done more in showing your love for him than any brother could. We all see that. And we know you love us and we love you. You get some sleep tonight. And this is just the beginning of your new life. You *let go* tonight of a lot of things, remember that. God was with us at the table and I felt his Spirit and I feel His spirit in you. So don't worry! We have the ability to overlook what people may say. They do not know what we know. And we will keep it to ourselves, just like we made that pact at the table, you can count on that tonight when you go to bed."

Ronnie also leans over and says, "We'll see you soon, and we love you."

I wave goodbye. I'm so glad they drove off, because I can't even go into the hotel. I have to walk around the hotel and catch my breath for I have deep emotions in releasing the truth to my brother. I never cried so hard, walking out in the middle of the crops that surround the hotel grounds.

I look up at the sky and say, "God, I'm in the town where I was born. Do you see me here, again, a second time? I want to know what you want from my life and why I'm still alive. And why I'm just finding all this stuff out now, after asking for the truth all my life. I wondered when I was small if I would ever be found. Now, I am found. How long, Lord, will this last? How long will you let me have this love?"

I get on my knees, out in the middle of the parking lot on the side of the movie theater.

I pray out loud, "Lord God, Heavenly Father! Please give me the opportunity to never be alone again in my life and that I won't have to continue dreaming that I belong but *knowing* that I belong. I thank Heavenly Father, that You have never left me or forsaken me. And I ask you to forgive my sister Teresa and my brother Kevin for responding in the way they have chosen. And please forgive the mother that bought me for not wanting anything to do with me because of what I have chosen to do. And yes, I *have* chosen to do the right thing and they all have *still* walked away except my Aunt Marion."

I tell the Lord, "So, protect Aunt Marion and protect me, from all backstabbing and malice and jealousy that I have found where I was born, God. Please give back what the world took away from me. And I thank you, Heavenly Father, for putting love in my brother's heart and my sister-in-law's heart and their two children,

EMBRACED

for me. Because for once in my life I got to eat and be with people that have the same blood that I have inside and be accepted *just as I am*. Through Jesus Christ, I pray that this trip will be a trip that will be life-transforming for all of us. In Jesus Name I pray, amen."

I get up, still crying. I walk to the hotel room to take Charity out.

I still whisper, "Lord, my life doesn't work without you. Nothing does! I was basically an orphan. I have been an orphan and I know that you have walked beside me and I thank you for not giving up and letting me die without this opportunity to know that I have been found and that I have been remembered."

Immediately as I get back into the room. With Charity, I fall into bed and sleep so well that I am just relaxed, with so much peace from what my sister-in-law and my brother shared, and the fact that I was able to release the secrets that I have had to keep inside. It gave me so much peace! I did tell them how much I regretted letting another man in my life convince me to take a name *Jordan Jantz* and to believe that Jordan meant "crossing over" into a new life. Anyone in my shoes at the time would have been desperate for a new life and Mr. Jantz knew that.

I think again of that moment, on a Christmas eve at the family home on Mount Hood in Oregon, when Mr. Jantz asked me if I would become a member of his family. I will *never* listen to people and believe what they say is true again until I receive spiritual confirmation from God because not everyone who goes to church is a believer in God.

I finally expressed that when speaking to my brother tonight. What a relief to let go of the Jantz name. The nightmares of performing to be accepted is something that I wish I could just erase from my life. They are just like the nightmares I have experienced these past two weeks before the trip, of *not hearing from Teresa* after her invitation to celebrate her life. She just threw me under the bus for not liking her badmouthing of my brother Ronnie and members of his family. I will not tolerate this in my life and I know that Jesus will not leave me stranded here in Decatur in backbiting that could take place. He will remove me from the snares of people who are deceitful; like my biological sister deceived me into believing we have a connection but that is removed. I know I wish I had therapy right now, but it is not possible at this time. It is the middle of the night and I have to go to bed and then see Aunt Marion in the morning. Aunt Marion is like ointment to my wounds.

You see, I would never try to control Teresa's words nor her actions, but I had believed her and my brother, Kevin, too. I believed her words that she expressed to me in my last visit that she valued family celebration, as I was celebrating my Aunt Marion's life and birthday back in May. I know my biological dad and my biological great grandmother would have wanted me to be with my Aunt Marion, of all the people in the world. Because the way Teresa and Kevin responded to Ronnie and his wife and two children, I knew that I did not want to get in the way. I knew that I there was a lot that was being manipulated and it wasn't the right thing to do, even just seeing my brother Ronnie have to be embarrassed. I felt overwhelmed in my heart for the actions that I was witnessing and experiencing throughout the two weeks of my first visit and this part of the three weeks of my second visit.

I believed Teresa then and I believe *she believed herself.* But what her words caused me to have faith in is not here and everyone can see it. Kevin did the exact same in dropping me like a hot potato soon after letting me know his feelings about our brother, Ronnie, and what Ronnie did when our father passed away and when their mother passed away. In a way their anger was as hard as a rock. I felt both of them wanted to separate me from Ronnie because obviously I was nothing to them and they wanted Ronnie to *be without,* for they felt he had been given everything and took charge of everything. This is truth and they would deny it because they know that Ronnie was very close to his mother and she loved him very much, for Ronnie protected her in every aspect.

On this second visit, I have been so overwhelmed with embarrassment and shame from Kevin not opening his heart for anything good to happen and Teresa closing her spirit to stop anything positive to come about, which made it impossible to say anything except the truth that we all here have the same blood in us, *but that's all*. I can tell personally in my heart exactly what I have in common with them, for I will not tolerate what I heard about my brother, Ronnie, and I will not repeat it in this book. I want no part.

So immediately that morning when I wake up, I use my cell phone (the only way I can call long distance with only a few minutes, because I am on Verizon and it meets my budget.) I can only call for a few minutes with my therapist until she calls me back in the room, because she does not have Verizon.

My therapist tells me when she calls that it is amazing how I am able to make the best of what I have and make it stretch to touch the lives of others with so little information that I have been given about my past. It is an incredible medical miracle and, "I will not let this process of healing be destroyed for you."

She speaks peace and focuses me on what I have experienced from the first visit, and tells me to keep journaling and that, "this definitely is going to be an incredible healing process for many people when you share the truth." Her words make me think of how I will choose to tell the story of your life.

My therapist says, "Everyone anticipates your return in group therapy wants you to continue this journey with your biological family. The truth of what you find out will set you free."

JORDAN JANTZ

As we end our therapy session, we both reconfirm that we were meant to work with one another, to be able to be the change I wish to see for the lives of children such as me. My therapist reminds me that she is committed to my life and my wholeness. She is committed to my comprehensive infinite value.

Still, here in Decatur, when I am not with Aunt Marion, I feel ashamed in front of everyone because of what Teresa has done. I am having trouble with the truth of those hateful actions, and her telling me things that don't uplift me about my biological mother, or even when Teresa just talks about my brother, Ronnie. I'm having the best brother-relationship with Ronnie that I know I am capable of having, and I told Ronnie and Lisa that on my first visit.

Remember you said that to Ronnie and Lisa, my therapist reminded me on the phone, *and that Teresa and Kevin don't like that. They want you to <u>not</u> hold Ronnie up as you do.*

CRACKER BARREL AND SHOPPING THERAPY WITH AUNT MARION AND CHARITY

~31~

CHARITY AND I PLAY WITH HER TOYS in the room during therapy, and then it is time to go outside again for another potty dance, but this time she runs into something and I do, too. I have never seen animals quite like this before. As she is out there going potty, all of a sudden she's jumping up and down and I'm like, *What are you doing, Charity?* And she sees and I see what it is. It is *frogs*. Frogs are jumping up and down in the grass and Charity is jumping up and down like the frogs. I am just blown away. I cannot believe it. It is *country* out here; I can't believe the turtles all over the place. They are called snapping turtles and they will bite your fingers off, from what everybody tells me. So I'm holding close to Charity, but she's sure intrigued with these frogs.

As she finishes her potty dance and jumping up and down like a frog, I laugh so hard and hold her and pick her up in my arms in the beautiful sunlight of Decatur and the fresh dew of the morning. It is nearly Labor Day and the temperature and humidity remind us that summer has not decided to leave, yet.

I don't think Charity's ever smelled so many things, all *doing their business*. This time it is turtles, frogs, corn fields, all types of crops under the Midwest sun. I want to open the windows to the room as the sun is shining and bright and it is beautiful country like I have never seen.

As I am thinking about Charity. I recall my conversation about my dog with Ronnie and his family.

I said, "I never thought that I would think of ever living in the country. I have never been in the country nor did I ever desire to be in the country. I am a city beach starved southern California type of guy." I think I could even live here in the country, where my brother and his family live. It is a cute little village that reminds me of Little House on the Prairie. Lisa was born and raised out there. I am Ronnie's first born brother but I am a *babe* on the farm!

Lisa commented to me about Charity and how connected she is to me. She said to Ronnie, "Can you see that? What do you think of that?"

And he said, "I think that my brother senses that Charity is responding to him. When I held Charity she responds to me and I respond back. I can tell she likes that. What do you think, Jimmy?" he asks.

I said, "She really likes you and Charity is a kind soul."

I get Charity into the room, away from the frogs. She runs to the window to look outside and see the frogs jump up and down in the grass, she tries to let me know she wants to go play with the frogs. But I'm OCD and would not want her to be around dirty frogs with diseases.

EMBRACED

I tell Charity, "I'm jumping in the shower, I've got your breakfast made, and we're going to go to Cracker Barrel with Aunt Marion for lunch."

I call Aunt Marion up and say, "I am so excited to spend the day with you. We are going to have a great day and a lot of surprises! I will be bringing over some gifts that I brought for you! We'll have a great lunch and we'll even go to the mall and go *shopping*."

Aunt Marion says, "I haven't been to the mall in years!"

Our cab takes us first to the Cracker Barrel. It is my favorite place to eat in Decatur. I love country fried food like fried okra. I tell Aunt Marion our *farm adventures* while we sit with Charity, who sits at her own seat at the table.

The waitress is surprised at Charity's fine manners, sitting so courteously until we are finished eating. The waitress asks if Charity could have a treat, but since she is fourteen years old that is not a good idea. I thank her anyway.

Aunt Marion tells Charity, "You are the most beautiful dog and you have better manners eating at the table than most people! Jimmy, I've never seen a dog that minds so well and she just loves you whenever you leave she cries! It just breaks my heart. She is filled with love for you and I am so glad because you need to be loved, and I know that you do not have the love you need. I should have taken you from Bud when we offered me the opportunity, but your Aunt Marion just wasn't able to and we didn't think it would be a good idea, because of being in the same town with your biological mother. But I sure do enjoy our time and our talks and you have had me do more things in the time that I've spent with you than I have done in the past two years of my life! I have enjoyed you since you were three years old and I loved your dad and he would be so proud to see you being the man you

are today, and the way you have turned your life around to help children that are just like you and your father.

You both were left between the ages of four and five, by your mothers. You and your dad are a lot alike in so many ways. And everyone loved him, Jimmy. And, I have always loved Bud and Ina McNear has always been my best friend since I was a young girl who grew up with her. She loved you more than anything and wanted you away from your biological mother who left you and would forget where she left you at for weeks, and nobody could find you. And, the entire family would be in hysterics trying to find Bud's son, James Lee Bond, who was missing frequently and that's why your dad never believed that your older sister was truly his daughter and I can understand why. There was time when your dad with him in his car most of the time trying to keep you away from your mother and you were so good about living in the car. It broke my heart, that you were such an easy little boy to please. You grew up pleasing people and today I don't think anyone has ever not been pleased with you, but has just taken many expectations out of your life and replaced your life with an eraser that could erase the memories that others could forget but you had to live with. <u>And I'm sorry!</u>

I affirm that Charity sooths my heart in ways that no human can see, and she is a gift from God. The Spirit encourages me to open to my Aunt Marion and tell her a little bit more about my memories. She is not surprised but she is very grieved because she had hoped that I was too small to remember the worst, which, in fact, I didn't share.

She says, "Please forgive your Aunt Mary, for I never wanted any of the things to happen to you that Bud and I found you in! I'm so sorry that you remember. **I will never let anyone hurt you again!** Your great grandma was so good to your dad, and she loved him and took him when he was four years old and he knew and was afraid for you because you reminded him of what happened to him. He just never was able to talk about it. But Ina told me all about it. And so, your dad and I became friends because of Ina. Please don't let this hurt you, Jimmy! Let go of this pain of being sold, however you can!"

All I could do was say, "I forgive you, because I <u>really</u> do. It's not your fault. It is not my dad's fault. It is not my great grandma's fault. It is all a part of God's plan. And Aunt Marion, at least I have a true heart brother, with a true spirit and honesty, that when he tells me something he will do it. And the same goes for his children and his wife. I'm all about standing up for the truth and the truth is, I am not longer lost or have to be someone else to all people. I am my brother's brother!"

Aunt Marion shines, she is so happy, "And I like your brother. Ronnie, a lot, too! And his wife, and I adore your nephew, Zach, and I want to see your niece, Hannah. Those are your family, Jimmy, your blood family! And I'm sorry you never had been given the truth."

Aunt Marion, Charity and I then walk *both* ends of the mall *twice* to find the cab to drive us back, the two of us now realizing we are *both* having a little bit of forgetfulness. We are both experiencing together our *senior moments.*

I tell her, "I need some *shopping therapy* in the mall!"

She says, "Well, Jimmy, I don't know if I can make it up and down the mall now, too. You'll help me won't you?"

I say, "Of course I'll help you with anything in your life. I am going to take you shopping and buy you some pretty outfits of your choice."

EMBRACED

As we arrive, I realize this shopping mall is the smallest shopping mall I have ever seen. And I never knew that it would look like a ghost town. Hardly anybody is in it. I feel like I am walking in to a place that is vacating before being demolished. It is just a weird feeling. Most shopping malls have music and are filled with people with food courts and an opportunity to shop many stores instead of going into a couple.

But I have no problem with that because it is all about making sure I am able to get Aunt Marion some personal things that she may like to have that she doesn't have already. And I know that she is a clothes horse just as much as I am. We both love fashion and we both love the finest of apparel. She knows I know her color wheel very well and that I am not only one that dresses myself in a proper manner, but I have been taught to dress other models also in a proper manner, from head to toe, from hairstyle to nail polish, to lip color to hair highlights, turning and transforming appearances into artwork is my forte. Aunt Marion knows I am *the best* at this very special quality of help that my friends seek out from me. And I have the opportunity to do this now for my own aunt. What a blessing this is.

I wish I could take her to a runway show and let her pick out the clothes she wants on the runway, but I don't think Decatur would have any fashion shows or fashion buyers or models marketing new designs. So, I'm just grateful to get Aunt Marion the simple things that will make her feel happy, because to me she is the most beautiful woman in my life today and she deserves beautiful things. I keep this all to myself because I'm not the type to expose what I want to do for people, I just act upon it.

It surprises her when I pick out pink (because pink is *definitely* in her color wheel) and I tell her, "This pink sweater is gorgeous, and it would go great with these pants and the dress. It would look great for church this Sunday!"

I hold it up to her and say, "You don't even need to try it on. I know it is going to be perfect. I'm buying it."

"Are you sure?" she says.

"YES, I am buying it and you need to have this other shirt to go with it just in case you need a backup. You always need to have more than one of everything. That's how I was taught," I say.

We pick up me a pair of pajama bottoms. I let Aunt Marion pick them out for me, and I say, "I love them, I want them, and I'm buying them. Thanks for picking these out, Aunt Marion."

She laughs as we go to the register and we both leave the mall with our bags and head home after a lovely lunch and a beautiful time shopping at the ghost town shopping mall of Decatur.

My favorite part of Decatur is definitely still Lake Decatur. I just love crossing the bridge and seeing that man-made lake. There is so much history inside that lake. And the stories that I have been told will be forever remembered. Most dear to me are the stories about Aunt Marion herself, and how she grew up and then stayed in Illinois throughout her life and became a very forefront runner for women in the political world in the Midwest.

I remind her about that as we cross the bridge, but add, "Not only were you a forefront woman for running in politics, Aunt Marion, but you also were very successful in doing your own business as a beautician. I'm so proud of you, and I always have been. You have encouraged me more than you'll ever know, with the Make a Wish Foundation. I can't believe you and I have so much in common in wanting to help save children and make their wishes come true. And all you did for the children at the Make a Wish Foundation has touched many lives."

EMBRACED

She says, "Jimmy, there is nothing more important than loving a child. Not only when it is a little baby, but throughout its entire life, and that's the most important thing I can give you, love, and you've <u>got</u> that from me, always. You gave your Aunt Marion a wonderful day today, and I can't wait to relax with you at home and watch the Golden Girls and take these shoes off because Aunt Marion's not used to walking so much in all these years. But you helped me all along throughout the mall, and sat down with me and got me something to drink when I was thirsty and you took care of me, and I want you to know I really thank you. I love my pink sweater and the little gifts that you picked out at the mall for me. Our lunch at the Cracker Barrel was really good and Charity was so well-mannered, you could tell she is professionally trained to assist you with your panic attacks and it is amazing how in tune she is to your emotions and feelings. Jimmy, I am so glad you have her, but she is so old! I don't want anything to happen to her, because it will devastate you."

I say, "Oh, Aunt Marion, nothing's going to happen to her. And the reason why I say this, Aunt Marion, is because her name, Charity, *means* the pure love of Christ. That's the kind of love I want to have in my life, the pure love of Christ. I am fallible and make mistakes, but that's what I desire in my life and for people in my life to experience along with me this type of peaceful reality that giving Charity to others is showing pure love and true love ...Christ's love, in fact. That's the page I'm on today, Aunt Marion. Charity is going to stay with me for a long time."

Aunt Marion says, "Jimmy, that is the best page and only page you want to be on. And that's why you do what you do for so many people. I have witnessed this throughout your whole life. You are a people pleaser like your brother, Ronnie, said, and there is nothing wrong with that as long as you let others return the favor of being able to please you and treat you with the love and kindness that you give out."

Soon are home at Aunt Marion's assisted living center. We get out of the cab, and I get her walker out for her, so she can get to the door. We laugh at Charity doing another potty dance, so well-trained and behaved.

Aunt Marion says, "I miss having a dog, Jimmy. I miss that so much. I just love Charity."

Then she adds a bit hopefully, "You know they are still serving dinner here."

I say, "Well, maybe we'll go down there for dinner and have some dessert."

We sit down in her home and watch *Everybody Loves Raymond*. She just loves that show. I laugh with her and she laughs with me. I realize how tired we both are, when she starts to discuss my cousins, her children.

She tells me, "Mark wants to come and pick you up. Your cousin wants to do more than just see you, he'd like to take you to his house."

I have always admired my cousin, Mark, ever since childhood. He always loved to do those *guy things* that I did not know how to do. He loves camping and hunting and I would *love* to experience hunting but I've never been able to hold a gun without having a panic attack, severely. So, another guy thing bites the dust for a new adventure.

Aunt Marion tells me that there is something special planned from my cousin, Mark, is looking forward to me visiting to his home. Aunt Marion says Mark's wife, Robin, is beyond kindness and has a true heart.

EMBRACED

Aunt Marion says, "You will feel immediately comfortable at their home, just because of the way you are, with your honest and open heart. Mark and Robin and your cousin, Sandy, in Florida, respect honest integrity. And I want you to know that your other cousin, Renee, makes time to bring me little things that I might need, every now and then. She and her husband have bought and restored a historic house, which is like living in an art project, or a construction project."

Special time is set aside for me to go home with Mark.

Aunt Marion tells me that all my cousins are happy to see my open heart and love that it is transparent for my Aunt Marion and Uncle Dale. As I plan and talk to my cousins during this trip, it is the happiest catch-up time, ever. Nobody cares about what we can't do, just about the value of what we choose to love. It is heaven for me, being with the ones who love me and celebrate me and not tolerate me. They all know my story of my childhood (like everyone does) and they know how much I have been removed from the truth of ever knowing the reality there *is* biological family in Decatur, but that was something *then* and *now,* "I've got what God promised," I tell everyone, "God will not let an orphan's prayers go unanswered. He says this in the Bible, that orphans and widows are protected and I know that I have had the presence of God even through the darkest, darkest moments of my life, so I am here to celebrate because it is behind us all now."

Aunt Marion says, "It is a miracle we are all alive to even share the truth, Jimmy. And that you have your brother and that he gave you the opportunity to have the grave that your great grandmother Ina, who you called Gram, bought that was given to you. Your brother, Ronnie, is a remarkable Christian man. By his actions you can tell what kind of person he is. Remember, you will know a person by their actions and not their words, because actions speak louder than words. That's what you are experiencing right now with your biological family here in Decatur. God's got a plan, and *you* will have this plan revealed to you because you have gone the distance to make it happen and so let God know how important it is to you that he saved your life today. And as you say, *that's why you continue to go to church,* even though you have same gender attraction or whatever you want to call it. That is just something you deal with, but you have chosen to keep everything in your life in order so that you can live in light and not darkness anymore."

I know who Aunt Marion means when she says, "So don't ever listen to anyone who tells you, *you chose this life*. They are wrong. God knows what they have done to you by making you believe that you chose *all* of this that you have been through."

Aunt Marion comes right out with it, "*Don't* let my sister tell you ever again that you chose this life and you chose to live with same gender attraction, because that is just not true. You were abused and abandoned and left to be sold by a very mean biological mother who continued to let a mother-son relationship rip your life apart as she profited from selling you. I would say you have overcome what most would never be able to. You were traumatized when I first found you. It is a miracle you can speak today and have any ability to even trust yourself. So, you let whatever my sister or any destructive person says go, because you did everything you could to perform and be the best and *overcompensate* to please people, just to make them love you and be happy with you. You are better than they ever thought to be. And you are a good, kind man that loves God. Just as David in the Bible who had a heart after God."

And I say, "Oh you are totally right, and so let's just end this TV show and go on down and getting us some ice cream with caramel on it, and some nuts and have a sundae before it is time to go to bed."

EMBRACED

And she says, "I would like that, Jimmy! And maybe I'm a little hungry too."

We go down for dinner and end up ordering BLTs and soup and having another meal.

I tell her, "Aunt Marion, do you remember when I was taken to California? Do you remember when you were with me on the first meal that we had out there, in Compton, where I moved to with your sister? I remember it because I had a hard time holding silverware and eating with silverware. So, we had tomato soup and grilled cheese sandwiches. Do you remember that?"

She says, "I do remember the first night, having the grilled cheese sandwiches and tomato soup, because you couldn't eat your soup with a spoon. You were never taught to eat like a child before you were sold. So, you were given grill cheese sandwich and tomato soup, and we dipped our sandwiches into the soup. You watched us all do it, and then you did the same thing. You remember all that, don't you."

I say, "I remember it all like a Polaroid picture. And it really was a Kodak moment. I was actually sitting at a table, getting to eat with a family for the first time at 5 years old. It was so different but I was glad you were with me, because I was so scared. I didn't know what they would do to me, but I trusted you. So I'm glad we did it together. You didn't leave me, you stayed with me throughout my life, and you are here with me and I am here with you and we are having a wonderful time. And by the way, that pink blouse looks beautiful on you."

She lights up and says, "I've already had two compliments on it just coming down here for dinner, I want you to know that. I think I'll wear it for the Labor Day concert by the Kidd Kaddilacs."

I say, "Well then, I'll be prepared to *match* you."

EMBRACED

She giggles and we finish our sundae and go back up to her room and I realize that I have to get home to meet my niece and my nephew and my sister in law, to go see the movies. So, I tell Aunt Marion that I love her and we'll get together soon, and I need to go back to my room.

She says, "You aren't going to stay for after dinner?"

I say, "I wish I could. As it happens, I promised Lisa that I would meet them for the movie."

She says, "Oh, I remember! I want you to have a wonderful time. I will see you tomorrow and call me when you wake up. And sometime, remember, I would like to meet Hannah, I just haven't gotten the opportunity yet and I would be honored!" and then she waves to me and blows kisses as I take myself back to my room, with her watching over me.

While doing Charity's potty dance, I think about the upcoming movie with Zach and Lisa. I want them to be proud of me, because I'm definitely proud of them. I just adore my sister-in-law.

Charity and I leave the hotel to meet Lisa and everyone for the movie and have a wonderful evening together, at the movie theater across the street.

I arrive before they do and get the popcorn and tickets for the movie.

I see them approaching the theater with smiles and I tell them, "Come on, let's go on it, I've already got the tickets and here's the popcorn!"

Lisa is blown away and I say, "It is Family Home Evening and this is how I want to spend it with you!"

Zach wants a drink and I say, "Well get a drink, whatever you want."

I have a blast sitting next to my sister-in-law and my nephew, Zach. Hannah couldn't make it. We enjoy a family home evening together. I am so tired, I believe I fell asleep, but I'm not sure if I snored. They sure are being polite about it.

As we depart, they walk me over to my room, and we say goodbye.

We make plans for another time later in the week for it is Labor Day coming up and I have made plans with my Aunt for the Kidd Kaddilacs and Lisa, my sister-in-law, told me that the Kidd Kaddilacs are her relatives.

I say, "You are kidding me!"

She says, "Not at all. Some of the people in the band are really my friends and relatives!"

I think *whoa, this is going to be a lot of fun.*

She says, "Jimmy, you will *really* like them a lot. Have FUN!"

My family drive off.

I go to my hotel room and call Aunt Marion. First thing, I tell her that the Kidd Kaddilacs are related to my sister-in-law!

Aunt Marion says "Well, Jimmy, they are fantastic, just like I told you they were!" and now I really know we are going to have so much fun tomorrow.

She says, "I am so glad you had time with your family, Jimmy. You really deserve for you and your family to *be close.*

EMBRACED

Jimmy, I want you to have a lot of fun with him while you are here in Decatur. You need this connection with Ronnie and his family, because they are your family, too. He has made it be that way for you, because he obviously loves you very much."

I tell Aunt Marion, "I love him so much, more than words can ever say. There are no words that can ever even be spoken to describe my admiration and respect and love that I have for my biological brother, Ronnie, and my sister-in-law, and their two children."

And she says, "Good night! I can't wait to dance and have a fun time with you. I will call you in the morning or you call me!"

I take Charity out before bed to do her little potty dance and outside I pray on my feet because I'm so tired. I hold the leash with one hand and throw up my other arm and say, "I just thank you Lord for this beautiful moment, and I also pray that You will bless the event tomorrow and Aunt Marion will have the best time of her life! It is very important to me to know that my Aunt Marion is happy and well, for she is the most important woman in my life today. I don't know if anyone has ever loved me the way Aunt Marion loves me today. And it really doesn't matter because what I have now is more than I had yesterday. And I am grateful to have what I have in my life and I thank you, God, for it. I have a brother that embraces me, I can't tell you, Lord, how grateful I am for giving me my brother, and I can't thank you, Lord, enough for my sister-in-law, and I want you to bless by niece and my nephew and to touch my sister's heart and my other brother's heart with your peace. And God, protect them also. And that is my wish, dear Heavenly Father, I pray and I thank you for *today*, in Jesus name, amen!"

You see, prayer is very important to me because it is the only thing that sustains my life. When you've been there and done that and worn out the t-shirt, I realize I need to put on the whole armor of God and become who He has created me to be. That goes for anybody.

I feel, personally, that if anyone calls out to God, He comes running, because I wouldn't be here if it wasn't for crying out to the Lord. He answered and came running for me and brought me and carried me throughout my life's journey.

I am so thankful to realize what it is like to live in truth. That's the biggest gift I could receive: truth. The truth of what God wants me to become, the truth of who I am and the truth that I am a child of God. I live for Him and I live to please him, and I am content for the first time in my life that I know where I belong. As I lay there in bed and hold Charity next to me and fall asleep, I am so at peace, a sweet peace that I have not ever felt before. It is nice to know that I do belong to somebody. And that somebody is my brother and he loves me. Charity and I fall asleep immediately.

Ronnie's Swing

LABOR DAY FLASHBACKS WITH THE KID KADDALACKS

~32~

As THE SUN RISES IN MY ROOM, I lay in bed and sleep in a little bit longer than normal. Charity stays peacefully snuggled right next to me as I plan in my mind the best way of bringing my Labor Day gift to Aunt Marion. I have a special quilt that was made by the Relief Society in my church, and I have it all wrapped up, just for her. It is something very special. I picked the colors out and the women at my church made the most beautiful quilt.

When I have got the packages ready and the bows on them, I am driven across the street. Today, Aunt Marion is outside, smiling.

Catching sight of all my packages she says, "What is that all about?"

I say, "It is for you, Aunt Marion, it is your Labor Day gift, and I want you to know you are loved. And this was made just for you by the ladies at my church in the Relief Society, and it even has your name on it and I want you to know that I picked out the colors and the fabric just for you. And I hope you like it."

She opens it up and just starts to cry, because she can't believe the look in my eyes as I watch her open her present. Tears

EMBRACED

fell down my face, too, as I want to embrace my Aunt Marion for I want her to feel the love that I feel and I want her to be happy in her life, for she has been so good to so many people and reached out to so many children at Make a Wish foundation, and I cannot keep my eyes off of her smiling, joyful face, as she takes the quilt and wraps it around her and says, "this is the most beautiful quilt I have ever had."

I tell her, "You better get your dancing shoes on, 'cuz we're going to go dance and have some hamburgers and hot dogs on Labor Day and they are already setting up outside for the big event!"

And she tells me, "You can't forget your cousin, Mark, he wants to do the bee thing with you, remember that."

"Of course I remember," I say "Mark is the most honest man I have known in a long time, and his wife is so kind to me. You let them know, Aunt Marion, I cannot wait to see them, and spend some time with them."

Aunt Marion goes and puts on her outfit for the Labor Day celebration, and I think to myself, *how fun it will be to spend some time with mark, my cousin, who has known me since we were both young kids because we would come out to Decatur and visit every now and then.*

Honestly I never put the two together, that I was actually in the town I was born in. I just dissociated myself from the reality that this was where I was born, every time when we would come visit and Mark and Sandy and I always enjoyed our time together, and so did my cousins, but it was something we just would do every now and then.

When I was a little boy, Aunt Marion and Uncle Dale meant the world to me. It is kind of strange to think back now that my biological family was in the same town as I was and it was never mentioned or ever talked about. I realize how I dissociated so much, now that I am back in Decatur and it is Labor Day and I am thinking about Mark and Sandy, and I *realize* that what my aunt is *telling* me is that my *brother worked with my cousin*, Aunt Marion's daughter, Sandy, at the mall that we just went to, and Sandy *also* knew my *biological dad*, "Bud" Bond, and would that Sandy always enjoyed my father when she might see him every now and then, Aunt Marion had said. Aunt Marion also mentioned that Sandy enjoyed working at the mall with my *biological brother, Ronnie.*

I couldn't get a word out of my mouth. I was dumbfounded thinking about this reality. This is where I was born, and I *have* been in this town a few times throughout my life and *never once* did I think, *this is the town where I was born* or *I am visiting town of the father who gave me life and the mother still live in.*

And *everyone knew it*, except it didn't make sense to me at all at the time. Maybe it is because I was a child, why I didn't think of those things. But then again, I never knew that there *was* family. All I knew was a little girl that would put mandarin oranges under the door. I would eat them, but I never saw a face or a connection to any brother or sister at that time, until this moment, I realize. I have misunderstood a lot about my life and the reason and purpose for it, until now.

Aunt Marion walks out of the bathroom, as beautiful as an angel in pink, she says, "How do I look?"

"Absolutely beautiful," I say, and she is all set and I take her with me by the arm, with her walker and open the door for her as always, and lock up her apartment and we head for the barbeque.

We hear the music playing, GO JOHNNY GO, GO! Aunt Marion is ready to get out there and says "I can't wait, I haven't danced in years!" and, "You are going to have to hold me up now!"

EMBRACED

The ladies and the men and the staff are all outside and the Kidd Kaddilacs are jamming to the music of the fifties and sixties.

"Aunt Marion, do you want something to drink?" I ask her.

She says, "Yes, honey, but let's first find us a seat."

So I take her over and get her a seat right by the dance floor outside, and she sits down and I go to get her a drink and as I am getting her a drink, I look over and I see *all* these little old ladies all around her, wanting to know what she is doing and how she is, complimenting her on her outfit. She always did steal the show, Aunt Marion, because she was like a light bulb. She lit up the room when she walked in it. I just grin and smile and take a picture of her and her girlfriends and take her drink over to her. She introduces me to all her friends, and lets everyone know that I am her nephew from Portland, Oregon, and the ladies all ask me if I want to dance.

I say, "Of course I do! That's why I am here to celebrate with all of you! And I am so glad to see that you girls have gotten to know my Aunt Marion. She's a very special woman to me, one of the most special, kindest ladies you will ever meet!" and they all of course agree that she is just incredible, because she is.

I say, "If I had the opportunity, I would just take her home with me to Portland, but I can't do that, because I want Aunt Marion to be able to have the things that she needs here in Decatur."

And the girls just giggle and laugh and say, "I wish my nephew would want to take me to his house."

I say, "Well, Aunt Marion has always been my voice when I couldn't speak, when I was young. She has always been there for me, come rain or snow. And it is an honor to be here today and celebrate this incredible moment with all you wonderful ladies! So, let's get out there and dance, and show them how to do it, Aunt Marion! Let's take all these ladies on the dance floor!"

Aunt Marion grabs my hand and I pick her up and she gets her groove on and starts to do a little shimmy and I just start laughing and dancing all around, holding her up, and we have the funnest time, and all the ladies just start clapping at my Aunt Marion, for she has always been a dancer and can dance up a storm!

Sensing a pause to come in the music, I tell Aunt Marion, "I think this Johnny Be Good stuff is about ready to be over with, for the moment."

She says, "I could sit down for a hot dog."

So, I go and get her and me hot dogs and refresh our cold beverages, and we visit with all her friends. We have Pepsi and brats, too.

Then, I take each one of her friends and dance with them, and they just love it! Some of these little old ladies say that our dance was the first time any of them had danced, since their husbands died. They thank me for having the heart to go dance with an old woman.

I say, "You aren't an old woman. You all are just angels! *That's* what you are."

Aunt Marion just grins and tells me, "You make so many people happy, Jimmy. Those little ladies have not had anyone hold them up like you did. And the ones in the wheelchairs, you took them out there, too, and held their hands around the wheelchairs and danced with them. It just touched their hearts, and it touches my heart to see it all. You really do love people. You really have a heart."

I say, "It is a blessing to be able to give to these people here, Aunt Marion. It is my honor to hold them in their wheelchairs and dance with them."

She starts to cry. She says, "I am so sorry that things are not what you had hoped for with your mother. But just maybe you might be able to see her. I don't know. But I want you to know that you are worth more than what you have ever been told. And there is no price tag that you can put on yourself. And there is not enough money in the world to be able to buy you! Remember that. What you have done here today is something most people don't even know how to do."

I hand her a tissue and she wipes her eyes and says to me, "Jimmy, I am so glad that you are here. You don't know what this means to me."

I say, "You don't know what this means to me, Aunt Marion. You will only find out just what you have done for my life when you and I get on the other side, because there are no words I can use to describe to you how I feel about you and Uncle Dale. You have not given up on me. And it is fifty years later that we are still going strong. So when you finish your hot dog, you better *find some strength* to go dance to that Dianna Ross and the Supremes, the best of Motown," and I sing along, "*STOP IN THE NAME OF LOVE! ...before you break my heart. Think it o-o-ver!*"

JORDAN JANTZ

Aunt Marion gets right up with me and says, "Let's go show 'em how to do it, Jimmy!"

I take her out and we do the swing and be-bop all over the place. I can't believe the energy of my little ol' aunt. It just blesses my **heart** to see her smiling and dancing up a storm and boy was she movin' and *working it out.* She is exercising more than I thought she could. She is incredible and it is amazing to see her move at her age. But then again, I encourage her to get out there and get her boogie on and she *did.*

I love Labor Day, and this was beautiful. It will always be the best Labor Day I have ever had. I have never felt so much joy being around these little ladies and dancing with them, knowing in my heart how happy there were inside. Seeing the joy inside of these beautiful senior saints made my day special.

JORDAN JANTZ

EMBRACED

I visited with my cousin and saw his bees!

And it looks like Aunt Marion's right!

PRESIDENTIAL ELETION YEAR DECATUR COUNTRY CLUB

~31~

AUNT MARION TELLS ME that she wants to take me down to Lake Decatur and see the beauty of it again, this time just her and me. We decide to leave the assisted living center with Charity and go to the beautiful lakefront near the Decatur Country Club, where Decatur's upper echelon still meet to partake of golfing, swimming and other activities.

Aunt Marion tells me more stories from her years growing up as a young child right on the lake. It is the center of so many beautiful memories from ages ago. "Your grandfather swam across it once. He also farmed – like everyone farmed - and used the water from this lake for irrigating his crops."

It is wonderful to hear about my adopted grandfather. I am shocked to hear her tell me that he was born from a Jewish mother: Goldman was their last name. It is surprising and yet my few memories of Grandpa were always in line with the typical Jewish Grandpa. I just never put it together before. Some things are right there but we don't see them.

JORDAN JANTZ

Many people lived and worked in the fields near Lake Decatur because of the Depression, Aunt Marion explains. The lake was a source of life. The land kept them alive. Everyone was desperate but Aunt Marion told her friends and family that she was *not* going anywhere to go find work, she was going to stay right there in Decatur, Illinois, and she did just that. The rest of her family migrated to California, leaving her alone. I take more pictures. We stuff ourselves on our picnic food, the Midwest air in America's breadbasket making us hungrier. Our bodies say, *Let's eat!* and we sure do.

On the ride back, we both are commenting on how many corn and soybeans fields are all around us. We are a small dot in the middle of them. I am overwhelmed by the *miles* of fields. It is so far from what I have known in my life. I find I enjoy the constant smell – cut grass and warm vegetable scent.

As we are on the road driving back, Aunt Marion says to me, "Did you know that Decatur is the soybean capital of the world?"

I say, "No, I didn't know that."

She says, "Did you know that *Decatur* is the *real* home of the Chicago Cubs?" *She always does that.*

In her room again she swoons, "Oh, I LOVE MY CUBS, and Jimmy, they are the best team and they are going to win this year. They are going to take home the cup, Jimmy!"

I laugh, because she is so cute. I am embarrassed to tell her that I don't watch television, I only watch movies, but I do remember the Chicago Cubs *always* being her favorite team even since I was a child. I can see that what a person holds onto in life just grows deeper in with time. The Chicago Cubs and the Chicago Bulls and the Golden Girls have always been a major part of life.

EMBRACED

ILLINOIS HOUSE OF REPRESENTATIVES

CAPITOL OFFICE:
200-5S STRATTON BUILDING
SPRINGFIELD, ILLINOIS 62706
217-782-8398
FAX: 217-782-2528

DISTRICT OFFICE:
132 SOUTH WATER, SUITE 628
DECATUR, ILLINOIS 62523
217-428-2708 or 1-866-453-2066
FAX: 217-428-3419

EMAIL:
bobflider@repflider.com

COMMITTEES:
VICE CHAIRMAN:
• LOCAL GOVERNMENT
MEMBER:
• AGRICULTURE & CONSERVATII
• ELEMENTARY & SECONDARY EDUCATION
• ELECTIONS & CAMPAIGN REFORM
• VETERANS' AFFAIRS

ROBERT F. FLIDER
STATE REPRESENTATIVE
101ST DISTRICT

Mrs. Mary Lee Brown
26 5th Drive
Decatur, IL 62521

Dear Mary Lee,

Congratulations on your 80th Birthday. I hope your special day was filled with joy. My wife Jean and I extend our best wishes for many years of good health and happiness!

With warmest personal regards, I remain

Very truly yours,

Robert F. Flider

Robert Flider
State Representative

Aunt Marion was a forefront runner in the political arena in the state of Illinois. She continued to have relationships with many politicians after her retirement from the political office that she held for many years as a representative in the state of Illinois. She gave much to the city of Decatur. She continued to transform the politics and challenges that faced the state of Illinois and embraced her government work while tending to the needs of her family and others throughout the city of Decatur. Aunt Marion is a trailblazer for other women in politics and society today. Equal rights throughout the USA have been given to me by powerful women like my Aunt Marion and men who endorse freedom in Illinois.

JORDAN JANTZ

My Amazing Aunt Marion, in her day.

EMBRACED

To Mary,
Movements for real and lasting change are sustained by the relationships we build with one another.
Thank you for your support.

Michelle Obama

JORDAN JANTZ

I'D APPRECIATE YOUR VOTE
MARY LEE BROWN
DEMOCRAT CANDIDATE
MACON COUNTY BOARD, DISTRICT 1

HAIR DRESSER - OWNER MARY'S BEAUTY SALON 22 YRS. MARRIED, 2 CHILDREN, 3 GRAND DAUGHTERS. MEMBER FIRST BAPTIST CHURCH, DECATUR. ATTENDED MARY W. FRENCH, JOHN'S HILL JR. HIGH AND STEPHEN DECATUR. TEACHERS CERTIFICATE FOR HAIR DRESSER. LIFE LONG DEMOCRAT. CURRENTLY PRECINCT COMMITTEEMAN.

Nov. 2 Will Work For You! 1982

EMBRACED

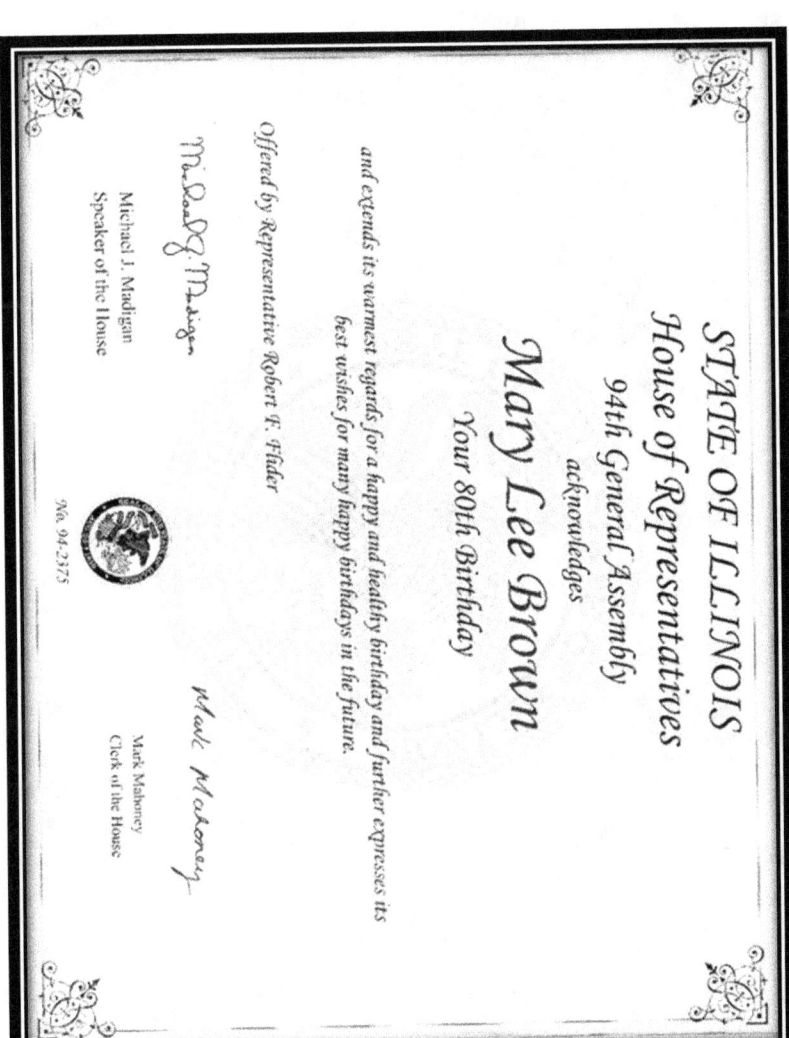

JORDAN JANTZ

To Ms. Brown,
    On behalf of Bo and myself, please accept our gratitude and thanks for your leadership and support at this critical juncture in American history.

EMBRACED

The Clintons in Decatur

JORDAN JANTZ

"Let me say this, hypothetically speaking, I really do hope we have a woman president in my lifetime."
Hillary Clinton
June 20, 2013

EMBRACED

To Mr. Brown,
On behalf of the Democratic Party, please accept our gratitude and thanks for your leadership and support of our ongoing work.

Debbie Wasserman-Schultz

JORDAN JANTZ

EMBRACED

BISHOP'S BLESSING IN DECATUR

~ 34 ~

LATER THAT EVENING I share my feelings with my minister in Portland through a phone call. He feels that since the shame that I feel of being treated as *not there* by my sister (by the very person I had come to celebrate) is still almost overwhelming me, I need a blessing. My minister is right; I *do* need a blessing.

Soon, I get a message that my minister in Portland has contacted the minister in Decatur. The minister in Decatur would like to get together with me and take me out to dinner, so that he and his wife can meet with me.

I am a little bit stand-off-ish, but my 'stake president' minister in Portland tells me that the Church of Jesus Christ of Latter-day Saints is the same all over the world. I still worry. My minister asks, "What is the Spirit telling you right now? Can you trust me?"

The Spirit is confirming that I can trust this and I tell him so.

My minister continues, "The Bishop in Decatur wants to give you a blessing, and I believe you need a blessing to help with clarity, with your emotions and give spiritual knowledge of God's direction that He wants your life to go and what He can do in your life, today. Please, open up your heart and call this minister. He is waiting with anticipation to take you out for dinner, counsel with you, and give you a blessing."

So, the next morning, I call the Decatur Bishop and introduce myself. He and his wife are making plans to meet that evening to go to Ruby Tuesday for a steak dinner.

But I nearly miss them when they come. One of the hotel staffers catches me in the hall and says that some couple in suits is looking for *Jordan Jantz* and they are driving away.

I jump, "Oh, please! Could you please help me catch them?"

The staffer runs out and flags them down. I run back into my room to settle Charity who is not feeling well at all, and I come back out to find the hotel staffer right there at my door.

She says, "Now, please tell me, Jimmy, are you hiding because you are a *movie star*?"

Oh, that is the most precious thing!

"Not at all," I say, "That is just a name that I am also known by, but I want to be known by my birth in Decatur. Can you understand that?"

"Oh, of course, Jimmy. That makes sense." The staffer and I walk out together to meet the Bishop of Decatur and his wife.

I introduce myself again, and we depart for the restaurant. I am so grateful for this hospitality and generosity.

At the restaurant, I tell the Bishop and his wife the basics of my story, and they both are just about ready to fall off their stools. They seriously look in danger of keeling right onto the floor. They tell me that they spoke to my minister and watched my Voice of

EMBRACED

Hope video. They still are feeling the power of my mission so much, they just want to listen while I talk.

We discuss the situation and I express my emotions. This entire second trip to Decatur had a purpose to build a true bond with biological family – a bond as strong temple work – and the Bishop and his wife seem to feel for my family what I feel for my family, my hope and pain together.

I realize that they are not eating and I ask them, "Why aren't you eating?"

They say, "This is all too emotional to be able to swallow food. You *really* went out on a limb blindfolded, with hope for your family. This takes a lot of faith and trust. We were told you were abandoned, left behind and forgotten by many and those wounds still continue in your life today. And, on top of this, you are *so loved* by your minister in Portland. He wants to make sure that you are protected and not abused by people again. So..," the Decatur minister looks at his wife who looks back, "we want you to call us for any reason. We also want to share the joy of your grave marker and your grave that has been gifted to you, by your great grandmother and your brother, Ronnie Bond. All that says, right off the bat, that God has had this planned since you were born. This is God's plan, Jordan, no man or woman could *ever* create a plan like this."

He and his wife wring their hands together on the table. Stress and hope, I see they have felt this together before. The Bishop says, "We were told that you go out on a limb to touch a person's life and we can see it, here at the table, tonight. It is contagious, what we see here, Jordan."

He continues, "We wish for all that is in your heart to come true, while you are here experiencing this terror and nakedness of putting yourself on the table to experience judgment or acceptance, not knowing what to expect because of what you've been told in the past and what you have experienced just surviving to get you where you are at today, right back here in your hometown where you were born with your biological family. WE hear you. God hears you. Oh, Jordan, *know* that Heavenly Father is looking down and He sees your heart. He is holding your hand through this. I know it."

When we have finished the meal, the Bishop says, "I will go back with you to your lodging to give you a blessing, and then I will let you give your service dog, Charity, a blessing, only because I have never given an animal a blessing before."

In my hotel room, his wife sits in the chair as I sit on the edge of the bed. The minister pulls a vial of oil, consecrated for healing, to touch the hearts and transform the spirit by connecting into God's healing presence. A few drops are put on the crown of my head, and he puts his hands upon my head and speaks the blessing through the Holy Spirit.

After my blessing, I am filled with God's reassuring, confirming Spirit.

We turn to Charity. I anoint her with consecrated oil, and pronounce that she will feel the peace and healing presence of my Heavenly Father. I say this prayer for her, through the power of Jesus Christ, who is my Savior and finish with an Amen – so be it. Both the minister and his wife stand with tears saying, "We felt the spirit during the blessing of your precious Charity and we have never experienced anything like this before, ever."

I say, "I know that new spiritual experiences are powerful. I've learned that sometimes I just have to walk by faith because I can't create what God can create, and I can't even try. And that is what my sister-in-law, Lisa, says, that I just have to *walk by faith*."

EMBRACED

It is very late, now. I thank them again, for their great kindness in taking me out to dinner. They say again that they are very excited to celebrate the grave marker and the fact that after fifty years my life has come to a full circle, continuing "You know, these things *don't happen*, except in the New Testament, when a son has gone, but returns home, and the father throws a feast for forgiveness and celebration and inclusion. The father won't tolerate *anyone's* negative comments because the value of family love is more valuable than the reputation of love.

I recognize the story and laugh, "Only one of those *loves* is real, and the other is *plastic-fantastic*."

The words of the blessing to me sink into his heart, too. The Bishop turns serious and says, "Your devotion to the church and to the Savior is high. Your brother, Ronnie, may be the only one that knows how to walk with the love you are speaking of with the vulnerability that you are choosing to live in. It is very possible that the other family members will guard everything they have, including sharing their life, because you know, they always knew you were *somewhere*. They have had time to think about this. Your father let everyone know that you were sold away, which he had to do to keep you safe from your biological mother. But God does not allow his love for children to be mocked. And your mother, I understand, mocked you consistently by hiding you as though you didn't exist, and using you to benefit herself. All these things mocked God's love for you. You never knew whose home you were at, or what babysitter your biological mother dropped you off at, or what man's house she was at the night before, and she left you again and again."

I can see that the Bishop's heart is opening to the understanding of what the lies that children are told *mean*. He is learning from the words and intelligence communicated through the

Spirit in the blessing he pronounced upon me from my Heavenly Father.

I say, "I was told back then that many people wanted to keep me, but I remember that all they wanted to do was to play with me in a painful and inappropriate way. So even when I was left in an odd place, it was better than being mistaken for an object of pleasure. It has been a constant battle throughout my life to shut the door on men like these, which I was exposed to as an infant. Many people will ignore this reality and back then many people knew and *did* ignore the reality of a parent wanting money for their child. My conversations with Ronnie, even, bring up some uncomfortable circumstances that they remember were told to them that start with: *Whatever happened to James Lee Bond?* It was never a real question because the answers were always right there, in the open. I was not put up for adoption. I was basically sold, which was illegal. Later, the court system had to fix it right, so that I could grow up in California with a new culture and better standards of living. The people in California that chose me wanted me more than any amount of money. They told that to my biological dad and biological great grandmother, Ina McNear who I always called Gram. The new family said that they would never let me go. They promised that I would have the finest of upbringing any boy could ever dream of. I would lack for nothing."

I continue, "But there are intentions and there are facts, and facts can be messy and conflicting. This last May, I was shocked that *any* of my biological family knew of the communication breakdown with my adoptive family. Then, I was in so much pain when my biological sister came right out and asked me if I was gay and if I had AIDS. I was shocked by that total violation of respect and boundaries. I was, like, tortured and left for dead. I never thought anything like that would happen when I came to Decatur. And she said that my *biological mother* called her up and told her all kinds of dirt during the time my biological father passed away in

EMBRACED

June 2006. When my biological sister did that, I wanted to say, "What type of response are you looking for? It seems to me that you have avoided everything of substance about me, except wanting to interrogate me about my existence, as though I have a hidden agenda. But you are the one that has left your biological brother and your niece and nephew and sister-in-law and raised your family separate. You've made your choices to separate yourself and I'm making my choices to connect, now that I am in my fifties and nobody will ever tell me to live under their expectations or answer their questions *that are inappropriate to anyone's integrity*." I didn't say all that to her, but I wish I had. I really just said, "I love you Teresa, but I do not like the way you have treated me." It felt the way she might treat a dog in the Humane Society, and honestly, that is just the way that my biological mother treated me. "

The Bishop says, "These things are so *distorted*. They cannot be unwound from your side alone. They cannot even be healed from God's side alone. It has to be in cooperation, spiritual and social healing has to be desired."

I answer, "But how do you open up the heart of someone who you want to love and be a part of, and they don't respond to you, like you don't even exist? I have tried to respond to my biological brother Kevin and my biological sister and nothing comes to the surface except pain and rejection from them, as though I am not worth responding to. I feel abandonment and rejection *and* I don't like what I see happening to my brother, Ronnie, for I'm sure they have hurt him, too, and I don't want to see it happen to him ever. I don't want it to happen to my niece or my nephew or my sister in law. These actions are horrific. What do you *do* with people like this? They have not even taken the opportunity to see the truth of what they have done to my brother and that makes me very upset!"

JORDAN JANTZ

I ask the minister, "What would you do? How do you handle this? What would you say to my sister or my brother? What would you have me to say to them, if you were me?"

The Bishop responds that I need to just pray for them, and not call them because *they know how to hurt you, and they already know that you have been abandoned, so shame on them.*

I answer, "You speak the truth, Bishop. My heart has been hurting because of Kevin, too. In this visit I had such high hopes to connect with Kevin, and he only seems to connect through Teresa, and Teresa has made her decision and it seems to be making Kevin's decision too, somehow. I have called Kevin every day since I have gotten here in Decatur again, using up my minutes. He does not have the desire to open his heart or even say, *Thank you for thinking of me, for calling, and I'm glad you are here.* All these things tell me the true story of what really is going on, and has been going on, and even maybe why I was the only child sold. Maybe it is true that the fact that I was sold and he was not sold gives him self-esteem. All these conversations are left behind, not developed, because of Teresa's current lack of ability to communicate with truth."

The Bishop and his wife leave my hotel room as friends. I look forward to staying consistent with these two new friends in Christ.

EMBRACED

Jordan with the Bishop of Decatur

The AMAZING and kind staff of the hotel!!

HUNG OUT TO DRY

35

My SISTER'S BIRTHDAY dawns bright, and I can't move in the bed. All through this visit to Decatur I had been making phone calls, leaving messages, and I was not even getting a response from Teresa. I would have liked a picnic, or a visit to the lake, I would have brought the birthday cake. But not even a chat in the lobby. To Teresa and Kevin, I didn't exist or they didn't know who I was somehow. But really, *all of them* know where I am and how long I will be here.

I get up and get ready to face the day. I realize that this *part* of the family has *no intention* of embracing me as a human being that deserves communication. And that is exactly what occurs.

On the other hand, Ronnie calls me and communicates pure acceptance and value to me for my life and my heart, which wanted to embrace my biological sister. I tell him that my hopes cannot come to pass. My presents will sit here, as if I never came to Decatur and never even followed through on my promise, which I made to answer Teresa's heart's need that *she expressed* to me during my first visit. I cannot even keep my word.

I next call Aunt Marion who of course hopes that I will come have breakfast with her. I will never want to say no to this precious woman, my favorite woman in the world.

EMBRACED

While I'm over at Aunt Marion's, my nephew, Zach, calls and says, "Uncle Jimmy, I heard about you having presents for Aunt Teresa. I get it. I will be honored to take Aunt Teresa's birthday dress and birthday purse to her house. I'll drop it off for you."

When Zach comes into town, I walk over to the hotel again. It is a great feeling to have my family share my needs and my pain. Zach gives me a hug, and dashes off with the two brightly wrapped gifts, bows and cursive all over them.

Later, Zach calls me. He tells me that when he arrived at Teresa's house, the front door was open. He knocked politely, but nobody came to the door. He could see Teresa through a doorway, but she did not move from her spot. Zach left my sister's birthday-wrapped designer dress and designer purse at the door and quietly drove home.

Zach's words sting all over again. Teresa <u>did</u> give me the impression that if I would celebrate her birthday, as I was celebrating Aunt Marion's, we would have a wonderful time because we are blood family. She implied that I could count on her love because of her Reiki guides and clouds and spirits directing her life by angels sent to her. She said all that on a voicemail I've got saved on my answering machine. The spirits went so far *as to write in the sky* to communicate with her, telling her to "embrace and love James." Uh huh.

The hotel staff is able to take me to Lake Decatur, where I throw rocks into the lake for each individual that has led me to believe false truths about my life, false truths about who I am, false truths about my value, and false truths about who *they* are, false truths about ever being wanted or found. I throw all those feelings *out*, and they sink down in the smelly muck, where they belong.

AUNT MARION FINDS THE BLIND SIDE

36

AUNT MARION IS GLUED to the Cubs game, as I bring food up to her room.

She has so much fun cheering on her Cubs as I fall asleep on the couch, so peacefully tired from draining events. Some *empties* are good.

She knows my visit is already more than half over, and she really wants to make sure that I have a good encounter in Decatur and that I will be going home with happy memories. "Memories are important," Aunt Marion says.

Aunt Marion reminds me of her advanced years and tells me that of all ages, the eighties are the hardest years of life, "because that's when you can tell that the body starts to shut down. I just can't do the things that I used to do and there is no fixing it. It is very hard to accept, Jimmy." She is so glad that I am there.

As we finish our pizza I see that we have eaten the whole thing again. Aunt Marion is so relaxed after her Cubs winning, so happy and proud, when I realize that it is once again midnight and I have to get to sleep for another day.

So I walk home with my dog, Charity, to the hotel. It is so sweet to look back and see my Aunt

EMBRACED

peeking out the window, watching over me to the hotel to see that I get home safely. She tells me that Decatur is different from Portland because of everything else is different. Money is hard to come by, the state is bankrupt and so some people are more desperate. With her eyes she follows me from the window. I wave her good night at the door, and walk in to sleep.

The next day, Aunt Marion and I are on a mission to find antique stores that had mother of pearl. We find a beautiful ring and bracelet, and we find feelings of such satisfaction and fun, as we take our treasure which is so appreciated. My Aunt Marion actually experiences joy, now, beyond her dreams, just eating with me for lunch. We fill ourselves up with breadsticks so that the next day we are only barely recovered from our food coma, and we go out *again*.

Aunt Marion has always been very unconventional, adventurous and inspiring. She talks about what it was like back then, being a beauty operator: the people, the feelings, the hair, nails and needs.

One afternoon, we get *The Blind Side* on DVD. I just know we have got to see it together. So much of me is still the boy who can't expect, Aunt Marion will recognize it immediately. Sandra Bullock is always worth seeing again, too. Aunt Marion is glued, the volume is up, and she is hitting the 15 second "repeat" button to cry over this and that section again and again.

Aunt Marion says, "I've never seen a movie like this before. It is so encouraging, Jimmy. It makes you want to just *go out* and *help* people."

I think of her in her nineties with her walker and wonder if maybe I've gone too far, but she turns and says, "Honestly, I think

2016

this is what you do, Jimmy. Everybody here where I live just talks and talks about you, because they like you and they like how you treat people. If you aren't here, they ask me *when you are coming back*. You really touch the hearts of the people that work here, Jimmy. You see them. I think that is what this movie is showing us to do."

During all my time with my Aunt Marion, there were communication touches with from my brother, Ronnie, and my sister-in-law, Lisa, my niece and nephew, and my cousins that I knew growing up. Sandy and Mark and Mark's wife, Robin, were all very gracious and welcoming. Some calls were just to say hello and check in, and those phone calls are moments when I find integrity in a Christian who thinks of others as they do of themselves.

These phone calls contrast so much with other memories that I have of calls from people claiming to love me, then turning around and hanging up the phone on me, because I didn't say what they wanted me to say. That kind of call has happened often in my life, growing up. Fitting into a pair of tap dance shoes and making music and showing my credentials of what value of person I am, and waiting for the judgment of their response, these are sensations I can't forget. I experience this all over again with certain biological members, and realized as tears fall from my eyes that my brother Ronnie has also had to endure family members claiming that he dishonored them. I can see that the truth is that these people need to take responsibility. They should leave me alone and they should leave Ronnie alone.

And it better happen quick, because I'm falling in *love* with my brother and my sister-in-law and my niece and nephew and in fact, I won't tolerate people hurting them. I'm in my fifties and I was taken away from my family at five years old and I feel the pain and embarrassment that these biological family members have rearranged the blame of their dysfunction onto my brother's positive and consistent, ethical life choices. And by the way, his life choices are appropriate choices that I would trust him to make for my life because I feel and see the truth of what he is, who he is, and the way he loves. *That's integrity* and I embrace and support him.

Lisa, my sister-in-law, respects my choices. The words that come out of her and the acts that she chooses show me all the time what is real in her.

One morning Lisa calls me up and says, "Jimmy, I have been thinking about your tattoos. They mean so much to you, and you express love through them. You express love and gratitude of the ocean and God's gift of baptism to wash away our wounds and I can't get that thought out of my head. I am thinking that I want a tattoo. I've never gotten one before so I don't know how to do it."

I say, "Oh, LISA! I would be honored to go with you! You have nothing to fear and I will get a tattoo to mark this moment that we honor expressions of gratitude and faith!"

I know my way around this industry and call her back with our appointment.

On the day, we get matching *Walk by Faith* ink. Mine is a little larger because I am more experienced and love the expression of color on my skin, but my sister-in-law and I have now got permanent statements of what we believe, which we believe *together*.

SABBATH IN MOWEQUA WITH MY FAMILY

~ 37 ~

SUNDAY IS COMING. As Lisa is dropping me off at the hotel, she opens the topic of coming to church with their family. I am undone all over again by the offer of intimacy in spiritual connection with God and with biological family. I can't help it; I break down crying. Lisa says she and my niece, Hannah, will be pleased to pick me up for church, and we can meet Ronnie and Zach there. They go to church in Moweaqua.

The next morning, I go to the front desk of the hotel asked a staffer to just help me *find* this place on a map. The staffer pops it in the computer and we are surprised to see faces of people of Moweaqua, people who are loved but who are gone after a terrible mining accident.

The staffer says, "This must be a special place because there are accidents in every town in America, but this tiny little place *still* loves those who are gone and talks about how they miss and value their own people. That's a pretty special place."

I ask her if it is big and she says, "No, but look at the pictures and see that the people live right next to each other and know each other and that's really interesting and unusual."

I thank the hotel staffer so much, because I know what to expect and I have wonderful clarity of the village of Moweaqua. I'm still thinking about my dream which I am still looking for, where there is respect and peace and restfulness.

Lisa and Hannah come to pick me up on Sunday morning. The drives out to the country seem shorter and shorter, as we have more and more to talk about. Hannah hears all about her mother's tattoo experience and sees the larger version on my shin. There is no desire to cover up the joy we feel.

The little village seems to operate with stop signs only. The yards are as well-kept as the metal roofs are tight. This town does not waste energy on what doesn't matter, and it splurges on what does. There are churches in sight of each other. In perfect harmony, the people load inside.

The name of the village church is First Christian Church. *Draw Near and Go Far* is on all their pamphlets. They give me a little welcome bag with positive messages to carry away and keep forever. Inside there is a book with stickers. It is a perfect memory bag for me. My brother takes me up to the counter of the church and asks me to sign the welcome book as Jimmylee Bond, and I did. That record means that today at church, my brother's Bond family (me!) came to support him in his spiritual life. This is very important to me.

It is incredible, to sit and sing and worship the Lord with biological family. I feel the Spirit all over me. My emotions are very sentimental as I sit next to my nephew who sits next to my sister-in-law, with me looking at her and her looking at me, to see that I am okay. I wink at her and mouth, "We *walk by faith* right now," which is the wording of our tattoos. The little smarting from the tattoo procedure just keeps it present to me, in the very moment that I proclaim to walk by faith with biological family. Throughout my life, I have been walking in uncertainty, never knowing tomorrow's plans. Walking in faith feels so different! I can't control much more

EMBRACED

than I ever could, but I'm not supposed to control. I am *asked* and *covenanted* to walk by faith.

It feels like white light is coming out of my heart. I am embedded with a permanent, pure acceptance. I know that I am found and not ever forgotten, even after five decades. I find myself looking at my brother, the way he walks, the way he talks, the shape of his eyes and face and characteristics. I just fall in love with the gift of having a brother that *is true*. What more could any brother ever ask from another brother or a sibling ask from another sibling? Truth, honesty, integrity and faith, these are the hopes that bonded us the first time we met. On this, the second trip what cements our hopes into reality are the actions we showed to one another. Loving intention was followed by loving follow-through. Respect and empathy refined feelings into appropriate loving acts, *kindness!*

We stand to shake hands in all directions, to say *God be with you* to the stranger and friend alike. God's spirit is in any church that seeks Him. That is the promise and we can trust it.

Lisa invites me over to meet her parents. She has to stay but I am glad to stop in and say hello. Lisa proudly introduces me as her brother-in-law. That shows *everything* about how she was raised, and what type of heart she has. I will protect her as if she is my own blood, and I know more of what that means, now.

At the end of a day of spiritual overflowing, I find myself back at the hotel, cuddling Charity, absorbing God's gift of family.

JORDAN JANTZ

MAMA'S MISTAKE NO REFUNDS AND NO RETURNS

38

MY ADOPTED MOTHER (Mama) calls Aunt Marion several times during my visit. Mama does not call me. Communication between us is still an enormous challenge. Mama no longer lives in California but she does not live nearby. My Aunt Rose and Uncle Ray offer to drive my adopted mother and her husband half-way to Decatur to meet me.

Making life happen for the residents, my favorite maid at the Hawthorn Inn can drive me the other half of the distance, on her free day in her own car. This task will take Miss Ruth's whole day that she has off from work, just to be so kind to me. I owe this angel woman more than gas money, I know.

If we can accomplish this, this meeting will be only the second time that I have seen my adoptive mother in thirty-five years. The last time was when I got Charity as a tiny puppy.

There have been so many things that Mama has done that have hurt me, most of all because I felt that she wanted to hurt me. When she got foster sons, I heard all about how they do *just* what she tells them to do, how they attend to her wants and needs first, and how masculine and boyish they are, and that they are not sissies.

JORDAN JANTZ

We agree to meet in public, at a restaurant called Ryan's. I am terrified but I know that God wants me to at least reach out and connect to her.

When I look at her beautiful face, I can't put my finger on why we have these dynamics but today.

I have a lump in throat. My throat is dry and I am fighting back tears. I think how much she has changed, how much I have changed, and I realize how *very young she was*, at the age she got a beautiful and very abused and neglected little boy. She had no knowledge of the severity of the abuse, before I was received. How big and impossible a puzzle – and how broken! – I was when she received me into her life.

I think and think again. I must have compassion and forgiveness. And perhaps she will someday have compassion on me, as Jimmylee never was able to be the best little boy in the world to her. I think that is why she took in foster boys. I never could please her and make her happy, although I danced as fast as I possibly could to every beat that would make her proud.

I know that one thing is for sure, my Aunt Rose knows the truth because she did tell my adoptive mother (her sister) while we were eating and talking about the fact of my biological mother would probably wish to see me since I found my biological family, but I respond, "I want no part of her, for what she did."

At that point, Aunt Rose says, "I'm sure your biological mother did love you, Jimmy."

And I say, "No she never loved me by her actions. That's how I feel, Aunt Rose. If she did love me, it was a weird love, because the church did my genealogy and there are things that she did that nobody knows, in fact. She tried to extort money all the

Aunt Rose and Jordan. She was the aunt that helped Aunt Marion get Jordan from Decatur to California at four years old.

"I'm so proud of Aunt Rose and the truth she speaks!" – Jordan

way 'til I was almost seven years of age, for selling me at the price she did. She wanted more and more and more."

My mother immediately says, "How can *you* even talk about this? How can you even *remember* this?"

I say, "What are you talking about? Children know what is going on when they are three, four, five years of age. I came here today and sitting across the table here is Miss Ruth who drove me across this country to see you, and have lunch with you after thirty-five years and I get this?"

My Aunt Rose says to Mama, "Actually, I **do** remember some challenges that you were dealing with, sis, with Jimmy's mother. I remember she wanted to make sure her and Jimmy's sisters, Robin were *set up*. I do recall that."

Mama says, "Well, you are misinformed."

I feel like I'm about ready to have a stroke. I have to get up and leave the table and go to the bathroom and put water on my face. I collect myself out of *embarrassment* that Miss Ruth from the hotel drove me for this event for this special lunch, across the country, on Miss Ruth's day off, to hear this is the most painful, shaming demonstration that I am *meaningless* to my Mama...

When I return, Mama says, "You had Botox done, didn't you? How can you be in your fifties and look the way you look? You *can't fool a fooler*."

I say, "I don't have a clue of what you are talking about. You know that in the model industry when doing photos for advertisements, you have to look and be what they want you to be and that is the way my life has always been, so for my financial security I have to be all things to all people in order to be able to get a job at what I know how to do, which is the only thing I have ever

EMBRACED

known how to do. So, Botox: Not. A facelift: Not! Taking good care of what I have, *Yes!* because of the best medical support in the Pacific Northwest and my physicians take care of my medical and physical needs because I would be dead if it wasn't for the love of my doctors."

She says, "Well, then, you should just get on the plane and fly right back to them, and avoid going back to your Aunt Marion and let her *grow old in peace*."

And I just think, let it go let it go let it go, like the words in the movie, Frozen.

I look at her and turn my chair around, and say, "Aunt Rose, Uncle Ray, I am so grateful for this moment that you have brought my mother here, and I will always remember this lunch here and it was the best southern food that I have ever had. Thank you so much and I love you, I have always loved you, Aunt Rose and Uncle Ray, and your children have been the sweetest to me throughout my life as cousins, and I thank you for that. But I can tell that Mama does not want to be a part of my life. And she continues to believe that I tell people that I have molested by all of her brothers and I do not do that. I have not said that."

Miss Ruth asks me if I would like to have a picture taken of my adoptive mother and my aunt and I say, "That would be really nice. Aunt Rose, would you like to do that? Mama, can I get a picture with you before I leave?"

Mama says, "Yes, because this will be the last picture *you'll* ever see of me."

And I say, "That's fine, memories are what I have existed on, so a photograph is something more than a memory. It is tangible to hold and embrace. Just because you choose to not love me doesn't mean I will ever let go and let you be the winner of my soul, because

JORDAN JANTZ

God knows I have given you all I have to show you how much you mean to me. Thank you so much for taking time out of your life to come and have lunch. Aunt Rose is an honest, truthful aunt and I love her. And I thank you, Aunt Rose. You know the challenges and the reality and I do not want to cause any problems, so it would be best for me to leave and let you guys get back to where you came from, because Aunt Marion and I and my biological family have much to accomplish."

What a memory this has been, and still is today, as I am reflecting on this, and recording this on my tapes that I use to remember special valuable moments that pertain to my well-being and this definitely has been a tape that I will put away and listen to and take to my therapist, which we will work on for a few months to get this behind me. Once again my therapist knows the pain of my mother telling me I am nothing but *used shoes*. So this will be an opportunity to let go and let God be in control of this circumstance because I release it and erase it from the chalk board of my life.

Both love and forgiveness are choices. What we do with our lives is a choice, though many of us do not have many choices. I did the best that I could, although my choices in life were all about making other people happy. Even so, I managed to find a great deal of happiness through knowing that I made other people happy.

And maybe when she ponders the life that I have – the life I am so grateful to have - Mama will realize that love truly isn't love until you give it away. It's *Pinocchio*, puppet or pretend love, until that love is *given* – without conditions and without strings – to the other. Many people practice false love and use the words without ever practicing love. Conditional love is meant to manipulate and shame, to keep a "loved one" in line, not spiritually included.

EMBRACED

I love her, and I love the whole family that I was sold to. I am grateful for what Bud and Ina did fifty years ago because I know that giving me up and getting me away from my circumstances was only done to give me a life.

Even though life is challenging, God finds a positive purpose in what we go through. I don't understand the miracle, how God transforms negatives into positives that can bless the world. This is why God is so much greater than man.

This wonderful woman drove me on her day off, so that I could try to do what Jesus would have me do. What an amazing person!

UNCLE DALE'S FIRST TIME OUT

~ 39 ~

THE NEXT NIGHT IS MY LAST EVENING with Aunt Marion. Aunt Marion has been on my side longer than any other soul on earth. She never demands answers but always calls me her little boy.

As I am preparing to depart, I do not have to tell her specifics about my oath-dinner with Ronnie and Lisa to give her the understanding that we have made commitments to one another, to be true family, to include without conditions. In my heart, I know I never have to worry about Ronnie and Lisa. They vowed to keep their promise and I believe them. They vowed that nobody in Decatur, through loose lips of theirs, will ever read the book or learn of Jordan Jantz, *Out of the Closet, Into the Light*, and I know that when it comes out, no one there will read my second book, *Embraced*. Those who may know through me will have respect for privacy. I know the value of my brother's love for me and the kind of person he is: honest, open, truthful, committed. And I know my sister in law's love for me and the person she is: discerning, compassionate, inclusive, and hard-working. Because they are so unified it is hard to know who has what traits, more.

I will have dinner with my aunt, warmed inside with the love that I will embrace. My biological family has helped mend

With Aunt Marion and Uncle Dale, there is always love.

my broken heart and teach it that home is where the heart is. This is the kind of love Jesus has for you and me.

My heart is light. Dinner is lovely. Aunt Marion's friends are unbeatably precious and never fail for a moment in their grace and kindness. I think older folks show me lessons they have learned and the wisdom they have acquired in their "let it go" and love everyone with gratitude. My Aunt Marion has always been a bright light in the world.

In the morning, I call Aunt Marion before breakfast, which she has waiting for me, again. We go, as we have gone every morning, to see Uncle Dale in the memory care unit down the block for one last time before I leave. This trip has been so up and down, so high and so low.

But here I am in my last hour in Decatur for now, spending it with my Uncle Dale and Aunt Marion. We take Uncle Dale out to his favorite restaurant, Gabby's, where the owner remembers him. Years ago, it had been Uncle Dale's favorite place to take Aunt Marion for chicken fried steak, southern style.

Aunt Marion and I still can't get over the miracle that Uncle Dale, who retains very little new information now, has all sorts of memories of me. He talks on and on about me being "a little whippersnapper," holding on to him so tightly, wanting to learn to swim but so afraid to let go. And now I realize as I sit with dear Uncle Dale in his age, struggling with Alzheimer's, and Aunt Marion in her advanced years gently accepting that things are not going to get better anymore, that we will all have to let go of this life at some point. We all have to eventually be ready to join together in the celebration of our new life, after this life is done. That's what I learn my last day at Gabby's restaurant with Uncle Dale, Aunt Marion and even my sweet, elderly dog, Charity, as I sit there, eating fried southern food, the best fried food in the world.

EMBRACED

As Aunt Marion and I settle Uncle Dale back into his unit, she looks at his black cowboy hat. "You know, Jimmy, Dale wore that hat every year, for all the six months that we lived each year in Corpus Christi. I want you to have that hat, Jimmy. Wear it as you go. Wear it for good luck."

I board the tiny plane. The ride will be bumpy. It always is, in tiny planes. You get to feel every gust of wind and every drop, because you are small in the big ocean of air. And yet, I feel complete spiritual clarity and wholeness for the first time in my life. Most of all, I feel all found.

I'm headed back to Portland. I know I have a lot of decisions myself to make for my life as I will soon now become a senior citizen. My brother and I together will experience this opportunity along with my sister-in-law. We will have the blessing of becoming senior citizens together, if our hearts are open to sharing the commitment that we made as family, not just for today, but forever. This prospect does not worry me as it once did. It does not worry me at all.

MAMA STATES: WHY DON'T YOU STICK IT UP YOU'RE A**?!

SISTER STATES: I MUST DISCONNECT FROM YOU. YOU ARE UNHEALTHY.

~ 40 ~

A*RRIVING BACK HOME* in the port of Portland, the sea breeze reaches throughout the misty, rainy city, which I so much have missed. I'm more of a sea-level type of guy that loves the fresh water and smells of the ocean throughout the Pacific Northwest. The green mossy trees bring delight to my service dog, Charity, as I immediately take her out to enjoy her potty dance on the moss that is growing on the sidewalks throughout Portland State University, across the street from where I live, which is Charity's favorite dog park. I can tell she is so happy to be home. We both have to take our first days back slow and easy.

EMBRACED

I look forward to the fine moments of relaxing and recalibrating all my history and piecing the puzzle of my life experience together from this incredible miracle of my life.

I see as I am entering my home that there is a message left for me, on my answering system. Immediately I check the message and it is my sister-in-law, Lisa. She has read the whole book in two days. My sister-in-law always embraced my disabilities regarding my post-traumatic stress disorder that I have lived with and never knew how to handle anything until my medical team came into my life. She knew through Ronnie that I had been dealt experiences that challenge me to this day, and that I lean on professionals who provide me with care and nourishment from day to day. I work hard to have clarity and hope for my future. Lisa has the gift of discernment.

My brother reads a chapter a day so that he can embrace each moment of the book. He has integrity for choosing to embrace each chapter and make it a part of his day. He is *so* not plastic fantastic. The chapters in my book are not difficult to read but are painful to accept. He had heard about some of these activities that did happen when I was a child. In all the communicating with each other and biological family, nobody ever brought up or mentioned my embarrassing reality of being the only child sold.

Unfortunately, that doesn't pertain to everyone.

The peace with Mama cannot be kept from just my end. In her mind, I abandoned her and rejected my adopted family, which anyone who knows me would tell you Jordan would never do a thing like that. But with my adoptive mom, that's not the part that is upsetting right now to her. She feels the whole circumstance should just be not spoken about, and let go of forever, as she continues to say to me, "You have made my life choice and you

JORDAN JANTZ

2016

have chosen my lifestyle, and you have made your own bed and you need to lie in it, no matter what condition or circumstance is." There is no grace for me in any format with her. I have always had this reality of a relationship with my adoptive mom and this is nothing new.

I have always trusted Aunt Marion and she could always trust me to keep her own doings in confidence. It has come out that my mother has found out that many years ago Aunt Marion and Uncle Dale came to visit me in Milwaukie and went to dinner with me and my partner. All this happened, after my adoptive mother had declared me to be dead to the family (because, in her memory, she never told me to leave.)

So, today my adoptive mother calls me, livid, "You mean to tell me that you have been in contact with Aunt Marion *all this time?*"

Actually, I had lost Aunt Marion's contact for many years, which I don't explain, because Mama is angry that I had been in contact with Aunt Marion during *any* of the years that Mama had declared me unwelcome.

I try to reason with Mama, but she isn't mad that she didn't that I had no contact with her. Her verbal abuse continued throughout my life and was only lightened if I brought her opportunities to shine as a mother of a wonderful son. If I did that, everything was fine and dandy for Mama, but Mama didn't understand me and my challenges from the day she bought me, for, like any child that has been abused, I had difficulties in trusting and learning because of fear of being hit or put in a place that I could not get out of. Mama never really understood me or my fears because in her eyes, I was the perfect child *on the outside*. When she saw the picture of me in my sailor suit, that was the selling point. She didn't know what was inside of the package of the little boy in the picture standing next to the Christmas tree. She just knew what a pretty little boy I would grow up to be. She never understood how deeply wounded I was, before I came into her life.

Mama says, "*You* don't need to communicate with Aunt Marion. You do NOT tell me that. I have good sons now and you have just gone to your Aunt Marion's and *ruined everything!*"

It is heartbreaking to hear this. I say, "Mom, why are you saying all this?"

Mama says, "I don't believe you. I *don't believe* that Aunt Marion talked to you. That is not true!"

I try to reason with her, "Mom, Aunt Marion has always been in my life. When I was living with my partner in Milwaukie, Aunt Marion and Uncle Dale came out and spent time with us. Their visit was so precious to me."

Mama says, "Aunt Marion would *never* have done that. I have good people in my life and Aunt Marion isn't *that kind* of person. And you don't need to be calling up your Aunt Freda or Aunt Rose. *You* don't. You do *not* do that. They don't *want* to talk to you. They don't *ever* want to even hear from you again!"

I say, "Your opinion is your opinion, but I know that what you say is not the truth. None of the things that you have said to me were ever true about my sister and my father. They did not tell you that it would be best for me to leave. You are the one that wanted me to leave."

She says, "Well, I'm glad you chose your own lifestyle of being gay and you've chosen to be who you are and you are going to have to just live with your choices that you have made in your life and you choose to be gay and you have chosen that lifestyle and stop whatever is with my sisters and other family members that are

EMBRACED

my family. They are <u>MY</u> family! Why don't you just go ahead and be with the people I got you from? Go back and just see how good they can really be. Be with your *Aunt Marion*, if *that's* the best woman in the world. And let me tell you, the way you talk about how *she* saved your life? Well, she hasn't done anything for you! And your Aunt Freda, you act as if she is the *spiritual inspiration* in your life. And about my brothers!! I'm **sick and tired** of you *recalibrating your moments of abuse*. And ***telling*** **people** about it. **<u>Instead of sticking it up my a** why don't you stick it up yours!!!</u>** YOU *are not* my son, you *never have* been my son, I don't want anything to do with you, <u>I am *sick* of you</u> and I'm sick of the fact that you are alive and telling people your '*challenges*' you have live with. **I want nothing more to do with you!**"

"Mom," I reply, "how can you say this when we have only seen each other *twice* in *thirty-five years*? You once planned for me and then decided my future would be disconnection, dumping me when I was still vulnerable, after keeping me for a season in your life. I did everything I could to make you happy. I tried but it wasn't good enough. As you said, I was nothing but a sissy, a cheerleader, a model. Yes, I did things that most boys don't do. So, you get foster boys to throw me under the bus by comparison, because I can't do the things that other boys do because of the fear I have of loud noises and the intimidation of never knowing how to play basketball, football. I even tried to play baseball, but *couldn't* play baseball, so I became the best at what I *could* be, and I was the best at all I set out to be, receiving trophies and awards to put on the shelf for you to display. But nothing has ever been good enough for you as far as I am concerned, as your son. You have made that very clear to me and your sisters. So, I'm letting you know that I will no longer let *my love* just rest because of *your anger* towards me. I am doing the best I can in my life today with the challenges of abandonment and rejection that I have been put through. I *thank* you for meeting me and sharing one last meal together. That meal was heart-touching and will all be cherished by me, whether you appreciate my time and love, I don't care anymore. I just pray we can share our next meal at the eternal table in heaven where we will feast with love, if you will allow God's love to come into your heart for the little boy you picked out who wore a little sailor suit just for you."

She hangs up on me.

I call Aunt Marion and let her know a storm is coming down her phone line.

An hour later, Aunt Marion calls me, "Your mother doesn't want to hear reality, Jimmy. She wants to yell and yell her reality into the air and make it happen by daring us to talk back to her. She is so jealous of you! She has told your sister things that I know are not true. And, I'm sure she has said things to all of us that are just absolutely not true. I don't understand her doing this to you, after she knows what you went through your entire childhood before she got you. It was hideous and that's why Bud made sure you were sold to a family that would give you a good life. And I followed through with his request, or I would have kept you, myself."

I say, "Well, what did you say to her?"

Aunt Marion says, "She was going on about how *I DO NOT talk to Jimmy* this and *I DO NOT see Jimmy* that and carrying on hollering and I just got fed up and said, "I do too see Jimmy and talk to Jimmy and I did back then," She howled, "YOU DO NOT!" and I yelled right back, *"I do, too, and I did that,* **because you didn't want him!** *and you don't love him today! How can you talk to him the way that you do? You destroy people by the things that you say to them!"*

It pains me to hear Aunt Marion defending herself from Mama. But it also sooths a part of me that always wanted someone to speak up for me. My heart is pounding in my chest.

EMBRACED

Aunt Marion continues, "That is what I told her, Jimmy. And I don't want you talking to her anymore. She has not one bit of respect for you and what you do in your life. She makes sure other people see her side of the story and she will press and press and press you 'til you submit to her. Stop submitting and know your *Aunt Marion* loves you, and your *brother* loves you, and I just pray that your brother never finds how mean and challenging it was for you to grow up trying to pleasing your Mama every morning and never being able to measure up to the expectations of what she paid for. I am so sorry, Jimmy! I regret this more than anything!" and Aunt Marion just falls into tears

It just makes me so angry to see my poor little Aunt Marion be abused verbally by Mama like this.

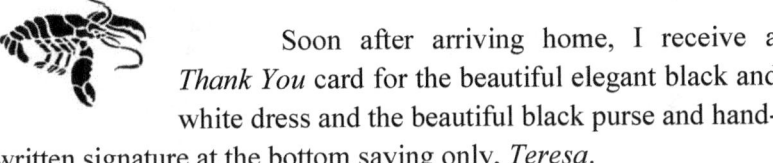

Soon after arriving home, I receive a *Thank You* card for the beautiful elegant black and white dress and the beautiful black purse and handwritten signature at the bottom saying only, *Teresa*.

I think about that, for a while. Maybe that is the most honest thing she can do right now. I do not have to understand her to love her, and I do not have to connect with her beyond her ability to reach out in a healthy, appropriate way.

Another letter from Teresa followed. In it was a note she had written, stating:

Jimmy, I'm writing to hopefully help ease your pain and to let you know I love you. I have listened to your messages and ask for your forgiveness for any suffering I may have caused you. The Lord knows this was not my intention, only to bring you peace of mind, love and joy, if only for a short time. I thank the Lord for allowing the time that we spent. I will treasure it. But, it is time for me to step back and disconnect from you. Always know you will be in my thoughts and prayers, much love, Teresa

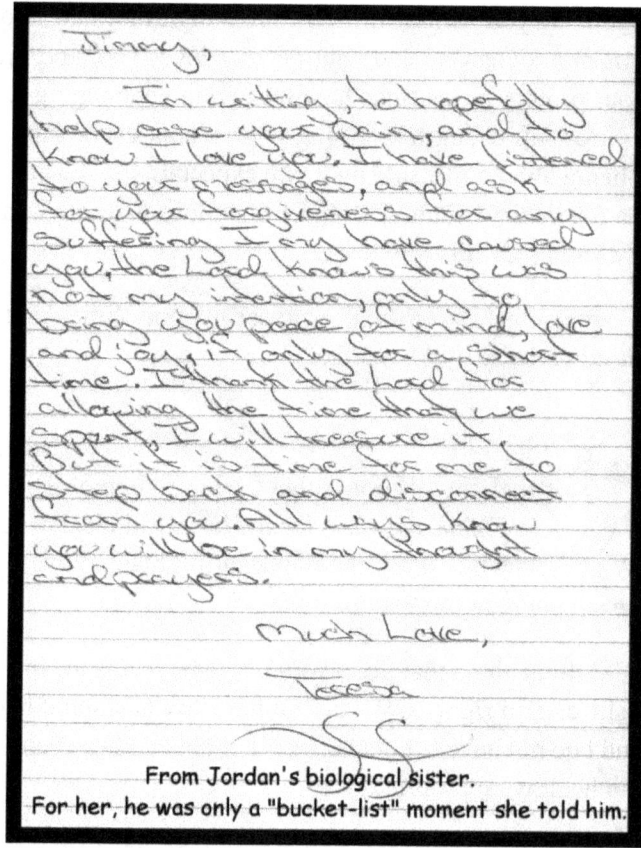

From Jordan's biological sister.
For her, he was only a "bucket-list" moment she told him.

I needed her letter explained to me (it doesn't even make sense).

I know she has to realize probably that abandonment is the best way to torture a person.

I tell her on the phone- Y*ou are treating me the exact way my biological mother treated me, and that is, your love is*

EMBRACED

conditional. And anything I do will never measure up to you and Kevin.

You and Kevin have done more harm to my brother, Ronnie. I will not tolerate this activity. My nephew went all the way over to your home to drop off the presents for your birthday that I came with, thinking I was throwing you a birthday party celebration, because you told me no brother has ever thrown you a birthday party. I felt sorry for you.

So I am the one that has the bird poop on his head, not you, because I trusted your words and your love that you say you have for me, and how much you care, but I realize words are so easily spoken and actions are what is reality. Words are cheap. And you have hit me below the belt, and so has Kevin, but I will tell you right now, nobody messes with the big brother of the family. And I am that brother. And nobody messes with my little brother, Ronnie. And nobody messes with my niece or nephew or my sister-in-law. Period. I am as much of a brother to Ronnie as you are but I pray I never have the heart or use the words that you have used to tear this family apart.

How in the world you convinced Kevin to dishonor me and to dishonor my brother, Ronnie, I don't know, but I know for a fact after what I experienced on this momentous moment with you. My light bulb being turned on. I see the cockroaches running for safety.

Then, I heard her hang up the phone on me.

And that was the last conversation she and I have ever had, and probably ever will have.

Kevin has no consciousness to realize how mean it is to do to me, what he has done in ignoring the truth that I have tried to love and reach out and be a brother to him and to Teresa. There comes a time when you can only handle so many slaps in the face from people and most importantly, people that are family.

Recalling all this makes me realize how my mother's anger and manipulating ways have really broken my life even more today. Maybe I'm even a little bit set back and emotionally broken from what I have experience throughout my life with people. You see, it is hard when someone wants you only for your physical appearance, not that I'm not grateful for the shell that my spirit rests in, but it is just a shell. What is more important than anything is my soul. That is what lasts forever.

It's amazing that the people in this world are able to live and exist treating people in such painful ways. When people know your history and turn it on you to be very mean and hurtful as to, for instance, ask you if you are gay or if you have AIDS, coming from a sister, stating that your biological mother called her up to inform her about me, I find this overwhelmingly painful to respond do and I'm frozen in fear of abandonment. I also feel exactly the same way about another woman who has maliciously made me a protégé to bring her youthful attributes as a mother much adoration for the way her little boy was able to perform and dance and sing the way he did, was meant for Hollywood and that always made her feel like a super-star mom and that is where my foundation of who I was and what I was meant to be as a son, came from. So I learned to let the sun shine down on my tap dance shoes for those shoes and my voice and my talent **was** the value of my existence for many of my years of my life. And still, today, I realize the expectations people have on my life.

So, now letting go and *letting God heal how I have just been wounded.*

EMBRACED

FEEDING THE HOMELESS IN DOWNTOWN PORTLAND

~ 41 ~

My city of Portland has seen me in all formats. The people of this city have rejoiced with me for more than thirty-five years and when my Aunt was found in Decatur they prayed for her and supported these good things in my life. Everybody here values time with each other in my life.

My city taught me that –strangers, even- can see people and help them live. Portland is a mild-weather city, and not too dry. People who can't make it hit rock bottom and they get themselves to Portland for it. They would freeze to death in Utah or Wyoming or New York. Portland is the city where I saw my first homeless person living on the streets, so many years ago.

I stayed away then, because I had been taught that homelessness was a choice of laziness and grifting. When I was a young model I thought that I could really have my own American dream in my industry. I even took many planes and trains to big cities to pass out my business cards at fashionable functions. My career as a model also had to be perfected to be competitive, because the agencies never used Photoshop back then, nor did we even know what it was. We were the real thing, and if you weren't they made you become the real thing through food and diet and physical transformation. I knew people valued the real thing.

Whatever the homeless people were doing, I thought that if they consistently did the real thing they wouldn't be homeless. The homeless people just didn't have a very good work ethic, I was always told.

Experience changes our young convictions, and it should. Eventually, exhaustion and illness kept me from work, and without work I had no income. Without nurturing and safety everyone gets more and more sick. My rock bottom was on the streets also, just like the people I see today.

I could never, ever have gotten up again on my own. People helped me. People make the difference for people. People set other people free, because we remember our own traps. It's wrong to say *God will help them* if we aren't willing to be God's hands and feet to make that happen.

So, this year I do what I do every Thanksgiving for the last eleven years.

Early November I visit the dollar store, where I can buy and carry away bags of potatoes and boxes of colored foil. I coordinate the means to share hot baked potatoes all over the city. The black Pentecostal church is mobile. The workers at Voodoo Donuts are on board. The women at the Salvation Army Women's Shelter are ready. The Mormon missionaries are excited and bewildered and yes, ready. One of my early-morning prayer partners, Sophie, would never miss this. The men's therapy group, my doctors and dentist, and even my pharmacist, everyone knows that the day of thanks is coming up. No one has to specifically love God, to love the *goodness and kindness* God teaches us to practice between each other.

EMBRACED

At dawn, I put the potatoes wrapped in foil in my oven and call everyone else to do that same. They call themselves Team Jordan and we all arrive together with our bags of baked potatoes at my home, with wheelbarrows outside to have the baked potatoes put in them, for dispersing to the streets of downtown Portland.

We all pull on our raincoats, boots and umbrellas and head out into the low-traffic streets of early Thanksgiving morning. We visit the underground parking lots, behind the buildings, and bridges, and find the homeless cuddled into their tarps. Some are cuddling their dogs and some are holding their loved ones. Some are cuddling children who are cold. We put a warm potato in every hand and give a smile and encouragement. Their eyes light up, to receive a warm Thanksgiving treat first thing on Thanksgiving morning.

I remember what it means to be seen as unhuman and <u>unvaluable</u>, as a homeless person. The moment that shattered and nearly cost me my life was <u>complete rejection</u>. When the Jantz family realized that I could not, and would not say that I was delivered from the spirit of homosexuality, my disowning from the family was complete. I lost my bed, most of my clothes and possessions. They didn't care that they had led me on to depend and trust them that I had not prepared at all or known in advance what would happen. They depended on their perfect trap to hold me where they wanted me, but it wasn't even possible to please them. God made me same gender attracted and it isn't possible to change any more than it is possible to substitute my eyeballs or my heart for cardboard replicas. What they asked wasn't hard, it was impossible.

They did not care that it would kill me. They meant to put me in that position. And when the scene played out, they were just fine carrying out what would likely see me dead anyway- disowning me without resources. When I stood at the door, hungry, hoping to be invited in for Thanksgiving dinner so that I could eat and retrieve even a few of my possessions, I was told, "Never come back. Not today. Not at Christmas." It was somewhat like a plotted murder, by people that I had loved. Nothing in my life has hurt me more than this moment.

I couldn't let anyone know that I was homeless because then I would never work in my industry again. Reputation is everything in the fashion and modeling industry. You get the price you can demand, and desperation means that you will never get ahead again.

If I wanted to live, I had to keep it all a secret. If even one of my friends knew, I knew they couldn't keep it to themselves. It was too juicy that Jordan Jantz the fashion model and industry king, was homeless. The phone lines would be on actual fire.

I had enough in my pocket for a blue plastic tarp to cuddle up on the bare ground under the legs of the Burnside Bridge that I had jumped off of years prior, desiring to be free from the work and life. For, I knew of nothing else but to utilize what I had been known that would make a good living, and that took me back to the time when I was paid for, as a child, and I realized that was the key to my career as doors opened and continued to open more and more throughout my life, bringing in much notoriety for abilities and talents I never asked for.

I could think of only one friend who could keep my secret. He brought me dinners and let me shower at his house once a week, but I was afraid to take any more, with others in the house. I thought I could just work and get ahead again, but you can't if you don't have the resources. That was when I learned. The homeless *never* choose to be homeless. It just got worse, and colder.

Sophie was a single mother who is and landscape artist at McMenamins. Sophie would never let her child feel hunger as she

EMBRACED

had. She knew what it was to be thrown away. When she had heard about someone hiding from the public in the bushes by the waterfront trying to stay warm on a windy, wet December morning, *she* brought me in. I couldn't be upstairs with her child because she didn't know me at all, but she knew I was a person, and a valuable person. She helped me with a sleeping bag in the basement, a light, water, a jar to pee in, and some food. She could do that for as long as I needed it.

Today, someone has told the Willamette Weekly about Operation Thanksgiving Hot Potato and a reporter wants the story with photos. Charlie and I show our baskets.

The reporter asks, "So, where does this come from?"

Charlie responds, "A long time ago, a sick and exhausted male model walked right off the catwalk. He got fired, and I found him in the street. A lady that didn't even know him took him in, but she had heard of him as many people in Portland had. Some don't realize that *all* people on the streets have backgrounds that have made their life become broken. That's why Jordan started the Potato Drive every Thanksgiving and why so many people help support this. Jordan does not place his life on the value of a dollar but the value of the ability to touch one life each day."

The reporters are so grateful to share the story of Portland's Baked Potato Man, a sweet whodunit. They are glad to tell just how much the annual potato run has touched the downtown homeless people. They end their reports with, *We are here at Dignity Village Homeless camp where many are waking up to hot baked potatoes by a mystery man. Every one of these people is wondering how a toasty warm baked potato got into their sleeping bag, and here is the answer this mystery. Happy Thanksgiving in downtown Portland!*

JORDAN JANTZ

If any of you have done it unto the least of these, ye have done it unto me.

It has been God all along, rescuing souls to goodness and wholeness, into loving each other and valuing each other. And it is a rescued soul like me that knows it. I can't earn the good things I have, because I myself can't create them. I need to share all the goodness with all the people, if I want to belong to God. That is the commandment.

Jordan, when he was homeless.

EMBRACED

EMBRACED

JORDAN JANTZ

I HAVE AN UNCLE AND IT IS MY FATHER'S BROTHER!! I LOVE HIM!!!

42

WHAT A WONDERFUL THANKSGIVING it has been! I'm so exhausted, I lay down and fall asleep.

In the morning, I realize I have not checked my messages. Then I realize that because of my activities, I haven't checked my messages for a few *days*.

I check my phone's answering system and I hear new a voice:

*JIMMY? This is Bill Bond. It's **your** Uncle Bill. I'm your Dad's brother. I can't believe you found us. Ronnie called me and told me that you have been found and you are alive. Do you have time to call me? I would like that very much.*

I immediately take down the number.

"Oh my Lord have mercy on me!" I say to myself and to Charity, "What are we going to do? My biological dad has left behind a brother that I can get to know. What a miracle that has

EMBRACED

come my way! Another person that knows my biological father and can tell me about my dad, who gave life to me!"

When I call, he picks up at the first ring.

I tell him, "Uncle Bill, this is Jimmy, your nephew."

He says, "Jimmy!! Do you remember me? You are my first nephew. Do you recall your Uncle Bill? Do you remember me bouncing you on my knee when you were a little baby?"

Oh, no! I hate to say it but, "No, Uncle Bill, I don't recall that, but I'm excited to know I have an uncle."

He says, "I am so glad that you are *alive*! We all wondered what happened to you. Everything was kept so secret and my brother didn't talk that much about what was going on in his life at this time, for I was in high school, a senior, when you were born. *You are very important* and I want you to know that right away. You live in Portland, Ronnie says."

I say, "Yes, I sure do, I've lived here for thirty-five years, since I graduated from high school."

"Oh my goodness," he says, "Well, I want to see you and would like you to know that you have cousins that would want to see you. You have an Aunt Brenda also, and your Uncle James who you might have heard about."

I say, "I was told I was named after my uncle, but I never was told where or who he was."

Uncle Bill says, "He was the nicest man and I loved him very much. He died last year of cancer. And, your dad and I got to spend the last eleven years of his life together and that meant so much to both of us, especially me. For he also had cancer and I just want to know if you're okay and if you are doing well."

And I say, "I'm doing fine. This phone call and talking to you are absolutely miracles to me."

He says, "I can tell that this is touching you, emotionally, right now. It has to, it would anyone. After all these years, aren't you in your fifties?"

And I say, "You are right, you are absolutely right."

He says, "I remember the day you were born. I remember what it was like to find out I was an uncle. But you were taken and it was very strange for all of us because of circumstances that nobody wanted to discuss. You know what you've been through, yourself. And I want you to know that I love you, and I don't want to be just your uncle. Now that your dad is not here for you, I would like to step up to the plate that my brother was not able to, and not only be your uncle and friend, but be like a father to you. That's what my brother would have wanted, Jimmy. And I want you to know that I want to see you and you are not forgotten. I have always remembered you but never knew what happened to you, for your dad was so hurt over a lot of things in his life that he kept bottled up inside. He had a lot of things that were not that great happen to him, as a little boy. Kind of like you. And so, would you be open to meeting me? And my family?"

Immediately I say, "Of course I would, I would be so happy to know you and get to know you. I love my brother, Ronnie, so much, He has embraced me and he just loves me to pieces. I am so grateful to have his wife and his two children embrace me, Uncle Bill."

He says, "I am so proud that Ronnie has embraced you and loves you. His dad would be very proud of him, as much as you are and I am also. I want to let you know that it hasn't been easy but we all have managed since your dad passed away in 2006, but I know that it has really hurt Ronnie a lot, especially since his mother also

EMBRACED

passed in 2012. So, I am so glad that you are there for him. How about Kevin?"

I say, "Well, Uncle Bill, Kevin doesn't really want anything to do with me. I've sent him Thanksgiving cards, Easter cards, birthday cards, letters and I haven't received one phone call from him. And then there is a sister named Teresa and another brother named Troy. Teresa has asked me not to be involved in her life and asked me to let go of her because she needs to disconnect from me, Uncle Bill, and she wants me to go on and live my own life and leave her out of it." *And I honestly cannot face any abandonment again.*

His voices cracks and it sounds as if he is in tears, "Jimmy, don't let that affect you and how you have your brother, Ronnie, and you have your Uncle Bill. I am so sorry that Kevin and Teresa are like that, and that they treated you this way. This is not right, and I am so sorry, and their dad would be so ashamed of them, if he knew what they have done to you in not treating you the way that you deserve to be treated. You are my brother's son, my biological nephew, and I remember you very well. I want you to know that I want to make plans to see you."

I tell him, "We can make this happen. I want you to know that I would love for us to get together, soon, also."

He asks me, "Do you have a family? Is life happy for you?"

I say, "I have a family that bought me when my biological mother sold me and tried to also extort money from that family, after they had already gotten me from her, but she made it where they had to come back and get an adoption through the state of Illinois, legally, instead of an adoption in California. So, it was so complicated."

He says, "I remember much of your challenges Jimmy, and I am so sorry but I am so glad to know you are alive. And I am so glad that Ronnie called me. Everyone is so excited to know that you are alive and you have found us. How did you find us?"

I tell him, "My church did some genealogy work and my friend, she is a genealogy specialist. She looked up Dad and Ina McNear, Dad's grandmother and my great-grandmother."

He says, "I remember Gram!"

I tell him, "My grave is right next to my biological dad! Ina McNear purchased two extra plots right next to her, one for Dad and Ronnie said the other one was for me. It's as if it was waiting for me, when I was found."

He is so shocked to hear this, that he says, "This is like a movie. I feel like I am reading a book, but I know this is all true for I was able to be at your dad's grave and see him buried next to his grandmother. I can only imagine what it must feel like for you today, and for Ronnie to gift you with this very special gift from Gram and your father."

I tell him, "Ronnie and I developed the grave marker to say 'Lost Son Found, Home with Jesus' and it has my birth name and my adopted name."

He asks, "Are you close to your adoptive family, still?"

I say, "I have been there Uncle Bill, and I have done that and I have worn out that t-shirt, but my adoptive father and I are close as far as being able to know that we have a love that will last forever. He and I are the only ones in the adopted family that continue to be consistent in our communicating love for one another. Other than that, I have my Aunt Marion who was Bud's friend along with Gram, who got her hair done at my Aunt Marion's

EMBRACED

beauty shop. Gram and my Aunt Marion were especially close. The three of them worked together to get me away from my biological mother, and that's how Aunt Marion became the most important woman in my life today and throughout my life she has always been my guardian angel. I got to spend time with my Aunt Marion *twice* this year and these were the happiest moments because I found out that I have a biological family that is alive and I was told more of the details of my life this year that I never knew. It is so good to know the truth about my life. I feel more free and more whole and able to let go of the people that do not do me justice, and do not choose to walk by faith in my life. So, I have chosen to be where I am celebrated and not tolerated. Even if that means being alone."

He says, "Jimmy, you don't have to be alone. You've got family. You have blood, biological family, and if Kevin and Teresa are going to be this way, shame on them. I never thought Kevin was that type of a person, but then again, he doesn't talk to me or call me, so I don't really know about Kevin. Everything changed when your dad passed away."

I tell him, "I could tell that, because Ronnie told me none of them have ever been to his house except me and Dad."

He says in a broken voice, "Jimmy you are welcome at my home, anytime. I would love to take you out for some nice Italian food and spend some time with you. I want you to come and stay with me and visit. You would really like it out here, and your cousin is here at my home and so is another cousin and they would love to meet you. In fact, my daughter is the one that got your dad and me close again, after a few years of not really communicating. I don't want this to happen to you and Ronnie."

I tell him, "That will *not* happen. Ronnie isn't like that. He's a lot like me. We love each other and we let each other know that."

JORDAN JANTZ

He tells me, "Jimmy, I feel the same way about your dad and I wish I could take back the things that happened but I can't. That's why it is important for you to hold on to what you can while you are alive and don't let go of it, now that you have it. I can only imagine what your life has been like."

I tell him, "I've always dreamed of finding out about where I am from and who I really am inside, meaning, Uncle Bill, who I am inside *biologically*. This is because so many deceitful things occurred from my biological mother. I was a child and didn't ever know all the details, but the biological mother told me that she didn't get enough money and that she wanted to know how I was doing *financially*. It was horrible to experience that reunion with her because I was still very young and naïve and I did not know what she meant about me being *financially set*. So, immediately I knew that I wanted out, away from her, as fast as possible. And others saved me and took me back to the airport to get away and go back to California."

I generally keep this to myself because of the shame it makes me feel, as though I was a protégé in her pocket that she felt <u>she</u> was owed money to because of what she did. It made for much sadness and emptiness in my life for many years. I have felt so ashamed of the reality of who my biological mother really was and what she really did. My adoptive mother gets very angry when anything is discussed like this.

I just say, "I have constantly walked on eggshells to please the world."

He says, "Well you don't have to walk on eggshells with me, and you don't have to worry about me hanging the phone up on you, and I want you to call me, and we will keep in contact."

Then he asks, "Do you have plans for Christmas?"

EMBRACED

I say, "I have a church family that invites me out every Christmas and they love me very much and they know that I do not have a family that wants me for Christmas or invites me to their home. I do not go, ever, to my adoptive family's home, for I am not invited. It is not because of my doing, but because they feel that they did what they were to do and now I must go and live my own life as I have done since a very young age. You see, money is not my main dream and focus in life, but to do good and do the right thing for children is what my life is all about. Saving the lives of children who have been abandoned and abused is what I do in my life. It is a philanthropist mentality that I live for, hoping that one child won't have to cry that day and be left behind and forgotten. That's my life purpose, Uncle Bill, and that's why I'm doing what I do for children in my life today. Before I got into doing philanthropist work for children, I was a male model for many years. I did runway and I made a good living at the time of my employment in the fashion industry. So, if you have any questions, I'll just tell it like it is, because that's the kind of man I am."

He says, "I can't wait to see you."

I say, "I can't wait to see you either."

And then we exchanged addresses and we say goodnight, goodbye, and *I love you* at the same time.

As I get off the phone, I am in tears to think that I have an uncle that is alive and that actually held me when I was first born and knew me and saw me and was a part of my infant years as a baby when he was a senior in high school.

This just encourages me to want to go shopping and get my uncle a package put together for Christmas, and make him *feel very special* for he is very special to me and the fact that he can honestly be so transparent and honest with me just like my brother Ronnie, makes me realize I have *good* blood in me.

JORDAN JANTZ

I have a good biological uncle and good biological brother and an awesome sister-in-law and I adore my niece and nephew and I can only imagine what my cousins are like, or my Uncle James and his wife would have been like, if I could only have met them before he passed, also, like my father. But God saved the best for last. And now I embrace what I have found. And that will be the best Christmas gifts of all gifts of my life. Nothing can compare, no money can ever measure what I have been given this year for Christmas and that is an uncle and a brother that have my father's genetics along with me. I am so excited to put together three packages: one for my brother and one for my uncle, and my Aunt Marion.

I never dreamed I would get this opportunity to send a Christmas card or a present to any of my biological family members or even know that there are around on earth. I will go the extra mile and make this new life worthwhile.

If I could only find a way to bring Uncle Bill and my brother, Ronnie, together. All these little secrets separated the family and now I'm learning the truth of so many things from my family, Ancestry-com and the Holy Spirit opening the heart of my uncle and my brother and my sister in law. I am ready to move to Moweaqua but I am scared out of my mind that I would be abandoned again and *that* would just put me in the nut house, at my age. So, I know I'm safe not taking any more chances letting love into my life or people into my heart, but I can't help but open up to Ronnie, Lisa, Zach and Hannah! So I leave the doors open to the Holy Spirit and let the presence of God's love land where is destined for my life. I know it will take me to where God can shine His everlasting light on me and all those around me to receive the light within from being set free from the torture* of being me.

*People-pleaser, people pleaser!!!

EMBRACED

CHRISTMAS IN UTAH WITH MY SPIRITUAL FAMILY

~43~

CHARITY AND I PREPARE for the holiday. My case manager helps me imagine transitions at the airports and helps me organize my documents so that others can help me navigate under the American with Disabilities Act. I can't say how often I bow my head in gratitude to live in a country in which we do not throw away people with disabilities and challenges. Because of this and only because of this, I am alive today and I am not surviving, I am thriving.

My ride to the airport is a wonderful friend. My service dog, Charity, and I are greeted by my sister from the Relief Society at church. She embraces me and Charity and helps get my luggage and takes us to the airport. She has an early Christmas present for me that she wanted me to open before I go and it is a beautiful blue coat, waterproof, and it is even pouring down freezing rain this minute! I am so grateful because I did not have a waterproof coat! I can't believe I didn't own one in Oregon, but now I do. And that is so warm and comforting to put. It is like being wrapped in love, which in all reality, that's what I have experienced in 2015, for the first time, a consistency of being wrapped in love, over and over and over. I think of that blue on the flight to Utah.

EMBRACED

Before I know it, my feet are booted up, nice and warm, on the salty shoveled walks in downtown Salt Lake City's Temple Square. These blocks are famous for surrounding the beautiful temple with Christmas tree lights adorning *every* tree-limb, so, it does look like Disneyland. I am with my spiritual brother and missionary, Spencer, and his wife and her family at the Christmas lighted events at Temple Square. We enjoy the children and the family as always. This is the moment my soul wants to belong to. It is another world, a different world. Downtown Salt Lake Temple Square on Christmas Eve night is truly the most beautiful place I have ever been on Christmas Eve night.

I feel so loved by so many. All around me know the honest truth of my life. People walk up to me and ask, "Are you the man on Voices of Hope?" they cannot see my long hair inside my winter hat to know for sure. When I smile and greet them, their hearts pour right out to me. My truth out into the world brings back truth many fold.

They ask, "Are you one that wrote *Out of the Closet, Into the Light*? Is that your life story? Are you the *Jordan Jantz* that we've about?"

(Actually, Jewel Adams <u>wrote</u> the book, *Out of the Closet, Into the Light,* and I am so grateful for all that she did and taught me about communication this way. But when people meet me and first ask about the book, they are usually asking if the book was about me, and I just say *Yes* and explain about Jewel Adams' incredible work.)

I say, "Yes, that book is about my life story. And there is more coming, too, because God's plans are greater than my plans!"

They say, "We have watched your videos on Voices of Hope! Your firesides are incredible, that's what the young adults are saying!"

JORDAN JANTZ

I am a bit embarrassed because I'm with spiritual family. I never asked that this would occur in my life, but for some reason I have always been put in front. These moments can make a small scene, and it does happen often that they are crying. We humans need so badly to see one another and to be seen that *one* person who sees you can save your life, and relief is expressed in tears as they approach me.

None of these moments when souls are open and healing would even have been possible without the **many** that supported my desires with a spirit of love, hope and charity. *Out of the Closet, Into the Light*, and Voices of Hope, and *Embraced* all involve hidden armies. Except for <u>living</u> my life with all the courage I can bring to it, there is nothing about these projects that could have been accomplished on my own.

And why would I even attempt, when I have a medical support team who wants my mission statement out there for someone like me with a past like me, who has become a true beacon of light to many "in church and out of church," is what one man said to his wife, standing in front of me, as her children were around us. They told me they have a daughter who is a stripper in Salt Lake and has a hard time believing that God is in her life and questions if He ever was. *What should we do,* they ask? I tell them to please go on the websites that the church people have developed for others to pull themselves out of darkness like the story of my life. I let them know that they are loved and God hears their hearts.

Then I continue on with my spiritual family. While there, I run into one of my favorite friends, Todd Christofferson, who is a leader in my spiritual community. I just adore him and especially his brother. I just love his brother to pieces because he reminds me so much of myself.

EMBRACED

Back at the house with my spiritual family, we have a beautiful Christmas celebration and enjoy our tradition of Christmas breakfast pizza, which is always the biggest and happiest moment of Christmas morning, besides seeing the beauty of the smiles on each person for the happiness we all have for the birth of our Savior. I'm not used to seeing people seeing Jesus as priority in their lives, and putting Him at the top of their lists. Maybe some might make Jesus their bucket list this year. Wouldn't that be something? I think, in fact, that would be a great fireside, *making Jesus be the bucket list for 2016 in your life....*

In all the years of visiting with the family men and singles of the special same gender attraction group in the stake president's office in Beaverton, Oregon, I only managed to have <u>one</u> real and true friendship come out of it all: Jared. Even though he is not just like me, we enjoy the value of our differences. He was born into the church and I wasn't. That gives us so much to cherish in how we see the world and how we can treat each other with respect for our backgrounds. We are different in age, spiritual age, spiritual maturity and street maturity. We have both same gender attraction and have the same hope to embrace the Savior in our life and throughout our life because we value Him. With my spiritual brother I experience faithfulness in friendship. We would not dream of holding secrets or devaluing one another with untruth.

Today Jared and I enjoy my favorite Mexican restaurant in downtown Salt Lake City, the Red Iguana Café. This is my favorite place to eat Mexican food, besides my spiritual Aunt Janet who makes homemade Café Rio, to which the Red Iguana takes a backseat.

At the Red Iguana, I always order pozole. I LOVE pozole during the Christmas season. Jared and I talk and eat and I learn about his new life in Utah, having just recently moved there from Portland, Oregon. He tells me about what is happening in his church ward. He has not shared his same gender attraction yet because he hasn't received the trust of those around him. I totally understand. He is going to college for his PhD. He is chasing his dream and I respect that and encourage him. I want the best for him. He deserves the best. He's been one of my truest friends, ever. He has never manipulated or backstabbed me or used me to bring attention to himself. I am so grateful to have a friend that is like that. I am so tired of being used for others' associations to benefits.

After eating, Jared takes me home to my spiritual family. He has to get to back to the hospital for work and my spiritual family and I make gingerbread houses out of graham crackers and frosting. Charity gets frosting all over her! She's just *Christmas'd out* with the activities and she could care less how much icing and sprinkles and tinsel she has all over her when she is at her spiritual family's house.

They always spoil her so rotten. Now that I think of it, everyone in my family does. She especially loves Cally and Dallin, the two youngest, because they love to play and chase her around and she just adores the two of them, maybe even a little bit more than me, at times, while we are there at Christmas.

They know me. At some time they ask me, "Do you have plans for the Christmas Box House?"

I say, "No, I went with Jewel during the summer, and it is so busy that I wouldn't have the opportunity to have private time and I don't want to go out to the orphanage and have everyone ask me about my contributions for children and me and end up being the center of attention. It is Christmas, and it is all about the children. When I do go, I want to be able to have my own time and bring my own Christmas gifts or personal blessings to the children. I don't like doing things to show off what I am doing in front of people. I like to do it privately before God."

EMBRACED

We sit around and enjoy the Christmas spirit. We have a tradition that we all watch *While You Were Sleeping* with Sandra Bullock. That is one of my spiritual family's favorite movies. We have a peaceful time, always, as if we had never seen it before, but when you are with people that all love each other, everything we do together is shared with joy and happiness.

I get a phone call from another member of our spiritual family who is a stake president, Paul, asking me if I would like to go Christmas caroling with him and some missionaries. I would be delighted to, if the boys will watch Charity.

Of course, Cally is always right there and so is David. Cally prays for me all the time. He is the little wild child with the prayers that shoot arrows directly up to heaven and for some reason God always hears his prayers of healing for my life. I value children and I respect their boundaries and I wish more people could do the same. Charity is so happy with these boys.

As I get ready to go Christmas caroling, I realize that it is so snowy and cold, but the joy of bringing hope to others pushes me out the door and into the car to go out into the neighborhoods, do some Christmas caroling and sharing a Christmas message to neighbors throughout the city of Ogden, Utah.

I always love being with Paul, my spiritual family member who has been a part of my life for over eight years. I do not take him for granted, for he has communication with my stake president back home in Portland, who I love more than anything and who has been consistent in everything he says and everything he does in my life.

It is a pleasure and a joy to sing to people who may not know the true meaning of Christmas, and for some reason people always ask me, *why are you so happy?*

JORDAN JANTZ

The answer is that I find joy in knowing that this life is so temporary but when I pass on into the next life, it is for all time and eternity and I value that opportunity for that is the one thing I know that will not be temporary in my life but will last forever. Just like the message of Christmas will last forever in many of the hearts of my friends and family.

And that's what Christmas is to me. This is always topped off just days later with the ending of a year with the beginning of a new year.

I know I will be returning shortly after Christmas to go home for the New Year's Eve celebration, sponsored by several child protective services throughout the Pacific Northwest. I will have the opportunity of sharing my mission and what it has done in the life of a child. I'm so excited and can't wait to experience this moment! Not everyone gets an invitation like this, for such a private event. I do not boast of the places that I have been invited or have been a part of, because I feel it is important to not provoke others into feeling they have been left out of something fun or special. I keep my events to myself for this very reason. I know what it is like to hear about others being invited to so many different events and when they boast they exploit their events of joy.

Another truth about these holidays is that many are recovering from many sadnesses in their life, just as I experienced when I found my partner in the bathroom shower on Christmas Day, hanging from the showerhead by a sheet tied around his neck. I don't share my sadness for people to feel sorry for me, but I do know and remember that many people have it very hard at Christmas time. I know what it is like to be alone at Christmas time. That's why I am so grateful for my spiritual family and their love for me. I will forever respect the continued embracing love that I receive throughout the year from people like these that I cherish.

EMBRACED

The family gathers the next day and we all have a last celebration at my spiritual family's house. We have so much fun singing, eating Christmas cheeses and then as a spiritual family we pile on the *Christmas bandwagon* on bales of hay in the back of an old truck, and sing Christmas songs through the neighborhoods. *Do you hear what I hear? A song, a song... He will bring us goodness and light.*

It is an annual event that I embrace with all of my heart. If I didn't have my spiritual family, I would not have anyone, now that I am single and have been single ever since I chose to make God my main devotion. He will not leave me or forsake me like others have. That is something I can hold on to, even though my fallible, sinful nature. I embrace him because I know that nobody could ever embrace someone such as I, except Jesus. That is what my life is all about today, because He gave me a new life.

I love this verse, especially at Christmas time, it is

John 3:16,
For God so loved the world
that he gave his only begotten Son,
that whosoever believeth in him,
should not perish,
but have everlasting life.

As I am leaving Utah, my spiritual family saves a little extra time to drive me by the Christmas Box House. This time I don't go in because they are not prepared and they have their mission to perform without distractions. I am grateful that I can celebrate this holiday with my spiritual family and that I have been given the opportunity to share God's love and be accepted just as I am, and I think of the little ones inside who don't have what I have right now.

JORDAN JANTZ

Near the door, I take off my new gloves, and lay them there for anyone who needs them. I can replace those soon and I have a new warm coat. That was all I had to give at the moment, besides to kneel down and say a prayer for this sacred house that I embrace. I can only imagine what it is like being a child inside the Christmas Box House right now. What would my heart have done, if I could have seen people who care, people who wanted to show me that they care, when I was so small and defenseless?

I don't understand how I survived my abuse and even today the mental aspects of enduring the past paralyze me, but tonight I know that I've been found. My soul has known it since Decatur. It is real. I'm not one of the children inside the Christmas Box House anymore. I'm on the *outside,* singing to them.

At the airport again, as always, I am so grateful for assistance. This time a pilot walks with me down the ramp and into the plane and he wishes me well. I think he knows me.

Later, when we are disembarking the plane, he walks with me again. He says, "I pray always for your mission, Jordan."

I ask where we know each other, and he says he was there when I received the award at North Star. He tells me how he loved the video and he has shared it.

He leans down and says in my ear, "Have a wonderful new year and make this year count, because you have a voice, you have something very few people have to give and I am forever affected with the positive transformation of your life. Thank you for sharing your life story. I will share it like I have throughout this year with many who struggle to become whole."

Merry Christmas and Happy New Year, we both say to each other. I thank him for his assistance in the Portland airport with my service dog, Charity and he departs to meet the other pilots.

EMBRACED

This truly has been the best year and the best Christmas for anybody like me who has been lost from their family and has lived a life basically as an orphan, never measuring up to the other boys or the other men, except on the runway. But now the runway ends at my brother's front door, because there are no more performances that need to take place for others to be happy with me. The desire of being wanted or needed has been dissolved now that I can live in truth for the first time in my life. I'm set free from other people's judgments and my own judgments on myself.

NEW YEAR'S EVE
SOME LIKE IT HOT, HOT HOT!!!

~ 44 ~

NEW YEAR'S EVE IS ALMOST my favorite holiday, next to Valentine's Day. New Year's Eve is about new beginnings and second chances. This evening will host many charity events throughout the world. This year the charity I've been asked to attend is at the Pittock Mansion, called by everyone I know, the Peacock Mansion. The event is the "Stars Come Out in Portland," a Charity Ball hosted by Doernbecher's Children Hospital and Make a Wish Foundation. The stars, musicians, actors, producers, authors and artists will arrive to draw those who have a heart for children who are in desperate need. They tell me *I am needed.*

My doctors know my anxieties are high. They rent me a tuxedo and even a limo so that I am able to be presentable and discuss the Christmas Box House and my new book, coming soon, for benefiting children. God gave me a voice to speak and a heart to share for these broken little ones.

Many people have the impression that my life is easy. But they don't live inside my mind or even have a clue of the words that are spoken about them under anyone's breath. As I see the limelight being presented and coming towards me, I turn to avoid all aspects of attention drawn to me. I realize that this New Year's

Eve is going in a different direction. I meet up with many incredible, talented production artists and actors that come to the Pacific Northwest. My favorite series filmed here is the Grimm series, which brings all the actors to this event. I see many artists and the criticism that they live with every day, that is the attention that they *have* to keep, and I know it is part of the territory of marketing, something I could not be more grateful to lay down, for myself. I am so grateful that I am no longer on the runway or in clothes that I have to continually be on a diet to wear. I'm relieved tonight to be known only as the person who champions a charity for children who have experienced abuse, neglect and abandonment.

I am grateful to glide between the pockets that are filled to the brim prepared for donations to charity. This is so whole and healthy from other things I've been a part of on New Year's Eves of years gone by. Many of my past upper crust friends that worked with me in the industry ask me to sign my book that they had out on the tables for this evening's event. Most are impressed with the relationships of healing in my life. can only agree.

I listen to colleagues continue to tell me they cannot believe how my life has done "*a 180*" and that I am the poster child of change. They want to know more about my secret and how I was able to get out of the industry. I smile with love and tell them that there is another life waiting for me that will bring me more than I ever dreamed of and it is on the other side and the veil is very thin and I want to be prepared for this beautiful opportunity that is offered to everyone but only a few have the ability to follow because the road is long and very narrow and few have the ability to follow it all the way through. I realize that I need to ask one of the catering staff if they have any pomegranate juice, please, just as the champagne glasses are preparing to toast the new year.

My friends hand each other glasses of champagne, as my juice is brought out right out in front of everyone. I talking and toast the group of all of us who have been working the industry, who are now in our fifties. We are all so grateful that we are together this evening, sharing a momentous moment for children. We never dreamed any of us would be at an event like this after all the years that have passed. Many of them were at my baptism and many of them knew my ex-partner and continue to ask how I am doing since Mark took his life. I let them know that I am fine and managing to go forward.

They comment, "You were such a cute couple, very complementary to one another. We are so sorry that he is no longer with us."

I thank them for remembering him. I let them all know that he will always be remembered and cherished.

They ask me, "What are you drinking? Is that wine? We thought that you were not allowed to drink because of your faith."

I say, "Guys, I've never been told I'm not allowed to drink, that is not the truth. It is that I choose to drink pomegranate juice. I don't put my expectations for myself on to others by any means, you guys know that."

They say, "We were just checking because we know you've come a long way, and it is just so surprising to see that you don't party anymore, the way you have been known to do in the past. You partied like a *rock star*!"

My best friend who did the catwalk with me makes a profound statement, "Jordan's past is past. He doesn't live the lifestyle he did before. Although many seem to say, *He chose his lifestyle*. And they still to this day try to bring it up, but it is impossible to bring up Jordan's past when he has been out of the

lifestyle of our community, guys, but continues to walk with all of us and not abandon us who do. He is remembered and he is a part of this community, but he is not living the lifestyle that he did before. So it is New Year's Eve, and Jordan has made new beginnings and it is time that we might want to think about doing the same thing."

I smile at my colleague and tell him "You and I always *stole the stage* but now that I'm not the diet pill king with bulimia, we could make a hit or a come-back as old men! What do you think about that? We can model old men's pull-ups."

He laughs, "Don't put us in wheelchairs and walkers yet! I can just see us on the catwalk with our walkers, modeling the new men's pull-up undergarments for Depends! That would be a real hit."

We all laugh. Our memories from over a decade ago have definitely changed many of the faces that are in my company. We are all now in our mid-fifties.

I tell them, "I'm grateful that I have in my life the lifestyle I have with God. That's the only thing that keeps me going in my life, because my life is not complete anymore without God. It doesn't work, you guys, for me."

They say, "What in the world made you decide to believe in *God*?"

I say, "I've always believed there is a god, my whole entire life I knew. I've even experienced moments when I felt the presence of angels around me and I knew it was the Holy Spirit, which is very real, "

They decide to toast their glasses to my lifestyle change and transformation in my life, *To 2016!* We toast as I hold up my pomegranate juice to their champagne glasses, and I thank them all for embracing our friendships from years gone by as if it was yesterday. We all can realize that time has flown by so fast and the future holds many promises for some of us and some, I can tell, have lost their way from the industry that has tainted so many who never become free.

You see, for some of us that have worked by getting by on our looks, it is hard to feel any value or worth when everything fades away that ever brought you hope and light. But for me, I realize the peace I see inside my eyes. I do believe it is true that eyes are the windows to the soul, and I can see through the eyes of my friends that many desire to experience the same opportunity that I have embraced.

As I give them all hugs goodbye, I let them know that they mustn't cry as the guys wish me a Happy New Year. Many of them say they never thought they would see me again because of the way my life had been. My response to them is that someday we will *all* be together again.

Josh Groban's music is playing Auld Lang Syne, and I realize that I want *one more last time*. **I can transform my experience of New Year's Eve** and share with them all that how they can be on New Year's Eve, by example. I use my cell phone to call the driver and ask if he can take me home early. I want to be with my *most faithful and loving relationship* before the fireworks go off: I want to leave the perfect and gracious Stars of Portland and spend New Year's Eve with Charity.

Arriving home, I thank the limo driver for all he has done to ring in the joy of New Year's Eve with me.

He says, "It was my pleasure to be a part of this evening's event and celebrate the charities that set children free."

EMBRACED

He drives off. I walk into my home and see my little Charity, just where I placed her before I left her, still all wrapped up in swaddling clothes upon her throne. I walk up and embrace this beautiful gift and that God has given to me for another year.

All my greatest blessings are together tonight. I hold Charity and we watch the New Year's fireworks go off from our balcony over Portland, where we watch the bridges and the people from a world of our own. God definitely has blessed me with doctors and housing management that are close to my heart that have worked together for the better good of my life to move me in to a one-bedroom apartment overlooking my hometown where I can see across the city of Portland all the way into Washington state, with a view of Mount Hood and Mount St. Helens that is breathtaking. This blessing is only because of a wonderful housing specialist that helped build my life into what it is today. Her name, I would love to tell you, but she is so valuable to my life, we'll just call her Pam for now. I want to respect all of my doctors and housing specialists. You can't explain some things that you don't even understand yourself, such as why are people so nice and kind to me? Why is it that my dog is still alive and well *and* turning *fifteen* years old in 2016, this New Year?

I have so much to be thankful for. I am in my home and another year has passed. I contemplate what this new year will bring, knowing now that I have an uncle that loves me like a father would love his son. Thinking of Uncle Bill brings back the memories of all I have experienced this year.

Dreams do come true! I think on my years as a kid for a moment and realize how much I played being Peter Pan, and I think how much all this last year and tonight is as if I have *experienced* Peter Pan's return. The animation of the party and the celebration of events of children's characters that were there, representing the communities throughout the Pacific Northwest with child protective services sponsoring many of the booths that showed what is taking place this new year for children… And all this I experienced among friends who have theirs hearts open to me.

And what a grateful blessing it was to see so many of my books presented for everyone I have shared my life with to receive.

HOLIDAY OF LOVE, SHARING FAITH, HOPE AND CHARITY

~45~

It is Valentine's Day 2016 and I can say I have definitely seen so many nice things that I have dreamed. As time rolls by throughout my life I realize the dreams have come true for me. I open my eyes to such an early surprise to see Valentine's Day in everyone's eyes. The love is surreal and comes to life as I board the trolley to my surprise. I have been invited to celebrate this life on a day that I have set aside and as I walk through the doors of at party's surprise I find all my friends all lined up in disguise. I ask what they are doing and they all reply, "It's Valentine's Day and *you're the surprise.*" I ask them why it is a surprise and they say to me, "Just look and see what you have given to all of us this Valentine's Day!" As I gaze at the table I am surprised that in front of my eyes, I see love and hope in the children's eyes that they have received from my embraced surprise. Happy Valentine's Day to all of you, and thank you *for embracing the life of a child* with this surprise.

I'm keenly aware that every day is a gift, that time is fleeting. Another Valentine's Day has passed and is so quickly gone. No moment but this one is guaranteed. I wanted a plan for my life and here it is, today. I've stepped up to the life that has been waiting for me. If you like, you can come and join me and make Valentine's Day a vibrancy of love for yourself and then we all can spread the love around for one another. That is what Valentine's Day means to me.

You know what I'd like to tell you? I want you to do something really good for yourself today, but better than that, do something really cool for someone else, and surprisingly, you will be blessed, I promise you that!

Third Edition Bonus Section:

THE HEART OF THE SEA

LOVE CAN TOUCH YOUR LIFE ONCE AND CHANGE YOUR DESTINY FOREVER

~46~

VALENTINE'S DAY IS OFTEN the happiest of times and the saddest of times. For some people, Valentine's Day can have recollections of warm celebrations with family and friends. For others, Valentine's Day triggers memories of loss and feelings of loneliness. If you have disabilities, you may experience mixed emotions that you may not be able to cope with in the seasonal pressure to be joyous and participate in festivities of love.

Believe me, I know all that too well. But nevertheless, I've never been without a Valentine until this year, for the first time, so I am embracing my dog, Charity, and the lives of children. You have the opportunity to be the light and the magnet, no matter what your circumstance is. The biggest mistake I can make is to assume I know what others want or what is best for them. As a Valentine and as a friend, the greatest gift I can give is to acknowledge performances and respect and honor other people's wishes but I can only do that if those wishes are spelled out for me. Make time for an honest conversation with your relatives about your holiday priorities.

Now that the holiday season is over and the new year has begun

EMBRACED

with Easter and Passover near at hand, I would like to share with you some open-hearted truth of what I feel is most needed, in a successful life for myself. Through the holiday season as I watched so many people do their own things in life, I realize that time on this earth is so short. Seasons change one after the other so fast and so the seasons of one's life keep changing, also. How wonderful it is that we can trust God's word for it never changes. God said he would send a Redeemer to Zion, and if what He promised the first time happened, how much more should that encourage even more to believe the promise of His coming again in glory will come to pass?

If I had been around before the nativity, and if I could have had it my way, I would have said, "Lord, please don't trouble yourself. Don't take on human form. Don't allow yourself to be humiliated and killed, for it is beneath you, Lord, to do all that!"

But the truth is, God's way was not my way and He knew that my way was not the right way, and He knew that I was fallible and would never be able to live up to my promises as a human being. I am not in any way able to walk in perfection. Nobody can and nobody ever will, only one person ever walked perfectly on earth and that is Jesus, who has left me His Holy Spirit, to comfort me, as He has through abandonment and neglect for not being what is expected. We all have a choice. I have not left anybody. I never would leave or forsake anyone I love, unless I was told to. And that is what has happened in my life. And Jesus has comforted the pain of having to leave memories I wanted to hold on to.

I understand that God had to do it His way. The difficult and painful way. For you and for me. It was our sins He chose to bear. God will continue to do things His way when he comes again it will be with power and great glory. I must take heart that He will come back again a second time, according to the promises in the Bible,

JORDAN JANTZ

Hebrews Chapter 9:28 "Christ was offered to bear the sins of many, to those who eagerly wait for Him, he will appear apart from all sin for it will be salvation." This is the hope I must hold on to, for this is proof to me that I win in the end.

The Lord says to me, "The truth will set you free." I have seen a variety of people in my life that take the truth and twist it to meet their own needs. They try extremely hard not to face the truth of who they are and what they are in this crazy world. They continue hiding the truth. Truth is the only virtual reality. Truth cannot be tamed or domesticated to serve us. Truth is not being someone who tries to control others who we can shape or who can be made to behave according to our own manners and morals. "World-class" is crap to the most-elite, and believe me, I know the most elite. And they honor and respect the humble and the meek spirited people. Arrogance is not tolerated in my circle.

For me, finding out truth is merely What IS, What WAS, and What will BE, truth in itself is neither pleasant nor unpleasant. I daily must face the truth in my life. I am nothing without Jesus.

Christ is the center of my life. My life-experiences with people from every background in life have taught me that many of us, including myself, have missed out critical ministry that sits right underneath their nose, and that is taking the time to be a friend to people outside of their comfort zone. For many people I know personally in ministry are simply lonely. Worst of all, most people really don't have anyone to share the truth of their life and problems with. I have seen across the board all lifestyles turning the challenge of facing our Heavenly Father on their death bed with me by their side, screaming for Jordan, to ask if there is a God, to please come immediately and reveal thyself. I am totally thrilled and encouraged of this reality, that I realize I am not alone. But you can't bring hope to someone that doesn't understand hope or listened to what hope

EMBRACED

could do for them.

The hope that I have, that they want, cannot be bought or found, it is given to me from Jesus. I wish many of my friends on their deathbed could have realized for months what I had been trying to explain, the peace that comes from within. Someday, before I die, God will teach me how to ease the fear of death for my friends who have died of AIDS. I am grateful to have been there with them. What I pray the church will understand is that just because you are in church doesn't mean you are immune from the sins of the world. AIDS is everywhere and it is not a sin to have AIDS.

In fact, I'm nauseated to think that I would ever be a part of a church that would call someone with AIDS "They chose that lifestyle" or "They chose to get that disease." What a Pharisee. So many tell me I am not in a Bible-teaching church because of their gay support groups. I'm amazed when I look at their support groups and see how many men have hooked up with one another. I can only shake my head at the reality of mistruth and just because a person is married with children doesn't mean that they are closer to God than the man or woman that has the identity of someone that struggles finding God's love for them, as a person who lives with same gender attraction. That, my friend, is false teaching and God loves you and I ask you to forgive the many ministries who come down on you for claiming the identity as a gay person and don't meet the requirements for membership or involvement in their programs. This is bullying. And that's why I stand up for women like Ellen DeGeneres who says every day, "Share a little love and be kind to one another." Maybe that's what God wants many to learn to do in church today in Bible studies throughout America.

Life cannot contain honest formality without experiencing the Holy Spirit at least once a day in your life. And, the Holy Spirit, I have found, desires this encounter with me at least once a day.

JORDAN JANTZ

Maybe that's why my life is where it is at today. I do know, we all must do our part to love and to support these people who are separating themselves from their old lifestyles. God is raising new people all over the world to take the truth of Jesus Christ to all types of people. God's children have stopped playing games with their salvation, including God's children who are gay and lesbian. They realize God loves them and accepts them, and they are ready to turn and embrace God as He desires to embrace them.

The tide is turning, and I believe for a purpose. I believe the tide is turning in my life. The last ten years have been growing ones. I have learned more from the people that the Lord has brought into my life, things I have never dreamed. I will never forget my experiences or the many people that have touched my life and opened my eyes to the Lord with a new perspective. It is people like YOU that will influence and help my life maintain my balance in being honestly the leader God created me to be for his kingdom.

Without steadfast influence of fellow leaders in my life, I am easy prey. The dark side has tried to lure me and prevent me from reaching the destiny the Lord has chosen for my life. I see it is vital to put on the whole armor of God. Having a covering of leaders in my life, like I do, is something I do not take lightly.

I'm grateful to have prayers and support for the love of my ministry to children. Together with the son of God, we can reach the lives of children from every background on earth. We will break the bondages, addictions, and past hurts in every child through the blood of Jesus Christ. God is an AWESOME God. We have victory in Jesus! I have written this in order for you to realize where my life is at and what I want to do with the rest of my life while I am here on this earth. I pray that I will influence our society and this frightening world we live in for benefit of the lives of children, that

EMBRACED

they can become whole and healed and restored after they were over-looked by the people that should take the responsibility that God had given them, as a parent.

God's word states in John 15: 16 "You did not choose me, but I chose you and appointed you that you should bear fruit and whatever you ask the Father in my name, He will give you." God has done just that, in my life. And He continues to do that. And people ask WHY would Jordan ever go back to Decatur and meet his family?? Ninety-five percent of the people have doubted God's ability to transform my life from the show-business industry of movies, fashion and being a pawn in this society of politics, escorting the most elite from the Broadmoor Hotel in Colorado Springs to the Hyatt Regency of Hawaii, to the Hamptons and Hyannis Port, Massachusetts. Throughout the world, I gave my all and have been an open book; a child protégé once who is now free, as an adult in my fifties, for the first time in life and I feel like I am just learning to walk, not knowing the direction to go. Do you think I need guidance? Of course, but God has one hand and the Holy Spirit has the other hand, and they know I am learning to walk on my own for the first time. I can learn to love again.

We must all love the sinner. With love, we can face all fears. I won't find it unless I try to see the hurt and pain in others. Now is the time to open my eyes to the truth. I pray life treats all of us kindly, and I wish all of us joy and happiness. Most of all, I wish all of us LOVE. Whatever road you choose, know that I'm behind you, win or lose. May Christ be your guide and may good fortune be what embraces your life, as you embrace this beautiful gift on Valentine's Day.

Thank you for reaching out, and being embraced.

JORDAN JANTZ

COTTON CANDY, SUGAR DADDIES AND PLASTIC FANTASTIC

47

I'M ELATED TO BE IN TOUCH on a personal level, and not a plastic fantastic level, for my heart and spirit thanks God for my brother and his wife. A lot of wonderful and sometimes challenging thoughts have opened and touched my heart since I have found my biological brother and my biological uncle. I was closed off from fear, because I was sold and I was the first born. So I always thought that I was the biggest mistake and it gave me the mentality that I was the biggest loser of the Bond family, and that's why I was sold and that's why I was a people pleaser, even to this day, working very hard to make others find joy in my company.

Sometimes challenging things have been happening in my life since I have opened up my spirit to my biological family. I am grateful for the experiences I have been blessed with. Getting to know them, I have gained intense reality of what family really is and what a true friend really means. My brother, Ronnie, is a true friend. God only knows what it would have been like to have grown up together. I can tell already; I would have been his protector. After these past few opportunities of opening and sharing my life with a truthful heart and open spirit, praying that I would be received and not abandoned a second time by this biological family (unfortunately not all dreams turn out the way they are dreamed and hoped for) it is phenomenal to me to have the opportunity that has been birthed. It is all about taking back ground.

It is like a fresh choice in my life, a life that will be restored with a brother, where all can be blessed, and a sister-in-law that is filled with love, with a niece and nephew that walk in meekness and kindness. A family that is built upon health, love, and the value of honesty is what I am experiencing. This could only help in the restoration of anyone's life, to experience a family like this. This is beyond my comprehension.

Sharing all this truthfully on the table, this will bring a meaningful life to many. No more plastic fantastic. I watch families and friends abandon their love for anyone that is different from them. Grief and sadness are common hours in a broken person who has been left behind because of their being different from the rest of their family. This is normal for so many of us. It is hard for families to stay together because of this shame of same gender attraction in spiritual settings. It is hard for families to stay together because they have no hope or understanding. I've lived this and been there since fourth grade, because of ignorance and lack of understanding in the churches around the country. The tables are finally changing for downtown Portland. I have leaders in many churches and my LDS family is breaking ground for those who struggle with same gender attraction and are ready to take back ground in their lives. My spiritual family calls me weekly just to touch base and to remind me that I am valued and loved. And it all started with their son, the missionary, who gave me the reality that I can go to church if I am gay and that I won't be thrown out of church like people have thrown out gay people in the past for being gay. The Church of Jesus Christ of Latter-day Saints does not throw people out of church for being gay. They do not throw

you out of the church if you have the identity of being gay. They do not throw you out of the church if you are questioning your gender identification. They are not hard and crass, but loving like the spirit of a dove, descending from heaven and landing upon the sinner who feels they will never make it. Imagine what that dove would mean to that sinner, when landing on his shoulder to remind him that He is there with him, to forgive and to love him, for better and for worse, richer or poorer, and death will not part. That is the only promise you can count on in this world. That's the only man that has never broken a promise to me. And He's the only man that has never left me abandoned, neglected and stranded or ever made me feel that I had been forgotten. I guess you could say, I've been rescued. And now it is my duty to show the truth, for I wouldn't be a true and faithful friend or family member if I didn't share the truth of my life with you. Who else in all creation can forgive the mistakes that Jesus did? It doesn't come from any other source.

God now has the leadership in our world to make this happen. Thanks to all of you who will no longer tolerate the opportunity for those who continue to seek help but have the door closed on their lives. BULLYING! To me, this is bullying in the church and I will never be a part of that. Most people have not received the blessings of leadership as I have where iron sharpens iron which leads to Elder Todd Christofferson putting men in my life that truly transformed the love of the Savior for my life, personally. God does go the extra mile. No matter who you are, and no matter what you are. You have got to get over this or you are going to lose and never win. It will only be your fantasy and your dream.

I've been throughout the world for decades searching for God's comfort in my soul, always wondering, was I born with same gender attraction and is there not a chance for anyone like me to see heaven, because I don't have a soul?

EMBRACED

My sole purpose in for me to write my life-story and this particular message for the world IS TO is for people who are like me, for children's lives like mine- abandoned, abused and neglected – who hope to be set free from the bondages that set us apart from embracing life and being embraced by the love of God. If you have never been abandoned, forgotten, neglected or abused, this book would be a waste of your time. I'm direct and honest. I'm broken and I've realized in my fifties that God loves to repair old, broken things and make them new again. But that doesn't mean putting someone back up on the runway to walk down in a pair of depends and a walker, at my age, ha ha just kidding. In all reality, God does renew all things and makes them new again.

I need my friends that do not know the Lord to come together with me because you are just as important to me as anyone else, whether you are gay or straight. I want you to come together for all of God's children to take back the ground that was taken away from you and from me, because people told us we were not worthy to be loved by God. WE need each other and we need to learn to walk in love.

I overcame the fear and obstacles that resulted in self-abusive activities that were not dealt with in church, because I was so angry that I could not pray the gay away. I was even told I was soul-less and didn't have a soul. I was told that if I couldn't marry a woman and become a husband with a family, I would never make it because that is an outward sign of an inward transformation. LIES LIES LIES, once again. I started looking for the perfect wife and immediately that next day, I had two offers to be married, immediately in the temple. It is amazing how many women at church are so anticipating the moment of their entrance into the temple to be married, feeling and thinking so much of their problems will be removed. But according to my knowledge of God's word, I have been lied to, by many gay people that call themselves Christians for God loves a contrite spirit and a contrite heart and He knows what man has done in my life, throughout the history. I have no right to cast stones but I can honestly say, it seems to me, I have dragged a boulder from birth all the way into my fifties. And it is time to be free and fly with someone who wants to fly in the direction as I do. And maybe I found that home that I've been dreaming of. Where ever it is, if there is real love, love that embraces me not for just the moment, but for all time and eternity, that's what I am seeking, something I've never had. And maybe, just maybe, before I leave, I will have the opportunity to know what a real family really is, even though I didn't make or create a family on my own. I'm leaving that up to God. He knows how plastic fantastic family has been.

I have learned about transformation and the role of the cross, especially at Easter time. My new identity as a Latter-day Saint Christian means that I live with forgiveness, no shame, or self-hatred (I have let go of). I have developed a very good devotional life over the past ten years with men and women that do want to take back ground and not just sit on solid ground. I can claim my place in the body of Christ. Many religions have life-altering conditions that tend to hold the ability back from being used for many that are gay to see themselves as viable and contributing members in the church of the body of Christ. I, at times today, experience this reoccurrence. Their energy and desire to pursue life gets thwarted by compromised health, anxiety, fears and isolation. For me, if I have no encouragement and I have no equipment spiritually from my brothers or sisters, I become an individual Latter-day Saint Christian *struggling to live the gospel.*

And yes, everyone has asked me if I have asked Jesus Christ into my life and if I have said the sinner's prayer. Of course I have. People have asked me if I have ever prayed or speak in tongues. People have asked me if I am born again. Of course I am all that and

EMBRACED

more. I am a child of God. And I believe in everything about the Savior and what He teaches. I do not follow Joseph Smith. I follow Jesus Christ. And so does the CHURCH of JESUS CHRIST of Latter-day Saints. Maybe these other churches are trying to corner me into believing that hell is waiting for me, because I am a Latter-day Saint Christian and they cannot fellowship with people not like themselves. How unfortunate.

I know Jesus Christ, personally, and He was not this type of man. And I will seek out His characteristics to employ them into my life as much as possible, no matter what the Catholic, Baptist or Pentecostal has to say. I am a child of God. Just as the Jew and the Buddhist and the Church of Christ. And the wonderful group of Pentecostal people that gave me my five-star review. God is with us all. Let's just put that on the table right now. And leave it at that. I have no more room for discussion on this topic, because it is closed with a stamp of approval by Jesus Christ. I know that much is true. Bullying is not of Jesus. And it happens inside of churches. But many turn their heads. And they do that because it is the *adults* that are doing it, and *not* the children.

SOME MEN WERE NOT MEANT TO BE FATHERS ...AND THAT'S OK

~ 48 ~

I KNOW SOME GUYS would have been better off without their fathers around. It is a case-by-case of, "Did you get loved too much or not enough?"

I now look back on my childhood and the people I come from, and I have a better appreciation. It is kind of scary. People have intimacy to bring a child into the world. You think people are going to be there, but ultimately you just have yourself. No matter what your age is, you are honestly God's child and I realize that I never had security as a child except the security of the Holy Spirit to comfort me when I boarded the plane to leave Decatur when I was sold.

I am blessed that God opened up a loving spirit for me. I think every parent has that moment when they think, "Oh, maybe this was a bad idea! We don't know how to do this!"

Well, guess what? This isn't something you can put back in the hospital if it doesn't fit. You can't exchange it or sell it, or abandon it, which would be the easiest thing to do. But one thing is certain, things don't always go the direction you think they should. There is no other way to say it.

EMBRACED

I love being a son. My father has shown me things about myself today that I wouldn't have paid attention to before. Sometimes I think, "Oh, my! That is *so* me! Right there!"

But I don't know if I am good at being a son. I say this because my father who raised me has a gentle spirit and would do anything for me, as he always did. He protected me. He and I remain close to this given day. It is challenging at times because he does not know about this book or about the pain I hold and can't get out of my heart. It would hurt him to know the pain continues on in my life. So I continue to be his shining star, and I will shine the light upon his life, no matter where he is and no matter how far away.

Am I successful at being a son? That is a question I ask myself and have asked myself every day of my life. I had the desire to be the best son, to be the best brother, to be the best grandson, to be the best at everything that was laid out in front of me, in order to be the best little boy in the world and the best man in the world, I had to be all things to all people. That put me in the Betty Ford clinic and I was not able to contain myself in any format because pleasing controlled every bit of my life, from eating disorders to addictions that would shame your mama under the table and give your papa a big fat heart attack. I don't think I want to go there. I am nothing and neither are you, without forgiveness.

It is deeply gratifying for a man to see the happiness of his life in his father's eyes! My adopted father has a heart of gold with eyes so tender they caught every tear that they possibly could, and then I know Jesus caught the rest, and has them all saved in a jar. At least, that's what my father told me when he held me at night when he first bought me; Jesus saves up the tears of all the children. Then, the tears were like a fire hydrant and my emotions were devastating. But he was the one that couldn't sleep and he was the one that today still walks with me. So, in reality, when I look back on what truth is, my dad gave my biological dad nothing but truth, that he would be a father to the fatherless. I thank them both for having the ability to both agree on something about my life before they both took a piece of it apart.

I have a special blessing. I think so much has happened in my life and my life has become more than what anyone expected it to be. God is bringing many fathers and sons together and the priesthood is being shared throughout the world. I am blessed to share the Melchizedek Priesthood with all my brothers and sisters throughout the country, especially for those who have ears to hear and a desire for a transformation in their life with their own personal issue. We all have personal issues. We are human and every day we make a mistake and commit a sin toward our Heavenly Father, if you want to put it all in real terms. Nobody is perfect. Get over it. And that is the only purpose of Jesus Christ when He atoned for sin. I have always thought, *without Him I am burnt toast.*

Jesus says, "You will never be alone and I will never abandon you."

I know a lot of people make these statements and continue on in their life journey, but God did not make me like other Christian and every spiritual man that calls themselves a follower of Christ. I cannot say something that is questionable. For what I do behind closed doors is the character of man I truly am, in front of other people. You cannot hide who you really are. I have learned the reality of that, and it has haunted my life, trying to live for God while living a double life as an entertainer in the industry that was so easily accessible to me, personally. But there are boundaries, and they simply can't be crossed.

I've been pleasing people throughout my life. As a little boy, in the beginning stages of childhood from infancy when I was sold,

EMBRACED

I was immediately immersed in tap dancing with a pair of tap dance shoes to become America's new tiny little trooper. And now as a grown man, I still continue to please the world but I direct my life to being the change I wish to see in the lives of children who have lived a life such as I, or to adults today are still working through their abuse and abandonment. I am truly a people pleaser. And I guess I was born that way, for my life is not complete and never has been complete unless others found happiness in my life. Thank you to those who found something of value in my life. Because if you ever question why you have spent time with me in your life, I want you to realize it is only the reflection of your soul's reflection in mine. It has been a joy to please and comfort the children at the Christmas Box House International. Because of this ministry, I have learned to *live the desire* and transformation of touching so many lives.

LETTING GO OF HOLLYWOOD

~ 49 ~

I AM GRATEFUL TO PEOPLE across this world, who have shared your life with me. Like a beautiful sunset, life passes away too soon. No clock can tell your time left on earth. Through the reality of one's journey, I can realize my words and actions affect everything in my life and the lives of others. I pray this journey of my life encourages all people to love and give gratitude through all walks of life.

Everything can be accomplished if hearts receive forgiveness. It is the first step of healing but this is not the nature of most people. Our eyes are blind to this, but I must see all things through my heart. As a child, I smiled though my heart was breaking, smiled though my life was hurting, and smiled, for what's the use of crying? I smile, and it will make others smile. When I smile, I'll be happy too. That's what I always thought and that's what I was always told. Repeatedly.

Making other people happy *first* was the most important thing. My existence was to be the entertainer, the showman, the life, the tap-dancer, the little Shirley Temple, the little Disney protégé. This approach to happiness – the Disney approach – is short-lived. You will see my life's final curtain call to eternity. How I treat others will be my eternal judgment. I must live my life in respect and integrity for the way God created me. I'm concerned for the well-

EMBRACED

being of others.

    I will always realize that I am innocent until proven guilty, but if ever asked, you can always count on the truth of who I am, what I am, where I've come from. To this date, even my closest friends know the story of my life, the story of the past and the present and my history of shameful acts that I have been involved with to survive the expectations of my life. I've never misled or misguided anybody.

    Most people will turn their life away from me, even though my life shines truth from my soul, because they cannot handle the reality that they also may be living with the same characteristics that I do. And they just don't choose to admit it. They continue to look down upon me because they know they are no different from me, even as they show up for church activities with their wives and children. I still get a few looks as though as if I am not fully clothed in the gospel from some judgmental brothers and sisters who feel the importance of marriage is for everybody. How judgmental and not uplifting. I'm so grateful none of my non-Christian friends know my Christian friends, because my non-Christian friends would think my Christian friends are very mean and judgmental. So, I balance the two because putting the two together is a good mix for me and a good balance for my life, because I'm a man that desires to be sharpened against iron where, iron sharpens iron. That is what I am learning to become when standing next to many who claim to be walking in the light of God's love. Really, their secret is revealed and opened by their actions when they choose to create negativity in people's life.

    God, my life has been lived, it was once a life of avoiding truth, and I will never be ashamed of what I had to do to survive and make a living ever again, for God has redeemed my life and no human being can ever condemn an honest man with integrity. I honestly did the best I could or knew what to do, but… I'm confident that there is life after life on earth for me, and it will be a celestial life with no abandonment.

I have a certain responsibility to my relationships that are fighting their own struggles, who may be able to benefit from learning about the truth of my journey on this earth. I'm completely elated that the Holy Spirit re-invents my life for others to learn of the creator's love for me. He truly has re-invented every decade of my life, with friendships, family, American medical professionals around the world, religious associates, college professors that ask me daily *why I keep caring about others and opening my life up like a book, so easily read.*

I can truthfully answer to all who question my life and why I have shared it, *where there is love, I will be there.*

Always, the doctors answer, *if only there was a book about your life, there wouldn't be one left on the shelf and the movie rental would be sold out, when it is made!*

I just smile, knowing in the back of my mind what God has planned.

SPEEDO MODEL

~ 50 ~

EVERYONE IS TREATED A CERTAIN WAY, based on how they look. I, myself, don't think I'm treated too bad. From some people, you get the vibe that they just want to sleep with you or take advantage of you, whether you are a Disney star or a runway model. But some people truly are genuine in the modeling business, if they have not been jaded by the fashion statements and the photoshoots they have been gifted to share with the world.

For me, I modeled speedos since I was a child. I was always asked why I was so photogenic, *and* why I was so hyperactive. It was in my blood, I guess. When modeling, I saw myself the way the camera wanted me to be, at an early age. And when I was up there, the stage was my pedestal and I was untouchable. I learned this at a very early age. They showed me what they wanted me to do and be, so I became all things to all people at a very early pre-adolescent age.

I never really saw myself like a model. I didn't realize it back in high school when some of the upper class girls were coming on to me. I always thought it was just because I was on the cheerleading squad. One of the first comments I remember getting was, "You have amazing teeth!"

At that time, I thought that was pretty strange to comment on my teeth, but they have done this throughout my life. I have always stood out. My teeth and my hair and my eyes have always the three main focuses besides the way I speak, that people comment on. People ask me about my raspy voice and find it intriguing. People sometimes love to dish out garbage and fluff you up to make you feel something you may not feel within, but I have always had confidence in my outer appearance. That is the only thing I was ever able to count on in my entire life. Nothing has ever been able to be counted on except what I saw in the mirror. At times, that still exists in my fifties, unfortunately. To think that I have lived this long and walked many miles in these shoes of what others have wanted me to be. And finally, in my fifties, I can take these shoes off for the first time and find my own pair that are my style and not someone else's style for me to wear and market for them. I am no longer a protégé, but am a peace-maker, the peaceful warrior that God created me to be, if I can find the way.

People comment on my appearance a lot and they have done this my whole life, since I was an infant. I was always picked out and pulled aside because of my appearance. Girls especially appreciated my long hair. It gives me somewhat of an androgynous vibe, and people prefer that in many modeling ads today, especially those ads that have no turned into computer generated models (which is taking the jobs away from us long-term fore-front runners. Now they are computer generated on the red carpet. It seems even the fashion industry will soon be losing jobs. And the perfect looking person will become a computer-generated person.) So, with all due respect, even with good looks, are you not guaranteed anything that you have worked so hard at.

Embarrassingly, I have been mistaken for a girl a couple of times. But it has shed some light on what the girls who model with me throughout the many years have had to go through. The pretty face stands out, there is no doubt. The world is *consumed* with your features from your eyes to your teeth to your hair to your nails, to the clothing you wear and even the finishing touches, and the

EMBRACED

resilience that you have to bounce back after working many hours, exposing the reality of what your professional life is all about: marketing yourself and your outer appearance to all buyers. Your value and worth become a price tag. As the years come and go and you become older, you're introduced into new venues in life, venues that can either make you rich or make you poor.

Maintenance of your physical body is the only required asset for anyone who desires to be the best in the fashion industry. I have pulled 14 hour days working through photoshoots up in the middle of the night in 25-degree weather, but when your validation is all about the next print and the next contract for a new season catalog, you become all things to all people at a very early age, because competition starts in elementary school. At least, that's how it was for me.

I've been catcalled because of standing out at times when all I really wanted to do was blend in. At times, being attractive isn't as pretty as people think. It can be downright painful and hurtful, many nights crying, while vomiting over the toilet of fear of weighing too much at tomorrow's photoshoot, crying because you ate that pasta that had *all* those calories in it, so you purge it all out of you, shaking all night until the photoshoot the next day. How glamorous of a life. Don't you just want to become like this? People don't understand the drama in the soul of being a public figure. I dream of living where nobody even knows my name or knows who I am.

Sometimes people say things like, "I guess as far as women, you probably have your pick."

All I've dated are models that I've worked with, though the majority of the female models are lesbian and the majority of the

male models are gay. We all kept together as family, because in this vocation of life you work every holiday and every runway catalog that comes out for every season of the year. I have always been in every season of every catalog since childhood, until retirement from the industry after getting physically sick to the point where I collapsed on stage and was removed from the industry. That was my final walk on the runway, realizing I had emaciated my body with diet pills and purging, causing my body to shut down, although being thin, I always felt I was obese, even during my embracing the porcelain alter, crying my eyes out, as an adult, shaking, knowing that if I don't lose enough weight I won't get the job.

You see, the older you get in this industry, it is all about *who you know*, not what you know. And I knew everyone around the country, and I was not about to gain even one pound. So that porcelain altar became my best friend every night until I ended up with feeding tubes in me at the hospital, being treated for malnourishment. And that is the challenge of continuing to grow older and be successful as a speedo super-model and living to make the world happy.

I personally find for myself that beauty is in more than what is prescribed in the commercial world. Beautiful things and beautiful places are not always already made but developed into beautiful, orchestrated opportunities for appreciation. I personally find beauty in more than what is prescribed throughout the world, whether that be Botox or facelifts, I am content in growing old as a retired model and now a child philanthropist.

I personally have enjoyed the fashion industry for what it has taught and given me. People think models are not very intelligent. That frustrates me, because there are a lot of artists out there who just happened to be picked up as models, where they were already pursuing something else in their life for an occupation, but when you are discovered, well, it just happens. You are picked and I never dreamed I what I saw on paper, which the photoshoots created, which was something out of menswear magazine. That could actually be me? Well, brothers and sisters, it was my life for over forty years.

All of the sudden you *take on* the image of what they have adorned your body and your appearance with. But in all honesty, if you don't have what it takes within your own self to be able to embrace the camera and the career, you can never be successful.

Many people take their appearance more seriously the older they become. You don't take your looks for granted as you did, when you were a younger model. I have much gratitude to be where I am today, not competing for the *best aging man* modeling the new Father's Day apparel for sale at department stores this Father's Day. I am so grateful to have the blessing to focus on other things now. It is a blessing to not be in the advertisements this year, and to let go of *all* of them and be free from the expectations. This year there will be no father's day modeling advertisements for Sears or JCPenney's or many other menswear catalogs for me. Today my life is transformed and I have two books out for the charity of my heart; my dog days are gone!

I have finally been able to let go of pain in my fifties because I am no longer responsible for anyone but me and I am free from having to meet the needs and the obligations through the perfect mediator in life. Meeting all the needs of all the people that call out for help, whether they are family or friends, I realize I have been told I have found my voice, finally. They say to me, *"You no longer need to explain your life and the reasons why people abandon you or the reasons why you live with the challenges of trust or abandonment today."* This has been my on-going life desire to come to a place where I *do not owe explanations* and I do not owe my

EMBRACED

reasons for choosing to do the things I do. I only owe Jesus Christ all explanations and I am free from other people's judgments from here on out.

I was not given a choice in my life for many decades. I made everybody happy, just like Shirley Temple did, throughout her childhood. And, you grow up confused about your value with a price tag attached to you. Growing up in California, you're born to hold an image. That image is something people would not let go of and they expected the image to stay and me to always be content, but I always knew there was something different.

The truth has set me free and I am able to be in a place in my life where I can celebrate my life and not tolerate any more questions of why things have turned out the way that they have. All of this is true because I know Heavenly Father knew of my life and the value of it and the people who would come into it and what my life would give to them, before I ever came to this earth. I am grateful to share the story of my life with you.

So, as I continue to receive questions from all over the world about this book, *Embraced*, I hope you will ask yourself *"What would I do, if I knew somebody in these shoes?"* and *"What could I do, to make a change?"* Just asking yourself to be the change you wish to see in the world opens up a whole new reality. You then desire to become the best **you** God created. And that's why you have read this book. God's plan for you is greater than your plan for yourself.

I promise you that.

MY SHAME AND PAIN IN SHARING THE TRUTH OF MY LIFE. WILL IT EVER STOP?

51

FRIENDS, FAMILIES, MEDICAL PROFESSIONALS and loved ones near or far, you all know who you are, for you have given me my dream. You have taught me and shown me that I can go on. You walked with me and you know who you are. Near or far, no matter where we were at, you were by my side.

I was waiting for anybody that would *let me* let go, let loose and just be me. That never has been an event I have ever experienced, being so relaxed you can just wear anything or be content just being in the moment with others without entertaining, serving and pleasing. I guess love can touch you one time and end up lasting a life time. That's what I experienced when I met my biological brother, Ronnie, and his wife, Lisa, and their two children. Never before had I felt that I could let go and open my heart and share *these books* with anyone in family, like I did with my brother and sister-in-law.

Trusting is like plastic surgery. I am so afraid that I will never be the same if I trust somebody. But I know, like plastic surgery, you end up feeling and looking better in the end, that's how it is with my brother and his wife and two children. It is better to be honest with my brother and his wife because of what has come out of it. Honesty and respect and the pact we made, we are now all three of us closer with a committed lifetime relationship as family. I believe this is my reality for the first time in life, maybe family can desire me without perfection. I don't know for that has never been a part that people talked about, but I'll never forget the pact we made at the dinner table in their kitchen, out on their farm in Moweaqua. Until that moment I shared, not even my family, my aunts or uncles or anyone that I know, whether they be Grubbs, Bonds, or Jantz, have I ever spoken a word about my life-transformation in the books, none of them knew that God has poured out redemption into the lives of others, for the purpose of helping children's lives be transformed, hopefully saving them from what I have lived through and experienced as an infant and a toddler and a young child, growing into adulthood, trying to find my place in this world, but not knowing where north, south, east or west would take me.

I was only guided by the hope of finding love, love that would last a lifetime. Someday I will walk up and just stop and realize I am at a place in my life where I have found love, and no longer have to walk another step to find what I have been looking for, my whole life.

DOCTOR'S ORDERS

~ 52 ~

FEW PEOPLE HAVE HAD THE CHANCE to share the things I saw and learned … the memories are as moving as they are astonishing. No matter what I do today, there is a broken-heartedness over something or someone, or even something I have done. **It is an empty space that came from the empty closet.**

It may not ever come out in this lifetime, whatever it is. Whether or not it is really from the empty closet or the empty life or an empty home, it will no longer be empty as soon as I am found. When I am found, the emptiness will be filled. And that is all God has asked me to do, is to wait until He brings me to the place He has called me to be, the place where I am to be celebrated and not tolerated.

For He wants to celebrate just as they did in the Bible, when the son who was lost but is found comes home, and they threw a big celebration for him, for they had thought he was dead. I'll always remember that, for I always dreamed that I would be found, and I know that I am now found, because of my brother and my uncle and they are my blood who have embraced me. And I am grateful for this opportunity to know that biologically, I was not sold because I was not worth anything. I realize today that I was sold by my father because of love.

I was taught to be captive to the memories of the past and the limited expectations I had for my future. And unless I am willing to

EMBRACED

deal with the painful experiences that life brought and still brings my way, the pain becomes a burden and a wound inside my heart.

I have finally let go of enough suffering to embrace the doctors and their techniques that have manifested goodness. I believe in western medicine, fully. I believe God created medicine for a purpose and I am grateful to have the expertise in all facets of my life, medically and spiritually in my life. Whether we identify ourselves as healers or those needing help, in pain, or those who seek awakening in their own life, there are providers of compassion with courageous hope for you and me. Spiritual methods have opened my life, never knowing where it would take me today. Once, I just knew my life could no longer continue, for I would break for

the long hours I gave to people, for their own happiness and security, and I removed much stability from myself, working and traveling throughout the world as I continued to dial for dollars, desperately, in an industry that was eating people up, left and right. That **had** to change.

SPENCER, NO MAN HAS GIVEN ME THE GIFT OF LOVE AND FAMILY UNTIL I MET YOU. I WILL NEVER BE ABLE THE SAME AGAIN.

53

How did so many missionaries wind up trapped by complicated visions at the Missionary Training Center in Provo, Utah? It just happens, when you have so many coming from all over the world. Why do we push the missionaries past our limits in pursuit of more work than any reasonable Pharisee has demanded?

I cannot run at a pace somewhere between maddening and insane to prove I'm among the faithful. For myself, I waited 365 days to check out the faith of The Church of Jesus Christ of Latter-day Saints, because it was the only church that would let me be honest about being gay, being born with same gender attraction, and letting them know that I prayed and prayed and fasted and to pray the gay away. I even went to have hands laid on me and be anointed with oil to pray the spirit of homosexuality out of me. I have had groups of men and women circle around me, laying their hands upon my head as they moved my head around in a circle on my shoulders,

EMBRACED

rotating my head around and around and around, praying that God would remove homosexuality and that I would no longer be in the arms of Satan, being used and abused since I was a child. And since I was abused as a child, I became a homosexual, they said. What a lie. As Marie Osmond would say, "What a pile of bullcrap!"

And she also says, "Might as well laugh about it now." She's right, because who in their right mind would out of the blue, say, "Oh, I think I'm going to become gay!" and go and seek out a lifestyle that is <u>so challenging</u> and <u>so competitive</u>. You can't make it if you are not prepared. And let me tell you, in the 'gay' arena, if you are thirty years old, you are considered a senior citizen. So anybody out there that is over thirty and dealing with same gender attraction, who might be just thinking about wanting to go into the life-style, you better get your wrinkle cream out right now. If you are over thirty, start saving for those false teeth and the ageless glow. Isn't this going to be a nice lifestyle to become a part of?

But let's fast-forward this some. Let's make it easy. If you are going to do this, don't play both sides of the fence. Because, that just displays your truthful dishonesty, and who you really and truly are, in character, and it will lead you down a rabbit hole that just goes straight down. I've been there and done that. You can't do it and feel good about yourself. It will only last for a season and then destruction will follow, because the truth is revealed to all, one way or another.

I do not choose things on a whim. I am into an exhilarating Latter-day Saint Christian Faith. A cage is no place for a Christian. My missionary, Spencer Wallentine, taught me that.

With Spencer, there were no more bells and whistles, no more phony masks, no more rat-race Christianity. Spencer is true people just like you. So it was that people could, in a time of need, find themselves in the loving presence of beings who led them out of the threatening darkness and into the light of hope on the streets of Portland. Spencer was a missionary that gave explanation and description in our everyday terminology. He communicated with every type of human being that he encountered. These people in Portland have cherished the extraordinary experiences that came from Spencer. He taught them that the goal of life must satisfy the highest of personality, our desire for living life, our craving for truth, and our desire for love. The human will is satisfied not by a love that grows cold or has phases like the moon, but by a love that is a pure white light of ecstasy without bullying.

A perfect life, with perfect truth and perfect love is what Spencer Wallentine gave to Portland, Oregon. His wisdom and comfort to be honest and open almost beyond measure gave people a way to happiness and a way to inner peace, teaching many people such as me the subjects of love, character, forgiveness, freedom, hope, happiness. He always went through the Bishop and did the most perceptive and brilliant, mindful personal acts of love to everyone he met on his mission. The yearning within Spencer for truth and love and beauty and perfection indicated that something big and great was yearning to be opened and it is the simplest form of love. No spade would ever be dug into the earth or pen put to the paper, if there were not some good thing expected of it. And with all you have done, Spencer, you have done to the least of these. That is what my missionary did throughout parts of his mission, as my brother and friend.

Spencer was compelling to me because of having the gospel within him, which was a peaceful light, not abrupt or aggressive, different from other missionaries that I had met. That's the kind of missionary God needed me to have. I don't *do* aggressive abruptness. I run from that, as I ran from other missionaries. But with Spencer, he knew I was not well and very sick and he was very

EMBRACED

gentle.

    I had never seen such tender kindness from a man until I met his father, Kent, who is just like him. I love Spencer's father, for he is a good man and very good to me, and treats me as a brother. Kent knows that I love his son and his children, and I am so grateful for what Kent has taught his son, Spencer. For, when he taught his son, Spencer, he was also teaching me, and didn't even know it. Through Spencer, Kent was teaching someone that never knew there was something else out there available in life that could make a difference in their life, a complete transformation that could change the course of life forever. But the decision, ultimately, was up to me. For me, change was the most fearful thing for that is what I had experienced my whole life, throughout many relationships and with many people, wanting me to become all things to all people. I couldn't think of God finding a place where that *could* end, but it seems to be something that has taken place over time and is in the process even today.

    Spencer, if you are reading this, thank you for not being abrupt or aggressive. Thank you for loving me the way Jesus would love me, instead of loving me because you wanted me to become a person you wanted me to be.

    Predictable in sharing friendship and love and gratitude from within, and very dependable as my spiritual brother and friend today, Spencer has always had a deep understanding of the many losses throughout my life, and his big-heartedness is rendered with vivid utterly convincing depth of a true man of God. How blessed I am to have Spencer in my life, and have all his family as my spiritual family. All I can say is how I personally feel about Spencer who has been such a wonderful influence in my life and continues to walk by my side to this day, along with his entire family.

JORDAN JANTZ

If you could imagine one of the nicest gifts anyone could ever receive, you would begin to understand what this wonderful friend and his presence in my life means to me.

Spencer, I will always have a special place for you and your family in my life and I honor you with this special book tribute to you for truly embracing my life as a true friend and brother really would do. This has been the best ten years we have shared as a spiritual family, and we will continue to share, throughout eternity. How blessed I have been to have you, Spencer, and all of your family in my life for the past ten years. I will never leave you or our family. I promise you that. **I attribute this book to having family and love in my life, and this is totally because of you.**

With much value and respect from my soul, we have really grown in truth and in wisdom for what really matters most. Ain't no plastic fantastic going on here. Ain't nothing like the real thing. And when you got it, you got it. And we definitely got it, brother. Thank you and Brittany and our entire family for making this book possible. We are all as family eternally embraced.

EMBRACED

MY LIFE GROWING UP IN SOUTHERN CALIFORNIA

~54~

It doesn't require a PhD from Princeton to assess that we are all busy human beings, forever on the move, doing things, eating stuff, working, jumping, jogging, writing, marrying, divorcing, buying, biting… you name it. Our country is doing it and in no place in our land are people doing more of it, more this hub of humanity where I grew up until I became an adult, Southern California. This was my life. And it definitely was a lifestyle for me. The pace is somewhere being somewhat different for me because whenever I'm up on the stage I was working and perfecting every attribute and I was untouchable. The stage is your pedestal. Everybody wanted to be someone or something else. That was my lifestyle.

The freeways and runways would choke the life out of you if you were not strong. People are going and coming twenty-four hours every day, working every hour of every day. In fashion, the industry will not let up. The lights are on you twenty-four seven and everyone is ready to find the first fault and the first imperfection in your life. You can't even breathe without the next model having their nose in your business. Their faces always reflect tension, with no let-up in sight. The air is polluted. The earth shakes. The malls are crowded. Everybody's nerves are shot. Many of the streets are dangerous. Interestingly, the more I've been in major population centers, the more I find similar scenes around the world, not just in California where I grew up.

I don't get tired of all the people. And I was not concerned about the impact that California lifestyle had on my modeling profession and my hurry-up mentality became more pressure from the Screen Actors Guild in Hollywood, 5757 Wilshire Blvd, 7th Floor Los Angeles, CA 90036.

That's why I so seriously considered permanently re-locating to Portland, Oregon. I imagined escaping the public eye by removing myself to some quiet, rural wooded piece of land by Hood River, windsurfing capital of the world, free of hassle and demands of the city and the demands of what people expect you to be and the way you are supposed to actually maintain your youthfulness throughout your life – that's IMPOSSIBLE – but that is what they expect from the career of being behind the camera. Although I know Hood River is filled with wind-surfing models, modeling many formats of surf gear and surf boards that would be right up my alley, for the opportunities for doing print ads but it would put me back into the business that I so long to be off the pages of the magazines.

You get to a point that you are afraid to turn the page of any magazine that you may end up opening up a men's magazine that has you wearing someone's designer clothing and boom, you are staring yourself right in the face, wondering why did this have to be this way for me? When I had always been told I should be grateful to be a good looking man and be on the covers of magazines and modeling that I don't appreciate anything and that I'm spoiled rotten and that I've always had everything I've always wanted and it is time to realize that I have to rely on my looks to keep up my finances properly and respectfully, as a respectable spokesmodel and speedo model would respond as the individual like yourself who is repeatedly asked to come back for cattle calls at universal studios for another call-back for a print ad for ocean-pacific, somewhere. Yes, it seems glamorous but very exhausting because once again, your appearance is what puts the money in your wallet to pay the bills.

If you are going to make a living you are going to work long hours, long days and long years. And your legs better be strong enough to handle the catwalk, because in California, that's what the red carpet is all about. Fashion at its finest. At the peak of California's high fashion, you will see every fashion designer showing their fashions for the season and yes, I was right in the middle of it all, throughout my years of growing up in California.

They said, "DO THIS, DO THAT, wear your hair this way, color your hair that way, cut your hair, grow your hair." If you are a model and successful at maintaining what you were born to do, you will be very fortunate with a healthy, long career, if you can hold up to the pressures of Southern California lifestyle.

Men like myself in Southern California were searching for something to ease the ache and soften their heart, if they are in the limelight of modeling. I never could imagine what life would be like for anyone in some sleepy, slow community where people talk of things like the weather and the tide, and get all hot and bothered over whether the pansies and the petunias will bloom early or late in spring. If that is the kind of stuff that turns your crank, fine. But not in California. All I ask is that you not feel sorry for us because we are stuck out here in wild and wooly crazy-land. And we're really not stuck here. We are all called to live here in a part of the world gone mad, full of frowning people who have lost their way. What a privilege it is to communicate reality of my life in California.

We all have elements in this story of our life, situations we either ignore or escape. Some storms are inevitable and bring downpouring rain. Some stories force us to face reality: life is difficult for all of us. Storms are inevitable. Pain and discomfort happen. Growing up in California I knew I must prepare for the winds and the rain and the floods to come into my life at some time. But the contrast of the story is eloquent. With the ultimate outcome, realizing I have so constructed my life that no amount of difficulty could bring me down. My principles and the instruction of experience on this runway of life gives solid secure foundation.

If you are only hearing and reading the truth, you are not prepared for life's reality, *because how can you explain something that you don't understand yourself.* It is easy to become fascinated, interested and intrigued by the concepts when you are a speedo model. Fashion runs through your blood like money runs through your fingers. The lights the music, being five feet up on the stage and the buyers who are all around, with the photographers consistently flashing as you try to hold your professional pony-walk down the runway or the glide with the slide at the end of your walk, which is very "in" today in most runway shows at high-end resorts. I am stronger and more experienced and I have gone far since I first started struggling to find harmony and love in the midst of those turbulent times, particularly scenes and roles you would be ashamed for your own mother to ever know about.

As disastrous as the fashion world is - on your body when you are expected to be on top of it all - the truth of all this is brought home beautifully when I am behind closed doors and can literally leave multitudes of people behind me. I appreciate freedom from people even though they have impacted my life in a positive way. I'm elated to be free from plastic fantastic. A lot of wonderful, and sometimes challenging situations happened for me in California.

JORDAN JANTZ

My life was filled with experiences where I gained intense reality of what life really means. California offered me phenomenal choices with a fresh choice of opportunities and not just anyone would have them offered to them. Many struggle with despair, with circumstances of seeking work in the industry with doors closed on their lives, sending many people back to the states they came from, hoping to make it in the modeling and fashion industry.

It seems you must be born with the talent to make it. I will never participate in bullying or manipulating ever in my life to get ahead. It has happened to several people I know in and out of magazine covers. I realize I am best where I am at, and that is living in forgiveness of the past, which today for me means forgiveness is giving up the hope that my past could have been any different!

I was meant to be a California boy! And that's why God took me all the way out there. And fifty years later, I find my life back in Decatur. I never thought how extensive and valuable my life would be and how enriched my spirit is in knowing truth and transparency, carrying peace and love and happiness. I've learned today from my life in California that the reality of forgiveness is a necessity in my life. *Reality is giving up the hope that the past could have been any different.* I'm grateful for California's beautiful beaches and people that I was surrounded by for that time in my life. I'm elated to be in touch with my life now on a personal level.

What wonderful experiences I've gained from the intense reality of phenomenal difference circumstances for the direction of my life. I'm very grateful I chose to move to Portland, Oregon. The difference has been night and day from the life in Southern California. I have learned the concept of change with confidence but I will always miss the beaches.

A phenomenal opportunity was birthed in my life, growing up

EMBRACED

in Southern California. It has made my life a meaningful life. Maybe a little different life from others, some may say. In California and later, I watched families and friends abandon their love for anyone that is different from them, growing up with much grief and sadness. People struggle with despair. I am prepared to take back ground, as I always have in my life. I have more now than before I left Decatur the first time as a child, because coming to Decatur the second time as an adult, I have a real spiritual family that invites me to stay at their home and share their home and be a part of their home, as if I was their own flesh and blood. I guess blood does make a difference, though. It is still hard for me to believe that I am blood family to someone else on earth. Knowing this brings more emotion than anything could ever bring because I feel I may have (embarrassingly) found real love for the first time. And, the objects of my love have my own blood also, running through their veins. Astonishing and amazing. It could make you stay up all night when someone realizes this reality in their life. It has for me.

It does touch my heart when I know I am asked to stay with family in Decatur, instead of checking into a hotel. But I'm afraid that if I did stay, I would never be asked back, because growing up in California, the family and everyone I knew always financially had money to never impose, or you just didn't go anywhere. That's the California lifestyle. If your wallet isn't thick enough to provide for yourself, you don't go. I was also taught that you never stay at a family's house. It is just not right. So, we always were in hotels throughout my life.

Even today, the thought of staying with my brother and sister-in-law or *ANYBODY* is daunting because I've never done that. I've always gotten my own hotel because that's the only *respectable etiquette* to represent yourself and your respect to others by not imposing yourself onto anybody for anything. This, today, is the hardest change for me to accept because to this day I have always

JORDAN JANTZ

gotten my own place somehow, someway without embarrassing myself by imposing. That is simply improper.

I've traveled the world for decades searching for God's comfort in my soul, always wondering where I belonged. Was I born for a purpose, sending my soul out into the universe?

I dream for the desire to be set free from the bondage that sets me apart from embracing life. The energy and desire to pursue life gets thwarted by compromised health, anxiety, fears. Uniqueness is primary for its success. Discovering an abundant life is possible as a model. I believed that. Models are empowered to embrace and exercise their God-given authority in the structure and uniqueness effectively transforming and healing their bodies.

I'm grateful to be affiliated for many years with California and its purpose and its vision that it had in my life. I will always return and know that I am welcome.

PS just thinking about California reminds me of the Katie Perry concert "California girls are simply undeniable" oh my, my what a song and what a life it was.

NEW YEAR'S EVE IN TIMES SQUARE

~55~

WHY IS IT THAT EVERY YEAR on New Year's Eve billions of people around the world come together to celebrate the hope of a new year, more than any other holiday celebrated on earth? How do you explain the whole world coming together in one night to celebrate the dreams and the hope they have for the new year? Many of us dress in silver and gold to symbolize the wealth of a new future. The world knows this is a day to *let go* of the past and embrace the future, and that's what New Year's Eve is to me.

You will give meaning that no one else has found in the new year. Another year you made a promise and another year you have a chance to turn it all around. The end of the year is at hand and we all need to fix what we have broken throughout the years. This is part of my mission statement in my life - to help others remember that we all get second chances. It is okay to listen to your heart and your spirit. Some things we can't control. The only thing that turns the world into a beautiful place is love. All we can do is reflect to be a better person. Second chances – they don't expire until midnight New Year's Eve. I'm blessed to have relationships that are not plastic fantastic. They walk with me, not ahead of me or behind me. Remembering our triumphs and missteps, our promises made and broken, some may even be grateful to get another chance to forgive this New Year's Eve, to do better, to do more, and to stop worrying about what if and embrace what will be.

The slopes in life lead me to realize there will be a magical evening this New Year's Eve. Take the opportunity and open your life to something beautiful that the world will celebrate. I'll never forget my new year's eves in times square when the ball dropped, I was there. So bring out the paper and the pens and make your resolutions and don't wait. Write down the changes that you want to see in the world in your life. BE the change you want to see in the world. Start to live that change as only you can. Life is short and we all get another chance to do things right, not just New Year's Eve, but every day throughout the new year.

Check off that list! Meet me in Times Square next New Year's Eve and see the ball drop with me, again! It is the greatest night of the year for me. Even though I have pressing matters that need attending to throughout my life, I know for myself in order to receive healing and repair my life and my relationships, I daily must give people meaning, including the homeless and lost children in the world. And so can you.

On New Year's Eve, I always remember to have a little faith in myself. Proper timing is everything on New Year's Eve. I will be where I am celebrated not tolerated. I embrace living in light with a voice of hope in this world. Charity and I will always celebrate New Year's Eve as we have over the past fourteen years. This year, my New Year's first resolution is to choose commitment over comfort. My second resolution is to make more eye contact with people, knowing that my eyes are the windows to my soul, reflecting the truth of my heart.

Love is the only thing that turns the world into a beautiful place.

EMBRACED

Love gives me hope on New Year's Eve transforming my heart and spirit to accept the opportunity to become kinder to my next door neighbor and kinder to my family and friends.

I don't care what your age is, or who you are, where you came from, or what you did, you will receive your greatest potential if you summon the courage to embrace it. It is risky to listen to your heart. New Year's Eve gives me the opportunity to repair relationships. Throughout the world resolutions will be made. My awareness of the meaning of New Year's Eve makes me lean into this way of life.

Some people believe there is no beauty or magic left in my two favorite holidays, New Year's Eve and Valentine's Day, change and love are what these holidays are about. Yesterday is a memory. I stopped and reflected on the years gone by. That's what new year's eve is all about. So take a cup of kindness for Auld Lang Syne, raising your glass, toast to your New Year's resolutions, second chances don't expire until midnight. Open your heart. I unconditionally love you and celebrate with you all this New Year's Eve.

Thank you for having Charity and me join the festivities. May your New Year touch your life the way you have touched mine. May Valentine's Day become a way of life. May you be embraced!

EPILOGUE

> "The church is not a place where perfect people gather to say perfect things or have perfect thoughts or have perfect feelings. The church is a place where imperfect people gather to provide encouragement, support and service to each other as we press on in our journey to return to our Heavenly Father."

This quote means a lot to me, because it helps me understand that despite how far I have come I will never be perfect in this life. I will still struggle with post-traumatic stress and emotions that overwhelm my life from my childhood. What matters is that I keep trying and never give up. I will never forget to help one another, to mourn with those who mourn, or to suffer with those who suffer and to build each other up to be the best that we can possibly be.

I have made a vow to myself for the years to come that I am here on this earth that I will be obedient to God's commandments and never speak ill of God's people. I will never justify things that are wrong to make others feel better about their choices. I will be the best child of God that I possibly can be. One thing I know now with certainty is, I must never forget that when Christ does return, I need to have my house in order. I glory in my God. I will praise him all my days and I eagerly look forward to his Son's coming. Through my trials I have learned to just be still and let God do His work in me.

EMBRACED

MY FAVORITE DREAM

At times life appears that you have no control over your environment. The slightest change could turn the course of your life forever. I cannot control what the world chooses to do. Or, what the people in it choose to be. All I know is I've always loved to think of the freedom of a dolphin. Throughout my life, I have dreamed that I, too, might turn as a dolphin and swim out to see to find my pod. Never knowing the dangers it would take to search for the depth of the deep blue sea, but down far below where there is no sound but the tranquil love when I find my pod and swam away from all life's judgments, set free with the other dolphins like me. This has always been my continuous dream, to be set free from judgments.

JORDAN JANTZ

EMBRACED

FINAL THOUGHTS OF REALITY

IT USED TO BE THAT THE WORD "HOME" was very frustrating to me, mainly because I didn't know where home was. I believed that it was my fault. I believed my personality caused a rift in my life and I deserved to be punished. Because no one was saying anything different, I accepted the lies from many throughout the history of my life on this earth and started to hide my personality to protect myself from others' opinions. I felt the fear and pain not only from losing the place that I called home, but not ever finding the way back to my heart's hope and dream to have a home where I belonged. My life was ruled by insecurities.

I never have understood these feelings inside me because they scared me. I felt that I had nobody safe to talk to, so I buried everything away from people, friends, family and relationships. I just kept it in my head. My confusion about where I belonged made me a very broken man. I didn't know how to process any of my feelings. Through all of these happenings in my life, I learned a way to avoid rejection and abandonment and gain acceptance of what God created when he made me. Because it's easy to wear a mask of perfection to be *world class* as people love to say, "That's what you were made for," I believed the lies.

People don't know what is underneath your reasons for life because some people don't want to feel uncomfortable. They hear, speak, and live for themselves. I used distraction as my main tool to avoid my internal struggles. There was no safe place to go to take off my perfection mask. Everywhere I went this mask became the biggest burden. There was not a place to go to safely take off my mask. I gave up hope that there would ever be a safe place for me where I could ever be honest about my hope for a home, my place to belong.

The only option for me was to keep up the façade that I was all things to all people. I could not keep going anymore, making others happy. I didn't trust people, I doubted their love and acceptance of me, because I believed that if all they saw of me was my mask, then that's all they could love. I had also learned through my experiences that people would reject me if they knew who I really was. I stayed up many nights tossing, turning and fearing the next day. I was losing sleep, eating poorly, and eventually began to have thoughts that if family is not wanting me in their life, and friends kept questioning my life history, then how could God desire a love for my life, when I even was confused about the history of my life. How can you explain something that you don't even understand yourself?

I had never really dealt openly with any of my struggles and this felt terrifying. This was very difficult for me, as it involved realizing the lies I had believed my whole life, that God hated me for I was not worth anything. It became a daily struggle to walk in this life and to keep believing that I was a good person. Nobody said it is easy to serve God. It is a different lifestyle to be a Christian Latter-day Saint and to keep the word of God close to my heart. I have had trouble believing the truth about who I was in Christ and that he accepted and loved me. I was still wrong.

That tension even grew stronger in the years to come. I was slowly realizing, more and more of the hopelessness I had believed was contending with hurtful memories in my life. Dealing with this was hard. I began to make my own decisions. I thought I knew more about myself than God did. Eventually I realized that God's plan for my life was not my plan I had set for my life. God's plan is much greater than my plan for my life.

EMBRACED

It took me years to realize that the home I was looking for was not a place at all. I was looking for people who would love me where I was at. I was looking for family, truth, hope. The family I was searching for was one that was accepting and safe. It did not matter where in the world it was going to be. The Forever Family I dreamed of could have been in Africa or Australia. I desired an eternal family who wanted me forever. And honestly, that's what I told God. It's true. I prayed asking Jesus about this crazy family thing called Eternal Family and it is real people, I promise that. It's a challenge but to gain the world and lose my soul, no way!

Yes, the world did give me many earthly pleasures. Many times throughout my life I realized my outward appearance was my foundation of who I was and what I was made for. It seemed it was easier to survive a life on the runway with the mentality of what I knew of all the lies that came together, that shaped my mind for many years. But God has a plan for me and for all of us that live with challenges throughout life. I thank God for Jesus who has given you and me a new life, because this world is not my home, it is my temporary home. I did not know it, but I have been searching for something I didn't expect. I was struck by God's grace. God had been preparing a life for me for a long time. God had forgiven me and loved me. I am still discovering more about grace and the loving home God has for me in my life. Please take advantage of asking God to help you through a challenge in your life. He will be there for you. Just call his name and I promise you all, He will be there for all of you who call upon his name.

I myself, call out to him every day and he has not abandoned me like family and friends have. Just because a person stands out with the ability to be photogenic or attractive to the world, you still can live feeling so empty and never knowing what you were created for. Your love for me is a testimony of God's love for his creation, that God is not dead. God lives in the lives of those who follow him. Thank you all for giving me the ultimate gift, and that is your

JORDAN JANTZ

unconditional love and hope for new beginnings. Please be the change you wish to see in your life because other people are just waiting for your hand to be extended out to them. Grab hold, and don't let go. Walk them through the journey of this life.

With all my love for you!   - Jordan Jantz and Charity

MONTAGE OF EMBRACEMENTS

⚡ LETTER 1 ⚡

October 22, 2004

To Whom It May Concern:

Jordan Jantz was a victim of assault on 10/17/2004 on NW 15th and Glisan. During this incident he experienced a head trauma, was left unconscious and all of his identification was stolen. At this time Mr. Jantz continues to experience difficulties in his communication and with anxiety as a result of this incident.

If you have questions about Jordan Jantz's identity, here is some information that may be helpful to you:

Address: Jordan Jantz
731 SW Salmon Street #609
Portland, OR 97205

Please feel free to contact me to verify this information. You can contact me at Project (redacted) or my cell phone (redacted).

Thank you for your assistance,

Graham Harriman, MA, LPC

LETTER 2

January 22, 2016

Regarding Jordan J Jantz

On behalf of Jordan Jantz, his care team at (redacted) Medical Group would like to express our appreciation and gratitude to you for the ongoing supportive role you play in his life.

Jordan has consistently felt that his physical and emotional well-being has been valued and respected by you and your colleagues. Your organization has often gone above and beyond what would be normally expected and Jordan would like you to know how valuable and appreciated that support continues to be. His medical support team considers you to be very valuable in his life and we greatly value the support you continue to provide him.

Please accept Jordan's and his clinic team's most sincere thanks for the work and support you provide. As Jordan likes to say, "Some people can touch so many lives."

Sincerely,

Jordan Jantz & (redacted) Medical

(redacted) MEDICAL GROUP INTERNAL MEDICINE

Jordan's primary healthcare physician who I owe my life to, because she has given me a life I never dreamed I would have.

Simply, the best.

JORDAN JANTZ

Dentist for the past decade. My #1 female Dentist gives me the glow and helps with my doctors to make my life peaceful to heal.

EMBRACED

My therapist for the past seventeen years. Words cannot describe the value of this relationship.

LETTER 3

Dear Jordan,

I can't believe it has been nearly ten years since we met. I am certain that when God sent me to Portland, he wanted me to meet you. I would never have imagined how our lives would converge. When my angel mother invited you to visit, I heard God's voice in her invitation.

Through our numerous visits and phone calls, we became family. Difficult as it was, you learned to trust us. I look forward to your visits and the time we spend together. At the end of each visit you tell me that this visit has been the best, ever. I look forward to many more "best" visits to come. It fills my heart with joy to know that you feel embraced after all the struggles you've endured.

This journey started with me teaching you, but you have taught me. I've learned to be more forgiving and humble because of your example. For this I thank you.

Love always,

Your Brother,

Spencer

Jordan and his missionary, Spencer

LETTER 4

Dear Jordan:

    I have often reflected on our relationship with you, Jordan, and have thought how remarkable it is that you are even alive today. I think there are several things that have contributed to your being alive and contribute to the person you are now.

#1-   You sought out God. I believe that by giving him your troubles, your trials, your hurts, your pain, your grief, he has helped you to heal. Incredible and humbling to me is that in the last few years I saw you forgive those from your past who hurt you horrifically. That, I believe, is an amazing feat in and of itself. You gave your burdens to God and I believe this is how you were able to be free yourself and move on with your life. I love how Elizabeth's Smart mom said to her, "Don't let him take another moment of your life away from you." In other words, move on, let the past go and don't let those hurts and memories suck any more of life out of you. I think you were able to do that by giving your grief to God and forgiving those who hurt you.

#2-   I think one of the biggest things that has helped you is that you have a desire to serve others. From the first time I met you, you showed examples of service. For Instance, taking care of older people by cooking meals, cleaning, shopping for them, etc. You told me how you helped those around you who were abused and volunteered in many capacities. You gave to the Christmas Box House. You cooked warm potatoes for the people of the homeless community; those lived on the streets and under the bridges then delivered them out to them. You gave and continue to give firesides, talking about your life's events and how others can

JORDAN JANTZ

heal. Because of your desire to heal and help others, I believe this brought healing to you. Whenever we serve we become Jesus' hands...I believe this has helped you in the past and is still bringing healing to you.

#3- You have always been a good boy deep in your soul. You have a desire to help, to serve, and to love others. I think I loved you from the first time I met you because I saw in you such goodness.

I have watched you become the man you are today. You used to have such severe panic attacks and anxiety whenever you thought you had to leave our family. Sometimes when you stayed here I saw the little boy personality, the teenager, and the adult. You are more in control now... you have become a man who knows his place and knows he is okay in our family. I don't think this means that you don't ever revert back, but you are becoming more sure of yourself. We respect that you have a biological family but we will always claim you as ours, too! I love you like the brother you are and hope you find peace, joy, happiness and success in all you do! You are a walking miracle! May God help you live your life to the fullest. Love you Forever and always.

Your sister, *Linda Wallentine*

EMBRACED

The Wallentines at Lagoon

LETTER 5

Jordan,

It has been a wonderful adventure to get to know and love you over the past several years! What an adventure it has been to participate in family activities, firesides and conferences. I was especially moved as you received the light house humanitarian service award last year at the North Star conference in Salt Lake.

We've grown closer and benefited as a family as we've loved and embraced you and been able to personally witness your life's mission and passion to bless children and families through your book. Your Christian spirit of service and kindness to all people is an amazing example.

Thanks for going with me to leave a Living Christmas Card to some families in our neighborhood in December. It was neat to hear a young girl exclaim at one of the houses, "Wow, when Jordan prays, he's so happy!" You light up my life, too, Jordan!

What a living witness you are to the whole world that Jesus Christ can lift and love and heal anyone. When people truly love each other the world is a better place.

Good luck with your next book - sounds like it will be wonderful! I truly value our friendship and relationship!

Your brother and sister always,

Paul and Karen

EMBRACED

Paul and Karen

LETTER 6

Dear Jordan,

I had heard about you for years from my dad before I had the chance to meet you. You had made quite an impression on him, and he spoke very highly of you and your noble spirit. I also knew that you were friends with Ty Mansfield.

Several years ago, when we finally met as we participated in a fireside together, I was deeply impressed by you, your kindness, and your desire to help others. Your message and your voice clearly touched others and it was a privilege to witness it.

At the time, I didn't know your story. I hadn't read your book, and I had no idea the level of abuse you suffered as a child.

I am a licensed marriage and family therapist, and as such I have some knowledge of what the effects human trafficking, abuse, and neglect can have on someone. To be sold and have your worth reduced to an actual dollar amount is incredibly demeaning to the human spirit, as are the profound abuses you suffered as a child. My heart aches to know of the things you endured.

Despite those things, you have triumphed and I couldn't be more impressed by all that you have done with your life. Where others might have become embittered or simply unable to heal, you have taken progressive steps to find health. You have allowed God to bring wonderful people, treatments, doctors, and other professionals into your life, as well as religious mentors, and you have allowed those influences to be positive agents in rebuilding your life, curbing maladaptive coping mechanisms, and finding peace and harmony with those around you. You shine, and you let your light bless all who come in contact with you.

EMBRACED

Because of your strength of character, you are now doing all you can to help others, and that's what touches me most about knowing you: you are a truly Christ-like and giving person who wishes to help God's children. I hope to be more like you someday.

Lolly and I are lucky to have met you, served with you, and gotten to know you. Thank you for being our friend, and for all you do for others.

With love,

Josh Weed and Lolly Weed

JORDAN JANTZ

❦ LETTER 7 ❧

29 January 2016

Dear Jordan,

Geri and I want to express our gratitude to you. We have known each other for the last nine years. Knowing you has made our lives better.

When we first met, you were in very poor health. You were newly baptized as a member of the Church of Jesus Christ of Latter-day Saints. You had learned to trust in Christ. We remember how you expressed your faith in Christ that all would be ok.

It is your faith and determination that has impressed us. Each time, as we have seen you rely on your faith and determination to overcome obstacles, you have grown stronger. As you have encountered continued serious health issues, you have relied on your faith in Christ to help you overcome these health issues.

You have had to overcome nay-sayers and critics about your new way of life. You have been steadfast in your position. You have continued to rely on God.

You have used the word "transformation" to describe your changes. I would agree; you have truly made a transformation. Your influence because of that transformation is felt throughout the country.

In addition to your reliance on God, you have genuine friends because you are a genuine friend to others. I have never seen anyone who is more focused on helping others than you; especially young

EMBRACED

people. I'm sure your experiences as a youth greatly influence your actions today.

You have been an example to others about holding your ground and relying on God. It is that undying faith in God, I believe, that has made the biggest difference in your life. That love of God is what makes your transformation possible.

It is a privilege to be able to call you our friend.

Love, *Allen and Geri Oyler*

LETTER 8

Dear Jordan,

It's been a privilege for us to get to know you at the Market Street Branch. We appreciate your gentle soul and willingness to serve others, many of whom are overlooked, forgotten or ignored as lost causes. You, more than anyone I know, understand the suffering that comes when men and women follow their worst impulses. But, rather than bitter and broken, you're an example that there is hope and healing through humility, faith and faithfulness.

Best,

David Bodmer

LETTERS 9 & 10

Jordan Jantz,

It has been my privilege to be your Branch President and friend, for 3 of the years since you joined the church. You have come to learn that the Lord truly loves you and guides you in His path on earth. I have watched you speak to an audience about your life and blessings and felt the spirit of the Lord guide you on the words you spoke.

With this new book, I see maturity come out and your love of the Lord being genuinely presented to your reading audience. Your audience will come to love you as we do and to know that you are a very special person in our Father in Heaven's eyes.

Pres. Robert Nelson

Dear Jordan

I am so excited to hear of your new book and that the proceeds are going to help children who are at risk. Your life is such a guiding light to all people to help them to know that Heavenly Father loves all of us and He is there to help no matter what our situation is.

I have known you long enough to see the great change of heart, mind and in your physical being since you joined the Church of Jesus Christ of Latter-day Saints. You have truly done as the scriptures say, "Love the Lord they God with all thy heart, and all thy soul and with all thy mind and with all thy strength."

Thank you for being an example of hope to all around you. May you continue to be put in the forefront so that others may be uplifted by you.   Susan Nelson

JORDAN JANTZ

Bob and Sue Nelson

LETTER 11

Dear Jordan -

When I think of the first time Fred and I met you, so many memories and feelings come flooding to my heart. Can you believe that it was fourteen years ago that Fred and I went to the airport in Salt Lake to pick you up and bring you to our home to stay with us for three days? Since we had never met each other before, we had no idea what you looked like. We asked each other, "How will we recognize Jordan?" And yet, when we saw you coming down the stairs, we knew who you were. There were hugs of love given. We instantly knew who you were, and our feelings for you were feelings of love! We felt God had brought you into our lives.

At first, you were quiet and shy. As time progressed, you began to open up yourself to us. You shared your nightmare childhood. Fred and I were overwhelmed at the horror of your earlier life. We asked you how you could survive such a difficult childhood. The more you forget about yourself and offer help to others, the more we feel love, respect and admiration for you. You have come so far, and you are becoming so strong.

Do you remember when we asked you to speak at one of our monthly firesides, which we held for many who share some of your challenges? They were all mesmerized by your talk! So many people wanted to talk to you after the fireside. They wanted to know how you could move forward and not look back. You continue to have health challenges, but you never give up. Instead, you forgot about yourself and offered help to others. All of your time and energy has been devoted to trying to help children who have been abused. So many changes have come into your life as a result.

JORDAN JANTZ

And then, there was the time when we had invited a few friends to come to dinner to talk with you. While we were sitting at the table, your phone rang. It was a call from your Aunt Frieda Jane. You couldn't believe that she had called you. She was the one who helped you find God in your life. Someone once said, "God is the source of all truth - not Google!"

Know that we will always love you! Our prayers are always for you.

Fred & Marilyn Matis

LETTER 12

Hi Jordan! This is *Adam Treadwell*.

    I just wanted to send you a note to tell you that we love you and that we're so proud of you for the amazing person you are, and the wonderful way that you love and strengthen others. Thank you for doing what you do and being who you are. God is proud to have such a son as you, who has overcome so much adversity and found ways to serve and love others. Keep up the great work!

Jordan and Adam at North Star

LETTER 13

Jordan is an inspiring and obedient follower of Jesus Christ. He has taken the courageous step of sharing his story of abuse and despair and ultimately redemption to prove hope to many. Jordan is a great friend and a true blessing.

Brett and Dee

EMBRACED

Bond Men

LETTER 14

Jordan,

Over 3 decades of friendship, I have watched, prayed, carried you, laughed, cried, yelled and watched how the powerful touch of Christ who has carried you through your darkest of times, hard times, great times and a path no one should have to walk or crawl through.

You have a healing message that few "Christians" have talked or written about.

Jordan's non-religious life and his deep love of Jesus Christ and his very personable walk has been a very horrifying life, so dark at times that anyone would of given up...but Jordan's goal is to make *good* to all the children who have not found their faith, voice, or the long path to walk in the light of Christ and find truth, freedom and real healing to pass it **on to others.**

I know these books will be healing and helpful to children and adults alike. Jordan's message is not a quick fix or a *band aid*, but of hope for a better tomorrow.

You are my dear friend.

Billy

My BFF for friends on earth, we will always be and brothers in heaven is our eternal destination. This is our temporary home.

LETTER 15

Dear Jordan

Looking back almost 7 years, I would have never expected that we would have grown to be the "brothers" that we are today. You have taught me so many things, one of which is to never limit others' potential!

Much like your readers saw in your first book, your life story is a remarkable one. It is one that is full of anger, love, disappointment, betrayal, peace, renewal, and charity. I am amazed at the man you have become despite the things you experienced. I am grateful for the many frequent visits to Maya's for dinner, and the time we spent talking about the trials in life.

Jordan I always admired your love and concern for others. Even when you were having hard days, or disappointments were knocking on your door, you continued to help those who needed it most. I am happy to hear that the proceeds of this book are going to help those you care about so much, the kiddos who need love and support after experiencing abuse. Your work is noble and helping others is something I notice you do so naturally.

In the short time that I have known you I have seen a wonderful transformation, one that has brought light to you and others around you. Some people might say you are crazy with all that you are involved with, however I wish I could have the vision you have in helping everyone know they are loved, valued and needed.

I am glad that you have decided to write this second book

EMBRACED

and know that everyone who reads it will see that even with all the hard times, life can offer some pretty spectacular experiences.

Jordan your love is endless and I sure love you.

Your "Brother",

Jarrett Henderson

JORDAN JANTZ

❦ LETTER 16 ❧

My wife Tanya and I have known Jordan for more than ten years. We first met him before he had found God, before he found Christ, before he found the Church of Jesus Christ of Latter-day Saints at an Evergreen Conference in Salt Lake City. But Jordan even then was a quester, someone seeking healing and growth. He already had an inner humility that wasn't weak, it was incredibly strong. Jordan is a survivor; he has survived traumas that lesser people would be rendered helpless by. But he has more than survived, he has triumphed. His love of God and of other people is infectious. It is clear that Jordan loves the Lord Jesus Christ and that loves shines through him and onto others. It's that lack of guile, and that relentless love, that has touched so many people.

That is why we recommended to the Board of Directors of North Star International that he be awarded our Beacon of Light Award last year (2015). This is an exceptional award we give to people for a lifetime of devotion to a cause greater than themselves, whose lives are an inspiration and strength to great number of people. Jordan exemplifies this award, which he richly deserves.

JORDAN JANTZ

Jeff and Tanya Bennion

LETTER 17

Dear Jordan,

Our association of the last few years has embraced some of my favorite things - friendship, faith, family, love for children, and compassion. You have opened your heart to truly transforming the ugliness of abuse into the beauty of giving hope to others. We are all God's children, as well as brothers and sisters, deserving of kindness, dignity and respect

Thank you for being a wonderful example of giving your "all" to lifting others humbly and without judgment. May your journey continue to bring joy and fulfillment.

Forever Friends,

Mary and David McCulloch

JORDAN JANTZ

❧ LETTER 18 ☙

Our Dear Friend and Brother,

    Jordan, you have come so far in this wonderful journey. We are so happy that you have found Christ and the true meaning to your mission here on Earth. The Lord has truly blessed you and He has blessed our lives for knowing you.

    You are such an example of someone who has overcome personal challenges and strives to uplift and help others on their individual paths towards peace and happiness. As our friend Ellen says every day on her show, "Be kind to others," and "Show a little love." You truly have taken this advice from Ellen and from the greatest example of all, our Lord and Savior who says to "Love One Another."

    We love you for the example you are and continue to pray for your health and happiness.

"Charity never Faileth."

Lee and Lisa Harris

EMBRACED

Lee and Lisa Harris and their children

LETTER 19

Jordan has been our friend for over 4 years. We've enjoyed having him in our home and hearing and watching his journey on his healing path. He's been able to make his path easier by letting go of the secrets that have held him hostage his entire life. His strength has come from changing his dependence on mortals and himself to depending on Christ, His forgiveness, and His love. Feeling clean and 'new' has given Jordan energy to serve and help others, including many children. 100% of Jordan's book sale profits go to benefit the children.

We hope and pray that the obvious changes and growth that Jordan has chosen to make will inspire others on their healing roads to a functional life. Many adults with early abuse have felt 'damaged' and have not understood their full potential and gifts. Understanding Christ and His love, and undergoing therapy with a competent doctor and therapist creates space to receive and recognize the love of others. Healing is possible for everyone and Jordan is proof of this.

We have worked as High Priest Group Leader and Relief Society President in the Church of Jesus Christ of Latter-day Saints with Jordan. We have seen both his physical healing and his spiritual growth as he has chosen to give his will to Christ and to keep His commandments. Jordan understands his purpose in being on this earth and lets nothing get in his way.

Mike and Stephanie Cluff

EMBRACED

Mike and Stephanie Cluff

LETTER 20

Jordan,

I can't say I'm too surprised at where you are today. I've always known you as a dynamic Man of God. Sure, it has been a process, but anything of value takes a lot of work to obtain. When I was in high school, you made quite the impact on me and my Christian friends world. A gay guy with a serious lisp could come to God, just as he was. It was so cool! Our God was so big! No one was out of reach from the hand of God.

As I got older, we became closer. Not only were you an inspiration of God's grace but you were also a friend. You made it a point to Be Real, be who you are! I felt lucky, being straight. I knew it was nearly an impossible struggle that you fought; the pressure of the church and others to conform to their boxes was overwhelming. Sadly, in some of my weakest moments I'd do the same, try to change you, try to do the work of the Holy Spirit on my own.

Thank you for sticking with me. Thank you for forgiving me. Jordan, I don't know anyone with a bigger heart than you. You love people, just as they are. I'm still inspired by your life nearly 25 years later. I see God's gift of forgiveness, God's gift of redemptions, and the healing power of an almighty God at work in you. I look forward to our next 25 years and eternity.

Love you, *Paul Schmoll*

EMBRACED

Paul Schmoll and family

LETTER 21

I met Jordan when he was publishing his first book, *Out of the Closet, Into the Light*. In that book, he described his childhood story of abuse and eventually being sold for sex. Devoid of descriptive detail, the book is written with a detached honesty that exposes the horrors some children must endure from birth, through their teens, and beyond into adulthood.

Jordan's personal mission is to eradicate mistreatment of children. If he can prevent just one person from experiencing what he has lived through, he will consider his life a success. Of course, his aim is to save many more than just one. He fully supports, with every dollar he can muster, Christmas Box House International. He describes this special place as a safe, loving harbor for abused children. It brings love and comfort to those who have never before felt any security, acceptance or normalcy in their young lives.

Jordan's transformation from the confused, abused child that he was, to the compassionate, active crusader for children and their safety that he now is, must be called a miracle. I'm awed at how his individual spirit could not only survive, but rise above the mud, to emerge as a powerful, passionate agent for good. I'm looking forward to reading *Embraced*.

Sincerely,

Sherry Chew

EMBRACED

Sherry Chew

LETTER 22

Dear Jordan,

As we near Valentine's Day and the release of your book, *Embraced*, I look back at the almost ten years since I first met you and just marvel at all that you had experienced and accomplished.

I still remember the day I first met you. Elder Wallentine was the missionary serving at the Market Street Branch and he told us about a man who was learning the Gospel of Jesus Christ. I do not remember what else he said, but I remember he was very excited because you were learning to walk by faith and developing a relationship with Jesus Christ and that made him very happy. He asked if anyone would like to join him and his companion for your next lesson, and I readily said yes. I remember meeting you with your beautiful long blond hair, broad smile, and perfect teeth. I cannot remember what our lesson was about, but we shared experiences and testimony; I felt the Spirit.

Not long after that first meeting, Suzi and I left the Branch to attend our home ward, so we did not see you much until your baptism. Your baptism was very unique in our experience because so many people outside of church came to support you. A close friend of yours stood up towards the end of that special service to congratulate you and he said that when you decide to do something, you don't do it half-heatedly but you go all the way. I would find out later just how true those words were.

Do you remember how sick you were back then? It seemed that every week you were sick with the flu, with pneumonia, and so often you were not able to attend church because of it. I seriously

EMBRACED

thought you did not have much time left on earth. But, do you remember when I gave you a priesthood blessing in the Branch President's office one Sunday when you were able to make it to church and asked for a blessing of healing? In that blessing you were promised that *your life was in the hands of the Lord*, that you still had *much to accomplish* in this life, and that your *life will be extended for you to complete your work*. After that blessing, I had no idea how those promises would be realized, but I felt certain that the promises were true and that the Lord will fulfill those promises. As it turns out, the miracle of healing came through a group of special doctors that you would only tell me about months later who developed a series of treatments that would save and extend your life. How true it is that so often, it is through the people in our lives that the Lord accomplishes His miracles.

You are the most unique friend I had ever met. Your language, the way you thought, the experiences you shared, were all so foreign to me. I know you felt the same way towards me. You had SUCH a difficult time trusting. Our expectations were so different and often misunderstood. All of this made being friends so challenging, yet perhaps it is because of that difficulty, and our dogged willingness to set aside frustrations and hurts that our friendship grew strong. You showed me how to not hold on to the hurts of the past but move on. What's the use of opening old wounds anyway? You look for hope and love, to hold on to relationships, and to keep trying. I am still learning how to do that.

You joined the Church of Jesus Christ of Latter-day Saints because you learned about Jesus Christ through the missionaries and were spiritually reborn through His atoning sacrifice. You developed a personal relationship with Christ. You made a personal commitment to follow Him, and Him only.

JORDAN JANTZ

You never wavered on that commitment. You gave up so much for that commitment to Christ. You stopped smoking. You stopped drinking alcohol and coffee. You knew that having easy access to technology made it too easy to draw you into temptations that you knew was not compatible with your commitment to Christ, so you gave away your computer and threw away your cell phone. You are one of the only people I know living in the 21st Century who choose to not have a smart phone! When you do something, you go all the way!

Joining the church also meant being a part of the Mormon community...that was REALLY hard...again because of cultural differences. What was harder was that so many in the gay community deserted you because of your decision to join the church. It did not happen all at once...but one by one, so many trusted friends on whom you relied and to whom you gave so much left.

Then one day, you called in tears because your old boyfriend, whom you loved dearly, had just committed suicide. You were the one who found Matthew. Your heart broke. He was your lover and best friend for decades. You told me he grew up Mormon. His family ostracized him when he came out about being gay. He left the church. You were so outraged that his family did that. You knew that was wrong. Matthew was so torn and heartbroken when you were baptized because he could not understand how it is that you, his love, embraced the church he left so long ago. The day you found him, you had gone to give him a present. The one thing that has carried you through all of this turmoil and these challenges was your faith in and commitment to Jesus Christ. Your love for Him and the love you felt from His through the Spirit is what kept you constant. I have always admired your commitment. You are a man of integrity.

EMBRACED

We had a lot of phone conversations in which you told me bits and pieces about your life, about the abuses you experienced as a kid, about your work in the adult industry, about broken relationships and breaches of trust, about abandonment, about miracles and angels, about love and fulfillment, about loneliness, about fear, and about finding Jesus Christ and the joy that relationship has brought into your life. Those snippets of life experiences were like pieces of a jigsaw puzzle. Even though I did not know where some of those pieces fit, and many pieces seemed missing, I started to see a picture of the man that you are and all that you experienced that brought you to where you are.

You opened my eyes to what it means to be gay. You helped me to understand that being gay is not a choice. You helped me to see that it is not just about physical intimacy, but it is about the universal desire for emotional love and fulfilling relationship. You helped me to learn that being gay is not the result of abuse. You taught me that being gay cannot be "cured". You also showed me that you can be gay but still live the Gospel fully.

As I thought about these things, a distinct impression came to my heart and mind that you need to write down your life story because it is so unique and worth telling. A few days later, you called and told me excitedly that another friend said you should write your story and you were not sure how to do that. I told you about my impressions and that I thought this was part of the work that the Lord wanted you to do and encouraged you to take on this project. Neither of us knew where to begin. You mentioned you did not even have a computer to work on, but that maybe a typewriter will work. A few days later, I found an old typewrite and brought it to you along with ink ribbons and a stack of paper. Despite my nagging, progress was slow...well, actually, I think it was zero. You had so many other commitments to attend to that writing was just not possible.

JORDAN JANTZ

Then another miracle: you called one day and told me about meeting an author after attending a North Star conference in Salt Lake City, and she offered to write your story. That was Jewel Adams. The book, your first book, was *Out of the Close, Into the Light*. I bought it and read it in a night. The pieces of the jigsaw puzzle now present a whole picture. It helped me to understand and appreciate you better.

This is what I wrote after reading the book:

***Out of the Closet, Into the Light** is an authentic account of a person who has experienced tremendous pain and abuse in childhood, yet has found the courage and capacity to continue to love. One sad result of many who have experience abuse is becoming trapped in the belief that they are not lovable and worthless, thus imposing on themselves, after the original abusers have long gone, continued self-abuse through drugs, depression, and for some, suicide. Jordan's account of his journey through life shows that it is possible to "dare greatly" in the face of his abusers so that he is not held hostage forever by their actions His humility and willingness to give a chance to opportunities for growth and healing is a lesson everyone can learn from and emulate. Although the experiences shared in this book are some of the most heart wrenching I have read, ultimately, it is a hopeful book. Jordan showed that despite all that is evil in the world, there is also good...if you are willing to let love in. I highly recommend it to anyone, not just those who have experienced abuse, but for anyone who has experienced pain, betrayal, and loss.*

With the book published, I felt you accomplished a great work that the Lord wanted you to do.

You live your life with meaning and purpose. You could have a very peaceful and uneventful life given your circumstances. However, that is NOT you! You would feel life is meaningless.

EMBRACED

Instead, you seek for opportunities to share what you learned and the love you feel with others through firesides, through serving in non-profits, through feeding the homeless, and especially through serving abused children. You brought the message of hope in your book abroad to many states and traveled extensively as a motivational speaker despite the toll it took on your body. There were several times where after arduous trips, your health took a dive and you were close to death. With support and love of friends from the gay community and church, and the tender care of your team of doctors, you recovered and your ministry continued. You took on another major project last year to write a second book. I am looking forward to the release of *Embraced*, and to finding out what message you have prepared to share with the world through it.

I am grateful to know you. I am grateful you embraced Jesus Christ and His Gospel. I am grateful for your example of living true to your commitments. I am grateful for your example of living life with purpose and giving your life in loving service. I am grateful that you have opened my eyes to understand a whole community of people that I knew little about. I am grateful you have embraced me as a brother. I have no idea what else is in store for you in this life, but I embrace you and will walk with you as your brother in this life and in the world beyond.

With love, your brother,

Yiyang

JORDAN JANTZ

Yiyang and family

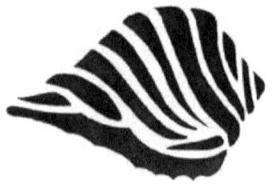

˞ LETTER 23 ˜

My Uncle Bill sent me a first Christmas Card, and a picture showing the gifts that I sent him, on his mantle!

Biological Uncle Bill

Jimmy,

May the warmth and joy
of the season
fill your heart and home
with happiness.

We are so happy you found us. Love you and looking forward to all of us getting together.

Love,
Bill & Sue

JORDAN JANTZ

⁃⟨ LETTER 24 ⟩⁃

Jordan,

We certainly remember the early days when we first met you. We were grateful that you allowed us into your life. We were amazed and overwhelmed at the story of pain and tragedy that you had to live through. It seemed that you were so open to finding healing and truth in your life. Hearing parts of your story helped us to understand your methods of survival, some helpful some harmful.

We have many memories and photos of you gathering with us and our family over the years. You have always tried to be a person who was vulnerable and honest yet your tragedies were so deep. No matter how many times you walked through certain doors with the hope of this being the time that you will be set free and that this is the way that will turn your life around, and it seemed to only take a few layers off, you never gave up.

We remember the day while walking through some stores that you asked my husband to walk in front of you and when I asked you why you said, "Because I want to see how a real man walks." And you practiced. We must say we even loved you more.

And here today, look at what God has done in your life. He gave you the grace to never give up and you used it. You are a story of hope and transformation in the midst of the deepest tragedies. Jesus has much more for you and He has always worked with you in the midst of the pain and carries it and holds every tear replacing all with the grace of healing.

May each person who has endured these horrors be strengthened knowing if God walked with you even in dark places,

EMBRACED

He will continue to walk with you until you also find your release and freedom.

No matter where you go or what you do we have God's love stored up for you.

You have the courage of one who knows you are loved by the One who matters most, and that Love loves through you. Thanks for letting us love you these many years.

Vic and Kathy

LETTER 25

Jordan,

I met you in March 2007 when you were baptized into the Church of Jesus Christ of Latter-day Saints. I admire you that you would be willing to give up a lifestyle that was different than the one that the church teaches, coming from a life of abuse, and you believed that you had no family and now to arrive at a point in your life where you have found a brother and now an uncle, is amazing!

I believe that the Lord loves you very much. To be able to be a tool for our Heavenly Father to hold the children and to be aware of all the gays in the church that need a voice, you had to have been very special in the spirit world before we all came here.

When I first met you, I nagged you about working on your family history. You declined my offer because it was all too painful for you. Finally, in 2014 you were ready to find your biological father's family. Having the conversations when we called those phone numbers that we found on Ancestry.com was the most emotional time in your life, for you never knew your family was alive and that they remembered you and that they even wanted to see you and embrace you as family should. My what a journey this has been! You couldn't even talk; you were so speechless when you heard that you were loved. To find your father and your mother's lines, it has been an unbelievable trip. We had help from your family on the other side of heaven, and I know we were guided along the way by the Holy Spirit.

We were able to obtain pictures and articles and felt that we came to know these people in your family history personally. We

EMBRACED

even went back to 20 years after the death of Jesus Christ. Your genealogy is incredible and the amount of money spent on this project was enormous, but very much worth it for me. I know your family in heaven wanted us to find them and let them know they are not forgotten by you. Sometimes in this journey I felt guided by the Holy Spirit and wondered, "Where did that come from?" but I knew it could only come from God. The information we obtained is unbelievable! And the fact that we found out that your biological mother and biological father were married on Valentine's Day in 1959, though you were told lies that they were never married and you were illegitimate! That very year that they were married, you were born 9 months later. So, you were planned and you were not a mistake. You are not a pair of used shoes, as the mother who paid for you, told you.

You have a great love of our Heavenly Father and Jesus Christ. You glow with that love. You have a very giving heart and always look for others and what you can do for them. You have opened the door to help a group of people that had no voice. I hope you always remember that God will always be there at your side. He will put people in your path that you will need and you are not alone. It is for all of us to move on to our new chapters in our lives. We have had our ups and downs but it was a lesson that the Lord felt we both needed to learn. Someday your biological parents and family will realize what a fine gentleman you have become. Your honesty and your integrity have a light of their own, and when you walk into church everyone stops and smiles for the light you bring to others in life is a light of love and truth. I've never met a more honest man. And I am so happy you found your Uncle Bill and your brother, Ronnie, for the two of them are going to add something to your life that you never dreamed of and it will come from God, as a blessing from your family.

May your life be a happy one, as we both move on.

JORDAN JANTZ

Your friend,

Jewell Burcham

LETTER 26

In honor of the first man that opened his life to Jordan:

Pastor Wendell Smith
1950-2010

Special memories of Dr. Smith who believed in me before I believed in myself.

"No matter what happens, we win!"

Wendell, I will never ever forget the love and friendship you and Gini shared with me. You were the finest *Dragon Slayer* of anyone. You taught me how to believe when I couldn't see. You were my voice when I couldn't speak. You gave me hope because you believed in me. You took me with you and Gini to Tucson, AZ and I was so blessed to share God's love with you and Gini and to others at your incredible youth conferences.

When I was in my twenties you told me one morning at breakfast that the Lord was going to have the story of my life bring glory to Him and that my life would be changed.

Remembering every detail you told me about my life and that I needed to name the story of my life *Out of the Closet, Into the Light*.

You never gave up and neither did Gini and I'm forever grateful to have walked with you in my life. I know that you're with God and I pray that you can see just what your life has done for me. I'm forever grateful for your life. Someday I'll see you and embrace you for life.

JORDAN JANTZ

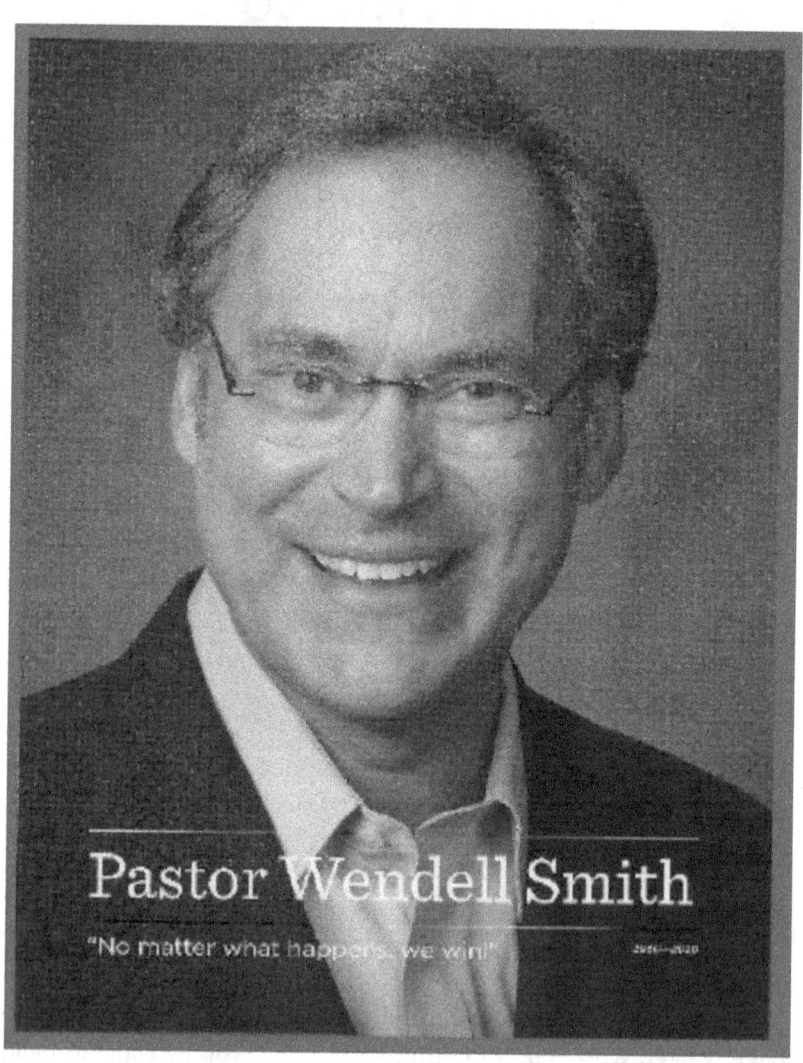

EMBRACED

One of my greatest mentors that taught me to become a dragon slayer and he and his family would invite me on trips with them to help share in reaching out to others less fortunate than myself.

JORDAN JANTZ

Wendell and Jenny Smith and I in Tucson Arizona. Their two children, Judah and Wendy, were in elementary school, so I went with Gini and Wendall to support the Dragon Slayer Conference. In Tucson is where this incredible journey of my book was birthed with Dr. Smith telling me the things the Lord plans to do with my life. Everything Dr. Smith shared about my life and what will occur when I let go of my controlled life and give ownership over to Jesus. My life would be unlimited, breaking the chains of darkness and setting the captives free. A true man of God, Wendell Smith and his wife, Gini, and their two children, Judah and Wendy will always be a family of light. You all shared good love with me.

EMBRACED

Gini Smith, You're one sister that will always have a place that God made open for me to realize that all women are not anything alike. You and I had a wonderful blessing going shopping in Tucson and I'll never forget you and I praying together for the taxi-cab driver who picked us up and took us to the Tucson Shopping Mall and you and I prayed for him after he asked us what we were doing in Tucson. And your reply was, "We are here for reaching Tucson Arizona for Christ. And he asked us to pray for him and we did it right then and there, asking all things for the cab driver to be touched by the Spirit of God's love.

Wendell, you were the best of men who taught me to love as though my life depends upon it. And you are always remembered, though you are with our Heavenly Father now, you have impacted my life forever and I pray that men who choose to love God can love others also, the way you and Gini loved me.

Forever grateful to be a part of your Dragon Slayer Conferences.

EMBRACED

Wendell and Gini Smith and me on one of many Dragon Slayer Conferences. Wendell and Gini were the ones who told me that God would use my life and through my life-story, people would have their hearts transformed through the power of Jesus Christ.

LETTER 28

To the girl I thought was my sister:

Wherever you are at today, I know I am so sorry as children feeding us both aspirin and 1-a-Day Vitamins and every pill I could find to stick in our mouths so that we could leave the world behind, for the pain of reality as a child, coming to Compton from Decatur, was overwhelmingly hard to comprehend and wanting to die was all I could do that morning. We crawled up on the sink and I fed us both pills to fall asleep from the dream no child should ever dream. I am sorry for trying to take our lives, and having to have your stomach pumped because of my own desire to leave. You see, you never realized what life was like before we came together, as family, for a moment in life.

It is better now, for you, and me. The truth has set me free.

It touched my life in many ways, never knowing what you thought or how you felt. I always hoped the best for you. I tried to help in many ways, but communication stood in the way.

You will always be remembered in all the many different events that I can remind myself of that were fun memories that we did experience. Considering circumstances today, I am so much happier today than I ever was before, because we no longer have the plastic fantastic lifestyle we've shared with one another. You are free and so am I. Never will I see on earth again what was lived in the past, but the memories always will last. Cheerleading was fun and such a blast, knowing how much I just kicked ass.

EMBRACED

Giving my all, I know, was hard when all I could see was the shame in giving you my all. I won't look back. I will not fall because I know I gave you my all. Let it go, let it go, let it go.

May you and your family share love into eternity,

<blockquote>
From the boy you
thought was your brother
</blockquote>

JORDAN JANTZ

LETTER 29

Jimmy,

    I wanted to let you know how much it means to me that you have found the time to spend with me and our family in 2015. You have become an important part of our lives, and our lives with forever be changed because of this. Looking forward to 2016 and being able to share Hannah's graduation and more opportunity to spend as a family. I can't imagine the overwhelming experience that you might be feeling at this time but what I do know is I look forward to sharing important moments to come in our lives.

    I wish I could change things in the past and I'm sorry things couldn't have been different for you. I can only think of how different our lives could have been if we had been able to stay together as a family, but know God has a plan for each of us even though we don't understand sometimes.

    We now have to focus on the time we have and make the most of every moment we can. I want you to always know you have a family regardless of what happens. Being involved in our lives moving forward and not losing touch is the key to being a family.

    One last thing before I send this letter to you... Remember I am your brother and you are a part of my family and a friend... I read somewhere that a true friend is not just a friend but a guardian angel from above and one who looks after you as the rest give up and run... I promise not to run.

Love you brother,

Ronnie Bond

Brothers, Jordan and Ronnie, above. ---Ronnie & family, below.

Uncle Jimmy,

   I'm so excited to meet you when you come to visit us! I thought I would tell you a few things about myself so you can get to know me. I turned 21 last year and I am a junior at Millikin University. I study Biology with a minor in psychology. I heard you work with children and that's really neat! I'm taking a child and Adolescent psychology course next ~~semester that I'm really excited about.~~ I also work at a pool during the summer. I am one of the pool managers and I also lifeguard. Once I'm done with school at Millikin, I am hoping to continue my education by getting my doctorate in physical therapy. Anyways, school and everything else is going great!
   Can't wait to meet you!
            ♡Hannah

EMBRACED

LOOK at my amazing niece and nephew! I'M SO PROUD!!!

JORDAN JANTZ

WHAT an amazing young lady my niece is!

Jimmy,
   Thank you for the lovely purse. That was very thoughtful of you! We are all excited to meet you on Memorial Day. I'm glad you found Ron. Family is very important to him. See you soon!!
           Love, Lisa

^ the sweet card Lisa wrote me before I got to Decatur.

Below, Lisa's tattoo! I have a matching version with a dolphin.

My very incredible nephew!

Ronnie and Jimmy Bond senior pictures. Both of us graduated from **Eisenhower High School;** Ronnie from <u>Eisenhower in Decatur</u> and Jimmy from <u>Eisenhower in California</u>.

Miracles, these are just miracles!!

Fig. 1 By Stephanie Wallentine "Best Day of Jordan's Life" Crayon on paper

LETTER 30

February 2, 2016

Dear Jordan,

I have been thinking about you and how much you have changed over the last ten years since we met you. When we first became acquainted there was one thing that was certain: you were struggling to find your way after having lived a challenging life. Even at the beginning, what was impressive was your determination to face the tests and not let them destroy you.

As you began to develop a personal relationship with Jesus Christ, your faith and hope began to grow and enhance the determination and resilience that already defined you. It brought us joy to watch you come out of the darkness that had shrouded your life for so long and emerge as a man of courage and faith. As a result, you have become a light to many people around you.

You have had to overcome countless obstacles and much prejudice because too many people doubted your commitment to allowing the Savior to transform your life. Although you experienced sadness and frustration over this, you continued to press forward in your assurance of Him who saved you from darkness.

It spite of the terrible way that you have been treated in your life and the darkness that you have experienced as a result of treatment from people who should have been there to lift you up, you have lived much of your life providing service to people in need, thus defying the bitterness you did not allow to control you. Once you came to know the Savior you were tireless in your efforts to share your light with people who are lost. Your community

EMBRACED

service of reaching out to children who have been abused or feeding the homeless has blessed the lives of many people in need.

You have also blessed our life by virtue of your sharing your life with us. When we are given an opportunity to share with others about someone who personifies strength and determination, we tell them about you. Your transformation through faith in Christ is an example of the changing power of His atonement.

We are honored to have shared our thoughts and feelings about you and are honored to call you our friend.

Much love to our brother in Christ,

Blake and Denise Smith

LETTER 31

Friends: Jeff and Jamie Burch

keepers of the
Macon County Memorial Park Cemetery
5700 West Main Street
Decatur, Illinois 62522
Garden of Memories

Jeff and Jamie are placed Jordan's grave marker on the grave plot next to his biological father on Jordan's favorite holiday just for love, Valentine's Day, 2016.

These dear friends, Jeff and Jamie Burch, were made aware by the Spirit that the writing of this book has exhausted Jordan terribly, and they called to communicate uplifting scriptures:

From Jeff: Psalms 27:23

> The steps of a good man
> are ordered by the LORD:
> and he delighteth in his way.

And from Jamie, Proverbs 3:6

> In all your ways submit to him,
> and he will make your paths straight.

On Valentine's Day these two friends will meet to dedicate my gravesite, and pray as husband and wife. They will anoint it with oil and bless it to peace and to the intent that when I am laid there, my soul will go straight to Jesus, calling on His name.

EMBRACED

LETTER 32

To the least of these, you have done it unto me, including the homeless.

Hello, this is Nicki Love, from Portland Oregon. I opened up my basement and my home to Jordan Jantz, realizing he had no one to go to and no family that he could show his face to, because of so many opportunities this man has overcome and the shame that he is able to be hope in life to today, realizing that family and friends were never around except when they wanted something from Jordan.

Jordan always has succeeded in sharing love for others that have been forgotten. Now that I know Jordan, I realize he, at one time in his life had seriously been abandoned and forgotten by his family.

That's why today I choose to remain in his life as a forever sister that will not walk away because I may feel uncomfortable. I'm committed and I'm grateful to have opened my home up to a man that is changing the lives of so many children like himself that need someone to believe in them. Even as adults, today, Jordan spreads his love before he thinks of himself, by sharing all he has with those who have nothing. We both are committed to transformation and as friends for nearly twenty years I know this friend, Jordan, is a forever committed friend to me and my life. I have never doubted Jordan's gratitude and the way his humble life has been able to touch so many lives today. He is a Voice of Hope.

Nicki Love

*Nicki is amazing **every** day.*

LETTER 33

Dear Jordan,

When we first heard your story, I was so moved by your determination and commitment to the Savior Jesus Christ. That was the thing that really attracted me to you and I had the desire to meet you and see if you were as incredible as my sister had said. I soon met you and found that you to have an exuberant personality and a love for everyone. You always told me that our friendship would be real not "plastic, super fantastic." I admire you for that. I found you to be all that my sister said and more. You have always been one hundred percent honest with me. That is a rare quality in today's society.

I think that the other thing that attracted me to you was your love for the children. You treat them as if they are very special. You always warned me to protect my children and never trust anyone else to be left alone with them. Your warnings were a valuable lesson for me. I am overly careful with them, as I should be. You have donated all of the proceeds of your books to abused and neglected children. That tells me that you really do value them because you are willing to give them everything.

Finally, I watched as you would go to the thrift store and buy enough clothing to fill your suitcase to take back to your less fortunate friends. You are always looking out for the other guy. Despite your own lack, you always want to share. Your love of humanity is your greatest gift. You always find the best in others. I feel elevated when I'm with you.

It amazes me how you have stayed true to your beliefs despite significant opposition and the difficult trials you continually

EMBRACED

face. You have shared your commitment to the Savior and your love of family. I am so blessed to have the opportunity to call you my friend, and my family.

All our love,
Rick and Janet

LETTER 34

To Our Dear Friend Jordan,

We were so excited to hear that you have been busy writing another book. You have been through so much and it is great that your story is being told. When we read your first book, we were so shocked and saddened to hear about your early life and the hardships that you endured. Your firsthand account of the child abuse that was heaped upon you at a very young age was very troubling. It is amazing that you were able to survive this tumultuous and horrifying treatment. It is even more amazing that you have overcome the inhumane treatment that was a huge part of your childhood, to become such a ray of sunshine to all of your friends and people that you come in contact with. We were so humbled to learn that you have contacted those family members that caused you so much pain and suffering, and were willing to offer them forgiveness for their sins against you. This magnanimous gesture is truly what our Savior would do. We are not sure that we have ever seen such a pure magnification of Living a Christ-like life, it is humbling to say the least.

In stark contrast to your early life including your young adulthood, which was so full of struggles that most people cannot even imagine, yet alone actually living through them, you have become a true servant to your Heavenly Father. You have given the rest of your life to do his will. We know of your love for children and the efforts that you make daily to help them and to make their lives better. Writing your books to show kids everywhere that there is hope, no matter how dark it may seem, as well as actually giving 100% of the proceeds to children's charities, really shows where your heart is.

EMBRACED

Your example of living by the Spirit has been quite evident as you have battled disease with an amazingly positive attitude. You have shown that medicine and prayers work together to heal our bodies and spirits. Your trust in Heaven has led you to the Best Doctors and Nurses available to help treat your body, and in turn your prayers and the prayers of those around you have been blessed those practitioners to perform to the best of their abilities.

Jordan, you are a great example to us of what we are put on earth to do with our lives. You give unselfishly and have such a great and magnetic child-like spirit about you that draws others to you. This is a gift from God and you realize this and are making the most of it to help all of his children, including young children, the elderly and the homeless. We can hardly wait to read the new book. Keep up the great work!

One of your many Brothers and Sisters,

Mark and Brenda Huffman

LETTER 35

February 14, 2016

Dear Jordan

It gives me great satisfaction to know that the housing projects we manage provide residences to wonderful people like you. Thank you very much for taking the time to write to me. I hope you have wonderful days at Rose Schnitzer Tower filled with happiness.

Jordan D. Schnitzer

> Look at this!!
>
> My life is so blessed at Rose Schnitzer Tower!!!

JORDAN JANTZ

⸻ LETTER 36 ⸻

(from her Christmas card)

Hi My Dear Nephew,

    Try to write you a line this morning. Mark and Robin came over Saturday and stayed 3 hours and watched the Hallmark movie with me. I was so happy. They had went to see Dale, said he is fine. I haven't went all week and not today either, my back hurts too bad for me to drive. I'm waiting to go tomorrow (Monday). Mark is getting him and Christopher is bringing him over. Hope he is up to it. It's getting chilly here now but has been just beautiful. Please excuse the writing for I can't see good to write. Got your cards and gave Mark his. Haven't got the package yet. Probably tomorrow, maybe. Hope you have a wonderful Christmas, we'll be thinking of you. Love you so much, God Bless.

*Aunt Mary and Uncle Dale **XOXO!!***

EMBRACED

Aunt Marion and Charity

LETTER 37

My friendship with Jordan over the past 10+ years has been both unique and inspiring. When I met him, he was physically weak and moving into a new and totally foreign lifestyle; he was scared, excited, and hopeful. Over the years, I've seen him blessed with much better health, evolve into an individual who can speak to large groups with poise and effectiveness, and gain great spiritual strength. Through all that he has experienced, and all he has accomplished, he has done it with humility and an eye toward serving and uplifting others.

This book is no different than much of what he's been doing all along. It will tell his story, yes, but the proceeds will go toward helping many who have or are going through similar traumas that he has experienced; he has not gained, nor will he gain monetarily from it in any way. He lives in humble circumstances and on limited resources and yet he plows forward and makes things happen that many would think him incapable of achieving.

With this publication, another chapter closes, and don't let him hear me say this, but there will be another chapter and another project - *probably not another book* - because that is the nature of his life. -Den

Den and Jordan

EMBRACED

My Aunt Frieda who found Charity for me!

(Charity puppy pic)

Hi Jordan,

I thought you would like these pictures. You are so photogenic! (I loved your outfit too!) Wasn't that a fun party? Jason's got a great house for entertaining. I'm so proud of him.

I hope you are doing well. I think of you often and always love your messages. You are always an encouragement!

Love, Joan

-P.S. Let's do pedicures again! :)

Friends like you make life sweeter than Honey!

Let it go, let it go, let it go!

04/05/2008

> Congratulations to my dear friend!

JORDAN JANTZ

> Amy Hampton
> Director
> Tiffany & Co.
>
> and
>
> Craig Hartzman   Mary O'Connor   Andy Davis
> and Jim John   and Kathleen Lewis   Patron Event Chair
> Honorary Chairs   Event Chairs
> Cascade AIDS Project
>
> invite you for breakfast
> to celebrate the launch of
>
> Cascade AIDS Project Art for Life 2005
>
> and for a special presentation
>
> Diamonds in Fashion: A Tiffany Legacy
>
> Sunday, the twenty-third of January
> ten until twelve o'clock
>
> Tiffany & Co.
> Pioneer Place
>
> R.s.v.p. by Tuesday, January 18
> (503) 223-9255
>
> Breakfast graciously provided by Food in Bloom and Starbucks

---

Today I aim to live my life giving back what CAP gave to me: <u>life-saving</u> compassion, kindness, assistance while affirming my value and never causing me to feel ashamed or like a service project. **Thank you for your care, for the years of devotion to my life that only make me want to return devotion and kindness into the world!**

EMBRACED

July 1, 2013 from your son,
Happy birthday dad,
I thank you and so very grateful also to be celebrating your life, and being

with you for the past 8 years is a blessing for me; dreams do come true on the Colorado river, and the fireworks create beautiful memories that enhance the reason and the purpose to be with you, Most men my age are not as blessed with a father that gave them special memories that they can never forget. I will have you with me in my heart and the memories you and I created together from childhood to adulthood for the rest of my life, And I will thank Jesus for your love and saving me when you took me as your son when I was 4 years old, I have

never forgotten that day. You will know just what you have done for me when you see Jesus. We are here for a short time and then gone. Dad you showed me each day is an opportunity to choose where to put my trust. Remembrance of your actions as my dad I use

to punctuate our time and enrich our walk upon the earth this single day. Many of us are exhausted by desperate search for answers. Some still have not discovered the answer to the purpose of their life. Dad you taught me that Jesus says, come to me, all you who are heavy laden, And I will give you rest....My yoke is easy, and my burden is light. To offer gifts is to affirm that, yes, we are a part of all this. Here, alive on earth, we receive and we give. We receive the care of so many, and we fertilize joy, kindness, and healing for ourselves, and

2013 Letter of love with gratitude for my adoptive father, pg 1

for all our family on the earth. You dad and your wonderful wife Liz have given me restored love that I've missed in my adult life. Thank you both for your honest hearts that I know I can trust. Good hearted people mean the world to me. You also taught me to be content with what I have, rejoice in the way things are when I realize there is nothing lacking, the whole world belongs to you. Dad hard it is to understand but you taught me in boy scouts by giving away food, we get more strength, by bestowing clothing on others, we gain more

beauty, by donating abodes of purity and truth, we acquire great treasures. Dad you always told me that the boy scouts motto be prepared And do your best. And the charitable man has found the path of salvation. True kindness is rooted in a deep sense of abundance you

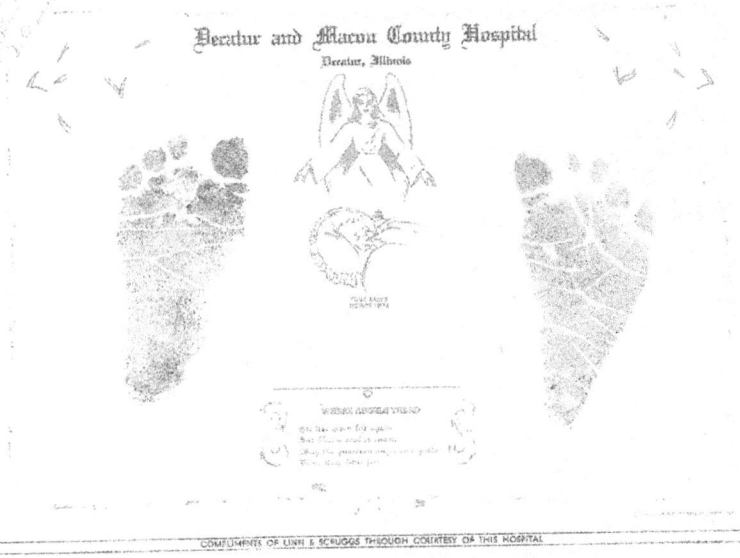

2013 Letter of love with gratitude for my adoptive father, pg 2

would teach this stuff to me dad. We are visitors on this planet. We are here for ninety, a hundred years at the very most. During this period dad we must try to do something good, something useful with our lives. Try to be at peace with ourselves and help others share that peace. If you and I dad contribute to

other peoples happiness, you and I will find the true goal, maybe even the meaning of why you adopted this 4 year old who has grown into a son who thanks god for his earthly father, you have taught me the meaning of life. Because if tomorrow is judgment day and I'm standing on the frontline, And the lord asks me what I did with my life, I will say I spent it loving your people lord. Dad you taught me how to show my love for god. And that god will never abandon me. Dad I remember how hard during the week you worked, But I didn't know it at the time. I remember when you came home from work, you set your briefcase by the door, and swoop me up into your arms. You would say jimmy are you ready to play? You would spray me with the hose, lead expeditions through the elementary school while you and I would go jogging around the school, you would read to me all kinds of

2013 Letter of love with gratitude for my adoptive father, pg 3

Fairy Tales. Your career didn't define you. When you were home, you were just my dad. I didn't even know what did for a living until I was much older. But here is what I do know. The briefcase didn't move again until you left the next morning. There was never any doubt about what came first for you dad. Thank you for spending your days with me .oh, dear daddy my dear dad, I wish sometimes we could go back and do it all over again, maybe someday in heaven. Happy birthday I will never abandoned you or stop loving you. You came to me from our heavenly father. You are the best earthly father any guy would want. God picked you and I out to learn and grow as father and son. And you are the best gift in my world. Sorry I don't tell you this more often dad, but it is your birthday so my heart wants you to know the whole truth of how I feel about you.

Happy Birthday Celebrating the past eight years of your life on the Colorado River! This will always and forever be my tradition celebrating your life each year on the majestic and spiritual Colorado River until the day I see you in heaven.

I love you. You've nevre left my heart, Dad and I will always love you.
Your son, Jimmylee Grubbs   503-223-3648
731 SW Salmon St., Apt. 203, Portland, OR. 97205

Enjoy these photos of the life you changed by being a father to the fatherless. You changed this 4 year old boys life forever. No father compares to you. I'm grateful for the values I've learned from you. No man on this earth could ever touch my heart and life like you have. You're simply the best. Dad, remember you are amazing just the way you are. Nobody will ever hold a candle to you ever!!!

2013 Letter of love with gratitude for my adoptive father, pg 4

This is the first time you saw me. Four months later I was on a plane in my sailors' suite. I will never forget this moment and how you changed my life into hope. No more abandonment. I love you for what you have done for my life.
I will always be your son,
Happy Birthday!!!!

2013 Letter of love with gratitude for my adoptive father, pg 5

JORDAN JANTZ
ABOUT THE AUTHOR

Jordan Jantz was raised in southern California, moved to Portland Oregon and has lived there throughout his adult years. His most valuable possession is his 14-year-old service dog, Charity, who has been in his life longer than any family on a continual daily basis. She inspires Jordan to advocate for children who have been abandoned, given up and forgotten from their families. Jordan's mission is to be Portland's advocate for saving the lives of abused children.

Jordan's mission is a lighthouse all over the Pacific Northwest. Jordan is known for support for his fundraisers including Make-A-Wish foundation and the Ronald McDonald House. Jordan has accepted awards for his first book about his life-story, *Out of the Closet, Into the Light*. Jordan's royalty proceeds went directly to the Christmas Box House. Jordan's consistent commitment is to be the best philanthropist for children who suffer child abuse. Because of this Jordan was offered the opportunity to have a second book published where 100% of the proceeds would go to the Christmas Box House International, if Jordan could share where his life is at today because of the blessings of medical doctors, case-managers and a variety of agencies in the Pacific Northwest that help support Jordan in sharing Jordan's process of healing and the God-given opportunities presented in his life to be the change he wishes for all children in the world today.

This second book, *Embraced,* also addresses the pertinent issues of Jordan's life and message and that is to reflect God's unconditional kindness and love for everyone.

EMBRACED

By the way, one secret about Jordan Jantz is that he has developed a reputation in the LGBT communities around the United States with his Voices of Hope project and by receiving North Star's Beacon of Light Award after his first book was released which went to the top of the charts so unexpectedly. With humility and humbleness Jordan has been given the gift of sharing his life to many conferences, firesides, benefits and child prevention presentations for public Child Protective Services.

Another miracle is that today Jordan has found his biological family. He has brothers and sisters, and he has just learned that he has an uncle and several cousins. Jordan has also embraced the love and kindness he has received from his sister-in-law and his niece and nephew, as this wonderful sister-in-law married Jordan's brother who is the only one that responds to the reality that Jordan is his biological brother who actually is kind and seems to have love for his lost brother, Jordan.

As Team Jordan we as a group realize that this new book, *Embraced*, will bring you *Out of the Closet, Into the Light* of what it is like to be found and never understanding what love really is about. You will feel your life's calling after becoming *Embraced*.

BIOGRAPHICAL FACTS

Born in Decatur, Illinois, Dec 2 1959 to Eldon Roy Bond and biological mother, as James Lee Bond.

Sold at age five to a family is California, was re-named Jimmylee.

Grew up in Southern California, a tap dancer and entertainer and model and in younger years, pep squad was Jordan's outlet for his sealed emotions. Jordan had leadership skills from early childhood, became polished in survival skills. Won the National Cheerleading Competition at Pepperdine University in Malibu Beach, California. Performed in various Disney productions throughout the country, including all Disney resorts.

Moved to Portland, Oregon for career change at age nineteen.

Enjoys watching cooking channels.

Favorite movies: *The Ultimate Gift*, *The Blind Side* and *Titanic*.

Favorite Male Vocalist: Adam Levine and Justin Timberlake

Favorite Female Vocalists: Katie Perry and Christian Aguilera

Favorite Actor: Leonardo DiCaprio

Favorite Actress: Angela Bassett

Favorite Gay Actor: Neil Patrick Harris

EMBRACED

Favorite Lesbian Actress: Jodie Foster

Favorite TV Programs: The Academy Awards, the Grammys, the Oscars and the Emmys, especially when Neil Patrick Harris hosts as he is Jordan's favorite comedian.

Favorite Colors: White, pink and green, with a splash of blue, crisp and glossy, glazed, strong but deep... an obsessively, compulsively perfect color-wheel that suits Jordan's life.

Scariest thing as a child: Getting his baby teeth pulled, because it was done the old fashioned way, with string tied around the tooth. Jordan was talked to in a soothing kind way, and then all the sudden, "Shebang! The tooth came out of my mouth! And I was so excited for the fairy (who took care of all the little boys' teeth) to slide money under my pillow and take my tooth. I knew I always liked fairies."

Favorite Birthday: Jordan says, "Celebrating my life in the jungle with no bathrooms, no electricity and filled with the most happy children on the earth! They made me a tropical ice cream birthday cake with fresh coconut cream frosting and fresh frozen mango ice cream with caramelized mango sauce. The ice cream never even melted, but everything caramelized into the most beautiful birthday cake, ever. It was an angel food cake filled with lemon meringue which gave it a tropical flavor of lime, mangos and pineapples with a caramelized mandarin orange sauce over it, after it was baked in the ground! This was the highlight of all birthday cakes, ever! I'm a jungle boy at heart!"

Favorite TV show: The Voice

Favorite beverage: Coconut water, which Jordan says is the most healthy and wholesome drink on the planet.

JORDAN JANTZ

Lifetime Goal: To give back all that was taken from the lives of children who lost their own voice while trying to protect themselves from the pain and suffering that others put on their lives.

Most Embarrassing Thing: Sharing the truth in front of the world of the misfortune and improper choices made by desperate circumstances in my life, making choices that forever carry shame. Through it all, I still have enormous amounts of embarrassment and I pray that people that have touched my life in a positive way will understand that I have had to hide the truth until now. But I haven't lost anything because many have walked away.

Favorite Gift: The grave plot next to Jordan's biological father, given to Jordan on Memorial Day 2015 by his biological brother, Ronnie Bond. The grave marker was placed on Valentine's Day, 2016. Ronnie and Jordan together chose what the grave marker would say, which is, "Lost Son Found, Home With Jesus." Jordan is so grateful that he did not have to use the name *Jantz*.

Biggest Regrets: Suicide attempt, with weights tied around ankles, jumped from the Burnside Bridge, Portland, 4am Mother's Day 1996, pulled out by Portland's lifeboat team, and letting people control my name and identity of who I am expected to become.

Saddest Moment: Being lied about to Jordan's sister and her family. Jordan says, "But I know that within her soul she knows what makes me tick, for she grew up as close as my twin, throughout many years, to some degree. I would call her family, though, I've been with my dog longer than I've been with any family on this earth. I guess, for me, it is a matter of the heart. I've got love in my life that redeems the lives of children, and I'm comfortable letting go. What a blessing to be free from the drama and leave it all to Mama, who created the drama." *Let it go, let it go, let it go!*

EMBRACED

Happiest Moment: Finding out the truth about Jordan's life's genealogy and history, that Jordan never knew existed, with no performances asked, none of them even know what Jordan's life severely encountered. This privacy gives Jordan so much pleasure to have the freedom to be able to walk in his hometown and with his family with gratitude and honor for being a philanthropist in his life today, transforming children who have been traumatized like himself. <u>That</u> is Jordan's biggest gratitude and happiest moment – to be a Voice of Hope and a Beacon of Light – unto the children of the world.

This is what Jordan wants to be remembered by, "For it will not matter when I am dead what I did for a living, how much money I made, or how big my home was, what kind of car I drove or what I looked like, all of this will be meaningless to life after I'm dead! Reality- the most valuable asset to embed in my heart is to embrace forgiveness as though my life depends upon it, for I've never before knew how to see myself properly, from the confusion of knowing that my value of my life in dollars.

Today, *I'm free, I'm free at last*. I am set free from the bondages, for God has opened my life more and I feel that my brother, Ronnie, and my uncle, Bill, have the keys and my brother's wife, Lisa, has the ax to break the chains that have held me captive in believing what others told me I was born to become. I feel that life surely will see transformation very soon for God uses the people who are prepared for spiritual war.

I'm ready for the frontlines to protect my brother and our relationship that is founded and built on Jesus Christ, with our brotherhood going into eternity, along with the love he and his wife have for one another and their two children. I feel like today I'm experiencing people that are able to love me deeply. I know this is foreign, but even my niece and nephew act as though *I have been*

JORDAN JANTZ

missed. Love is the greatest gift that creates the happiest times in my life!"

Most peaceful place: Embracing the Colorado River

Favorite spot to escape expectations and pressures: On Scudder Avenue, Hyannis Port, MA, there sits a simple white painted Cape Cod style two-floor home with a veranda that wraps around the front and sides, furnished simply and elegantly, with a pool and tennis court which Jordan used every day. From this home were many summer jaunts that Jordan used to go fishing. Walks on the beach provided much tranquility for Jordan, giving him meditation times during difficulty in life. No matter what calamity was going on in the rest of the fashion industry, Hyannis Port was a trademark for fishing and some of the best sea food fishing in the United States.

The people that lived on the sands of Nantucket Sound hosted wonderful tranquil parties and social events for the community. That is where Jordan first met John F. Kennedy, Jr., who was Jordan's age. John lived in Hyannis Port and also in off and on in New York, throughout his life. John very much had a wonderful spirit that embraced life. John and Jordan both enjoyed swimming and both had a passion for children who are handicapped and disabled. That's where Jordan's heart fell for John's kindness, in Hyannis Port, at the Special Olympics that were held in Cape Cod, which gave special meaning and value to this special man that would later produce a magazine called *George,* and to my surprise, was a wonderful magazine for business entrepreneurs.

A couple of times Jordan laughed so hard when John told Jordan about a time when John was being interviewed on the Tonight Show, along with Farrah Faucet. John said Farrah spent over an hour in the dressing room with a make-up artist and hair stylist, then came out on the show and was asked about her make-

EMBRACED

up and hair and style and told a LA Studio audience, "Oh, my hair? Oh, I just wake up in the morning, sort of toss it around, and *it is what it is*! It's just a mane. That's how it comes out to be every day!"

John said, "The rest of us were in stiches because we all knew how long she'd been in the dressing room, having her make-up and hair done. It isn't easy when people expect beauty twenty-four hours a day, without a break for a moment to find a flaw. People search for flaws, Jordan, so be glad you are open about your life, because once you hide it you have to keep on hiding it."

John had to do that throughout his life. Jordan will always feel blessed for his fishing and many political get-aways with people who embraced his life in Hyannis Port, MA.

If Jordan could be any man Jordan has experienced for a weekend: John F Kennedy Jr. He loved to rollerblade, loved the sun and outdoors. He was intelligent enough to represent George Magazine and was kind and engaging. He is missed since he passed away in an airplane crash July 16, 1999 while he was flying to Martha's Vineyard.

Favorite Food: Italian

Favorite Language: Italian

Favorite Hotel: The Broadmoor Resort in Colorado Springs, Colorado

Favorite place to snowboard: Lake Tahoe

Collections: Dolphin things

JORDAN JANTZ

Favorite dream: Jordan says, "To be where I am needed and wanted most of all, kind of like being where you are celebrated and not tolerated, would be nice. I'm tired of the competition, finally, at my age. I'm ready to be content just as I am. Let it go, let it go, let it go!"

Most spiritual encounter: Swimming with dolphins in captivity and in the wild throughout various where they can be found. Jordan says, "If I believed in re-incarnation, I would come back as a dolphin, no questions asked, because they have the character and personality of the man that I have always been and am today, whether or not my tail is broken, I still can swim with one fin!"

Adult: Well-traveled throughout the entire United States, except Alaska, and exotic locations and resorts doing modeling shoots for various magazines and clothing lines. Been on commercials promoting various products throughout life. Taught Cheerleading, as Jordan was the first male to be on the cheerleading squad in Southern California. Jordan always knew he was different.

Oldest Movie Contract: the Screen Actors Guild in LA, since age 14, when Jordan was thespian. Jordan was working hard dancing on American Bandstand on the weekends and would stay with people he never even knew, from the Screen Actors Guild, all of them living in Hollywood, trying to make it in the business. It was refreshing to Jordan to be centrally located, where Jordan was not stuck in the Hollywood scene, but had the benefits of making it in commercials and in entertainment opportunities that led to other opportunities, that led to *other* opportunities that Jordan would never want to even discuss. The opportunities became endless opportunities. Through the Screen Actors Guild Jordan was able to be promoted and photographed even though he was under-aged and Jordan's family had no problem letting him take off and go and do things that they knew nothing about, until after the magazine or the

EMBRACED

commercial would air. If they paid attention, they knew that Jordan was all that they had hoped for when they purchased Jordan, and Jordan just prays that he gave them all the happiness that Jordan only knew how to give, but Jordan will leave his hope for the best to come out of the most challenging circumstances of Jordan's life, to become a light for others.

Favorite song: "Like a Bridge Over Troubled Water" as performed by Clay Aiken

Favorite flower: Bird of Paradise

Favorite Author: Jewel Adams of Jewel of the West Publishing

Favorite Book by Jewel Adams: *Til You Come Back to Me Again.* Jordan says, "I love the fact that Jewel steps out of the box and has the ability to be in touch with a human emotion called Romance. Most people have not the ability to even show romance within their life, for another. But when I learned of Jewel Adams' romance books, I couldn't help but know she was the one to write the biography of the story of my life, *Out of the Closet, Into the Light*. I am grateful that she has embraced the love of this adventure in my life and celebrates happiness with me in the second book, *Embraced*, that completes the set by telling where my life is today. For men and for women, this author is amazing."

Favorite Film Festival in the world: Sundance, located in Park City, Utah, owned and operated by Robert Redford, owner of Sundance Film Festival. A great place to people watch!

Favorite Experience: Jordan says, "Dancing in the rain and embracing my spiritual family who know everything of truth regarding my life and they love me anyway for they love me just as I am."

JORDAN JANTZ

Favorite Female Politician: Mary Lee Brown of Decatur, Illinois (my aunt).

Favorite Disney Performance: Mickey Mouse Extravaganza. It is amazing how Disney can build confidence for children and adults who embrace opportunities. It was an honor to share my life with Disney.

Favorite Pier: The first pier Jordan was ever on, since he was five years old when he moved to California and that is the Newport Beach Pier. It is where the surfing competition every year is held and Jordan is at home. It is Jordan's favorite festival of the year, and Jordan is able to meet many people from years gone by that Jordan knew growing up in Southern California. Jordan says, "I wish I could bring my biological brother and my biological nephew and sister-in-law and niece to this beautiful festival where I first learned to surf, as any young California boy normally would gravitate to the sea to be free. Come and be set free with me and experience what the Southern California life is really like!"

Favorite Man in the World: "Running Bull," Jordan's father who raised Jordan after he was sold to him as a son, took Jordan ("Swift Arrow") to Indian Guides to have adventures with the best man God created for his life.

Favorite Musical Group: Reggae music from Ziggy Marlow and UB40. Jordan saw them both in Santa Fe, New Mexico for a Reggae Fest decades ago, and Reggae is still going strong!

Hardest Time in School: When held back in 4th grade, told that this would remove from me homosexual desire to hold hands with the boys instead of the girls. This ended up causing Jordan to go through school as a "twin" with the girl he thought was his sister.

EMBRACED

Happiest Time in School: When Jordan won State Champs at Pepperdine University hosting National Cheerleading for the NCAA. Jordan was the first male to be in the pep squad in the state of California back in the late 70s. Jordan says, "I never let being gay hold me back because like the song says, I was born that way."

First Concert Jordan ever Went To: Jordan was 15 and brought a signed parent's written permission form to Elton John's Goodbye Yellow Brick Road Tour-1975 at the LA Colosseum. Oh, those shameful oldies but goodies!

Favorite Sport: Professional Surfing

Favorite Friend Growing up: Terri, the best cheerleader, Jordan says, who "taught me to kick a**! I had fun, even if I was the only man who had the guts to support team spirit. I tried to play the gay away for many years until I broke down, though now I know I am the man that God created and I am worth loving by you and by God. Open your heart to me, for I hold the lock and you hold the key." - Jordan's favorite saying.

Current life: Philanthropist advocating for abused children throughout life.

Biggest Accomplishment in Life: Jordan says, "Receiving the Beacon of Light Award from North Star International, for I have never before been considered a Godly man. But I have never hidden the truth of myself. Because of that truthfulness, it made my life difficult. If I had been less honest, my life would have been a whole lot easier."

Books: First Volume of the Book Set of The Life Story of Jordan Jantz, *Out of the Closet, Into the Light*, authored by Jewel Adams of Jewel of the West Publishing in 2013. This book opens up

JORDAN JANTZ

Jordan's coming into the world, having no clue of the hand he was about to be dealt. First Edition of Second Volume of the Book Set of The Life Story of Jordan Jantz, *Embraced*, was released on Valentine's Day of 2016. This is the up-to-date telling of the life of Jordan Jantz and where he is at in his place in this world.

Favorite Inspiration: Children finding hope and being there for them as their families are able to embrace the responsibility of loving one another. That's when I feel most complete and that I have touched a life. That is my only inspiration for my life.

Best friend: Basenji, black and white, an exotic barkless breed from Africa, named Charity. Friends for fourteen years. Bow wow!

Long-time friend and **Favorite Pilot in the World** *and his beautiful family. Love you, Mark!*

EMBRACED

My favorite television show as a child: the Brady Bunch. I was, of course in love with Mike and I was heart-broken when he passed away!

Marsha, Marsha, Marsha!!!

The doll on the right was created to look like Jordan in connection with his tap dancing for Disney. The doll is a replica in every detail including the clothing Jordan wore.

JORDAN JANTZ

Favorite Book from **Favorite** *Author, Jewel Adams*

EMBRACED

*Aunt Marion and I take our **first selfies**, after Lisa shows us how to do it. A special <u>thank you</u> to my friends Mike and Stephanie who loaned a camera for these life-changing events!*

JORDAN JANTZ

APPENDIX

Daily mandatory routine care
and decoration of the body
including diet, exercise and clothes
for male models

This was my life. This is my history. This is what I knew that would keep me from day one to day two, throughout the week, throughout the month, throughout the years.

As a model, exercise is everything. Swimming is my favorite exercise. I usually swim sidestroke because I find that the crawl and breaststroke put too much strain on my lower back. My doctors put me on to that. Also, the backstroke and sidestroke keep my hair pretty dry. On days that I don't care about getting my hair wet, I do the dead man's float for as long as I have time, usually for forty or forty-five minutes, just hanging in the water, facedown, arms outstretched, feet floating, everything inertly hanging on the surface of the water.

Before I do the dead man's float, I will have backstroked twenty laps or more. Some people get in a pool, swim two or three laps and call that exercise. I don't. For people who swim regularly, twenty laps is a moderate work out. Swimming is the most complete exercise I do. I grew up with a built-in swimming pool, so I have lived in the water my whole life, diving off diving boards as high as they could be. These days there is no excuse for not swimming. There are pools everywhere, and a person can joy a health club like I have for a modest amount and swim all year round.

EMBRACED

Greatest tonic for anxiety and nerves that I know is the ultimate relaxer, and I also do some limbering up exercises which are designed to keep me loose. I always danced throughout my life thought I got a lot of knee problems, after fifty years of stage performances. Of course, many times on the catwalk I walked right off the stage (five feet up!) and would fall into the audience, forgetting how many steps I had taken or when to turn right or left or follow lead, or turn around and go to the back, and come straight back out for another entrance, at times landing on the side of the stage. How embarrassing! But to be in good shape, that was the most important on all injuries.

I usually hold on to the back of a chair and do a lot of kicks and squats, and toe and heel things that hark back to my old dancing school days. You can do it just as well, just move your legs around, trying to make them as limber as possible. You've seen dancers at the dance studio, getting prepared for their performance. It doesn't matter what you do as long as you have got your legs, knees and waist in motion. Next, I drop to the floor on all fours, let my back sag, completely relaxing, then I arch my back up like a cat as far as I can, then I drop everything down again and I do this motion five times, stretching up and back, as far as I can, each time. It is *mandatory* to keep your posture as a model or you simply won't have the job.

As far as face lifting and other surgical cosmetic aids are concerned, I'm all for them as long as you can afford a good surgeon and you can bear the pain and discomfort that are involved. A lot of male models say, "Well, I know my face has gone to pot but my wife loves me the way I am." Don't kid yourself. Not about the truth. No one wants to be unattractive. I weigh the very same today as I weighed at my lowest, when made my first cover-shoot for the Sears Catalog. I don't think exercising is what keeps my weight constant so much as the fact that I don't over-eat and barely eat at that. People who are too much into food for reasons other than hunger (to compensate for frustrations of one kind or another) I totally relate and understand, for I can sit and eat big portions at one time, if I am depressed that I did not get what I had been hoping to get. Depression affects each person individually and differently, whether it be over-eating or any other form of eating disorder. I've been there, done that, worn out the t-shirt. But food is vital to be a success in anything in front of a camera or in life, period. Food and water are necessities.

I eat simple foods but I often start the day with holistic teas. I also do not accommodate candy or ice cream for I never indulged in the calories, for I counted calories every day.

Male models always have some type of translucent make-up on while doing a photoshoot or showing up at a benefit. Outdoors-y type is what I am, and I don't like a lot of photoshoots that deal with make-up. I avoid them, personally. My pet dislike is the heavy pancake foundation that is applied with a sponge. It really wipes out any individuality your face may have. Many men use this because of facial shaving, and the camera picks up every whisker that has not been shaved.

Make-up is very personal and no two faces can really be treated in the same way. I have a friend who has very hard skin with a lot of dryness to it. He tried going without foundation at one of the photoshoots we worked together one afternoon, and we came up with a rose colored foundation that transformed him, and ended up changing the whole photoshoot of his look. His brown eyes, which I shadowed with a pale tan toned base to give him a deeper set of brown eyes, stood out in the photoshoot and made the set of glasses that we were modeling for optimum eye care clinics a hit at all the newsstands and it was a cover shot that made many optometrists very successful in their sales.

EMBRACED

The fact of the matter is that I don't spend much time on make-up myself. Today, it is out of the question, since I no longer do photoshoots or advertisements. But when I did, I was up and ready to go with the best of them. I simply don't have the time for the make-up. Modeling itself really wore me out. There were long hours, and of course almost all the time and attention is given the lighting specialist that is putting the heat lamps on the model, which is melting you with at least 90 degrees on your skin, while you try to feel as fresh as possible with a fan blowing on you, and wish for a gallon of water.

After many years of learning the industry, so many mistakes can be avoided, I know now. I could write a book. I feel that at times, I'm pretending to be somebody else when I'm on the stage because of what the people are expecting from me. I have to be all things to so many people that it is possible to forget who you really because I become what is expected, because I know what will pay the bills. All I do for myself is pray that I can just keep my appearance so that I can continue to live. Most people think modeling is glamorous and attractive but it is the hardest thing I've ever done. It was an honest living, with an honest paycheck. The older you get, the more you have to transform. So I did, all the way.

And I'm not mean to suggest that everyone go blond or follow my lead. There is a young man who works for my dentist who is very blond and has the palest skin I've ever seen. Everything about him is light. His skin and hair, they all match. You need to have a contrast if you are blond, and you need color to match. You can't get away with just being blond. You have to complement the blond with color.

Next, you have to choose the right cologne, to match your own personality. I was surprised that I could identify the scent of colognes so easily. There is really nothing to it. What is in practically every man's bathroom is a bottle of cologne. I realized that I had to get the message quick – cologne is a personal signature. For skin scents there are so many attributes from cleansing creams, to face creams that you use to apply with certain sponges, to keep the facial skin in order. I like to use a body lotion after my shower and I use one that has a very light scent that quickly disappears. Then I splash on my favorite scent: Acqua Di Gio for men, and that is about it.

I am affiliated with a favorite of mine, a cucumber skin freshener that I really like, and I use it whenever I shower. It is different from the regular cleansers. It is natural. I just rub it across my face and eyes while I am in the shower and let it sit for a moment, along with many various home remedies to keep the face looking its best. Once a week I use a mask. It is good for circulation and makes my skin tingle and glow. It has the consistency of toothpaste and it is easy to apply. I cover my entire face and neck with it, and leave it on for about twenty minutes, then rinse it off with tepid water.

I like to do my fingernails and toenails when I am in a good hot bathtub. I use a cuticle remover to get off the dead skin. And I use a terry-face-clothe to push back the cuticle. I never cut the cuticle on nails or toe-nails, because the more you cut it the more you have to continue to keep it up. I do my own nails and I always have, although I do enjoy getting together with the guys for a pedi and a mani. I like a clear-coat or the buffered look on my nails. Most male models always have a clear-coat, which is easier and faster to keep up and keep clean.

I wash my hair every other day and use only my fingers to towel dry and let the messy beach look fall into place. Some call it the *southern-cal* look. It is just a look of many that has always been a part my personality and character, and has made me a living with maintaining my profile.

EMBRACED

One night a week I make it a practice to cover my entire body – head to toe – with coconut oil. I buy coconut oil in huge jars for this purpose. I rub it thoroughly and apply it thickly. I then put on a flannel shirt and lightweight socks to cover my feet and go to sleep like that. Of course, if you are sleeping with somebody, you are not a very appetizing number in this condition. It is best to be in a separate bed on this occasion.

Coconut oil has a rather yummy smell, which is not at all offensive but very pleasant. It does wonders for the body, especially the feet. I like to walk barefoot which tends to roughen up the bottom of my feet and the back of my heels. Coconut oil will soak in and remove the dryness completely. The only danger connected with the over-night-coconut-oil-on-you soak is that you can slide out of bed, which I have done many times. This is because the oil wasn't just on my face, it was on my whole body, trying to restore it all back to the age of 21. *Keep dreaming,* I say to myself, as I prepare for my photoshoot the next day. (Thank god those days are long gone and over with.)

About clothing, if you do not have the body, you better work the clothes. One of the lessons I learned during my many years was how not to dress. I watched too many Doris Day and Rock Hudson movies with grandma to learn how important clothes are. Rock Hudson always made everyone want to be like him, and Doris Day made every woman want to be like her. That was the only rule I know is reality in the modeling business: Fashion. Don't dress for the sake of fashion, dress because you *are* fashion. Put only on your body what looks good on your body. Some people are able to put anything on and look fantastic. When I was young I was able to get away with wearing almost anything, but as the years went on I realized that I had to watch what I wore, for things were cut differently and fit differently the older I became.

JORDAN JANTZ

There are such prejudices about clothes, almost none of them valid, like the prejudice against the color grey. That is an ugly color to me, for some reason, but it looks really good on some people. And some people photograph great in that color, and the same way with whites and blacks, which are the most neutral and photographic colors on people (besides brown).

As far as jewelry is concerned, my taste is toward old pieces. I like silver. I have some antique bracelets that I like and some Indian jewels, though I don't wear them often. I have a lot of turquoise. That is a favorite and is my birthstone, and I love the mother of pearl stone. That, I like to wear a lot. I like the color of mother of pearl as well as silver or platinum bracelets and rings that are made with this beautiful stone. I am not big on the color gold for jewelry, but I love platinum. I don't wear big pieces that are heavy looking or that seem to carry me rather than the opposite.

I feel the same way about the clothes I wear. I don't want my clothes to wear me. So often I see men who are wearing overpowering clothes. You can't find the man if you can hardly see him, so lost in his big hat and his big coat. It is hard to see the physique and the cut of the pants and the cut of the shirt and the style, and that is what the buyers are looking for. I don't think any man is ever justified in wearing anything that covers up the cut and style of the clothes, for that is the purpose of modeling, to show what you are wearing and what you've got.

One last word about modeling throughout my life and the prerequisites that are required to be the best at such an early age - what really does the most wonders for a person's face and body – the greatest face lift, is a *thinking*-lift. Our faces reflect what we are thinking and when we have clouded, negative or bitter thoughts, thoughts with fear and hate in them, our faces and our eyes show these stressors of truth no matter what we do. Who we are inside and what we feel comes out no matter what we do to ourselves to

EMBRACED

look top notch and be able to become the super-model to make the mortgage and put food on the table.

Reality is that when thoughts are positive and loving, a person's entire face relaxes. Down lines go up. Worry lines ease out of the face and are removed. This is true reality. And a beauty secret to all men- the body lifts in spirit and soul, and the soul is uplifted also by the body's spirit being lifted. It is the greatest cosmetic of all and it doesn't cost a cent.

If you can contain this natural beauty from within, you can throw out the kitchen sink and be the owner of the runway and make a living without a lifestyle of daily routines that I have had to live with, which could have been avoided, as all are the benefit of living in happiness.

MEMORIES TO TAKE WITH YOU

BE WHERE YOU ARE CELEBRATED NOT TOLERATED

We all have experienced in our life inklings of truth. I have since I was a barefooted boy. I was always persistent and my most profound and meaningful memories are of people getting to see the light in themselves. I've been strengthened by the sharing of God's light, but most of all, His love to others outside my comfort zone. As I move into the next chapter of my life, I know that sharing my love will hold an even greater place with God. It is what I'm called to do. We're all called. If you are here, breathing, you have a contribution to make to our human community. The real work of my life is to figure out my function and my part in the whole picture of life as soon as possible, and not procrastinate and be a man of my word. And then, I must get about my business of fulfilling my word and honesty to the world.

Each creature God made must live in its own true nature. Part of my blessing and challenge as being human is that I honesty must discover my own God-given nature. This for sure cannot be some noble thing or abstract quest, but my inner necessity. For only by living in my own personal element can I thrive without carrying the baggage of anxiety. For me, it is imperative that I find that vital element that brings you and I alive and brings people of light together on this earth. For me, true vitality and integrity bring people together with an open heart to share God's spirit and his love. If I can discover what I honesty enjoy and love and if I can feel the energy and grab on to the excitement and the sense that life is

EMBRACED

happening for me better than ever, now, or even maybe for the first time in my life

I feel peace in my heart for all my friends on this earth. That means, to me, I am probably near my personal God-given calling and God's Holy Spirit is guiding me. Joy in what I do on this earth is not an added feature. It is a sign to me of deep health and growth within my own life. There is no greater gift I can give or receive than to honor my own personal calling. It is why I was born, and how I become most truly alive.

Now, let's be real with each other. You all on this earth who have given your life and friendship in so many ways, and you all know who you are, are very important to me and to many people. And remember, there are people out there who value you and you don't even know them. So I want to ask you to always remain confident and remember that all things work for the good for those that love the Lord. That's what God says in his Bible. I thank you all for going out of your way in my life. I have had the blessings in life from being honest and truthful. God put many of you in my life for His purpose and for His reason. I thank you for reaching out and pulling me out of the closet and into the light of God's love, When I couldn't pull my own self out, many of you were there. I would like you to remember that it is very important to speak truth and stand by your word for sharing your time and your life with me has been valuable to my life. We have shared the best years of life and they are simply the best. It has been wonderful making memories that I cherish today and forever into eternity because cherish is the word that reminds me of all of you.

What a tremendous price has been paid, more than all the riches in the entire world. This price was paid so that I could know the joy of being forgiven because forgiveness reveals the heart of God and I know that we all must leave at one point in our life and for me, I

JORDAN JANTZ

want to leave as a dolphin, swimming out to sea, swimming away from my pod towards the deepest, bluest oceans of all. That's when I will let go of my past and journey on to where I belong.

Thank you, all for sharing your life with me.

FINAL CURTAIN CALL

I have bitter sweet emotions over writing the truth and opening up my life. I thought of the first line and how would it start? So I started, preparing the book, working rapidly. Words would come out. I didn't choke until the end of each chapter. I survived many chapters that broke my spirit and heart. I documented accomplishments, achievements, showing broadcasting and journalism skills from my career as a model. As a man, written such vulnerable truth was such a deeply spiritual opening and I hope this true story speaks to each community.

As we turn the pages in the best stories of my life in this book, *Embraced,* an in the book, *Out of the Closet, Into the Light,* I am very up close and personal. I can't possibly thank the thousands of people across the world that helped me in this great project to bring freedom to the lives of children through the first production of Jordan's Underground 4 Saving the Lives of Children. That's what the purpose of my life is, 'til I leave this planet. In this book I do not try to convince. It is my aim to give you enough of my reasonings and evidence so that you can decide for yourself what you feel about all these issues.

My book, *Embraced,* reveals the inner life of millions of children.

Confessing the truth of my life came with a great opportunity to bring a about great charity for children. Now, I can comprehend and express better what it meant when I was young, when to my chagrin it seemed that everyone was drinking the invention of my new life: a new child protégé brought out for others. Though my second family came with luxuries, I certainly missed spending a misspent youth. I earned my reputation as the best in

JORDAN JANTZ

California, as I tap-danced throughout parades and auditions, which all came to me so naturally. I had to put in hours of practice every day and keep at it, always recalling my biological mom's words that in order for me to be ever be wanted and never have to be moved around again, I have to be the best little boy in the world. Fame was never the goal of my youthful years and throughout my adult years, though I needed great notoriety to survive. To this day I wake up in night terrors. Thank God for my happy pill from my fabulous doctors, who have worked as a team with me for seventeen years to address the history of my life challenges that were put upon me.

Never did I expect any of these accomplishments for myself, for I grew up never being affirmed of any accomplishment, except my appearance, and how good looking I was and, "What nice teeth and hair and what a photoshoot that was, on the first take!" In this book I pay tribute to my modeling/broadcasting survival system, taking everyone on that rollercoaster part of my life, while acknowledging impact of the many abandoned moments. I once carved a glamorous career out of the obligation to provide for myself.

Now, as a dynamic public philanthropist for children working with great giants, I can handle my own. What is most valuable to me is to believe in what I do and to be honest about what I do, and that is who I really am. I know that what I do behind closed doors is the God's measure of me, as a man.

I've always been honest. As a child, I came out of the closet in fourth grade, knowing that I was gay and going to the teacher to say that I had the desire to hold hands with the boys instead of the girls. My parents were called and they asked me why I would do such a thing. I said, "I've always been close to boys." I knew then that nobody in the wider world knew that I had been a black market baby, illegally marketed and sold until at the age of seven when I

EMBRACED

was legally adopted after my biological dad and adoptive father worked together after my biological mother had gone to jail for selling her child. And I obviously was not the first child to be sold.

Though the memories seem to have an encyclopedic nature like a polaroid camera in every frame of my life, because of the multiple personality disorders that the child within me was subjected to through the criminal activities of the biological mother that continued through childhood, transforming dynamics with others, I had no identity except for the identity that I was told and taught to play.

My first biography, Out of the Closet, Into the Light, went sky high because of Jewel Adams' incredible work. My friends gave the network stations all the material on my spiritual transformation and it ended up becoming national news in the gay community. Affirmation was one group that did not mock me, and I am grateful because I was told they would have been the first because of their spiritual faith and my spiritual faith not mixing very well. But I realize faith is not the foundation of a friendship. Truth, trust and communication are the foundations of a friendship. That's why men and women throughout the country have embraced my transformation as a Latter-day Saint Christian. The past is far from me now and my life will never go backwards.

I've written as much as I remember, though I'm sure circumstances will jog a memory a two that I'll wish I had recalled before the book was published. Straightening out my priorities in my life, I know I will have to return to the pages of this book. I know

JORDAN JANTZ

I have stood up today for principles and I have paid the price for writing this book. Some people that have known me for so long oppose my faith and the happiness of no longer feeling like I must belong in the arms of some man, for one moment. I know that moment is so temporary that the emptiness and tears lasts longer after being embraced after never experiencing what it really is like to be embraced just as I am.

To each reader, let me express that I am encouraged by every letter and every phone call I receive. I have wanted to be the voice that calls to those who have been like myself, to embrace the stranger who is not a stranger. "There is instant connection inside some kinds of experiences," said a person that was not fed on a plate but in a dog bowl. A few letters like this can touch your heart and change your life forever. I cannot ignore what the truth is. I will rely on you to become the relay runners in my life and let me know of the things that need catching up. Right now, the baton is in my hand and I am winning the race. In some ways I have become a mentor. I know I am not the same man you read about in *Out of the Closet, Into the Light* ... for I will continue to grow. I was given a gift and it is the gift of embracing you and your life, encouraging you to become all you can be, embracing disabilities to become abilities. You who are broken as adults and as children - who are Christian or atheist or Buddhist or Muslim - you were given this book only to encourage your life to become more than what you expected. And reality - you have encouraged me to write this book for you.

EMBRACED

I knew I was a popular figure for my transformation. The gay community honored me at the Gay Pride Festival, actually honoring the Church of Jesus Christ of Latter-day Saints with a kind of Voice of Hope Award, as they reminded me, because I was not only a Voice of Hope to the church but a Voice of Hope in the gay community throughout the world, because of the Church of Jesus Christ of Latter-day Saints. I have found my voice, they say.

One of my many contradictions about working on this book is that I didn't want to be disliked by my church people for sharing my love for the gay people and I didn't want the gay people to be mad or upset for loving the church people. Also, the journalism in writing my book is about telling the truth, and some people don't always want to hear the truth. Others want the truth bent to suit their ends, but to do so is to become worthless as a shameful serpent slithering on the earth, not able to get up and walk. I did not compromise my truth in either of my books. Some friends ridiculed and parodied my actions, for they wanted to know if I was making a commitment for life or if this was a mid-life crisis.

Producing this book was an impressive mouthful, even for me.? I know this is a very different book than the one I first wrote with Jewel Adams. And, this being the second edition is even more incredible.

I have already been asked and am in deep consideration for the right producers for a movie to bring glory for the redemption of children who have become adults like myself. I have been told to call back when I know what I want in a movie from my book, after my time in Park City at the Sundance Film Festival. My request was only that I not be alone in the room during the interview, for I am far more comfortable being where there are two or more interviewing me. It is a safer environment for someone with a past like mine.

My boyfriend left this for me in the hours before he hung himself Christmas Eve:

First was Matthew's favorite scripture also from the book of Matthew:

"The King will reply, 'Truly I tell you, whatever you did for one of the least of these brothers and sisters of mine, you did for me.'" (Matthew 25:40)

And a note:

Jordan, being with you for seven years I received purity from your heart. Remember all are broken and all have come short of the glory of God. None of us will enter heaven on merit, Jordan, only on the mercy we give to each other, especially the smallest, weakest and most lost among us, who are the people you love the most. You are God's child, Jordan, who has touched the lives of God's children, old and young, a loving messenger.

God is sharp on the details of his plans and his events for my life. I thank him for giving me life with him and I pray to ask Him to take care of things that are unresolved, and that whatever comes my way I pray this is not our final conversation. I will cover lost ground whether on earth or in heaven as long as Jesus has his footprints in the sand carrying me through the tidal waves of my life, where I will never be abandoned or forgotten again.

- Jordan and Charity

EMBRACED

655

Favorite Film Festival!

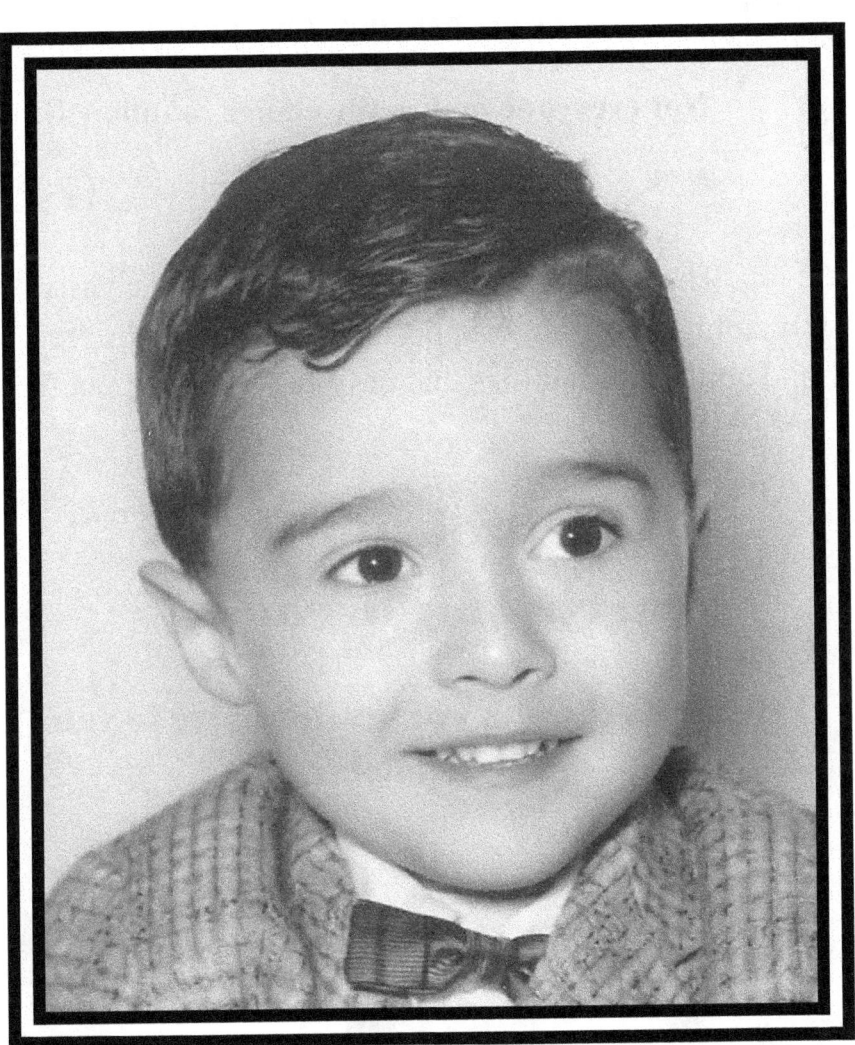

Everyone has their own destiny.

Not everyone makes the choice to follow it.

I'm lucky I did.

Thank you for purchasing this book of charity. By doing so, you are supporting the lives of children and adults and families that have been washed out to sea.

"With broken wings, I carried my dreams."

**With love, the story of my life I give to you.
Love, Jordan**

CONNECT WITH JORDAN

JordanJantzEmbraced.com

JordanJantzFiresides.com

JordanJantzNews.com

JordanJantz.BeaconOfLight.com

http://www.amazon.com/Jordan-Jantz/e/B019ELLHRK

www.ldsvoicesofhope.org

Jordans-light.blogspot.com

Jeweladams.com

northstarlds.org

Coming Soon:
Jordan Jantz Legacy Website by long-time best friend, Austin from New York Media

JORDAN JANTZ

In the history of my life to this day, many abandon my life over my first book and my second book as if they never knew I existed, including family and friends. I'm tired of trying to perfect my life to be valued in my relationships. I've revised my book three times, perfecting completion of marketing hope and love with mercy to all, embracing the abandoned lives of men, women and children, who are so often forgotten about.

I thank you for sponsoring *Embraced* with your purchase for protection of many lives that are hidden away through Child Protective Services throughout the world today. I will not turn my back, as I lived this truth and I will protect this truth that others have lived also, and not by choice.

Jesus has said,

"It would be better for them to be thrown into the sea with a millstone tied around their neck than to cause one of these little ones to stumble."

(Luke 17:2)

I'm letting go, and I surrender today plastic fantastic relationships by you reading this book. Jesus himself could not afford to be around those who walked with disbelief of His Life and what He did to change the lives of those who believed that He had been speaking the truth all the years of His life. That's how it is for me with many friends and family since Jesus came into my life.

www.ingramcontent.com/pod-product-compliance
Lightning Source LLC
Chambersburg PA
CBHW070831160426
43192CB00012B/2168